‘Is This Not the Carpenter?’

Copenhagen International Seminar

General Editors: Thomas L. Thompson and Ingrid Hjelm, both at the University of Copenhagen

Editors: Niels Peter Lemche and Mogens Müller, both at the University of Copenhagen

Language Revision Editor: James West

Published

Argonauts of the Desert: Structural Analysis of the Hebrew Bible
Philippe Wajdenbaum

Biblical Narrative and Palestine's History: Changing Perspectives 2
Thomas L. Thompson

Biblical Studies and the Failure of History: Changing Perspectives 3
Niels Peter Lemche

Changing Perspectives 1: Studies in the History, Literature and Religion of Biblical Israel
John Van Seters

The Emergence of Israel in Ancient Palestine: Historical and Anthropological Perspectives
Emanuel Pfoh

The Expression 'Son of Man' and the Development of Christology: A History of Interpretation
Mogens Müller

'Is This Not the Carpenter?': The Question of the Historicity of the Figure of Jesus
Edited by Tomas L. Thompson and Thomas S. Verenna

Japheth ben Ali's Book of Jeremiah: A Critical Edition and Linguistic Analysis of the Judaeo-Arabic Translation
Joshua A. Sabih

Origin Myths and Holy Places in the Old Testament: A Study of Aetiological Narratives
Łukasz Niesiołowski-Spanò
Translated by Jacek Laskowski

'Is This Not the Carpenter?'

The Question of the Historicity of the Figure of Jesus

Edited by

Thomas L. Thompson and Thomas S. Verenna

ACUMEN

First published by Equinox in 2012.
First published in paperback by Acumen in 2013.

Acumen Publishing Limited
4 Saddler Street
Durham
DH1 3NP, UK

ISD, 70 Enterprise Drive
Bristol, CT 06010, USA

www.acumenpublishing.com

ISBN: 978-1-84553-986-3 (hardcover)
ISBN: 978-1-84465-729-2 (paperback)

British Library Cataloguing-in-Publication Data
A catalogue record for this book is available from the British Library.

Typeset by S.J.I. Services, New Delhi
Printed and bound in the UK by CPI Group (UK) Ltd, Croydon, CR0 4YY.

Contents

Abbreviations

ANET	*Ancient Near Eastern Texts Relating to the Old Testament.* Edited by J. B. Pritchard. 3rd edn. Princeton, 1969
ANRW	*Aufstieg und Niedergang der römischen Welt: Geschichte und Kultur Roms im Spiegel der neueren Forschung.* Edited by H. Temporini and W. Haase. Berlin, 1972–
AThD	Acta theologica danica
AYBC	Anchor Yale Bible Commentaries
BASOR	*Bulletin of the American Schools of Oriental Research*
BibInt	*Biblical Interpretation*
BZ	*Biblische Zeitschrift*
BZAW	Beihefte zur Zeitschrift für die alttestamentliche Wissenschaft
CBQMS	Catholic Biblical Quarterly Monograph Series
CIS	Copenhagen International Seminar
CS	*Current Studies*
DKNT	Dansk kommentar til Det Nye Testamente
EI	*Encyclopedia of Islam*
EQ	*Encyclopedia of the Qur'an*
FBE	Forum for Bibelsk Eksegese
FFC	*Folklore Fellows Communications*
FRLANT	Forschungen zur Religion und Literatur des Alten und Neuen Testaments
HibJ	*Hibbert Journal*
HUTh	Hermeneutische Untersuchungen zur Theologie
JBL	*Journal of Biblical Literature*
JBTh	*Jahrbuch für Biblische Theologie*
JHC	*Journal of Higher Criticism*
JSHJ	*Journal for the Study of the Historical Jesus*
JSNT	*Journal for the Study of the New Testament*
JSNTSup	Journal for the Study of the New Testament: Supplement Series
JSOTSup	Journal for the Study of the Old Testament: Supplement Series

JTS	*Journal of Theological Studies*
JSP	Judea and Samaria Publications
LAI	*Library of Ancient Israel*
MdB	Le Monde de la Bible
MTSR	*Method and Theory in the Study of Religion*
NTM	New Testament Monographs
NovT	Novum Testamentum
OTP	*Old Testament Pseudepigrapha.* Edited by J. H. Charlesworth. 2 vols. New York, 1983
RB	*Revue biblique*
SBEC	Studies in the Bible and Early Christianity
SBL	Society of Biblical Literature
SBLSymS	Society of Biblical Literature Symposium Series
SBLTT	Society of Biblical Literature Text and Translations
SemeiaSt	Semeia Studies
SHANE	Studies in the History of the Ancient Near East
SJOT	*Scandinavian Journal of the Old Testament*
SNTSMS	Society for New Testament Studies Monograph Series
SP	Sacra pagina
StANT	Studien zum Alten und Neuen Testaments
StPB	Studia post-biblica
TANZ	Texte und Arbeiten zum neutestamentlichen Zeitalter
WUNT	Wissenschaftliche Untersuchungen zum Neuen Testament
ZNW	Zeitschrift für die neutestamentliche Wissenschaft und die Kunde der älteren Kirche

Introduction

Thomas L. Thompson and Thomas S. Verenna

> He left there and came to his homeland, accompanied by his disciples. On the Sabbath, he began to teach in the synagogue and many who heard him wondered, saying, 'Where did all this come from? What wisdom has been given him and what great things are done with his hands! Is this not the carpenter, Mary's son, brother to James, Joses, Judas and Simon? Aren't his sisters here with us?' They were offended by him, as Jesus told them that a prophet did not go unrecognized except in his homeland, among his relatives and in his own house. And he was unable to do any great deed there, except that he laid his hands on some of the sick and healed them, while wondering over their mistrust. (Mk 6:1-6; variants: Mt. 13:53-58; Lk. 4:16-30; Jn 4:44-46)

Mark's story brings together two central but distinct sayings of Jesus, each of which has a significant, thematically driven, sub-motif. The first embodies our title: 'Is this not the carpenter?', with its subordinate leitmotif of hands doing wonders, significantly emphasized in the story's conclusion wherein hands are laid on some of the sick to heal them. The other saying is Jesus' complaint that a prophet is unrecognized in his own home town, and the corresponding anger and dissonance that this provokes. These distinct thematic elements are treated independently in the variants of this story we find in the other Gospels. While the saying about the rejected prophet is given its own distinctive role in Jn 4:44-46 in support of the contrast John creates in the foregoing narrative between Jews, Samaritans and foreigners, who are represented by the royal official, who believes Jesus even before his son is cured in the following story segment (Jn 4:47-53). Even Galileans welcomed him, but, for John, the Jews insist on miracles! John's story, in fact, has little understanding for or interest in a historically viable understanding of Jesus' reception. He is so committed to a Christian supersessionist polemic against Jews that he freely compares the Jews negatively with Samaritans, Galileans and foreigners in support of his presentation of Jesus as 'the savior of the world' (Jn 4:42). Jesus' proverb that 'a prophet has no honor in his own country' is hardly about any Jesus of history, but summarizes for John contemporary Jewish opposition towards a newly formed Christianity's alternative understanding of an implicitly common religious heritage.

In the closure of Mark's story of Jesus in his hometown, as in Mark's presentation of the saying about a prophet in his homeland, motifs of rejection and disbelief are subordinated to the theme of Jesus' identity: 'Is this not the carpenter?' This episode in the synagogue of his hometown begins within the larger context of Jesus' growing fame, in which he is everywhere met with amazement and wonder at his wisdom and 'the great things done with his hands'. In the segment immediately preceding his arrival in his home country, Jesus has amazed a crowd of mourners by taking a young girl by the hand that she might rise from the dead (Mk 5:41). So also in Mark 6, Mark's prophet wonders over the distrust with which he is met: a distrust, which, although preventing him from doing any 'great deed', is nevertheless undermined by Jesus laying 'his hands on some of the sick and healing them'. This simple but ironic play on the hands doing great deeds effectively directs Mark's audience to wonder over the story's central question about this man who does wonders with his hands that they might ask, 'Is this not the carpenter?'[1]

One does well to consider, here, how the scene, with its pivotal motifs of the craftsman and his wonderful hands, readily evokes the figure of the Greek god, Hephaestus,[2] who was the god of craftsmen, who himself had forged the magnificent equipment of the gods and almost any finely wrought metalwork imbued with powers that appears in Greek myth. He too was—though crippled by Zeus—strong-armed. According to Hesiod's *Theogony*, he was born of the virgin goddess Hera[3] (though he is also described

1. The Greek word for 'carpenter', ὁ τέκτων, has the wider significance of 'Artisan', 'craftsman'; essentially one who works with his hands. Among other implicit references to ὁ τέκτων is that of the *Infancy Gospel of Thomas* 2:1-5, in which the five-year old Jesus plays with clay and forms 12 sparrows. 'A Jew', understanding this as 'work', complains to the child's father that he breaks the Sabbath rest. When Jesus is confronted with this by his father, he claps his hands and shoos his newly created sparrows away (cf. R. J. Miller, ed., *The Complete Gospels: Annotated Scholars' Version* [Sanoma: Polebridge Press, 1992], 363–72).

2. Rather than, for example, the figure of Asclepius, who had learned the art of healing and whose mother had been impregnated by Apollo (see G. D. Hart, *Asclepius: The God of Medicine* [London: Royal Society of Medicine Press, 2000]).

3. Hesiod, *Theogony*, 927.

as the son of Zeus and Hera by Homer[4] and indeed, in later tradition, the son of the Cretan sun god, Talus[5]). Does the question about the carpenter identify Jesus as a Jewish Hephaestus?[6] Within biblical tradition, a comparable figure can be recognized in the craftsman, Besal'el, who, like Jesus, is both filled with divine wisdom and the ability to create wonderful things with his hands (Exod. 31:1-11; 35:30–39:43; 1 Chron. 2:20; 2 Chron. 1:5).

> Yahweh spoke to Moses, saying: 'Behold, I have chosen Besal'el, son of Uri, son of Hur from the tribe of Judah and have filled him with the divine spirit, with wisdom and learning, with understanding for craftsmanship so that he might create artistic designs in gold, silver and bronze, engrave stone for inlay, carve wood and, indeed, carry out all types of handwork. (Exod. 31:1-5)

It is also in the Old Testament that one finds an early linkage between the creative identity which this thematic element gives to the figure of Jesus and his role as the prophet, unrecognized by his own people, which is fundamental to the construction of Mark's episode. The figure of the prophet as one who is mistreated by both friends and family is nearly ubiquitous in biblical literature and there are numerous passages which help us in understanding Mark's story (esp. Pss. 31:12bc; 38:12; 69:9-10; 88:9 and Job 19:13-19). Several Old Testament narrative figures have also been portrayed in this role. Joseph is scorned by his whole family for his ability to prophecy and to interpret dreams. He is thrown into a pit by his brothers and escapes death by being sold into slavery in Egypt (Gen. 37). A reiteration of such a rejected Joseph also structures the 'life of Jeremiah'. He, too, is hated by the people. Attempts are made on his life (Jer. 11:18–12:6). He is ostracized and rejected (Jer. 15:10-21), publicly persecuted (Jer. 19:1–20:6) and is barred from the Temple (Jer. 36:5-10), arrested and imprisoned (Jer. 37:15-21). Like Joseph, Jeremiah is thrown into a pit (Jer. 38:5-13) and finally forced to flee to Egypt after the death of Gedaliya (Jer. 42:18–43:7). It is, however, the less precise reiteration in Mark of the development of the figure of Moses which fully brings together the thematic figures of the prophet rejected in his homeland and the wonderworker whose hand creates mighty things. Although Moses' life, in the brief sketch of a story in Exod. 2:11-15, has been threatened by Pharaoh and he needed to flee his homeland, in Exodus 3 he is sent as Yahweh's prophet to Pharaoh to free his people (3:10). Yahweh knows that the Egyptian king will refuse, 'except that he be forced by a mighty

4. So, e.g., Il.1.578; Odyss. 8.312.
5. Pausanius, *Graeciae description* 8.53.5.
6. For Gospel variations of Jesus' parentage and family, see, Mt. 1:23's interpretation of the LXX's version of Isa. 7:14 as well as the different origin traditions implied in such widely varying passages as Mt. 1:1-16; 12:46-47; 13:55-56; Mk 1:1; 3:31; 6:3; Lk. 1:26-35; 3:23-38; 4:22; 8:19-20; Jn 1:1-14; 6:41-42; 8:41-42; 2 Cor. 5:21; Gal. 4:4-7 and Rom. 8:3.

hand' (Exod. 3:19, Gr.). It is therefore that—pointing ahead to the coming story of miracles and wonders—Yahweh tells Moses that he will strike the Egyptians with many wonders and that Pharaoh will let the people go (Exod. 3:20)! Moses is to tell the Israelites that God will strike the Egyptians with wonders: 'with great power and a mighty hand' (Exod. 3:20; 6:1; 32:11)[7]—a phrase which finds an echo in Mark's story.

Matthew's version of the story primarily distinguishes itself from Mark's through its context. The nearly verbatim reiteration of Mark's story in Mt. 13:54-58[8] finds its place in Matthew's Gospel with the help of Jesus' statement at the close of ch. 12. His 'true mother and brothers' are his disciples and 'those who do the will of his father' (Mt. 12:50). In contrast to Mark's use of the story in developing the figure of Jesus as wonderworker in the style of Moses and Hephaestus, with the theme of mistrust by the people providing its ironic support, the discourse in Matthew 13 presents the story rather as a 'living parable' about the kingdom.[9] Matthew's story of Jesus in the synagogue follows a series of brief similes about contrasts and distinctions related to the kingdom of heaven; namely, the parables of the weeds and wheat growing together (Mt. 13:24-30), of the little mustard seed becoming a great tree (vv. 31-32) and of the leaven in flour (v. 33). These are loosely organized similes, functioning as illustrative variants of the discourse's opening parable of the sower (Mt. 13:1-9), a story which Matthew uses to supply his parables with a reiteration of Isa. 6:9-10: a most defining passage of Isaiah, which supplies a structure for Matthew's Gospel and suggests a pedagogically oriented contrast between the understanding reader of this Gospel and the role that is played by the rejecting, misunderstanding generations of the story's Isaiah-like figure. Much as the author of Isaiah has his prophet sent to speak to the people of his generation, which Yahweh had himself made deaf, blind and without understanding that they not turn and be forgiven (Isa. 6:9-13; cf. Mk 4:12-13!), so that they might all the better serve their pedagogical role of a lost generation, so Matthew will

7. See on this, K. Martens, 'With a Strong Hand and an Outstretched Arm', *SJOT* 15.1 (2001), 123-41; I. Hjelm, *Jerusalem's Rise to Sovereignty: Zion and Gerizim in Competition* (London: T & T Clark, 2004), 181.

8. Among the thematically relevant differences is Mark's thematic question, which in Matthew is rendered: 'Is this not the carpenter's *son*?' Moreover, Mark's theme is not reiterated by Matthew as 'hands' does not form a leitmotif. The brother Joses becomes Joseph and Mark's ironically significant closure of healing some with his hands finds a somewhat diminished formulation in that 'he did not do many mighty works there, because of their unbelief'.

9. On the form and function of 'living parables', such as the miracle stories of Elijah and Elisha and their influence on the Jesus stories, see the discussion in T. L. Thompson, *The Messiah Myth: The Ancient Near Eastern Background of Jesus and David* (New York: Basic Books, 2005), 27-105; esp. 47-59.

have his hero speak to the 'great crowds', about the kingdom of heaven only in parables, that they also will not understand. He, thereby, rather evokes in his readers an understanding akin to Jesus' Isaiah-like disciples, who are given the role of understanding the secrets of the kingdom (Mt. 13:14-17)! Matthew has Jesus interpret the parable of the sower precisely in terms of understanding or not understanding parables (Mt. 13:18-23), and follows this with similar interpretations of the three similes for the kingdom of heaven (Mt. 13:24-33).

Matthew closes his discourse on parables with the help of the opening of Psalm 78, in which the psalmist defines the parable as a riddle of revelation in a striking reversal of Isaiah! Matthew will not hide the 'glorious deeds of Yahweh, his might and his wonders' from the children of his generation (Ps. 78:4): 'I will open my mouth in parables; I will speak of what has been hidden since the foundation of the world' (Mt. 13:35)! The next scene offers a further expansion as Jesus, alone with his disciples, is asked to explain his first 'parable of the weeds of the field'. Jesus responds with an allegorical coding of his earlier interpretation of the parable of the sower (Mt. 13:36-43), followed by three additional similes for the richness of the kingdom: treasure hidden in the field (Mt. 13:44), a merchant in search for fine pearls (Mt. 13:45-46) and a net thrown into the sea (Mt. 13:47-50) and closes his discourse on parables with a final simile, comparing his understanding disciples with 'every scribe who is trained for the kingdom of heaven' (Mt. 13:51-52). It is within this context that Matthew's paraphrastic version of Mark's allegory makes the story itself of his preaching in his hometown's synagogue into a parable. It provides a key to the brief discussion about Jesus' wonders and the scribes' request that he do a sign in Matthew 12. With Psalm 78's singer, Matthew will speak in parables to Jesus' true family of disciples and followers about the 'glorious deeds of the Lord, of his might and wonders', but few such mighty signs will be given to the disbelieving. Matthew's story radically transforms Mark's tale, but is broadly unaware of its mythic potentials. His orientation toward rewriting Isaiah and his preoccupation in creating a suffering servant for his own generation of readers precludes any historical interest in Mark's figure of Jesus.

Luke's version of the story is found within the opening chain-narrative of his Gospel, which is linked to the birth narrative with the plot-supporting leitmotif of the divine spirit which fills or leads the episode's central figure (Lk. 1:15, 34, 41, 80; 2:25-27; 3:16, 22; 4:1). So Jesus, filled with the spirit, comes to 'Nazareth, where he had grown up' (Lk. 4:16; cf. Lk. 2:39-40, 51). Luke's singular identification of Jesus' hometown as Nazareth reflects more than merely a simple identification of the unnamed *patrída* of Mark's story. Much as the opening of Luke's genealogy had identified Jesus as 'the son, as was supposed, of Joseph' in order to accommodate the fatherly role of the divine spirit in Jesus' birth story (Lk. 1:34), the naming of Jesus' hometown as Nazareth seems to accommodate Matthew's earlier narrative and create a harmony of the seemingly conflicting geographies of Matthew and Luke's birth narratives. Whereas Luke had Joseph and Mary travel from Nazareth to Bethlehem, where they unsuccessfully sought temporary lodging, Matthew has Jesus grow up in Nazareth, because, in their return from Egypt, Joseph and Mary had been afraid to return to their home town of Bethlehem in Judea and went rather to Nazareth so that a passage from Isaiah might be interpreted as a prophecy; that Jesus would be a 'Nazarene' (Mt. 2:19-23; cf. Isa. 11:1; 61:1), a role which Luke's own birth story—reiterating the role of the spirit from the Samson story—had given to the Baptist (Lk. 1:14-15; cf. Lev. 19:9; Num. 6:3; Judg. 13:4-5). It is the leitmotif-figure of the spirit which leads Jesus to Nazareth. There, Luke associates Jesus' sermon in the synagogue with both the driving spirit and Isaiah's figure of the suffering servant. The text of Jesus' sermon, reiterating the great ancient Near Eastern trope of 'the song for a poor man',[10] is used by Luke to define the proclamation of the good news, which had marked the opening of Mark's Gospel as an inauguration of the kingdom of God and which had already developed a stereotypical configuration of Jesus' role as miracle worker in Luke (Mk 1:1; cf. Lk. 1:19; 2:10; 4:43): 'The spirit of the Lord is upon me, because he has anointed me. He has sent me to bring good news to the poor, to proclaim freedom to prisoners and sight to the blind; to free the oppressed and to proclaim a year of grace from the Lord' (Isa. 61:1-2; Lk. 4:18-19).

The people, at first, react with wonder and acceptance at Jesus' interpretive claim that the text, marking the kingdom of God with the expectations of the 'poor man's song', now finds its fulfillment. However, the form of the question, with which Luke has them express their wonder, 'Is this not Joseph's son?', both turns the story away from the defining themes of the good news and healing reversals of the fortunes of the poor and centres it within the thematic element of the unacknowledged prophet in his homeland. This shift of focus is also stressed by the expansion of Mark's story with references to two miracle stories of Elijah and Elisha (1 Kgs 17:9-24; 2 Kgs 5:1-14). Although both are classic and fitting illustrations of the 'song for a poor man', both are strongly marked by an unfavourable contrast between foreigners and Israelites. It is this pejorative distinction which provides the cause for the people's wonder, which turns to anger and grows to fury as the story closes with the people driving Jesus out of the village and attempting to throw him over a cliff-hang which is strikingly

10. On 'the song for a poor man', see Thompson, *The Messiah Myth*, 107-35, 323-35.

similar to that which had been used in Mark's foregoing story to destroy a flock of demon-possessed pigs—a story that had also closed on the motif of Jesus being rejected by the people (Mk 5:11-17)!

Both the distinction between those who are saved and those not and the death-threatening fury the discrimination evokes the distinctive Christian supersessionist context of John 4's story which contrasts the Jews of Jesus' homeland so unfavorably with the Samaritans. This is akin to the comparable emphasis on the accepted and rejected in some of Matthew's parables. Only the people's inability to lay hold of him, his 'passing through their midst', allows Luke to continue Jesus' triumphant tour with a following brief, three-fold closing story of healing and driving out demons and fevers, through which both his fame and his popularity grow (Lk. 4:31-44): all illustrations of Jesus 'preaching the good news of the kingdom of God' (Lk. 4:43), which define him as 'the holy one of God' (Lk. 4:34), 'son of God' and 'messiah' (Lk. 4:41). Luke's narration is emphatically influenced by the other Gospel traditions about Jesus. Indeed, his dominant commitment to the central Old Testament folkloric motif of the spirit seems to draw him to ignore the historical potential of any of the significant thematic elements he develops. For Luke, the crowd's wonder offers an opportunity of asserting the theological and mythic values of his and Matthew's narrative above anything which might represent a description of events. His own Jesus was Yahweh's servant announcing the good news of the kingdom of God to the poor. The people's wonder over this son of Joseph whom they knew is interpreted by Jesus himself as a threatening demand to John's unrecognized prophet in his home town, as the episode turns from wonder to discord, threat of violence and mutual rejection.

In concluding this brief exegetical excursion, one must ask once again, with the marvelling people of Jesus' hometown in the Gospel of Mark, our historicist question: 'Is this not the carpenter?' And we must answer, just as quickly: Yes, even so! Those 'few sick people' on whom he laid his wonder-creating hands give us the key to our allegory, and we, too, can marvel with Jesus at the disbelief with which he was met by his own people! It is Jesus as Hephaestus, the myth, which demands affirmation. It is that which Mark writes of and which also forms the modest centre of focus for the present collection of essays.

The Quest for the Historical Jesus

For some time, New Testament scholarship has avoided direct questions regarding the historicity of Jesus. The assumption of a historical Jesus has been secured within a debate about the sayings of Jesus and the events of his life, as referenced in the New Testament, reflect either Jesus' own life and teaching or a construction of early Christianity. The dichotomous structure of this debate has typically made alternative explanations for the ubiquitous allegorical interpretations and narrative reiterations and allusions of a wide variety of both ancient Near Eastern and biblical motifs, themes and tropes irrelevant in the eyes of many scholars, in spite of the fact that an unquestioning acceptance of the New Testament figures of Jesus, Paul and the disciples as historical can at times be shown to ignore and misunderstand the implicit functions of our texts. While early critical scholarship has exposed many of the flaws in contemporary assumptions of historicity already in the eighteenth and early nineteenth centuries, the absence of a coherent comprehensive understanding of the New Testament literature at the time created a stereotype, which has not yet faded. As late as 1977, for example, Michael Grant could maintain that 'no serious scholar' would 'postulate the non-historicity of Jesus'.[11] Even more recently, Geza Vermes has remarked in his most recent book on Jesus' resurrection, in an affirmation of his own belief in the historicity of the figure of Jesus, set his own perspective as opposed to 'rationalist dogmatists' (2008).[12] Although no effort has yet been made to respond to recent efforts to focus on the question of historicity, [13] the question as such is dismissed without argument. While the assumption of historicity has prompted many to attempt to describe what the historical Jesus must have been like, it has also encouraged many to ignore both literary and theological issues central to an understanding of New Testament narrative. An analysis of this problem is important, as the current discussions about which of the many proposed historical figures of Jesus might be judged the more probable have become all too predictable. The question of historicity itself, however, remains unaddressed and there is, accordingly, little discussion of the central questions regarding the significance and function of our texts. One has begun with the unwarranted assertion of a 'probability' of a historical Jesus existing in ancient Palestine and freely presented one or other of such a possible figure as a viable alternative to the only known Jesus—the mythic one of our texts. Jesus has become a 'concrete entity with recognizable parameters'.[14] This was so thoroughly accepted that, when the Jesus Seminar was originally assembled, it was assumed from the outset that Jesus had been in fact a historical

---

11. M. Grant, *Jesus: An Historian's Review of the Gospels* (New York: Macmillan, 1977), 200.
12. G. Vermes, *The Resurrection* (New York and London: Doubleday, 2008), ix.
13. T. L. Thompson, *The Messiah Myth*; R. Price, *The Pre-Nicene New Testament: Fifty-four Formative Texts* (Salt Lake City: Signature Books, 2006).
14. M. Goodacre, *The Case Against Q: Studies in Markan Priority and the Synoptic Problem* (Harrisburg: Trinity Press International, 2002), 9; Goodacre addresses the academic opinion concerning the hypothetical nature of the Q document.

person. The Seminar, hence, could proceed to produce specific guidelines for determining the type of person he had been. 'Over the...years a flood of works...has inundated scholars and the public, as the range of portraits of Jesus broadens.'[15] Jesus became all of the following: an itinerate preacher,[16] a cynic sage,[17] the Essene's righteous rabbi,[18] a Galilean holy man,[19] a revolutionary leader,[20] an apocalyptic preacher,[21] a proto-liberation theologian,[22] a trance-inducing mental healer,[23] an eschatological prophet,[24] an occult magician,[25] a Pharisee,[26] a rabbi seeking reform,[27] a Galilean charismatic,[28]

---

15. P. Fredriksen, *From Jesus to Christ: The Origins of the New Testament Images of Jesus* (New Haven: Yale University Press, 2000, 2nd edn), xiii.
16. J. D. Crossan, *The Historical Jesus: The Life of a Mediterranean Jewish Peasant* (San Francisco: HarperCollins, 1992).
17. *The Historical Jesus*; B. Mack, *The Christian Myth: Origins, Logic and Legacy* (New York: Continuum International, 2003), *The Lost Gospel: The Book of Q and Christian Origins* (San Francisco: HarperCollins, 1993) and *A Myth of Innocence: Mark and Christian Origins* (Philadelphia: Fortress Press, 1988); F. G. Downing, *Cynics and Christian Origins* (Edinburgh: T & T Clark, 1992); P. R. Eddy, 'Jesus as Diogenes? Reflections on the Cynic Jesus Thesis,' *JBL* 115.3 (Autumn, 1996), 449-69.
18. J. M. Allegro, *The Dead Sea Scrolls and the Christian Myth* (Newton Abbott: Westbridge Books, 1979).
19. G. Vermes, *Jesus the Jew: A Historian's Reading of the Gospels* (Philadelphia: Fortress Press, 1973); idem, *The Religion of Jesus the Jew* (Philadelphia: Fortress Press, 1993); B. Thiering, *Jesus and the Riddle of the Dead Sea Scrolls: Unlocking the Secrets of His Life Story* (San Francisco: Harper Collins, 1992).
20. S. G. F. Brandon, *Jesus and the Zealots: A Study of the Political Factor in Primitive Christianity* (New York: Scribner, 1967); G. W. Buchanan, *Jesus: The King and His Kingdom* (Macon: Mercer University, 1984).
21. B. D. Ehrman, *Truth and Fiction in the Da Vinci Code: A Historian Reveals What We Really Know about Jesus, Mary Magdalene, and Constantine* (Oxford: Oxford University Press, 2004).
22. J. M. Robinson, 'The Jesus of Q as Liberation Theologian,' paper presented at the Jesus Seminar (25-27 October, 1991).
23. S. Davies, 'On the Inductive Discourse of Jesus: The Psychotherapeutic Foundation of Christianity,' paper presented at the Jesus Seminar (22-25 October, 1992) and *Jesus the Healer: Possession, Trance, and the Origins of Christianity* (New York: Continuum, 1995).
24. E. P. Sanders, *Jesus and Judaism* (Philadelphia: Fortress Press, 1985); J. P. Meier, *A Marginal Jew: Rethinking the Historical Jesus*. II. *Mentor, Message and Miracles* (New York: Doubleday, 1994).
25. M. Smith, *Jesus the Magician* (San Francisco: Harper & Row, 1978).
26. H. Falk, *Jesus the Pharisee: A New Look at the Jewishness of Jesus* (New York: Paulist Press, 1985); Hyam Maccoby, *Jesus the Pharisee* (London: SCM Press, 2003).
27. R. Horsley, *Jesus and the Spiral of Violence: Popular Jewish Resistance in Roman Palestine* (San Francisco: Harper & Row, 1987); M. Borg, *Jesus: Uncovering the Life, Teachings, and Relevance of a Religious Revolutionary* (New York: Harper San Francisco, 2006); B. Chilton, *A Galilean Rabbi and His Bible: Jesus' Use of the Interpreted Scripture of His Time* (Wilmington: Glazier, 1984).
28. G. Vermes, *Jesus in the World of Judaism* (Philadelphia: Fortress Press, 1984).

a Hillelite,[29] an Essene,[30] a teacher of wisdom,[31] a miracle-working prophet and an exorcist[32] and the list continues to grow. Jesus is as fluid a figure as is our understanding of early Christianity. 'The mistake was to suppose that Jesus could come to mean more to our time by entering into it as a man like ourselves.'[33] '[A]ttempts to say what we could really know about the historical Jesus actually told us more about their authors than about the person they sought to describe. The authors seem to have looked into the well of history searching for Jesus and seen their own reflection.'[34]

Such projection represents the crux of the problem this book hopes to address. Historical Jesus research did not come about through the discovery of an actual historical Jesus as focus for such research. Despite what many have suggested, the data we have is no more useful for an understanding of a historical Jesus today than it had been a century ago. Even what little had been understood as known to scholars of the nineteenth century—such as the existence of widespread Jewish expectations for an apocalyptic messiah—has been found wanting.[35] The ancient world's many mythic and theological representations of a figure comparable to the Jesus of New Testament texts are not alone decisive arguments against historicity, but they are part of the picture, which needs to be considered more comprehensively. Literarily viable figures have been represented—historically—in many clarifying ways.

The role genre studies play in investigations of the Jesus of the New Testament rests largely on an analysis of intertextuality, which is well defined in terms of an analysis of the functions of tale-types, stock figures, sayings, motifs, narrative patterns and thematic elements through a process of reiteration, refraction, allusion and emulation. A historical Jesus is a hypothetical derivative of scholarship. It is no more a fact than is an equally hypothetical historical Moses or David. To the extent that New Testament

---

29. Maccoby, *Jesus the Pharisee.*
30. Maccoby, *Jesus the Pharisee.*
31. M. Borg, *Meeting Jesus Again for the First Time: The Historical Jesus and the Heart of Contemporary Faith* (San Francisco: HarperCollins, 1995).
32. H. Koester, *Introduction to the New Testament*. II. *History and Literature of Early Christianity* (New York and Berlin: Walter de Gruyter, 2000, 2nd edn).
33. The central conclusion of A. Schweitzer, *The Quest for the Historical Jesus* (London: A. & C. Black, 1910), 397-98; German original: *Von Reimarus zu Wrede: Eine Geschichte der Leben-Jesu-Forschung* (Tubingen: Mohr Siebeck, 1906); cf. G. Bornkamm, *Jesus of Nazareth* (New York: Harper & Row, 1960), 13, and J. D. Crossan, *The Quest for the Historical Jesus*, 398.
34. B. Witherington, *The Jesus Quest: The Third Search for the Jew of Nazareth* (Downers Grove: InterVarsity Press, 1997, 2nd edn), 9.
35. J. H. Charlesworth, ed., *The Messiah: Developments in Earliest Judaism and Christianity* (The Princeton Symposium on Judaism and Christian Origins; Minneapolis: Fortress Press, 1992); cf. T. L. Thompson, 'The Messiah Epithet in the Bible,' *SJOT* 15.1 (2001), 57-82.

literature was written with literary, allegorical and, indeed, theological and mythic purpose, rather than as an account of historical events, there is significant need, not to speak of warrant, to doubt the historicity of its figures to the extent that such figures owe their substance to such literature. The best histories of Jesus today reflect an awareness of the limits and uncertainties in reconstructing the story of his life. Abraham, Isaac, Moses and Sarah, Ruth and Boaz, Jonah and his big fish are but a handful of characters found in the Bible, without the slightest historicity. They are literary creations. The figures of New Testament discourse must also be critically examined in the same light, for the New Testament is to be defined neither as a history of the early Christian church nor as an account of the life of a man named Jesus and of that of his followers.

An Effort to Define the Question

The essays collected in this volume have a modest purpose. Neither establishing the historicity of a historical Jesus nor possessing an adequate warrant for dismissing it, our purpose is to clarify our engagement with critical historical and exegetical methods in the hopes of enabling the central question regarding the function of New Testament literature to resist the endless production of works on the historical Jesus. Our hope is to open a direct discussion of the question of historicity much in the spirit of the more than decade-long discourse and debate by the European Seminar on Methodology in Israel's History, which has been so profitably engaged in regard to the historicity of figures and narratives of the Hebrew Bible and the related construction of a history of ancient Palestine.[36] The essays we collect here are presented by a wide range of scholars and deal with three central issues: (1) some problems and issues of past scholarship regarding the historical Jesus; (2) fresh perspectives regarding the figure of Paul and his epistles as our 'earliest testimony' of the figure of Jesus; and (3) intertextual literary reading and the significance of the function of a rewritten Bible for literary composition. These collected essays will close with a related, theory-oriented discussion about the history of Christian origins without a historical Jesus.

Past Scholarship on the Historical Jesus

Whether or not one wishes to use the term 'minimalism' to identify some of the questions which are addressed and the methods that are used in the essays

36. The European seminar has met since July, 1996 and its proceedings have been published in a number of volumes since 1997, under the editorship of L. L. Grabbe in the T & T Clark series, European Seminar in Historical Methodology.

of this volume, the first, brief essay by Jim West, 'A (Very, Very) Short History of Minimalism: From the Chronicler to the Present,' opens our discussion by pointing to some of the central issues engaged in different ways by most of the contributors. When one is dealing with biblical traditions, one is not dealing with texts that are historical in their orientation, however much they construct a past. Theology is rather the medium of biblical discourse. If one does insist on reading biblical narratives and the literature related to them as if they were histories of Israel and of early Christianity, from which modern histories of Israel and early Christianity can be constructed, one is quickly caught in a web of circular reasoning. The trap, West further argues, is difficult to avoid, as one is unable to write such a modern history without drawing directly on the narrative perspectives of the biblical text itself. The Bible, indeed, is both the most important source in constructing such a history and its only viable confirmation! On the other hand, lacking histories of Israel and of early Christianity which are independent of biblical perspectives, one cannot reasonably or convincingly identify a historical Jesus or an ancient Israel which existed apart from their story worlds. One can neither affirm nor deny their existence. One can only conclude that we lack evidence for such constructs. With this dilemma in place, West argues that the function of historical construction is neither biblically based nor appropriate for an understanding of the biblical literature.

Roland Boer's article, 'The German Pestilence: Re-assessing Feuerbach, Strauss and Bauer,' asks whether we have yet seen the end of the Bible's territorial dominance over rational thought or, indeed, German dominance over biblical scholarship, which had been furthered through a *Kulturkamp* fought with and through theology, the then *lingua franca* of public debate. He reminds biblical scholars of their well-known irrelevance to nineteenth-century intellectual life in France and Britain and draws out some relevant implications of our field's long flirtation with what had been once known as the 'German pestilence'. Instead of 'dismissing the Bible as a document of outmoded superstition', nineteenth-century German intellectuals developed their theories of society in terms of biblical criticism. Boer's discussion, for example, of the diminished humanity resulting from Ludwig Feuerbach's understanding of God as a projection of what is best in ourselves, David Strauss's mythic representation of Jesus as 'a poetic expression of deeper truths' and a natural way of understanding life and religion and Bruno Bauer's critical historical perspectives about Christian origins in the second century CE, which defined Christianity as a form of sectarian, *exclusive* monotheism, all develop a discourse which deconstructs the orthodox understanding of early Christianity. Boer, because of his understanding of Bauer as a forerunner of 'minimalism', may surprise some readers by his assurance that Bauer continues to be relevant to our discussion. However, his assurance rests on the caution Bauer's work maintains even for today's scholarship that 'one must be very careful with using the Bible for any historical reconstruction'.

Lester Grabbe, in his contribution, '"Jesus Who Is Called Christ": References to Jesus outside Christian Sources,' underlines such caution with his unfortunately—but appropriately—brief survey of the few and ambiguous extra-biblical references to the figure of Jesus which exist apart from the Bible: our present, quite limited, store of early Jesus testimonies which is unfortunately neither large nor growing. Beginning with the known Roman sources, he refers to Tacitus' use, nearly a century after the date of Jesus' alleged death, of what are presumably Roman sources, which enable him to describe the success of Nero's efforts to punish a group called 'Christians', a name that was derived from one Christus, who had suffered the death penalty under Pontius Pilatus and who had become the source of superstitions in Judea and Jerusalem. Grabbe then turns to Tacitus' younger contemporary, Suetonius, who had also referred to Christians who had been punished by Nero (emperor from 54-68 CE). In contradiction to Tacitus, however, he refers to a Chrestus/Christus as an instigator of Jewish disturbances in Rome under Claudius, who had been emperor from 41-54 CE. This reference Grabbe judges 'problematic' for several reasons, not least that of chronology. Pliny the Younger (110 CE), speaking of his own (limited) involvement with the trials and executions of Christians, describes how these people had chanted verses in honour of Christ 'as if to a god' and made vows to him to live virtuously. Finally, turning to a more detailed discussion of Josephus, who wrote in the second half of the first century, and to his medieval commentators, Grabbe argues that Josephus, who might well have used one or other Christian tradition for his brief paraphrase, did have knowledge of the execution of James, who is described as Jesus' brother. He, however, also argues, on the basis the witness of Origen and Jerome, that Josephus' bold and famous assertion, 'This was the Christ!' (the *Testimonium Flavianum*), is to be understood as a later, Christian insertion. Grabbe goes on to offer his own 'hypothetical reconstruction' for what Josephus 'might have written'. He further argues that Rabbinic references to Jesus are secondary and based on 'Christian' sources and closes on an all too brief discussion about two attempts at an early 'Jewish' *life of Jesus*, the *Toledot Yeshu* and the *Hebrew Gospel of Matthew*.

Niels Peter Lemche follows Grabbe by taking up the classic question of historical Jesus study: the compatibility of the two faces of Jesus that one meets in the Gospels—the Jesus of Nazareth and the Church's mythic, divine figure of Christ—in an essay entitled, 'The Grand Inquisitor and

Christ: Why the Church Does Not Want Jesus.' Likening David Friedrich Strauss's Jesus, without myth, to Dostoyevsky's Christ in the hands of the Spanish Inquisition, Lemche discusses today's conservative and evangelical alienation from studies of the Bible which are both historical and critical, an alienation which undermines the idealistic independence of exegesis from the authority of church dogmatics that had been so sorely sought by the eighteenth-century theologian, Philipp Gabler. While the nineteenth-century's critical exegesis has often been accused of having alienated believing Christians from their Bible, its more appropriate role and self-understanding was determined by ridding the Bible of ancient beliefs and superstitions, so that it might more legitimately serve as a reliable source for the history of both Judaism and Christian origins. However, as in the nineteenth century, so too today, doubts about the historicity of the Bible's events and figures—not least those related to the figure of Jesus—and a return to an understanding of the mythic qualities of biblical literature is also intolerable, as can readily be seen in reactions to the deconstruction of biblical history by the 'Copenhagen school'.

In closing the first part of our book, Emanuel Pfoh's essay, 'Jesus and the Mythic Mind: An Epistemological Problem,' addresses the implications of a renewed emphasis on a mythic Jesus in his effort—from a historical and anthropological perspective—to distinguish knowledge about a historical person behind the New Testament figure of Jesus from what should be understood as an aspect of mythic creation. Pfoh addresses what he calls 'the mythic mind in the intellectual world of antiquity' on the one hand and the question of whether knowledge of a historical Jesus is possible at all on the other. Contemporary understanding of a historical Jesus is not based on evidence so much as it is rooted in theological necessity. The mythic character of the figure of Jesus relates to the perspectives ancients had of reality and the role which humans were thought to hold beyond what is known and tangible in this world. Bearing and illustrating a tradition, great figures of ancient literature reiterate each other in their behaviour, values and function. In such a context, the question of historicity, as might be implied, for example, in the Jesus Seminar's efforts to identify the *ipsissima verba* of Jesus, is wholly inappropriate. The matrix of biblical literature can hardly accommodate the rational presuppositions about reality that modern historicism has as its point of departure. Bultmann's understanding of *kerygma* precludes the theological function of a historical Jesus, however much the goals of the second and third quests for the historical Jesus assume just such historicity as their theological point of departure. As Old Testament studies has learned over the past forty years of critical research, the limitations of historical knowledge are hardly to be ignored and biblical texts allowed an understanding as historical sources. Pfoh closes this essay on perspectives with a discussion of some of the ways that 'cultural memory' can help clarify issues further.

Paul and Early Christianity

Part Two of our book comprises three articles which take up the New Testament's purportedly earliest references to Jesus and the question of their relevance to the historicity of this figure. The first essay, by Robert Price, 'Does the Christ Myth Theory Require an Early Date for the Pauline Epistles?,' addresses fundamental methodological questions concerning the dating of the genuine Pauline epistles. Price begins by examining some of the assumptions of 'mythicists' today by using George Wells and Earl Doherty as his primary examples. He draws the conclusion that the originally mythic saviour of Paul's epistles was gradually historicized and then found its place in the later Gospels, one of whose central functions was the legitimation of early Christianity through an origin story. In this effort, the Gospel stories expansively fill a void left by the epistles. Acknowledging the traditional early dating of the epistles, such scholars see an apparent lack of knowledge about Jesus' life in the epistles, even though, if such knowledge had existed, such references would have been highly relevant to many of the arguments of the epistles. Nor do they see Paul evoking Jesus' authority, when he might be most expected to do so. Turning to the history of 'mythicist' scholarship, Price first discusses the implications of the theories of Couchoud and Dujardin from the late 1930s concerning Paul's knowledge of a historical Jesus, in so far as such knowledge might be implied on the basis of their understanding of the authorship and date of the Pauline epistles. Price then turns to Arthur Drews, a writer of the early twentieth century, in an effort to raise the question of whether a 'mythicist' theory requires an early dating of Paul. Taking up the questionable principle that sayings precede narratives and epistles Gospels, one might easily add that the more spectacular can enhance the less and one might arrive at the conclusion that, therefore, the Gospels expand on the themes of the epistles. However circular, the argument is rhetorically simple and unfortunately persuasive. Even if the epistles are late, the Gospels must be much later, because they are unknown by the epistles. Citing Robertson's argument that even if the epistles were later and had accepted the tradition of Gospel myths, this would not establish the historicity of these miraculous and heroic myths, Price goes on to argue that there is a lot less difference between the Jesus story of the Gospels and the Christ myth of the epistles than we usually assume. Following a brief discussion of the similarities between myths and legends, Price turns to the possibility of Marcion's authorship of some of the epistles in an effort to raise the question of whether he knew of the Gospel tradition as well as to turn his discussion to the anti-Marcionite structure of the Gospels as rewritten Scripture, an understanding of the Gospels which has long been argued by Thomas Brodie and others. He then turns to the apparent Marcionite influences on the Gospels of Mark, John and Thomas. Price concludes his essay by recognizing the self-serving character of the early twentieth-century 'mythicist' acceptance of an early date of the Pauline epistles and hints at what he sees as a (historical) priority of the epistles' 'Christ myth' to what he calls the 'Jesus epic'.

In the following essay in this section, 'Paul: The Oldest Witness to the Historical Jesus,' Mogens Müller, though also accepting both an early date for the letters of Paul and the highly 'mythic' or theological character of Paul's figure of Jesus, understands these letters as providing the earliest witness to the historical person of Jesus. The letters themselves reflect the process by which this figure has been transformed into a 'heavenly saviour' and transformed so thoroughly that the historical figure of the past has nearly disappeared from our texts. The process itself is viewed as evidence for the early dating of the genuine Pauline epistles, relative to the Gospels. Diametrically opposed as his perspective of the early dating of Paul is to Wells's and Doherty's 'mythicist' use of the early dating of the Pauline epistles, Müller argues that all four of the canonical Gospels reflect Paul in the saving significance of Jesus' life and death. Müller's use of Paul's letters as witness to the historical Jesus is not oriented to identifying specific elements of Jesus' life and teaching within the epistles which have been reiterated in the Gospels. He avoids that argument's intrinsic, circular argumentation by associating Paul's witness rather to the significance attached to his life and conduct in subsequent interpretations. Assuming that Paul had never met the historical Jesus, the whole of his understanding would have been derived through others, even as, in Paul's self-understanding, his own calling came directly from the 'mythical' Christ. That is, Paul understood Jesus according to the transformation of his own life. The argument for Paul as witness to the historical Jesus rests on the effect of his message on Paul. While one learns admittedly little about a 'life of Jesus' from the genuine letters of Paul, these letters rather witness to the theological consequences Paul drew from Jesus' life and death. What we meet in the epistles is Jesus as faith sees him. We only have access to him through this reception: as expressed in confessional statements. Through this indirect way, Müller finds the Jesus of history behind the letters of Paul, not so much in the mythic figure Paul developed, as—through his reception—'a charismatic interpreter of the will of God', an understanding of the figure of Jesus which is also cast in the Gospels. He closes his essay with the assertion that if Paul must be assumed to be a historical person, the same assumption must be made with regard to Jesus.

The essay of Thomas Verenna, 'Born under the Law: Intertextuality and the Question of the Historicity of the Figure of Jesus in Paul's Epistles,' also directly engages the question of Paul's witness to a historical Jesus and questions whether Paul in fact believed his Jesus to be historical, rather than an allegorical figure within the genre of 'rewritten Bible', reiterating Isaiah's 'suffering servant'. Beginning with a discussion of the Psalms, Isaiah and the historicity of the crucifixion, he considers Mark's representation of 'crucifixion' and 'resurrection' in the context of Ezekiel's reference to the myth of Tammuz, which, having roots in ancient Near Eastern traditions from as early as that of the Sumerian Inanna, is evoked in the Gospels through Mark's allusions to Psalm 22. Such insight into Jewish culture can also be recognized in Paul's keying the crucifixion to the Passover tradition, an association based not in history, but literature; also, the tradition of the atonement sacrifice of Yom Kippur found, namely, in Leviticus 16 and echoed in Psalm 22. Verenna argues further for early Jewish familiarity with mystery religions and early forms of Gnosticism with the help of Paul's discussion of Archons in Galatians, Romans and 1 Corinthians in an effort to explain, with the help of 1 Enoch, Paul's understanding of Jesus' death and rebirth as hidden and spiritual rather than historical. The reference in Galatians to Jesus as 'born of a woman' has led historical Jesus scholarship to two claims. He points out that the passage in Galatians is entirely allegorical and rooted in Old Testament rhetoric and, accordingly, hardly meant to be taken literally. A further example is taken up from 1 Corinthians 11, which is set in the context of a discussion of disputes in the community of Corinth, in which the author introduces the allegory of the last supper with its interpretive echoes on Exodus 24's covenant meal, which had been introduced in 1 Corinthians 10. In closing, Verenna takes up a passage in Galatians 1, which refers to 'James, the brother of the Lord'. This he describes as 'the strongest case' for Paul referring to a historical Jesus. Reminding the reader of the possibility that the term 'brother' is not necessarily to be understood literally and, at the same time, lightly suggesting that Paul's use of the term might derive from the fellowship language so well known from mystery religions of the day, and as, for instance, might be actually supported by 1 Corinthians 15, he leans rather apologetically on the much later Gospel of Luke to hold to the possibility that the passage not be understood literally. He points out that Paul's Christ is taken from his understanding of Scripture rather than from a historical figure living some decades earlier. Verenna concludes with the point that any attempt to locate a historical figure would inevitably only discover Paul's allegorical figure of Jesus, born not upon historical events but through reiterated themes from the Old Testament.

The Rewritten Bible

This third and final section of the book borders on the eclectic. The first essay, by James Crossley, 'Can John's Gospel Really Be Used to Reconstruct a Life of Jesus? An Assessment of Recent Trends and a Defence of a Traditional View,' begins by pointing to the long-standing habit of New Testament scholarship, prior to the last decade, of avoiding the Gospel of John in discussions of the historical Jesus. In more recent years, however, the work of the British scholar, Richard Bauckham, on the 'eyewitness' and on the Gospel of John as the work of such, the situation has changed considerably and this change is placed within the broader cultural anxiety and conflict over the growing influence of evangelical and conservative religion on the one hand and secularism on the other. In dealing with Bauckham's understanding of the importance of eyewitnesses for the Gospel of John, Crossley takes up the pericope dealing with Sabbath disputes in Mark 2–3 and the representation of Jesus in John 5 as a divine figure who recommends the breaking of biblical Sabbath laws. While Crossley points out that it is theoretically possible that both accounts are fictitious, he argues that if one of these versions were to reflect a typical halakhic dispute, it would undoubtedly be that found in the Synoptic Gospels, rather than that in John's story, which so clearly reflects Christian rather than Jewish interests and perspectives. Crossley, taking up Bauckham's claim that the raising of Lazarus, found only in John's Gospel, is a more logical provocation that might lead to Jesus' execution than the story of cleansing the Temple as the bearing cause as presented by Mark, points out the obvious problem that the history-defying miracle of raising Lazarus from the dead cannot be understood other than as fictive. John 3's story of Nicodemus is then taken up to show how John can be useful for sketching the development of the Jesus tradition in an effort to reflect later concerns. He also points out that Bauckham's method seeks to affirm the historical accuracy of 'unique, unusual, memorable and salient events' and is, thus, intrinsically problematic, particularly if this method were applied equally to other unique episodes of the Gospel. Even if one grants that John's Gospel is based in the memory of an eyewitness, the problems of historical accuracy and creativity are not thereby lessened. Turning to the more systematic treatment of these questions by the Society of Biblical Literature project on John, Jesus and History, Crossley sees a definite tendency to make the arguments too general, leaving out as they do specific and critical details. Seeing John's figure of Jesus in such vague and generalized categories as that of an eschatological prophet, a wisdom-related teacher or even a Cynic Jesus, Crossley points out that describing Jesus with the help of such categories hardly makes that figure more useful for the question of historicity. Taking up the project's discussion of specific features of John's

Gospel, he also makes the obvious, but, for his argument, important point that the uniqueness of John's departures from the other Gospels also does not make them more useful for such questions of historicity, however much they might enlarge the discussion. Finally, he takes up the often-used apologetic premise that theology does not hold historical inaccuracies implicit. However, the argument is in fact largely a straw one to Crossley, who sees the primary opposition to John's historicity in relation rather to the later historical matrix of that theology. In closing his essay, Crossley sees no reason to challenge the consensus that John's Gospel brings little new to the discussion of historicity.

With emphasis on thematic elements and patterns of composition, the following essay by Thomas L. Thompson. 'Psalm 72 and Mark 1:12-13: Mythic Evocation in Narratives of the Good King,' analyses the untold story in the beginning of Mark's Gospel in Mark 1:12-13, in which Jesus had been driven by the spirit into the desert for forty days, where, living among the wild animals and—Elijah-like—cared for by angels, he is tempted by Satan (Mk 1:12-13). In contrast to the debate stories one finds in Matthew and Luke, Mark clusters these four thematic elements from the Old Testament, whose narrative functions are merely implicit, but all of which play an important role in structuring the 'biographic' form of Mark's Gospel. Within a context of rewritten narrative, Matthew's version is an allegory in the form of a stereotypical three-fold debate story, using Mark's cluster of thematic elements as context, while the debate itself is a classic reiterative narrative, thoroughly integrated through identifiable episodes and prophecies drawn with a clear interpretive coherence from the Pentateuch, Kings, prophets and Psalter. Luke's version is presented as an extension of an expansive baptism narrative, functioning as an etiological allegory identifying Isaiah's suffering servant as God's first-born. The story is placed as the first of four tales in which the central figure has been filled with the spirit and where the debate is presented as a reiteration of Moses stories in Exodus and Deuteronomy. Luke's most distinctive element comes with the emphasis he places on his narrative variation of Deut. 6:16 and his citation of Psalm 91. Each of the three versions of this episode is well integrated, but distinctively so, with each of the themes of the Gospels in which they are found. In spite of the lack of a meaning-bearing plotline in Mark's version, the cluster of motifs he presents identifies a stereotypical tale-type, reflecting both the symbol-system of the Pentateuch and former prophets and quite specific biographical tropes, evoking an implicit mythic narrative. This narrative is identified with two tropes belonging to ancient Near Eastern portraits of royal saviour figures; namely, the title of 'son of god' and the theme of 'former suffering' leading to a saving reversal. A comparable construction can be seen in the biographical sketch of Job's earlier life in Job 29, which Thompson understands as functioning as a parable. The biographical 'events' of this episode are then derived from a cluster of central thematic elements in Psalm 72; namely, the central motifs of 'good news', victory over the dragon, eternal kingdom and universal empire. The essay finds its closure in a brief discussion of thematic reiteration as a function of such composition.

Ingrid Hjelm's essay, '"Who Is My Neighbour?": Implicit Use of Old Testament Stories and Motifs in Luke's Gospel,' in its analysis of the rewriting of Old Testament stories and motifs in the composition of Luke's Gospel, exposes an insight into Old Testament theology and the ideology implicit in its narratives and language that is far more sophisticated, complex and profound than the relatively simple 'search and mark' method implicit in Matthew's identification for explicit proof texts in the construction of his narrative. Casting doubt on the common scholarly identification of Luke as a 'Christianized non-Jew', Hjelm questions our methods for identifying what is 'Jewish' in the New Testament. She argues that Luke's methods of reiteration and parallelism, though quite far from the Rabbinic traditions of marking specific 'utterances and fulfilments' as Matthew's Gospel continues, are rather typical of ancient Near Eastern and classical literature. While, from a modern perspective, the use of such reiteration has a tendency to undermine a narrative's historicity and in particular its value as reliable testimony and witness, the recognition of such reiteration becomes an indispensible aid to the interpreter to identify the symbol system by which the text is used to communicate a strategy of evoking signs of its 'transcendent' meaning. Centring her analysis on the theme of the return of God's glory to Israel and the identification of Luke's use of Chronicles' portrait of David as *Moses redivivus*, Hjelm discusses the narrative strategies supporting Luke's casting Jesus in the role of both Moses and Elijah's successor as lawgiver and prophet in order to create an allegorically based role for Christianity as superseding Moses' Samaritanism and Elijah's Judaism. The roots of Luke's theology are found in the role of the Davidic king as cultic and spiritual, rather than political. In Luke's theology, Samaritanism and Judaism are not rejected, but reformulated within the theme of reconciling 'all Israel', which she finds expressed in Chronicles, Isaiah, Jeremiah and Ezekiel. This central theme of Luke's theology is illustrated with a discussion of the biblical roots of Luke's 'good Samaritan' parable.

Joshua Sabih's essay, 'The *ʿĪsā* Narrative in the Qur'an: The Making of a Prophet,' which deals with the Islamic figure of *ʿĪsā*, not only helps further understanding of some of the theological functions of the intertextual discourse on the Gospel's figure of Jesus, it also points out a significant aspect of the reception, through its identification of the implicit function of 'mock narratives' as a counterpart to the Qur'an's use of the figure of *'Īsā*. In particular, the *'Īsā* narratives in Sura 3 and 19 demonstrate a clear lack of interest in any reconstruction of a 'historical *'Īsā*'. Moreover, such narratives in the Qur'an appear to be, but are in fact not, fragmentary. The narratives maintain, rather, their original, allegorical and pedagogical mode. They are composed 'to tell a different story' which is consciously and intentionally, ideologically motivated. It is as it were 'Allah who speaks, in a monologue. The accounts are not fragmentary; nor are they a mistaken retelling of the Gospel story. They rather deconstruct that narrative within an anti-historical discourse that specifically opposes Pauline theology! It is first of all the cue name of Jesus and its theological significance (עושי/עושוהי: *he saves/Yahve saves*), which the Qur'anic narrative of *'Īsā* disputes. In the process of constructing its prophetic histories as a salvation history, the Qur'anic discourse revived peripheral narratives which had been silenced or 'de-canonized' through the construction of an imperial orthodoxy. Accordingly, Sabih, rather than understanding Islam as one among many Christian or Jewish sects, argues that the *'Īsā* one finds in the Qur'an is not identical with the figure of Jesus in the New Testament, even though the *'Īsā* of post-Qur'anic Islam obviously is. The Qur'anic use of Maryam as the mother of *'Īsā*, for example, is not a confusion of a historical Moses' sister with Jesus' mother, but rather the opening of a discourse related to the question of the tradition to which the 'two Marys' belong. To understand the Qur'anic *'Īsā*, one must look beyond the question of historicity. For Sabih, the Qur'an is 'a corpus (an assemblage of text fragments), a text (with both unity and cohesion) and a discourse. These fragments belong not to specific literary genres so much as they reflect types of discourse.' In clarification of his reading, Sabih presents a discussion of the Qur'an's discourse on three themes: the name of *'Īsā*, the 'annunciation' and the 'nativity'. He argues that the name *'Īsā* is not the result of an Arabic translation of either the names Jesus or Jeshu'a ('savior'), but it is rather a reiteration of the name Esau—parallel to late rabbinic tradition which, using the contrasting pair of Jacob and Israel comes to use Esau as an allegorical synonym for Christians, much in the way that Ishmael became synonymous with Muslims. Turning to more 'bio-hagiographical' elements, Sabih sees Sura 19's discourse on the annunciation as a form of Gospel epitome, while Sura 3's double-annunciation narrative outlines *'Īsā*'s prophetic destiny in an anti-Christian narrative in which Jesus regains his identity and humanity. Similarly, Sura 19 on the nativity adds an independent polemic voice to the discourse of the nativity, in which the baby, *'Īsā*, takes an active, prophetic, role, speaking and acting on behalf of 'Allah. In conclusion, Sabih argues that the Qur'anic literature should not be read as a text that is dependent on the Bible, but rather as an independent voice within the larger theological discourse. His argument supports the principle that no text is original and to be read in isolation from other texts.

The closing theoretical essay by Kurt Noll, 'Investigating Earliest Christianity without Jesus,' takes up the central methodological question of the relevance of research into the historical Jesus for understanding earliest Christianity. Applying a model for the construction of central ideas which determine worldview and behaviour of, for example, the 'Jesus movement', Noll sets out to argue that the historical Jesus—assuming that he existed—was irrelevant to this movement's earliest stages. He presents the thesis in four steps: a description of his method, the identification of a key issue, an analysis and evaluation of the relevance of the role played by the historical Jesus and, finally, a comparison with early Muslim traditions, providing an alternative understanding of the data. After his initial description of what he refers to as a Darwinian method of analysis, Noll takes his key issue from the contrast implied in the choice of data between early orthodox and heretical Christian writings which have been analysed by Richard Bauckham, on the one hand, and the literatures of the ancient Near East, analysed by Thomas L. Thompson, on the other. After a critique of Bauckham's identification of the basis of the Gospels and early Christian writings in 'eyewitness testimony', Noll argues that Bauckham's assumption that the accounts are 'fully referential' is directly contradicted by Thompson's understanding that they reflect rather recycled literature written in didactic and allegorical genres which are uninterested in original sayings or founding events. The conclusions of these studies, however, only appear to be incompatible; for Noll understands Bauckham as having failed to trace his assertions about eyewitnesses to actual witnesses and points out that Thompson's arguments hardly rule out a conclusion that the referenced events had indeed occurred. What has not been asked is *why non-referential narratives about Jesus were promoted as eyewitness testimony*. This question he pursues according to his 'Darwinian model', with the help of an analysis of Paul's dispute with Cephas and James and its provocation of an eventual break with Judaism after the city's destruction in 70 CE. Noll then turns to an analysis of the development of ideas related to identifying Christianity's origins with conflicts related to its roots in Judaism, raising the argument that a 'historical' Jesus had become necessary for the success of Paul's doctrines, a pragmatic solution for defending doctrine by appeal to Jesus as authority figure. Comparing Bauckham's data on Christian 'eyewitnesses' with the more elaborate and systematic data related to early 'eyewitnesses' for Islamic traditions, Noll then discusses a scenario by which this literary Jesus might have been invented and then presented as a product of such accounts and draws the conclusion that a historical Jesus was indeed irrelevant to the construction and development of early Christianity.

Thomas L. Thompson/Thomas S. Verenna
Copenhagen/Philadelphia

Part I

Into the Well of Historical Jesus Scholarship

- 1 -

A (Very, Very) Short History of Minimalism:[1] From the Chronicler to the Present[2]

Jim West

'Minimalism'[3] is the supposition that the biblical text cannot rightly or honestly be mined for historical reconstructions of ancient Israel or earliest Christianity. The underlying assumption here is that the biblical text is not historically oriented. That is to say, the purpose of the Bible is not to offer twenty-first-century historians fodder for their reconstructive mills. It is to speak theologically to ancient (and I would also say, modern) communities of faith.

Though this definition is not necessarily the standard definition of minimalism, it does offer a more accurate understanding of what 'minimalism' is and will be the working definition for the words 'minimalism' and 'minimalist' in what follows. Furthermore, denoting ancient persons as 'minimalists' is admittedly anachronistic. Nonetheless, I will use it anyway simply because it encapsulates present reality. So, for example, Paul the Apostle may not have gone to Copenhagen or Sheffield to learn theology, but I describe him as a 'minimalist' for reasons I shall demonstrate below, albeit briefly.

---

1. Though its originators meant 'minimalism' as a slur, I retain it here as it has now become both familiar and in my estimation acceptable (in the same way that 'Methodist' was originally intended as an insult but is now perfectly alright).
2. An earlier version of this essay was published in *The Bible and Interpretation*, http://www.bibleinterp.com/opeds/hist357908.shtml, accessed on 8 September, 2010.
3. *The Bible and Interpretation* has published a number of essays on the theme, available here: http://www.bibleinterp.com/articles/Minimalism_essays.shtml and accessed on 30 August, 2010.

First, though, a few things have to be stated as clearly as possible. These are:

1. Most 'histories' of Ancient Israel and Earliest Christianity are simply examples of circular reasoning. Many 'historians' use the Bible as a historical source; they reconstruct a 'history' which is often nothing more than a recapitulation of the biblical telling; and the Bible is affirmed as 'historical' because of the history so constructed. Similarly, the life of Jesus, for instance, is gleaned from a reading of the Gospels. Said reconstruction is named a 'history of Jesus' life'. That 'history of Jesus' life' is then utilized to prove historically the life of Jesus as described in the Gospels. One need only pick up John Bright's *History of Israel*[4] or Joseph Ratzinger's *Jesus of Nazareth*[5] to see circularity in action. True, ancillary materials are added to these histories (on the very rare occasions that they are available), but these only reinforce the circularly circumscribed reconstruction.
2. Any attempt to construct a history of Israel or earliest Christianity without appealing to the Bible is virtually impossible. Even the heartiest efforts[6] to offer a history of ancient Israel or the early Church usually draw on the biblical text. There simply seems to be no way—at present—to write a history without recourse to the Bible which then, since it has become the source of the history also finds itself confirmed by the history it has constructed.
3. Do points one and two imply, as some souls would have us believe,[7] that there really was no historical Jesus or Ancient Israel? Μὴ γέ νοιτο! Absence of evidence is not evidence of absence; absence of evidence is evidence of absolutely nothing at all. What points one and two illustrate is that the Bible as Bible cannot be used for grandiose historical projects: nothing more, and nothing less. Something happened. We just are not in a position to say what. Not historically.

That said, we can now move on to assert that the Bible itself is the first and foremost witness to the propriety of minimalism as an approach. Think, for example, of what the Chronicler does to the story of David's numbering of Israel. 2 Samuel 24 clearly states that Yahweh impelled David to number the nation. The Chronicler, completely disinterested in the 'historical' situation,

4. J. Bright, *A History of Israel* (London: SCM Press, 1960).
5. J. Ratzinger, *Jesus of Nazareth* (New York: Random House, 2007).
6. See, for example, the herculean effort by M. Liverani, *Israel's History and the History of Israel* (London: Equinox, 2005).
7. R. Price is a prime example, see http://rationalrevolution.net/articles/jesus_myth_history.htm, accessed 30 August, 2010.

alters the tale completely and instead of describing Yahweh as inciting David to count the folk, describes Satan doing it (1 Chron. 21). These two accounts cannot be harmonized historically and the Chronicler surely understood that. The historicity of that tradition did not matter to the Chronicler because he approached the text as a minimalist: it was not 'history' that mattered, but 'theology'. In this regard, most redactional emendation can be seen as an adoption of miminalist literary technique, be it inner-biblical exegesis, midrashic interpretation or targumic reconciliation—all of these are examples of minimalist attempts to rewrite or properly explain history.

In fact, a cursory examination of the Chronicler's work demonstrates that he is not at all interested in 'history' in the same way that modern historians of the Bible seem to be. Rather, he was first, foremost and only, a theologian.[8]

But the Chronicler was not the only biblical author who did not care about 'historicity'. The Synoptic Gospels, too, each go their own way. Matthew recounts a Sermon on the Mount while Luke has a Sermon on the Plain. Neither cared where the sermon (or sermons) occurred,[9] they only concerned themselves with the theological substance of the sayings of Jesus—sayings they compiled and organized along lines purely determined by theological necessity rather than historical accuracy. In fact, even though Luke appears to be casting his Gospel in 'historical' garb, he only adopts that appearance in order to make his story of Jesus sound very much like the Septuagint's story of God's acts on behalf of his people. That is, Luke is writing in a style intentionally mimicking the Old Testament so as to make clear to his readers that the story of Jesus is just the continuation of the activity of God among his own. If Luke was writing 'history', he got a number of things mucked up (as all commentators and historians recognize—e.g. the census he mentions at the beginning of his Gospel[10]). The census could not have occurred when Luke reports it having occurred and in fact it did not. But Luke does not care about such things because he is doing theology, not historiography. Luke is making a theological assertion: Jesus and his family may have been under Roman authority—but that authority only served the larger purpose

---

8. J. Jarick's work on *Chronicles* is spectacular precisely because he focuses on the theological import of the text. See more at http://www.theology.ox.ac.uk/people/staff-list/dr-john-jarick.html, accessed 30 August 2010.
9. Though see Hjelm, who asserts that the location suggests that God has power over the whole world, the mountains and the plains. Also, cf. T. L. Thompson, *The Messiah Myth: The Ancient Near Eastern Background of Jesus and David* (New York: Basic Books, 2005), 51-52, 109-111, 132-135.
10. On Luke's census, see the very extensive bibliography of J. Nolland in *Luke 1–9:20* (Word Biblical Commentary, 35a; Dallas: Word Books, 1989), 94-96.

of God's plan being fulfilled. Jesus, Luke will show, is not only the Lord of the Jews, he is also the Lord of the Romans.

The Gospel of John, similarly, does theology without any interest in portraying 'things as they actually were'. John places, for example, the cleansing of the Temple right at the start of Jesus' ministry while the Synoptics place it right at the end. Unfortunately, New Testament scholars have needlessly debated which one was 'right' in their chronology.[11] Both and neither are right because both are interested in saying something theological and neither care about the historicity of the cleansing.

Paul, too, shows absolutely no interest in 'historical' matters. See 2 Cor. 5:16 where he, for all intents and purposes, undermines any 'quest' for the historical Jesus.[12] The verse says:

> Ὥστε ἡμεῖς ἀπὸ τοῦ νῦν οὐδένα οἴδαμεν κατὰ σάρκα· εἰ καὶ ἐγνώκαμεν κατὰ σάρκα Χριστόν ἀλλὰ νῦν οὐκέτι γινώσκομεν.

Paul thus asserts, it seems to me, scant concern for historical reconstructions of the life of Jesus. Were he interested in such matters he could have, and would have, not only not said what he said above; but he would have gone into great detail, especially concerning the empty tomb, which was the central factor in his proclamation of the risen and living Jesus. In fact, the letters of Paul contain scant 'historical' reference of any sort when it comes to Jesus. 'Born of a woman, born under the law' (Gal. 4:4) is about as historical as Paul gets when it comes to discussing the life of Jesus. Likewise, 'I am crucified with Christ...' barely touches the fringe of the historicist garment. Paul is just not interested in the historical details of his faith's earliest comings and goings. Rather, again, Paul's concern is theological.

In the Deutero-Pauline and Catholic epistles, there is no 'historical reconstruction' implied or indicated. Revelation, too, is metaphysical and super-historical (and maybe even too metaphysical!).

In sum, the Bible, from beginning to end, is primarily interested in God. The stage is set in the opening verse of Genesis where we learn, 'In the beginning, God...' The Bible's aim is not to tell a historical tale; its aim is to tell a theological tale. For that reason, its authors, minimalists all, recognized that their work and aim and calling were something other than to use traditions and tales for historical reconstruction. 'What, when and

---

11. See the very interesting debate currently taking place in the Society of Biblical Literature and spearheaded by the John, Jesus and History group, http://catholic-resources.org/SBL/JJH.html, accessed 30 August, 2010. And while sceptical of their results (because historio-centric), I am very glad to see John getting some positive press after all these decades of disdain.
12. R. Bultmann's commentary on *2 Corinthians* remains the most useful.

how' were of no interest to them; but 'why' mattered supremely. 'Why' mattered alone.

Time would fail us to consider Augustine and Jerome, Origen and Cyril, Clement and Aquinas, Luther and Zwingli and Calvin...men of whom the world was not worthy. They wandered in deserts and lived in caves (and in Luther's case, taverns); they were scorned, mocked, beaten and abused, and yet they never sought refuge in a false historicism. They and other exegetes up until quite recently (the eighteenth century essentially) understood that theology is the substance of things biblical and the evidence of things free from needing historical underpinning. The tyranny of the circularly arrived at *Sitz im Leben* had no power over them. To be sure, they were more certain of the historical 'truth' of the Bible than they should have been—but they still excelled in their ability to clearly perceive that the Bible's purpose was not historical, but theological.

Postmodern interpreters and post-postmoderners who use the Bible to ask and answer the questions about 'what, when and how' are asking the wrong questions altogether. If they were to ask the Bible 'why' they would at least be getting closer to the truth. As it is, that truth is obscured from them, since we all know (or should know) that the answers we get are utterly dependent on the questions we ask.

Minimalism did not begin with Lemche[13] or Thompson[14] or Whitelam[15] or Davies[16] or any of the other central or marginal players commonly associated with it: it began with the Chronicler and the prophets and the evangelists and the psalmists and Paul and John and was continued by the Fathers of the Church and their Reforming heirs. Minimalism is not a new phenomenon; it is as old as Scripture itself. For this reason we can only rationally conclude that maximalism, then, distorts Scripture. It distorts the theological message of the text by transforming it into historical source materials.

13. N. P. Lemche, *The Old Testament: Between Theology and History* (Louisville: Westminster John Knox Press, 2008).
14. T. L. Thompson, *The Mythic Past: Biblical Archaeology and the Myth of Israel* (New York: Basic Books, 1999).
15. P. R. Davies, *The Invention of Ancient Israel* (New York: Routledge, 1996).
16 K. W. Whitelam, 'Method and Madness: Some Remarks on Doing History with the Bible,' *JBL* 114.4 (1995), 699.

- 2 -

The German Pestilence: Re-assessing Feuerbach, Strauss and Bauer

Roland Boer

What is the relevance or actuality, as the French like to say, of David Strauss and Bruno Bauer (and for that matter, Ludwig Feuerbach) today? In their own time they caused outrage, were sacked from university posts and denied positions. Outside Germany (Prussia) they were known as part of the corroding 'German Pestilence' that would ruin almost two millennia of facts about the Bible. No less a thinker than Nietzsche made a shipwreck of his faith after reading Strauss. In our own time, especially with the so-called minimalist position in biblical studies, we find a return to many of their concerns. It is as though the implications of the radical work of these nineteenth-century scholars have yet to be realized.

This essay concerns itself with three topics. First, it considers the reasons for the theological turn of German philosophy in the first decades of the nineteenth century. Why did all of the major debates concerning reason, republicanism, democracy, the nature of the state, freedom of speech and of the press, the relations of church and state and even economics take place on the territory of the Bible, especially the New Testament Gospels? An exploration of the context in relation to other European centres draws out the reasons for this distinct German turn to theology. I also argue that this was the situation which launched a century-long global domination of biblical criticism by German biblical scholarship.

Second, it explores the specific (and at the time explosive) contribution of Ludwig Feuerbach's theory of projection that was to be so influential in subsequent thought, David Strauss's argument concerning the mythic nature of the Gospel narratives and Bruno Bauer's radically sceptical New Testament criticism, which went hand-in-hand with his radical politics and militant atheism. In each case I situate their arguments within the wider context of their thought and that of Germany at the time. Third, I sift through the dross to find a few gems that are still worth considering today. As for those items, we will need to wait for the close of the essay.

Context: The Biblical Terrain of Political Thought

> There are two kinds of facts which are undeniable. In the first place religion, and next to it, politics, are the subjects which form the main interest of Germany today. We must take these, in whatever form they exist, as our point of departure.[1]

So wrote none other than Karl Marx in 1844, but is a fair summary of the situation of public debate at the time. In what follows I draw a sketch of the intertwining of religious and political issues in the 1820s and 1830s in Germany.[2] Although it is going too far to argue that the idea of separating religion and politics was simply not possible in those years, it is true that there was a massive effort to make sure they stayed an inseparable married couple, however much they might have squabbled.[3] But we need to be more specific: at stake was not merely religion but theology, indeed not merely theology but biblical studies. As for politics, that took the specific form of the drive for a 'Christian state' under the pious Friedrich Wilhelm III and his equally reactionary son, Friedrich Wilhelm IV. Let me say a little about them before returning to biblical criticism.

When the new Prussian king, Friedrich Wilhelm IV, took power in 1840 he succeeded a father who had begun a process of ensuring the Restoration of authority in the monarchy. Frightened by those dreadful Frenchmen and their revolutionary fervour across the border, one after the other the two Friedrichs busily set about shoring up their domain against the hordes of barbarians keen to lop off their heads. In 1822 the devoutly Calvinist

1. K. Marx, *Letters from the Deutsch-Französische Jahrbücher*, in *Marx and Engels Collected Works* (Moscow: Progress Publishers, 1975 [1844]), III, 143.
2. I know it is common knowledge for anyone with a smattering of knowledge about German history, but 'Germany' refers to a loose conglomerate of independent states: Prussia, Westphalia, the Rhineland and East Prussia. Westphalia and the Rhineland had been under the French for almost two decades, had absorbed French culture and politics (including the abolition of feudal social relations) and often looked to Paris rather than Berlin. However, in 1815 they were annexed to Prussia.
3. For a good treatment of this period, although he tends to treat it in terms of the history of ideas, especially by means of the key motif of 'Christian personalism', see W. Breckman, *Marx, the Young Hegelians, and the Origins of Radical Social Theory* (Cambridge: Cambridge University Press, 2001). For an insightful treatment of the tensions between an archaic bedrock and the reforming push by a small group of liberals in the Rhineland, see S. Kouvelakis, *Philosophy and Revolution: From Kant to Marx* (trans.G. M. Goshgarian; London: Verso, 2003), 243-46.

Friedrich Wilhelm III had brought together the Calvinist and Lutheran churches to form the Prussian Union (*Preussische Landeskirche*). He enforced a single liturgy for the church, ensured a strict hierarchy and in all modesty promptly placed himself at the head of the church. One would have had to be a complete hermit not to notice the impression that theology and politics were united in a broad reactionary front, all of it concentrated in one person who was both political leader and Christ's representative on earth.[4] To use terms the Americans are fond of using, he was commander in chief and theologian in chief—all rolled up into one humble person. Despite a few vague hints at reform to keep the liberals hopeful, his son was perhaps even more reactionary, seeking to wind back the clock even more. The 'Christian state' would be restored no matter what stood in its way. One by one the reforms that had been imposed on his father in a moment of republican ferment after the unrest of 1805–15 (which in its turn followed in the wake of the French Revolution) were rolled back. In effect, what Friedrich Wilhelm III and then especially his son, number four, were trying to do was hold back the push for political power from a newly wealthy bourgeoisie. They did so by fighting rearguard actions to preserve political control in the hands of the leftovers of the feudal nobility and the idea of a Christian state (trailing the dust of the Holy Roman Empire). At all costs that anti-church, anti-aristocratic and democratic impulse had to be resisted in Germany.

For intellectuals this reactionary tendency had a real effect on livelihoods and opportunities. The monarch had a direct hand in university appointments, ensuring conservative appointments to positions in philosophy, law and above all theology. Feuerbach ran afoul of the system and ended up operating a porcelain workshop of his wife's family (Bertha Löw) in the small Bavarian town of Bruckberg. Bruno Bauer was removed from Berlin and then Bonn and ended up living on a farm. David Strauss struggled to be appointed in Switzerland. One of the most notable moments was the direct invitation from Friedrich Wilhelm IV to a retired and increasingly reactionary Schelling in 1841 to take up Hegel's chair of philosophy in Berlin in order to 'slay the dragon-seed of Hegelian pantheism'. The Young Hegelians, to which Strauss and Bauer belonged, were certainly not in favour.

So far the story is reasonably well known, at least for anyone with a passing knowledge of German politics in the early nineteenth century.[5] However,

---

4. It is this concentration that leads Breckman to speak of a type of personalism in German thought and practice, a personalism that became the focus of struggle.
5. For more detail, readers may consult any number of histories of the period, although see especially, F.-L. Kroll, *Friedrich Wilhelm IV. und das Staatsdenken der deutschen Romantik* (Berlin: Copress, 1990); R. M. Berdahl, *The Politics of the Prussian Nobility: The Development of a Conservative Ideology* (Princeton: Princeton University Press, 1988); D. Blasius, *Friedrich Wilhelm IV. 1795–1861: Psychopathologie und Geschichte* (Göttingen: Vandenhoeck & Ruprecht, 2000).

for my purposes the theological questions are even more interesting. In contrast to the radical anti-clericalism of the Enlightenment *philosophes* in France (where in response early socialism had a distinctly Christian flavour) or the Deism of English intellectual culture, Germany fought its cultural battles on a different ground, namely that of theology.[6] Or rather, theology was crucial to all three, but in very different ways. While the French radicals either rejected it and its institutions or developed a rather Christian form of communism, and while the radicals in England tended to slide from religious Dissent to Deism (with a good dose of anti-establishment polemic against the Church of England),[7] in a Germany still saturated with the Pietistic revival of the 1810s and 1820s as well as the well-known German backwardness in economics and politics, German intellectuals could hardly avoid fighting their battles with and through theology. Actually it was more specific than that: they waged furious controversies over the Bible, especially the New Testament and its Gospels. In short, the stories about Jesus in the Gospels were the gunpowder in the political powder-keg, precisely because political and ecclesiastical power hinged on this figure. If theology was nothing less than the *lingua franca* of public debate in Germany for most of the first half of the nineteenth century, then the Bible was the terrain of battle for the knot of political struggles—over the state, politics, freedom of the press, secularism, reason and religion.

This point seems to me glaringly obvious, so I find it passing strange indeed that those who write of the period speak of an amorphous 'religion' and its entanglement with politics. I hardly need to point out that religion in early nineteenth-century Germany designates the touchy relationship between various Protestant groups (most notably the Calvinists and Lutherans) and the Roman Catholics. But a careful study of what was being written and what generated the most controversy reveals that the key was biblical criticism.

The radical edge of the heated debates of the time came from the Young Hegelians, who met in the small Hippel Café in Berlin from 1837, drank copious amounts of alcohol, perused pornography and debated Hegel, politics and the Bible into the early hours.[8] One feature of the writings (and

6. Or, as F. Engels put it, 'the battle for dominion over German public opinion in politics and religion' is in fact a battle 'over Germany itself.' F. Engels, *Schelling on Hegel* in *Marx and Engels Collected Works* (Moscow: Progress Publishers, 1975 [1841]), II, 181.
7. See E. P. Thompson, *The Making of the English Working Class* (New York: Vintage, 1966).
8. For some strange reason, we seem to be living once again in the time of the Young Hegelians. As A. Toscano put it to me (private communication), we in our own time have not yet reached 1840. That may explain why interest in these rabble rousers and party animals has revived somewhat. Three decades and more ago, a stream of works on the Young Hegelians appeared (e.g. I. Berlin, *Karl Marx: His Life and Thought* [Oxford: Oxford

limited teaching) of this energetic bunch cannot be emphasized enough: a good number of them were biblical scholars or at least theologians, and their chosen ground of battle was nothing other than the Bible. The decades of the 1830s and 1840s trembled and indeed rumbled with the seismic shift taking place. David Strauss had lain down the challenge with his *Leben Jesu* of 1835,[9] only to find that he could no longer find a teaching post.[10] Bruno Bauer added his deep challenges to the Bible, in studies on both the Hebrew Bible and the Gospels throughout the 1840s. Add to this what was perhaps the most influential work—Ludwig Feuerbach's *Das Wesen des Christentums* of 1841—and we have a serious and sustained assault that was simultaneously biblical, political and philosophical.

The question, then, is why the Bible was so important for these debates? Let me suggest three factors, one from France and the other two relating to Germany itself. From France there came a distinct form of radical politics that the Prussian king and the nobles found so threatening: socialism with a distinctly Christian flavour. Or rather, arguing that the original form of Christianity was communist—as found in that legendary account of Acts 2:44-45 and 4:32—this French socialism sought to transform Christianity's teachings into codes of ethics without all the supernatural trappings. So we find Saint-Simon's critique of capitalism tied in with an argument that both the Protestant Reformation and medieval Catholicism had distorted the nature of early Christianity, which was really a religion of brotherly love and not a dualistic one that elevated heaven and debased earth. The communities that formed after his death established themselves as 'church' replete with a priesthood that proclaimed Saint-Simon himself as the messiah. Despite the inevitable fractions in the movement, the defections to Fourier, who had until then managed only a small band of followers for his phalanteries, and even the much-ridiculed venture to the Middle East to

---

University Press, 1978, 4th edn], 47-76; D. McLellan, *The Young Hegelians and Karl Marx* [London: Macmillan, 1969]; S. Hook, *From Hegel to Marx: Studies in the Intellectual Development of Karl Marx* [New York: Columbia University Press, 1994 (1936)] and the unreliable L. Kolakowski, *Main Currents of Marxism* [trans. P.S. Falla; Oxford: Oxford University Press, 1981], I, 81-95), but the interest waned. Breckman's study of 1999 is the first of a small revival, but see also D. Moggach, *The New Hegelians: Politics and Philosophy in the Hegelian School* (Cambridge: Cambridge University Press, 2006) and the anthology edited by L. S. Stepelevich, *The Young Hegelians: An Anthology* (Amherst: Prometheus Books, 1997).

9. D. F. Strauss, *Das Leben Jesu, kritisch bearbeitet* (Tübingen: C. F. Osiander, 1835), English: *The Life of Jesus Critically Examined* (trans. G. Eliot; London: Thames, 2006 [1902]). For an extraordinary discussion of Strauss and modernity, see W. Blanton, *Displacing Christian Origins: Philosophy, Secularity, and the New Testament* (Chicago: University of Chicago Press, 2007), 25-66.

10. Even in Zürich, when he was elected to the chair in theology, there was such a storm of opposition that the city pensioned him off before he even began.

find a female messiah, this type of early socialism washed over the border to affect some German radicals. It was the moral vision and sense of progress in human society towards brotherly love that inspired characters like Heinrich Heine, August von Cieskowski and an early collaborator with Marx and Engels, Moses Hess. It also influenced some of the early leaders of the German communist movement, such as Wilhelm Weitling, Hermann Kriege, Karl Grün and Gottfried Kinkel.[11] These radicals based their vision on the Bible, especially the figure of Jesus in the Gospels. With texts like Weitling's *The Poor Sinner's Gospel*,[12] a radical reading of the Gospels in a communist direction, the reactionary German authorities and the Church were ready to pounce on anything that smacked of the mildest radical politics *and* of radical biblical criticism.

As for Germany, it is often pointed out that it was economically and politically backward, with industry barely established and the state engaged in a last gasp of absolutism. For this reason it did not feel the full effect of the radical anti-clericalism of France or the extremes of Deism in England. Yet this is far from the full picture, for there are a couple of other historical reasons, one much deeper and longer, and the other more immediate. In one sense, the controversies of the 1830s and 1840s provided yet another turn in the rumbling history of the Reformation. From Luther's defiance (and assistance by the Duke of Saxony) in the sixteenth century to the Thirty Years War (1618–1648) that raged over the German states, Italy and the Low countries, during which the Roman Catholics wrested some of the southern German states back from the Lutherans, Protestants in the north and Roman Catholics in the south had dug themselves in to become deeply conservative. The Roman Catholics looked to the pope, while the Protestants (a mix of Lutherans and some Calvinists in the far north) drew upon conservative streams of Pietism, marrying an inner walk with God to a tenacious hold on the Bible as the 'word of God'. Despite all the best efforts of the state to keep both Protestants and Roman Catholics in a civil if often fractious relationship, the mutual polemic ran deep.

A more recent factor was the Pietistic revival in the 1810s and 1820s. It was a confluence of the revivalist waves that rose across Europe in response

---

11. See K. Marx and F. Engels, *The German Ideology: Critique of Modern German Philosophy according to Its Representatives Feuerbach, B. Bauer and Stirner, and of German Socialism according to Its Various Prophets*, in *Marx and Engels Collected Works* (Moscow: Progress Publishers, 1976 [1932]), V, 484-530; idem, 'Review (May to October 1850),' in *Marx and Engels Collected Works* (Moscow: Progress Publishers, 1978 [1850]), X, 528-32; idem, 'The Great Men of the Exile,' in *Marx and Engels Collected Works* (Moscow: Progress Publishers, 1979 [1930]), XI, 227-326.
12. Wilhelm W. Weitling, *The Poor Sinner's Gospel* (trans. D. Livingstone; London: Sheed & Ward, 1969 [1843]).

to Enlightenment rationalism and 'Godless' revolutionary republicanism and the longer history of German Pietism. The emphasis was on recovering one's walk with God, the inner life of faith, the priesthood of all believers and the all-important role of God's word, the Bible. The big difference from earlier moments of Pietistic fervour in the late seventeenth and eighteenth centuries was that the nobility and intellectuals took it up with not a little enthusiasm. This combination of the aristocracy and bourgeois intellectuals meant that it was not merely a revival from above, but that it also took a nicely conservative turn. Misgivings in the Prussian state—for Pietism could easily reject the state in favour of one's direct relation with God and others—soon gave way when it dovetailed nicely with obedience to God's regent on earth and the purity of the Reformation itself. Crown Prince Friedrich Wilhelm declared himself in favour (why would he not?) and theology faculties became watchdogs for orthodoxy. Among these was Ernst Hengstenberg in Berlin, against whom Bruno Bauer directed his attack in *Herr Dr Hengstenberg* of 1839—one of his less than astute political acts, for it led to his removal from Berlin. In this context, the Young Hegelians were both cornered and became the champions of the liberal and republican cause. Indeed, when Bruno Bauer was eventually dismissed from the theology faculty at Bonn in 1842 (whither he was sent from Berlin), none of them was ever to hold a teaching post again. No wonder, then, the radical journal of the Young Hegelians, *Deutsche Jahrbücher für Wissenschaft und Kunst*, often fought theological battles with conservative journals such as the *Kölnische Zeitung*, the *Rhein-und Mosel-Zeitung*, the *Münchener politische Bläter* and the *Trier'sche Zeitung*.

In sum, due to the proverbial tardiness of German economics and politics, as well as the Lutheran doctrine of *sola scriptura* and the long history of struggles between Protestants and Catholics, the debates over religion, reason, secularism and politics took place on the territory of the Bible and biblical criticism. There is a dialectical point to be made here: the radicalism of German biblical and theological scholarship, engendered from the deep conservatism of their context, gave that scholarship a radical edge it was not to lose for some time. The result: the struggles over reason and supernaturalism, religion and secularism took place on the territory of the Bible. Instead of dismissing the Bible as a document of outmoded superstition, these scholars, radicals and politicians worked out their theories with the Bible itself. German critics took up with vigour the various uncoordinated strands of biblical criticism from the likes of Spinoza, Simon and Le Clerc and turned them into a sustained approach, full of differences, arguments and advances. By the end of the nineteenth-century German dominance in biblical criticism was almost unassailable. Indeed, German biblical and theological scholarship was able to surge to the lead in biblical scholarship for about a century, until a good number of the leading figures moved to the USA before the Second World War.

Feuerbach's Divine Projections

No assessment of the biblical scholarship of this volatile period is complete without some consideration of Ludwig Feuerbach's *The Essence of Christianity*.[13] Even though he did not work directly on the Bible, it is a deeply theological work that influenced a generation of radical thinkers. In fact, rather than debunking Christianity, Feuerbach sets out to improve Christianity by arguing that its truth lay in the fact that God does not pre-exist us but is the projection of all that is best in human beings. Using this one new idea (more than most have in a lifetime) he explores the full range of theology and practice from creation to immortality, drawing up unlikely subjects such as celibacy and miracles.

So what exactly did Feuerbach argue? Religion, or rather Christianity, is actually the projection or abstraction of human subjectivity. It takes what is best in human beings only to hypostatize them all into an entity or force that is exterior to human beings. That entity becomes a figure, a 'god' who appears to human beings as a being in his own right, one that returns love, saves and directs human life through providence. As Feuerbach puts it, theology is really anthropology: 'the divine being is nothing else than the human being, or, rather, the human nature purified, freed from the limits of the individual man, made objective—i.e., contemplated and revered as another, a distinct being'.[14] One way of putting it is that religion is an expression of the unrealized wishes of self-transcendence that each human being harbours, that they have not quite realized themselves in full. With this definition in place, Feuerbach shows how it illuminates one theological topic after another: wisdom, moral being, love, suffering, the trinity, logos, cosmogony, providence, creation, prayer, faith, resurrection, heaven and immortality, which is the perfection of unlimited personality. In short, 'the

13. L. Feuerbach, *Das Wesen des Christentums* (Leipzig: Friedrichs & Bley, 1924); English, *The Essence of Christianity* (trans. George Eliot; Amherst: Prometheus Books, 1989 [1841]).

14. Feuerbach, *Das Wesen*, 18 = *The Essence*, 14. Similarly, 'In religion man frees himself from the limits of life; he here lets fall what oppresses him, obstructs him, affects him repulsively; God is the self-consciousness of man freed from all discordant elements; man feels himself free, happy, blessed in his religion, because he only here lives the life of genius, and keeps holiday' (Feuerbach, *Das Wesen*, 121-22 = *The Essence*, 98). His later work, *The Essence of Religion* (trans. Alexander Loos; Amherst: Prometheus Books, 2004), merely extends the insight to all religion and switches the projection from human beings to nature.

fundamental dogmas of Christianity are realised wishes of the heart'.[15] This at least is the argument of the first, positive part of the book. The second part focuses on a series of contradictions that are unresolvable within traditional theology; he claims that his own proposal does resolve them. In fact, he suggests that if one were to read only the second part, the conclusion would be that theology is mere illusion and falsehood. One needs to read the first part, too—which is why it is placed first—to see the benefit of theology.

There are a few points I wish to stress in Feuerbach's argument. To begin with, the controversial genius of Feuerbach's argument is that we do not realize what is going on. We may think that God is a more powerful and eternal being who creates us and guides our lives, but that assumption only moves from God to ourselves. There is a prior step, namely the projection of the divine from our own subjectivity. So there are in fact three stages: the projection of religion and God by human beings; assuming that this being is superior to us and that we are beholden to him; believing that we are secondary and inferior creatures in relation to this God. Or, as Feuerbach writes:

> God is the highest subjectivity of man abstracted from himself; hence man can do nothing of himself, all goodness comes from God. The more subjective God is, the more completely does man divest himself of his subjectivity, because God is, *per se*, his relinquished self, the possession of which he, however, again vindicates to himself. As the action of the arteries drives the blood into the extremities, and the action of the veins brings it back again, as life in general consists in a perpetual systole and diastole; so it is in religion. In the religious systole man propels his own nature from himself, he throws himself outward; in the religious diastole he receives the rejected nature into his heart again. God alone is the being who acts of himself,—this is the force of repulsion in religion; God is the being who acts in me, with me, through me, upon me, for me, is the principle of my salvation, of my good dispositions and actions, consequently my own good principle and nature,—this is the force of attraction in religion.[16]

A further point that is often forgotten is that Feuerbach stresses the way belief in a god diminishes human beings. The elevation of God leads to the depreciation of human beings: 'To enrich God, man must become poor; that God may be all, man must be nothing.'[17] This argument, modified and extended,

15. Feuerbach, *Das Wesen*, 174 = *The Essence*, 140.
16. Feuerbach, *Das Wesen*, 39-40 = *The Essence*, 31.
17. Feuerbach, *Das Wesen*, 33 = *The Essence*, 26. He also points out that the illusion of religion is 'profoundly injurious in its effects on mankind' (Feuerbach, *Das Wesen*, 349 = *The Essence*, 274). Indeed, Breckman (*Marx*, 90-130) argues that Feuerbach is far more politically radical than many take him to be, but then Feuerbach is the real hero of Breckman's book. On Feuerbach's radical politics, see also D. Leopold, *The Young Karl Marx: German Philosophy, Modern Politics, and Human Flourishing* (Cambridge: Cambridge University Press, 2007), 203-18.

would of course gain much greater fame in the hands of Karl Marx. Indeed, Feuerbach's lasting presence is much due to Marx, even if Marx felt that he had achieved an *Aufhebung* beyond Feuerbach. But it is actually a small step from Feuerbach's point that Christianity diminishes human beings to Marx's argument that religion is a sign of human alienation in this world. From there, of course, they would diverge in the solution: for Feuerbach it was a case of showing how this feature led to the doctrines of sin and depravity and that we need to realize our full potential through a proper understanding of religion; for Marx we need to deal with the oppressive and exploitative conditions in which we live.

Strauss and Myth

Only within this context, with the wide-open and furious public debates over religion and politics, spiced up with Feuerbach's argument that religion is a projection of the best in human beings,[18] can we understand David Strauss and his book, *Das Leben Jesu* (he is barely remembered for his many other works). Not so much a book, it was a bomb. After deliberately taking time off from his first teaching position at the theological faculty in Tübingen (where he taught for only three semesters from the summer of 1832 to autumn 1833 in logic, metaphysics and the history of philosophy since Kant and ethics) in order to focus on his writing, Strauss published in 1835 his *Das Leben Jesu kritisch bearbeitet* in two volumes. It really is the kind of work that most writers would dream of producing—a controversial, landmark text that makes its mark way outside the narrow confines of intellectual work.[19] I must admit, however, that I could have done without the stress. Although the liberals held Strauss up as something of a champion, he

18. Even though Feuerbach's book came out in 1841, he had been developing his ideas throughout the 1830s.

19. In the shadow of such a great book, Strauss was never quite able to repeat the performance. Apart from the four editions of the *Leben Jesu* itself, in 1835, 1836, 1839 and 1840, he kept producing support works, responses to critics and further explorations: D. F. Strauss, *Streitschriften zur Verteidigung meiner Schrift über das Leben Jesu und zur Charakteristik der gegenwärtigen Theologie* (Hildesheim, 1980; original edn, Tübingen: Osiander, 1837); idem, *Die christliche Glaubenslehre in ihrer geschichtlichen Entwicklung und im Kampfe mit der modernen Wissenschaft* (Tübingen: Osiander, 1840); idem, *Das Leben Jesu für das deutsche Volk* (Leipzig: Brockhaus, 1864; Berlin: F. Duncker, 1865); idem, *Der Christus des Glaubens und der Jesus der Geschichte: eine Kritik des Schleiermacher'schen Lebens Jesu* (Waltrop: Spenner, 2000 [1865]); idem, *Der alte und der neue Glaube: Ein Bekenntnis* (Bonn: Verlag von Emil Strauss, 1873). Apart form these works, he devoted 20 years of his life—a hiatus from biblical criticism—to biographies: D. F. Strauss, *Christian Friedrich Daniel Schubarts Leben in seinen Briefen* (Königstein: Scriptor Verlag, 1978; original edn, Berlin, 1849); idem, *Christian Märklin: Ein Lebens- und Charakterbild aus der Gegenwart* (Mannheim: Bassermann, 1851);

was surprised to find himself vilified and roundly attacked by both Young Hegelians like Bruno Bauer (for 'misreading' Hegel) and a range of conservative forces in theology faculties, the churches and government, so much so that he lost any chance of further offers of positions in either university or church (he had been briefly, in 1830–31, a pastor's assistant for a local parish in Kleiningersheim near Ludwigsburg, his hometown, after studying theology at Tübingen). The theology faculty at Tübingen sacked him as soon as the book came out. The closest he came to any university position at all was in Zürich the year after the book appeared. Some of the liberal burghers invited Strauss to take up a chair in Dogmatics and Church History. Twice their proposal was overcome by conservatives, but in January 1839, with a majority in the city government, they were successful. However, his arrival was anticipated with fear and trembling[20] and in the face of huge protests, the government gave him a lifelong pension in compensation. (I must admit that I wish I could pull off such a coup: a pension for the rest of my life in order to write, ride my bicycle and relax.)

So what was it about the *Leben Jesu* that so offended people? The book itself argued that the key to the Gospels and their depiction of Jesus lay in myth. He played off a double sense of myth: it did mean that we can never recover a distinct picture of the historical Jesus (fiction), but he also argued that myth should be read in a positive light, as a poetic expression of deeper truths that cannot be expressed in any other form. Focusing on the miraculous dimension of the Gospel narratives, from virgin birth through the various miracles performed by Jesus to the ultimate miracle of the resurrection, Strauss argued that both a supernaturalist and interventionist understanding was hopelessly wrong and that the rationalist effort to explain the miracles in naturalist terms (e.g. Jesus did not walk on the water but walked on a sand spit so that he seemed to do so) simply missed the point. If the former accepted the record at face value, the latter argued that the New Testament writers misrepresented or misinterpreted what had actually happened. For Strauss, however, what the New Testament writers did was draw deeply upon the mythical Jewish messianic traditions of which they were a part and used these to portray Jesus as the Messiah. Indeed, myth is the natural way in which life and indeed religion was understood

---

idem, *Ulrich von Hutten* (Leipzig: Brockhaus, 1858–1860); idem, *Hermann Samuel Reimarus und seine Schutzschrift für die vernünftigen Verehrer Gottes* (Hildesheim, 1991; original edn, Leipzig: Brockhaus, 1862); idem, *Voltaire: 6 Vorträge* (Leipzig: A. Kröner, 1924 [1870]); along with the odd satirical and very polemical political work: D. F. Strauss, *Der Romantiker auf dem Throne der Cäsaren oder Julian der Abtrünnige* (Heidelberg: Manutius Verlag, 1992; original edn, Mannheim: Bassermann, 1847).

20. I feel for Strauss, since 'fear and trembling' was once used to characterize my own imminent arrival for an invited lecture in Adelaide in 2002.

by pre-scientific peoples—Lévi-Strauss was by no means the first to come up with this idea![21] Strauss's challenge was to apply such a mode of mythic interpretation to the New Testament in as rigorous a fashion as possible.

The result: after a lengthy introduction that establishes the need for mythic interpretation, with a characteristically German propensity for trawling through all of the previous studies on both the Gospels and myth, Strauss painstakingly works through each episode in the Gospels. In each case he presents the supernaturalist position, negates it with the naturalist one and then offers a mythic interpretation in order to resolve the contradiction: in light of the lack of corroborating evidence, the contradictions with known physical laws, the presence of poetic language and the heavy use of prophecies from the Hebrew Bible, in both the narrative and in Jesus' mouth, what we have is mythic construction of the first order. If you picked up a Hegelian echo in his plan, then you are not mistaken.

He then takes the final Hegelian step in the third part of the book (the first two parts move through the Gospels) to offer his own positive proposal. In short, he wants to 're-establish dogmatically that which has been destroyed critically'.[22] His proposal is what he calls a speculative Christology, produced with a helping hand from Hegel. God is nothing other than the Infinite Spirit that moves out of itself to produce 'the Finite, Nature, and the human mind' from which it eternally returns to itself in unity.[23] Neither the finite spirit of man nor the Infinite Spirit of God has any reality without being in contact. So, the 'infinite spirit is real only when it discloses itself in finite spirits; as the finite spirit is true only when it merges itself in the infinite'.[24] The result is none other than Jesus Christ, for the following reason: 'If God and man are in themselves *one*, and if religion is the human side of this unity: then must this unity be made evident to man in religion, and become in him consciousness and reality.'[25] The catch is that such a union and such an appearance is not restricted to one person, as the Church would have it. By contrast, this dialectical unity of Infinite and finite can take place in every person, or preferably in the whole of humanity. Here is Strauss:

> This is the key to the whole of Christology, that, as subject of the predicate which the church assigns to Christ, we place, instead of an individual, an idea;

---

21. The key figures are the classicist Christian G. Heyne (1729–1812), and the biblical scholars Johann Gottfried Eichhorn (1752–1827), Johann Philipp Gabler (1753–1826), Georg Lorenz Bauer (1755–1806), Wilhelm Martin Leberecht de Wette (1780–1839) and Ferdinand Christian Baur (1792–1860).
22. D. F. Strauss, *The Life of Jesus: Critically Examined* (trans. G. Eliot; London: Swan Sonnenschein, 1902), 777.
23. Strauss *Life*, 777.
24. Strauss *Life*, 777.
25. Strauss *Life*, 777.

> but an idea which has an existence in reality, not in the mind only, like that of Kant. In an individual, a God-man, the properties and functions which the church ascribes to Christ contradict themselves; in the idea of the race, they perfectly agree. Humanity is the union of the two natures.[26]

The question remains as to why this book, a lengthy and detailed work in New Testament criticism, in which it has had a lasting influence, should have had such a wide political impact. And why was it the text around which much of the ferment of the time took place, a ferment in which even the likes of Marx and Engels were also caught? There have been far more critical works that have hardly had the same impact. Here I draw on Marilyn Massey, *Christ Unmasked*,[27] where she argues that it was understood, championed and opposed as a text that espoused 'radical democratic politics'.[28] Not only did its undermining of any verifiable historical record of Jesus of Nazareth challenge the basis of both Protestant and Roman Catholic assumptions about the Bible and Christianity, it also shook up the theological justifications for the hold of the old aristocracy on power and of the Prussian king himself. Even more, in developing a Christology in which the divine and human rested not with one man but with all humanity, Strauss was giving voice to a theological agenda with radical democratic tendencies. Rather than God's chosen ruler being, like Christ, a chosen individual, all may potentially rule. In short, Strauss attempted a reinterpretation of Christianity that questioned its cosy relationship with the power of the state. In making a shift from the heroic individual to the general community, 'the potentiality seeming to belong only to one exalted human belonged, rather, to humanity itself'.[29] Massey's conclusion is, then, that by 'unmasking' Christ not as the God-man of Christian doctrine but as the democratic Christ, as the one who shows that the human species itself is the embodiment of God-man, Strauss pointed to a model of popular sovereignty instead of the monarchy.

There are a number of ways of reading such a situation. A conventional one is to suggest that Strauss used the dominant language of his time—theology and biblical studies—to make political points. Should he have lived in a different time, such as ours or perhaps in ancient Greece, his language may well have been economic or political. The Bible thereby becomes a code for something else—in this case the politics of German self-determination. Another approach is to argue that Strauss's purely biblical work had unforeseen and unexpected political consequences.

---

26. Strauss *Life*, 780.
27. M. C. Massey, *Christ Unmasked: The Meaning of The Life of Jesus in German Politics* (Chapel Hill: University of North Carolina Press, 1983), 12.
28. Massey, *Christ Unmasked*, 79.
29. Massey, *Christ Unmasked*, 149.

Strauss's own surprise and dismay at the massive reaction suggest that any political consequences were unintended byproducts.

A third possibility—the one that Massey pursues—is that Strauss clearly articulated despite himself the key tensions of the time. She points to the differences between the first and third editions. In the first (the one I have outlined all too briefly above) Strauss pursued his radical critique of existing scholarship and understandings of Jesus, concluding with a democratic reinterpretation of Christology. By contrast, in the third edition he made many concessions to his critics and elevated the individual figure of Christ. In this 1838 edition, Strauss 'offered the palliative of an aristocratic Christ, a genius Jesus, who was the epitome of the perfection of the inner life'.[30] He gave up a massive amount of ground, allowing for the unique unity of divine and human in Jesus' religious consciousness of himself and even granting a category of miracles based on the unusual powers of nature. Partly an effort to secure a teaching post, Strauss soon regretted his back-peddling and in the fourth edition of 1840 he returned to his former hard-hitting arguments. For Massey this tension within Strauss himself gave clear expression to the struggles within Germany between the liberal, democratic movements and the forces of reaction which waged a consistent campaign against Strauss and the liberals.

I would add that it is no surprise that such an articulation took place in the realm of biblical criticism. As I pointed out earlier, all of these furious debates were not purely the fussy and pompous struggles of academics, the hot air of intellectuals vainly feeling that they were important for shaking up a few of their colleagues in the Faculties of Theology at Berlin, Bonn or Tübingen. These debates hit at the crux of the idea and practice of the 'Christian state' at the time. They also fed off the long history of bitter struggles between Roman Catholics and Protestants, with their resultant conservatism, and the immediate situation of a reactionary king, Friedrich Wilhelm IV, who sought to recover the lost glory of Christendom. Apart from having a say in university appointments, he also oversaw the tightening of censorship regulations. Besides liberal and republican movements, one of the main targets of this censorship was the Young Hegelian radicals. Wilhelm IV had in fact called for an answer from Young Hegelians in response to Strauss's claim that he had made use of Hegel. Bauer was nominated to take up the attack, but the king was not altogether pleased with Bauer's effort. The conservative papers had a field day, feeling that their assaults on the Young Hegelians were fully justified in light of the crown's support.

30. Massey, *Christ Unmasked*, 149.

But what about the value of Strauss's Gospel criticism? His arguments do not want to lie quietly in the grave with him. Many have tried to assassinate this argument, hurriedly burying it in a shallow grave and scampering from the scene in the hope that biblical criticism will soon forget it. But it was not to be, for this corpse at least keeps on gaining new leases of life—Lazarus has nothing on *Das Leben Jesu*. Indeed, recently we have witnessed a return not so much to Strauss's arguments as they stood in 1835, but to the mythical nature of such narratives, either in terms of their ancient Near Eastern background or in terms of social location, anthropology and comparative religion.[31] But then this renewed interest begs another question, namely the nature of myth itself. Does it become a distortion of language we need to resist? Is it a more sublime way of expressing truth? Is it a tribute to the greatness of the human imagination? Possibly, but I would suggest we might better understand these myths as playing a double game, operating with a fair degree of cunning and subterfuge.[32]

Bauer, Scepticism and Atheism

The second great polemicist and radical biblical critic is one of my favourites—Bruno Bauer. He was primarily a New Testament scholar and sometime theologian and political commentator. The works that got him into no end of trouble were those on the Gospel of John and the Synoptic Gospels.[33] Appearing during the first great wave of German critical work on the Bible that would launch German biblical scholars into a position of global leadership, Bauer's work was at the edge of that work and beyond. For a time he was widely regarded as the leader of the Young Hegelians. Bauer's genius was to combine painstaking attention to biblical texts within their historical and cultural context and his own development of Hegel's philosophy.

31. See, for example, T. L. Thompson, *The Messiah Myth: The Near Eastern Roots of Jesus and David* (New York: Basic Books, 2005) and B. Mack, *Myth and the Christian Nation: A Social Theory of Religion* (London: Equinox, 2008). I mention but two examples of these current works. Mack has been working on this question for what is a lifetime of scholarship; see B. Mack, *Who Wrote the New Testament? The Making of the Christian Myth* (New York: Harper, 1996); idem, *A Myth of Innocence: Mark and Christian Origins* (Minneapolis: Augsburg Fortress, 1998); idem, *The Christian Myth: Origins, Logic, Legacy* (London: Continuum, 2003).

32. See further, R. Boer, *Political Myth: On the Use and Abuse of Biblical Themes* (Durham: Duke University Press, 2009).

33. B. Bauer, *Kritik der evangelischen Geschichte des Johannes* (Bremen: Karl Schünemann, 1840); idem, *Kritik der evangelischen Geschichte der Synoptiker* (2 vols.; Leipzig: Otto Wigand, 1841); idem, *Kritik der evangelischen Geschichte der Synoptiker und des Johannes, Dritter und letzter Band* (Braunschweig, 1842); idem, *Kritik der Evangelien und Geschichte ihres Ursprungs* (3 vols.; Berlin: Gustav Hempel, 1850–1851); idem, *Die theologische Erklärung der Evangelien* (Berlin, 1852).

This combination led him to argue that Christianity only emerged in the second century CE, that the Gospels contain virtually no historical records, and indeed no record of a historical Jesus, being primarily the products of religious consciousness embodied in individual authors who composed them freely, that they are saturated with the spirit and thought of Hellenism (the key ideas may be traced to Stoic, Philonic and neo-Platonic ideas), and that the crucial tension was between free self-consciousness and religious dogmatism. He took consistent aim at the ossified established church and the repressive state, especially in light of their dirty and corrupt hold on power—so much so that his book *Das Endeckte Christenthum* (*Christianity Exposed*)[34] was banned, hunted down and destroyed until it was reprinted in 1927.

I will come back to the content of *Christianity Exposed* and his treatment of the Gospels in a moment, but let us now back-track a little in order to understand how Bauer approached the Gospels. While Bauer taught at the Friedrich Wilhelm University in the late 1830s, he published a two-volume work on the Hebrew Bible called *Kritik der Geschichte der Offenbarung: Die Religion des alten Testaments in der geschichtlichen Entwicklung ihrer Prinzipien dargestellt* (*Critique of the History of Revelation: The Religion of the Old Testament Explained according to the Principles of Its Historical Development*).[35] It was the only work he wrote on the Hebrew Bible, for the rest concerned the New Testament and politics. Here Bauer was developing his argument that religion, or rather, religious experience, is the result of (a Hegelian) self-consciousness. Not only was such religious experience a transcendental affair, but one could also trace in a phenomenological fashion the development of the various forms of that experience. Following the assumption that the legalistic priestly material (designated by P) was the oldest literary source of the Hebrew Bible, he argued that this material lies at the earliest stage of such a development. Here we find an authoritarian deity who demands a law-bound subordination. In contrast to this largely external relation, the later prophetic and messianic books mark a much higher stage: over

---

34. B. Bauer, *Christianity Exposed: A Recollection of the Eighteenth Century and a Contribution to the Crisis of the Nineteenth Century* (trans. E. Ziegler and J. Hamm; Lewiston: Edwin Mellen, 2002).

35. B. Bauer, *Kritik der Geschichte der Offenbarung: Die Religion des alten Testaments in der geschichtlichen Entwicklung ihrer Prinzipien dargestellt* (Berlin: Ferdinand Dümmler, 1838). At the time Bauer was also editing the *Zeitschrift für spekulative Theologie*, which ran only to three issues, and writing for the *Jahrbücher für wissenschaftliche Kritik*. Here he tried to develop an alternative theology that categorized Christian doctrines in terms of logical categories. In 1839 he also happened to teach Karl Marx a course on Isaiah at the university.

against the crass and oppressive particularity of the earlier material, here the universal is immanent in community.

In one sense, of course, Bauer simply sought to take the relatively new developments in critical biblical study he inherited a step further—Johann Gottfried Eichhorn, Wilhelm de Wette, Johann Vater, Heinrich Ewald and Hermann Hupfeld, and then later Wellhausen and the rest of the gang on JEDP. But then he also gave them a decidedly Hegelian twist—something for which he tends to be criticized and dismissed as a bit of a crackpot (which often seems to be par for the course for academics). Bauer came in at the earlier point of these debates, assuming that the Priestly material was the crassest and earliest. Religion struggles to rise above this state until it reaches the prophets and then the New Testament.

Yet soon enough, Bauer was to argue that even the prophetic texts of the Hebrew Bible had not yet arrived at the moment of overcoming the estrangement of externalized and legalistic religion. That, of course, would come with the New Testament, to which he was to direct all of his biblical concerns from the beginning of the 1840s. At this point in his thought he argued that the difference between the Old and New Testaments was that Christianity managed to free the religious consciousness from its limited and particular form in the Old Testament. What his work on the Hebrew Bible enabled him to do was define his key idea of religious consciousness, namely the un-mediated identity of particularity and the abstract universal, which he translated in terms of the immediate identity of the universal with a particular subject or community.

Now, while this position—the immediate identity of particular and universal—may seem like a positive assessment of Christianity and religion in general, Bauer was soon to argue that it is in fact the core of the problem. Already in *Herr Dr. Hengstenberg*,[36] published in the year he taught in Berlin, he had come to argue that the oppressive and narrow-minded sectarianism of the Church—especially the German Lutheran Church—lay in this claim by the particular to the universal. The logical core of his argument, which developed over his various works on the Bible, was that Christianity was a 'hubristic particularism' which made an unmediated identity between a specific subject (in this case Jesus Christ) or a community (the church) with the universal. What happens then is that the universal becomes completely other, divorced from communal and individual life. God and heaven become alienated and abstracted universals from human existence. This meant that any claim by a specific individual or group to be the exclusive representative of this universal inevitably produced a brutal, sectarian monopoly

36. B. Bauer, *Herr Dr. Hengstenberg: Ein Beitrag zur Kritik der religiösen Bewußtseins. Kritische Briefe über den Gegensatz des Gesetzes und des Evangeliums* (Berlin: Ferdinand Dümmler, 1839).

that excluded any other particular, whether that is religious or political. In short, Christian monotheism is an exclusive rather than an inclusive universal. This ultimate hubris of particularism, characteristic of the state Church at the time and the reactionary Friedrich Wilhelm IV (1840–61), let alone of both Christianity and Judaism, is the essence of religion as such. The Prussian state was only the latest manifestation of this brutal universal, for it traced it all the way back to the *polis* of ancient Greece.

This position developed over Bauer's studies of the Synoptic Gospels and the Gospel of John (written over an intense period from 1840 to 1842), only to receive full expression in his *Christianity Exposed*.[37] Through the writing of these works Bauer eventually recognized his own atheism, arguing that free self-consciousness must be released from the constraints of all religion and that the only way for self-consciousness to realize itself is through historical and social transformation. The Gospels themselves are a long way from historical records, being the products of creative and unknown individuals. Within the restrictions of the religious consciousness, these authors responded to the needs of the Christian communities for an understanding of their own nature and origins. So Mark, the earliest Gospel, presents a basic picture of Jesus' adult life and death, while the later Matthew and Luke fill out that story with birth narratives, additional material and the resurrection. By the time we get to John we already have the full expression of a dogmatic monopoly. But why are these stories problematic? Here is Bauer:

> The gospel reports are nothing other than free, literary products, whose soul is the simple categories of religion. What is specific to these categories, however, is that they reverse the laws of the real, rational world. They alienate the universality of self-consciousness, rend it violently away, and restore it in the form of representation as an alien, heavenly, or as an alien, limited, sacred history.[38]

Christianity denied the truth that could only come from self-consciousness by identifying such truth with another being and a heavenly realm alien to that self-consciousness. Even worse, Christianity claimed that its ultimate form of alienation was the absolute and universal truth, thereby exacerbating the problem. It cranks up such alienation until it becomes unbearable,

---

37. Bauer, *Kritik des Johannes; idem, Kritik der Synoptiker; idem, Kritik der Synoptiker und des Johannes; idem, Christianity Exposed*For an excellent discussion that traces the way Bauer's position developed over these works, see D. Moggach, *The Philosophy and Politics of Bruno Bauer* (Cambridge: Cambridge University Press, 2003), 59-79. Unfortunately D. Leopold (*The Young Karl Marx* [Cambridge: Cambridge University Press, 2007], 101-105) skips by the importance of Bauer's biblical criticism.
38. B. Bauer, *Hegels Lehre von der Religion und der Kunst von dem Standpunkte des Glaubens aus beurteilt* (Aalen: Scientia Verlag, 1967: original edition, Leipzig: Otto Wigand, 1842), 61.

thereby opening the way for a final resolution. Thus, in good Hegelian fashion, Christianity was both the best and worst of all religions. It may have provided a revolutionary breakthrough, freeing people from the ties of nature, family and spirits, but it was also the highest form of alienation. What was needed then was a sublation (*Aufhebung*) of the necessary stage of Christianity in order to see that the truth came from a free self-consciousness. Only 'criticism' is able to release such a universal self-consciousness. But it also meant that any state or church that laid claim to Christianity would have to go, too. Religious monopoly and the Restoration under way with the German monarchy merely reinforced his views, so much so that by 1840–41 he rejected all forms of religious representation in favour of an emancipated philosophical self-consciousness.

Needless to say, Bauer's radical biblical criticism and theology went hand-in-hand with a radical political republicanism. But in the context Bauer was an *extreme* radical. This one-time favourite of Hegel, who recommended Bauer for a royal prize for an essay on Kant in 1829, was removed from his post as licentiate at the Friedrich Wilhelm University in 1839. His crime: the aforesaid book, *Herr Dr. Hengstenberg*. Hengstenberg happened to be a leading Pietistic theologian, colleague and former teacher. Bauer, it seems, could not suffer fools gladly. Fortune was with him, for the Minister of Culture, Altenstein, was favourable to the Hegelians and moved him out of harm's way—or at least so he thought—to Bonn. But fortune did not smile on him much longer. Altenstein died in 1840, the same year Friedrich Wilhelm III gave up the ghost. Along with the new king came a new Minister for Culture—or as his title was known in full, for Religious Worship, Education and Medicine—by the name of Eichhorn. This enlightened bureaucrat had no time for the Hegelians and was certainly not going to protect the young radical. Bauer had lasted five years in Berlin (1834–39), but he lasted barely three in Bonn. At the end of March in 1842 his *licentia docendi* was revoked by Eichhorn and he was dismissed by direct order of the new king.[39] With no options left in a university, he purchased a small farm, ran a tobacco shop and wrote—as prolifically as ever—in the evenings until his death in 1882.

However, I am interested here is a particular feature of Bauer's work, namely the argument that the form of Christianity that has come down to

39. The story of his dismissal as Privat-Docent of Theology at Bonn is a little confused. Initially he was put under investigation for his radical views on the New Testament by a consultation that included the ministry of education and the theology faculties of the six Prussian universities, but the investigation was unable to achieve consensus. In an astute moment of ill-timing (a characteristic, it seems), he attended a banquet in honour of the South German liberal, Karl Welcker, in 1841. Bauer proposed a toast to the Hegelian concept of the state, but the king decided to sack all those who attended the banquet and who were in state employment.

us has little, if anything, to do with its earliest forms. Of course, once you have taken such a position, the next step is to account for that well-known final form. Bauer argues that what we know as Christianity now is the result of a combination of vulgar and popularized versions of the neo-Platonism of Philo of Alexandria, Seneca's stoicism and Roman imperial beliefs about the emperor as son of God. But why did Christianity catch on? Bauer argued that a part of Christianity's appeal lay in its reversal, for it despised wealth, power and privilege, seeking its disciples among the rejected—the poor and slaves. As we shall see, this is one of the most enduring contributions from Bauer, not least because Friedrich Engels took it up and gave it his own spin. But what of earliest Christianity? Bauer argues that Revelation is the best window into that strange phenomenon. Assuming a date of composition between late 68 and early 69 CE, it presents a group of Jews (not Christians) who believed the end would come soon. There is no Trinity, for Jesus is subordinate to God, and certainly no Holy Spirit. There is no doctrine of original sin, no baptism or sacrament of communion, no justification by faith, and no elaborate story of the death and resurrection of Christ. And there is no religion of love, for the author preaches sound, honest revenge on their persecutors. The author is unknown (certainly not the legendary disciple by the name of John) and all of the 'visions' find precursors in the Hebrew Bible and other apocalyptic documents that preceded it.

How has this reconstruction stood the test of time? It is easy to dismiss it as reliant on out-of-date scholarship and to suggest that Bauer was too extreme in his scepticism. We can hardly blame Bauer for immersing himself in the biblical scholarship available at the time. I would be in a similar situation if someone a century from now were to read a position I take today in relation to contemporary biblical scholarship. The strange thing is that the underlying assumptions of Bauer's work are the same in historical critical scholarship of the Bible today (which no longer has the hegemony it once had). The tides of some forms of scholarship may come and go, but the basic assumptions remain unchanged: one must be very careful when using the Bible for any historical reconstruction, since it is unreliable to some degree (by contrast to the Tübingen school—Ferdinand Christian Bauer, Heinrich Ewald, Friedrich Lücke et al.—Bauer takes a more sceptical option which is only now coming back in vogue); the overwhelming concern is with origins, whether that of early Christianity or early Israel; archaeology plays a crucial role, since it provides evidence external to the text; and one spends an inordinate amount of energy discussing authorship and dates, which, like the fashion in skirts, can go in only one of two directions—up or down. Bauer, the Tübingen School and historical critical scholars today all share the same assumptions. Further, some of Bauer's concerns are still very much alive in biblical criticism, such as the influence of Stoicism and the relation to Philo.[40] His argument that the letters of Paul predate the Gospels, which come from the second century CE, still holds water, although his theory on Revelation as the earliest document has little credibility. However, his radical scepticism has returned to biblical scholarship, especially through the so-called 'minimalist school' which finds little that is historically reliable in the texts of the Hebrew Bible and which has been making headway in New Testament research.[41]

Conclusion

What, in conclusion, is still of value in the work of Strauss and Bauer? As far as both of them are concerned, radically sceptical biblical critics are still not assured of employment or acceptance in the academy. The recent story of Gerd Lüdemann is a case in point. Until 2009 he was a professor of New Testament in the theology faculty at the University of Göttingen. In February of 2009, Lüdemann wrote a terse email message to many colleagues and friends, telling people that the German Supreme Court had decided to reject his appeal against the decision by the university to ban him from teaching. This was his last court of appeal and the decision saw the blogosphere run hot over issues such as academic freedom and church control over theology. But why was Lüdemann, a respected New Testament scholar and tenured professor in his early 60s, prevented from teaching students? The reason was that he had come to the conclusion that the claims of Christianity are a fabrication and have no basis in fact. Nothing new in that, for Strauss and Bauer had made similar arguments, but the catch is that Lüdemann was

40. For example, see T. Engberg-Pedersen, *Paul and the Stoics* (Louisville: Westminster John Knox Press, 2000). M. Lee, *Paul, the Stoics, and the Body of Christ* (Cambridge: Cambridge University Press, 2006); W. Loader, *The Septuagint, Sexuality, and the New Testament: Case Studies on the Impact of the LXX in Philo and the New Testament* (Grand Rapids: Eerdmans, 2004); B. Winter, ed., *Philo and Paul among the Sophists* (Cambridge: Cambridge University Press, 1997).

41. N. P. Lemche, *Ancient Israel: A New History of Israelite Society* (Sheffield: Sheffield Academic Press, 1988); idem, *The Israelites in History and Tradition* (London: SPCK, 1998); idem, *Prelude to Israel's Past: Background and Beginnings of Israelite History and Identity* (trans. E.F. Maniscalco; Peabody, MA: Hendrickson, 1998); T. L. Thompson, *Early History of the Israelite People from the Written and Archaeological Sources* (Leiden: Brill, 1992); idem, *The Mythic Past: Biblical Archaeology and the Myth of Israel* (New York: Basic Books, 1999); idem, *The Messiah Myth*; P. R. Davies, *In Search of Ancient Israel* (Sheffield: Sheffield Academic Press, 1992); idem, *Memories of Ancient Israel: An Introduction to Biblical History—Ancient and Modern* (Louisville: Westminster John Knox Press, 2008); idem, *On the Origins of Judaism* (London: Equinox, 2009); R. M. Price, *Deoconstructing Jesus* (Amherst: Prometheus Books, 2000); F. R. Zindler, *The Jesus the Jews Never Knew: Sepher Toldoth Yeshu and the Quest for the Historical Jesus in Jewish Sources* (Austin: American Atheist Press, 2003).

teaching students training for ministry in the Evangelical Church. Fearful that the frail faith of their students might suffer under the hands of such a scholar, the church leaned on the university, and Lüdemann was axed. And this from a university that was established on Enlightenment principles, has prided itself on free inquiry unhindered by external constraints and has boasted some of Germany's leading theologians such as Albrecht Ritschl (at least when German theologians led the world).

Apart from issues of academic freedom, of which I am sceptical, or indeed tenure, which seems to have the reverse effect and squashes originality, what emerges from the Lüdemann case is a crucial question. Can one be a student of sacred Scriptures and be an atheist? Indeed, can one be a theologian (as distinct from a biblical critic) and an atheist at the same time? In other words, does theology require one to be a believer first, so that, in the words of Anselm, theology may be defined as *fides quaerens intellectum*, a reasoned and systematic exploration and explanation of one's faith?

A further implication concerns the role of myth in the New Testament, especially in the accounts of Jesus. Many have wanted to argue that Strauss went too far, that there may be some mythical elaboration around the historical core, whatever that is. To my mind, there is far greater value in pursuing the argument from myth (taken in its dual sense of fiction and an alternative genre and mindset), for that gets us beyond the somewhat futile searches for the historical or unhistorical Jesus. What is the function of that myth, I would like to ask, especially in its political register? How does it function in terms of what I have elsewhere called a political myth, both in its original form and in its multiple uses and abuses?[42]

As for Bauer, I have already discussed the implications of his historical scepticism concerning the origins of Christianity and how he may be read in our own time as a forerunner of a minimalist position; alternatively, we may view recent arguments as part of an effort to recover the radical edge of Bauer's biblical criticism. But there is another, perhaps surprising, element of his work that remains very much part of the current debate: the appeal of Christianity to the lower classes, especially slaves, its despising of wealth and property, power and its exercise and its attraction to the dispossessed. That argument has a currency not directly due to Bauer, but to one who remained fascinated by Bauer and drew heavily from him for his own work on early Christianity. I speak of Friedrich Engels, who penned a number of seminal works under Bauer's influence.[43] Engels gives Bauer's

---

42. Boer, *Political Myth*.
43. F. Engels, *Bruno Bauer and Early Christianity*, in *Marx and Engels Collected Works* (Moscow: Progress Publishers, 1989 [1882]), XXIV = *Bruno Bauer und das Urchristentum*, in *Marx Engels Werke* (Berlin: Dietz, 1973 [1882]), XIX; idem, *The Book of Revelation*, in *Marx and*

arguments a twist, arguing that it was not merely the later, fully-fledged form of Christianity that appealed to the poor, but its raw, earliest form, before all the accretions. Or, as Engels put it, 'Christianity was originally a movement of oppressed people: it first appeared as the religion of slaves and freedmen, of poor people deprived of all rights, of peoples subjugated or dispersed by Rome.'[44] Apart from a few general comments about the effect of Roman imperialism, which he argues crushed older social structures of clan and *polis*, imposed a new juridical system, exacted punishing tribute, and exacerbated the hopeless state of the vast majority of slaves, impoverished peasants and desperate urban freemen, there is relatively scarce attention given to the details of this crucial point.

Despite this scarcity, it is the point that has stuck. In fact, Engels is also the source of the idea in New Testament studies and church history, especially in terms of class analysis rather than the dominance of ideas such as despising the rich (Bauer's position). Mediated and elaborated by Rosa Luxemburg and Karl Kautsky,[45] this position became by the early twentieth century the consensus among New Testament scholars[46] and among sociologists,[47] holding sway until the 1960s,[48] taking a dip for a while and returning with a vengeance in the new wave of anti-imperial studies of the New Testament. The problem, of course, is that which faces any effort to find some firm ground in the New Testament: the lack of conclusive evidence.

Finally, what about the issue of context with which I began this discussion? In the cases of Feuerbach, Strauss and Bauer, they found themselves in a Germany depressed economically and politically, a situation that generated a dialectical leap in biblical criticism that was to launch it into global

---

Engels Collected Works (Moscow: Progress Publishers, 1990 [1883]), XXVI = *Das Buch der Offenbarung*, in *Marx Engels Werke* (Berlin: Dietz, 1973 [1883]), XXI; idem, *On the History of Early Christianity*, in *Marx and Engels Collected Works* (Moscow: Progress Publishers, 1990 [1894–95]), XXVII = *Zur Geschichte des Urchristentums*, in *Marx Engels Werke* (Berlin: Dietz, 1972 [1894–95]), XXII.

44. Engels, *The Book of Revelation*, 447; idem, *Zur Geschichte des Urchristentums*, 449.
45. R. Luxemburg, *Kirche und Sozialismus* (Frankfurt am Main: Stimme-Verlag, 1982 [1905]) = *Socialism and the Churches*, in *Rosa Luxemburg Speaks* (edited by Mary-Alice Waters; New York: Pathfinder Press, 1970); K. Kautsky, *Foundations of Christianity* (trans. H. F. Mins; London: Socialist Resistance, 2007 [1908]) = *Der Ursprung des Christentums: Eine Historische Untersuchung* (Stuttgart: J. H. W. Dietz, 1977 [1908]).
46. See, for instance, A. Deissman, *The New Testament in the Light of Modern Research* (Garden City: Doubleday, Doran and Company, 1929); idem, *Light From the Ancient East* (Grand Rapids: Baker Book House, 1978 [1908]).
47. See E. Troeltsch, *The Social Teaching of the Christian Churches* (2 vols.; Louisville: Westminster John Knox Press, 1992 [1911]).
48. See R. Stark, *The Rise of Christianity: How the Obscure, Marginal Jesus Movement Became the Dominant Religious Force in the Western World* (Princeton: Princeton University Press, 1996), 29-48.

leadership. What, then, of our own situation and its return to the questions raised by Strauss and Bauer? The context is not quite comparable, for that scholarship comes from what seems to be the global centres of economic and political power. Or does it? Might it not be seen as a symptom of a slip in confidence, the loss of global leadership as the USA and Europe stumble in the Middle East and are burdened with the weight of an economic shift to the East, to China and India? And with those stumbles, perhaps even on the crumbling battlements of the West, it is a good time to return to a more sceptical position in relation to the founding documents.

- 3 -

'Jesus Who Is Called Christ': References to Jesus outside Christian Sources

Lester L. Grabbe

Articles and books about Jesus always seem to find an audience. This is not just a modern phenomenon, however. Once Christianity became dominant in the Roman empire, a considerable amount of interest was generated by the few references to Jesus in non-Christian literature. There were only a handful of these, and the many discoveries of new original sources in the nineteenth and twentieth centuries did not add to the store of Jesus testimonies, unfortunately. The result is that there is a long list of secondary studies on these passages, going back several centuries.

In a short article such as this, it is not possible to give an extensive survey of past studies.[1] Instead, my purpose is to examine the original sources that refer (or might refer) to Jesus and consider what they tell us about the presumed founder of Christianity, taking account of some of the recent secondary literature.

---

1. A good survey of studies on the Josephus passages was given by P. Winter, 'Excursus II: Josephus on Jesus and James *Ant.* xviii 3, 3 (63-4) and xx 9, 1 (200-3),' in E. Schürer, *The Jewish People in the Age of Jesus Christ* (revised and ed. G. Vermes et al.; 3 vols. in 4; Edinburgh: T & T Clark, 1973–87), I, 428-41. It has now been updated by J. Carleton Paget, 'Some Observations on Josephus and Christianity,' *JTS* 52 (2001), 539-624. See also further below. For texts and translations of the Latin writers and Josephus, I have used the Loeb Classical Library edition; however, the text of Tacitus is essentially the same as that edited by E. Koestermann, *P. Cornelii Taciti Libri qui supersunt: Tom. 1 Annales* (Leipzig: Teubner, 1952, 7th edn) and the text of Pliny, as edited by M. Schuster, *C. Plini Caecili Secundi Epistularum libri novem* (Leipzig: Teubner, 1950).

Roman Writers

Since Jesus allegedly lived under Roman rule, it is not surprising that our main 'pagan' sources are Roman. No Greek writers (i.e. non-Jewish and non-Christian) appear to refer to him.

Tacitus

Probably the most important Roman writer is Tacitus (56–c. 120). He was a historian of note and still regarded as the pinnacle of the Roman historians. He writes the following about an episode during the reign of the emperor Nero:

> *Ergo abolendo rumori Nero subdidit reos et quaesitissimis poenis adfecit, quos per flagitia invisos vulgus Christianos appellabat. Auctor nominis eius Christus Tiberio imperitante per procuratorem Pontium Pilatum supplicio adfectus erat; repressaque in praesens exitiabilis superstitio rursum erumpebat, non modo per Iudaeam, originem eius mali, sed per urbem etiam, quo cuncta undique atrocia aut pudenda confluunt celebranturque.*
>
> Therefore, to scotch the rumor, Nero substituted as culprits, and punished with the utmost refinements of cruelty, a class of men, loathed for their vices, whom the crowd styled Christians. Christus, the founder of the name, had undergone the death penalty in the reign of Tiberius, by sentence of the procurator Pontius Pilatus, and the pernicious superstition was checked for a moment, only to break out once more, not merely in Judaea, the home of the disease, but in the capital itself, where all things horrible or shameful in the world collect and find a vogue. (*Annales* 15.44)[2]

This is one of our most important references to Jesus. Unfortunately, it was written almost a century after Jesus is supposed to have died, according to the Gospel accounts. Yet Tacitus often had good sources, including the archives of the Senate.[3] His statement should be taken seriously.

What was his source for this particular piece of information? It is unlikely to have been Christians; indeed, it embodies mainly comments against the Christians, unlike the letter of his friend Pliny the Younger (see below) who got information directly from Christians. We have no reason to think Tacitus came in contact with Christians, who were still very much a minority group in his time. He could in theory have derived his information from Pliny, but Pliny's letter says nothing to hint at what Tacitus says. Could Tacitus have obtained the information from Josephus? Although this is theoretically

---

2. H. Furneaux (ed.), *Cornelii Taciti Annalium ab excessu Divi Augusti libri; The Annals of Tacitus. II. Books xi-xvi* (Oxford: Clarendon, 1891).
3. See R. Syme (especially, *Tacitus* [2 vols.; Oxford: Clarendon Press, 1958]), 271-303, for a discussion of the sources for the *Annals*.

possible, Tacitus does not indicate knowledge of Josephus' writings.[4] Where the two talk about the same points relating to the Jews, Tacitus does not agree with Josephus in the details. Thus, it seems likely that Tacitus' source is Roman. Tacitus is the only Roman writer to mention Pilate (though we have confirmation of his existence from an inscription[5]). If Pilate had reported to the Senate on the matter, this would likely have been available in the senatorial archives.

Suetonius

Suetonius was a slightly younger contemporary of Tacitus (c. 70–130). His *Lives of the Twelve Caesars* do not have the same reputation for accuracy as Tacitus' writings but are noted for their tendency to focus on the sensational side of their subject. Nevertheless, they are an important source of information and often draw on archival material. Both of the following quotations are found in a list of miscellaneous accomplishments or acts of the emperor in question:[6]

> *Iudaeos impulsore Chresto assidue tumultuantis Roma expulit.*
>
> Since the Jews constantly made disturbances at the instigation of Chrestus, he expelled them from Rome. (*Divus Claudius* 25.4)

> *afflicti suppliciis Christiani, genus hominum superstitionis novae ac maleficae*
>
> Punishment was inflicted on the Christians, a class of men given to a new and mischievous superstition. (*Nero* 16.2)

It seems that Suetonius has some information on the Christians. His reference to the punishment of the Christians under Nero is paralleled by the statement of Tacitus. But does he have information on Jesus? The name *Chrestus* (variant *Christus*) might indicate that, yet the reference to the Jews indicates the conclusion that this 'Chrestus' was troubling the Jews in the time of Claudius (or at least that Suetonius thought so). Although Suetonius may possibly have had some independent information on Jesus, the brief mention here is too problematic to make that assumption.

---

4. See the discussion in M. Stern, *Jews and Judaism in Greek and Latin Literature* (3 vols.; Jerusalem: Israel Academy of Arts and Sciences, 1974-84; 1980), 3-5.
5. See R. Syme, "The Titulus Tiburtinus", *Akten des VI. Internationalen Kongresses für Griechische und Lateinische Epigraphik, Vestigia* 17 (Munich: Beck, 1973), 585-601.
6. M. J. Harris, 'References to Jesus in Early Classical Authors,' in D. Wenham, ed., *Gospel Perspectives: Volume 5: The Jesus Tradition Outside the Gospels* (Sheffield: JSOT Press, 1985), 343-368.

Pliny the Younger

> *Cognitionibus de Christianis interfui numquam: ideo nescio quid et quatenus aut puniri soleat aut quaeri. Nec mediocriter haesitavi, sitne aliquod discrimen aetatum, an quamlibet teneri nihil a robustioribus differant; detur paenitentiae venia, an ei, qui omnino Christianus fuit, desisse non prosit; nomen ipsum, si flagitiis careat, an flagitia cohaerentia nomini puniantur. Interim, <in> iis qui ad me tamquam Christiani deferebantur, hunc sum secutus modum. Interrogavi ipsos an essent Christiani. Confitentes iterum ac tertio interrogavi supplicium minatus: perseverantes duci iussi. Neque enim dubitabam, qualecumque esset quod faterentur, pertinaciam certe et inflexibilem obstinationem debere puniri. Fuerunt alii similis amentiae, quos, quia cives Romani erant, adnotavi in urbem remittendos...*
>
> *Alii ab indice nominati esse se Christianos dixerunt et mox negaverunt; fuisse quidem sed dessis, quidam ante triennium, quidam ante plures annos, non nemo etiam ante viginti. <Hi> quoque omnes et imaginem tuam deorumque simulacra venerati sunt et Christo male dixerunt. Adfirmabant autem hanc fuisse summam vel culpae suae vel erroris, quod essent soliti stato die ante lucem convenire, carmenque Christo quasi deo dicere secum invicem que sacramento non in scelus aliquod obstringere, sed ne furta ne latrocinia ne adulteria committerent, ne fidem fallerent, ne depositum adpellati abnegarent.*

I have never been present at an examination of Christians. Consequently, I do not know the nature or the extent of the punishments usually meted out to them, nor the grounds for starting an investigation and how far it should be pressed. Nor am I at all sure whether any distinction should be made between them on the grounds of age, or if young people and adults should be treated alike; whether a pardon ought to be granted to anyone retracting his beliefs, or if he has once professed Christianity, he shall gain nothing by renouncing it; and whether it is the mere name of Christian which is punishable, even if innocent of crime, or rather the crimes associated with the name.

For the moment this is the line I have taken with all persons brought before me on the charge of being Christians. I have asked them in person if they are Christians, and if they admit it, I repeat the question a second and third time, with a warning of the punishment awaiting them. If they persist, I order them to be led away for execution; for, whatever the nature of their admission, I am convinced that their stubbornness and unshakeable obstinacy ought not to go unpunished. There have been others similarly fanatical who are Roman citizens. I have entered them on the list of persons to be sent to Rome for trial...

Others, whose names were given to me by an informer, first admitted the charge and then denied it; they said that they had ceased to be Christians two or more years previously, and some of them even twenty years ago. They all did reverence to your statue and the images of the gods in the same way as the others, and reviled the name of Christ. They also declared that the sum total of their guild or error amounted to no more than this: they had met regularly before dawn on a fixed day to chant verses alternately among themselves in honour of Christ as if to a god, and also to bind themselves by oath, not for any

> criminal purpose, but to abstain from theft, robbery and adultery, to commit no breach of trust and not to deny a deposit when called upon to restore it. (*Epistulae ad Trajanum* 10.96.1–4, 6-7)[7]

This is an important letter because it is the first non-Christian writing to give any information of substance about Christians. Yet it seems clear that Pliny has information only on the Christians in his own time (about 110 CE). There are references to 'Christ': he has those claiming not to be Christian to revile the name of Christ, while those Christians who meet in assembly chant verses in honour of Christ. It seems clear that the Christians believe in an individual called Christ whom they honour and worship, but it does not appear that Pliny has any information going back before his own time. All his information is on Christian actions and practices but nothing on the founder of Christianity. This passage gives no information about the historical Jesus beyond the traditional beliefs of Christians themselves.

Jewish Sources

Josephus

As so often, it is Josephus who gives us the most important information but in a way as to complicate the issue considerably. Josephus' life overlaps the middle and latter part of the first century CE, which means that he would have been a near contemporary of Jesus. His knowledge of the first part of the first century is mixed; for example, he jumps from 6 to 26 CE with evidently very little information. Yet from about 26 CE he does give us a considerable amount of useful information about the situation in Judah and the surrounding region, being more reliable than the New Testament Gospels, for example. This includes information about various groups and movements. For that reason, it would not be unusual if he had mentioned Jesus, and his comments on James the brother of Jesus are almost universally accepted. Yet Josephus' passage on Jesus, commonly referred to as the *Testimonium Flavianum*, is widely believed to be the victim of amendment by the Christian scribes who preserved the writings of Josephus (see the chart below).

During the Middle Ages and Early Modern Period, Josephus' statement was almost universally accepted at face value. But from the eighteenth century, even Christian writers began to question whether Josephus would have written such a statement. In more recent times, there have been essentially three positions: (1) a few scholars have continued to defend the

7. A. N. Sherwin-White, *The Letters of Pliny: A Historical and Social Commentary* (Oxford: Clarendon, 1966).

Testimonium Flavianum; (2) a number of respectable experts have rejected the passage as a complete fabrication; (3) the vast majority have believed that Josephus did mention Jesus but that the version preserved in the extant manuscripts has been worked over by Christian scribes to agree with and provide support for the New Testament account.[8]

Almost universally accepted as genuine is the statement in *A.J.* 20.9.1, §200: 'he [the high priest Ananus] convened the judges of the Sanhedrin and brought before them the brother of Jesus who was called the Christ, a man named James' (καθίζει συνέδριον κριτῶν καὶ παραγαγὼν εἰς αὐτὸ τὸν ἀδελφὸν Ἰησοῦ τοῦ λεγομένου Χριστοῦ, Ἰάκωβος ὄνομα αὐτῷ). An interesting aspect of this statement is that 'Jesus who is called Christ' seems to be the more prominent element of the sentence, perhaps because Jesus was better known than James or because Josephus had already mentioned Jesus in his narrative. This seems to be a definite statement that Josephus had knowledge of an individual of some notoriety named Jesus who had a brother named James important enough to be arraigned before the Sanhedrin and then sentenced to death by it.

One of the first Christian writers to refer to the works of Josephus was Origen (c. 185 to c. 254). He stated that Josephus had mentioned Jesus but also declared that he did not recognize him as the messiah: 'he [was] not accepting our Jesus to be Christ' (τὸν Ἰησοῦν ἡμῶν οὐ καταδεξάμενος εἶναι χριστόν [*Comm. Matt.* 1.17]); '[Josephus was] not believing in Jesus as Christ' (καίτοι γε ἀπιστῶν τῷ Ἰησοῦ ὡς χριστῷ [*Contra Celsum* 1.47; cf. 2.13]). Similarly, Jerome (writing around 400 CE) quoted the *Testimonium Flavianum* as stating that Jesus 'was believed to be the Christ' (*credebatur esse Christus* [*De viris illustribus* 13]). This all contradicts the bald statement of the *Testimonium*, 'This man was the Christ.'

Thus, those who thought Josephus wrote something about Jesus but not the extant version of the *Testimonium* seem to have the main data on their side. But after that things become blurred. Being able to conclude that the *Testimonium* might be a scribal reworking does not tell us what Josephus originally wrote. A good deal of erudition has been applied to reconstructing what is addition and what is original in the passage, but these reconstructions are inevitably hypothetical, however ingenious they are.[9] In the past few decades, however, another dimension has been added to the discussion, with potential new data to evaluate the question.

---

8. P. Winter, 'Excursus II'.
9. A good example is the recent analysis of J. P. Meier, *A Marginal Jew: Rethinking the Historical Jesus*. I. *The Roots of the Problem and the Person* (Anchor Bible Reference Library; New York: Doubleday, 1991), 59-67.

The new information comes from Near Eastern sources, specifically Arabic and Syriac writings of the first millennium of the Christian era. In 1971, S. Pines published a study of the statements of Agapius, the Christian Melkite bishop of Hierapolis in the tenth century, who wrote a chronicle in Arabic called the *Kitāb al-'Unwān* (*Universal History*).[10] Agapius mentions several writers in Greek who refer to Jesus, including Josephus; he then quotes a version of the *Testimonium*, but one that differs in certain essentials from the one in our extant Greek tradition. It is Pines's contention that this quotation comes from the Syriac tradition, and he compares the statement in Agapius with the Syriac text of Michael the Syrian and the Syriac translation of Eusebius' *Historia ecclesiastica* (see the chart).

Pines obviously leans to the conclusion that Agapius had access to a more original version of Josephus' statement about Jesus. He is not sure whether it is an uncensored version or one that has also been the subject of Christian censorship, though he thinks it is probably the latter.[12] He considers whether the version of Michael the Syrian might be the most original of the different versions. Yet he finally concludes that the version of Michael the Syrian is the result of a contamination between the Syriac original of Agapius and the *Testimonium*.[13]

Since Pines wrote, more work has been done on the sources of Agapius and Michael the Syrian. This is discussed by A. Whealey, who notes that both writers seem to have used the lost Syriac chronicle of Theophilus of Edessa (died c. 785) for the latter part of their work,[14] but this is not the section that contains the statement about Jesus. Michael quotes James of Edessa for the period before and up to the first century; this is more likely to be his source for the Josephus quote. It would also make sense if Agapius depended on it, but Agapius is more likely to have merely paraphrased his source. Michael, on the other hand, quite often quotes his sources word for word. Whealey argues that, contrary to the views of Pines, Michael is closer to the original statement of Josephus.

In trying to evaluate the different views, we need to compare the versions of Michael and Agapius. Agapius has three omissions in comparison with Michael:

---

10. S. Pines, *An Arabic Version of the Testimonium Flavianum and its Implications* (Jerusalem: Israel Academy of Sciences and Humanities, 1971), 20-21.
11. This clause occurs later in Agapius' version (in italics below), but this is where it would fit if it has become displaced. In any case, it will help the reader to see the parallel accounts in full.
12. Pines, 'An Arabic Version,' 70.
13. Pines, 'An Arabic Version,' 39-44.
14. A. Whealy, 'The Testimonium Flavianum in Syriac and Arabic,' *NTS* 54 (2008), 573-90.

Josephus, *A.J.* 18.3.3, §§63-64	Syriac Eusebius, *Hist. eccl.* 1.11.7-8	Michael the Syrian, *Chronique* 4.91	Agapius, *Kitāb al-'Unwān*
Γίνεται δὲ κατὰ	*hw' lm bhn' zbn'*	*dbhlyn zbn' 'yt*	*'nh k'n fy hḏ'*
τοῦτον τὸν χρόνον		*hw'*	*'lzm'n*
Ιησοῦς σοφὸς ἄνηρ,	*gbr' ḥd ḥknm'*	*gbr' ḥd ḥkym'*	*rjl ḥkym yq'l lh*
	dšm' yšw'.	*dšmh yšw'*	*'ysw'*
εἴγε ἄνδρα αὐτὸν	*'n wl' ln dgbr'*	*'n wl' ln dgbr'*	
λέγειν χρή.	*nqrywhy .*	*nqrywhy.*	
ἦν γὰρ παραδόξων	*'ytwhy hw' gyr*	*'ytwhy hw' gyr*	*wk'nt lh syrh*
ἔργων ποιητής,	*s'wr' d'bd' šbyḥ'*	*s'wr' d'bd' šbyḥ'*	*ḥsnh w'lm 'nh*
διδάσκαλος	*wmlpn'*	*wmlpn'*	*f'ḍl*
ἀνθρώπων τῶν	*dbny 'nš' hnwn*	*dšrr'*	
ἡδονῇ τἀληθῆ	*dbrgt' mqblyn lh*		
δεχομένων,	*lšrr'.*		
καὶ πολλοὺς μέν	*wlsgy" mn*	*wlsgy" mn*	*w'nh ttlmḏ lh kṯyr*
Ἰουδαίους, δὲ καὶ	*yhwdy' wlsgy'*	*ywdy' wmn*	*mn 'ln's mn*
τοῦ Ἑλληνικοῦ	*dyn 'p mn 'mm'*	*'mm' tlmdw*	*'lyhwd ws'yr*
ἐπηγάγετο.	*tlmd hw'.*	*mstbr'*	*'lš'wb*
ὁ Χριστὸς οὗτος ἦν.	*mšyḥ' dyn 'ytwhy*	*dmšyḥ' 'ytwhy*	*[fl'lh hw 'lmsyḥ]*
καὶ αὐτὸν ἐνδείξει	*hw'. wlh 'yk dmn*	*hw' wlw 'yk*	
τῶν πρώτων	*shdwt' d'nš'*	*shdwt' dryšnwhy*	
ἀνδρῶν παρ' ἡμῖν	*dšwhy d'mn yhbh*	*d'm' mṭlhd' ywbh*	
σταυρῷ			
ἐπιτετιμηκότος			
Πιλάτου οὐκ	*pylṭws lmsm brš'*	*pylṭws lmsbrš'*	*wk'n fy'lṭs qḍy*
ἐπαύσαντο οἱ τὸ	*dṣlyb' whnwn*	*dṣlyb' wmyt*	*'lyh b'lṣlb w'lmwt*
πρῶτον	*d'ḥbwhy l' šlyw*	*whnwn dyn*	*w'lḏyn ttlmḍw' lh*
ἀγαπήσαντες·	*mn ḥwb'. 'tḥny*	*d'ḥbwhy l' šlyw*	*lm ytrkw' tlmḏth*
ἐφάνη γὰρ αὐτοῖς	*lhwn gyr mn btr*	*mn ḥwbh 'tḥny*	*wḏkrw' 'nh ẓhr*
τρίτην ἔχων ἡμέραν	*tlt' ywmyn twb kd*	*lhwn mn btr*	
πάλιν ζῶν	*ḥy.*	*gywmyn kd ḥy.*	
			lhm b'd ṯlṯh 'y'm
τῶν θείων	*dnby' d'lh' hlyn*	*nby' gyr d'lh'*	*mn ṣlbh w'nh ''š*
προφητῶν ταῦτα τε	*wrbw 'yk hlyn*	*wd'yk hlyn 'mrw*	*fl'lh hw 'lmsyḥ*
καὶ ἄλλα μυρία περὶ	*'mrw 'lwhy*	*'lwhy tmyht'*	*'lḏy q'lt 'nh*
αὐτοῦ θαυμάσια	*tmyht'*		*'l'nby'h 'l''jyb*
εἰρηκότων.			
εἰς ἔτι τε νῦν τῶν	*w'dm lywmn' l'*	*w'dm' lywmn' l'*	
Χριστιανῶν ἀπὸ	*mgrd' 'm'*	*mgrd' 'm'*	
τοῦδε ὠνομασμένον	*dkrsṭyn'dmnh*	*dkrsṭyn' dmnh*	
οὐκ ἐπελίπε τὸ	*mštmh*	*w'dm' 'štmh.*	
φῦλον.			
LCL:	Pines:	Pines:	Pines:
About this time there lived Jesus, a wise man,	In that time there was one wise man named Jesus—	In these times there was a wise man named Jesus,	At this time there was a wise man who was called Jesus.

if indeed one ought to call him a man.	if [indeed] it is fitting to call him a man.	if it is fitting for us to call him a man.	
For he was one who wrought surprising feats and was a teacher of such people as accept the truth gladly.	For he was a worker of glorious deeds and a teacher of men: [that is] of those who accept truth with desire.	For he was a worker of glorious deeds and a teacher of truth.	His conduct was good, and [he] was known to be virtuous.
He won over many Jews and many of the Greeks.	And he turned many of the Jews and likewise many from among the other nations into his disciples.	Many from among the Jews and the nations became his disciples.	And many people from among the Jews and the other nations became his disciples.
He was the Messiah.	For he was the Messiah.	He was thought to be the Messiah.	[*accordingly he was perhaps the Messiah*][11]
When Pilate, upon hearing him accused by men of the highest standing amongst us,	[But] upon the testimony of the principal men of our nation,	But not according to the testimony of the principal [men] of [our] nation. Because of this,	
had condemned him to be crucified,	Pilate condemned him to the cross.	Pilate condemned him to the cross, and he died.	Pilate condemned him to be crucified and to die.
those who had in the first place come to love him did not give up their affection for him.	Those who had loved him did not cease to love him.	For those who had loved him did not cease to love him.	But those who had become his disciples did not abandon his discipleship. They reported that he had
On the third day he appeared to them restored to life,	For he appeared to them alive again after the three days.	He appeared to them alive after three days.	appeared to them three days after his crucifixion, and that he was alive; *accordingly he was perhaps the Messiah,*
for the prophets of God had prophesied these and countless other marvellous things about him.	For the prophets of God had spoken with regard to him of this and myriads of other marvelous things of this [kind].	For the prophets of God had spoken with regard to him of such marvelous things [as these].	concerning whom the prophets have recounted wonders.
And the tribe of the Christians, so called after him, has still to this day not disappeared.	And the people of the Christians, named after him, has not disappeared till our day.	And the people of the Christians, named after him, has not disappeared till [this] day.	

1. The first omission by Agapius is the phrase, 'if indeed it is fitting for us to call him a man'. This phrase is found not only in the Greek tradition of the *Testimonium* but also in Michael. Yet it seems unlikely that this statement would have been made by Josephus, as scholars have noted.[15]
2. Agapius omits entirely Michael's phrase, 'But not according to the testimony of the principal [men] of [our] nation', a phrase also included in all other versions of Josephus' statement. Yet this wording varies from the one in the Greek Josephus tradition and also the Syriac version of Eusebius. Judging by the other versions, this is an affirmation that 'principal men' testified against Jesus. What this suggests[16] is that the source common to Michael and Agapius had misread a Syriac *lh* ('to him') as *lw* ('not'). Michael included the scribal error in his text, but Agapius found it confusing and omitted it.
3. The final statement omitted by Agapius is the last one of the *Testimonium*, which the Christians continue until this day. This may not actually be an omission but rather that Agapius stopped his quotation with the statement about the prophets.

Two further points need some discussion:

4. The statement that Jesus appeared alive to his disciples on the third day (found in the Greek tradition, the Syriac of Eusebius and also Michael) also looks like a Christian statement. Agapius, however, makes this only the report of the disciples, which is more likely to be what Josephus would have written, if he mentioned this point.
5. Michael and Agapius differ from the Greek tradition in both having the statement that Jesus died. Both also lack the word 'again' of the phrase 'alive again', which seems to have dropped out of the Syriac tradition. Therefore, it was found necessary to add 'he died' or something similar to make it clear that Jesus died by crucifixion. This is why both Michael and Agapius have this verbal form, even though it was evidently not original to Josephus' narrative.

It strikes me that Whealey has an important point: both Michael and Agapius drew on a Syriac version of the passage in Josephus (which explains their similarities), but Agapius has paraphrased rather than quoting literally. This explains the omission of the statement about the principal men of the nation. She is correct that, by and large, Michael's version looks like a statement that Josephus could have written. Yet in a couple of places where

15. Winter, 'Excursus II,' 435-36; Meier, *A Marginal Jew*, I, 60.
16. So Whealey, 'Testimonium Flavianum,' 586.

Agapius differs from Michael, his text looks *prima facie* more like Josephus. The statement, 'if it is fitting for us to call him a man' (found in Michael but missing from Agapius), seems to me unlikely for Josephus. In addition, Agapinus' statement, 'They reported that he had appeared to them three days after his crucifixion', looks more like Josephus' arms-length approach than the more credulous 'he appeared to them alive after three days'. Thus, in the end I think Pines's preference for Agapius' version is justified, and his view that even Michael's statement has already been the subject of Christian editing is more likely. Yet, as Whealey suggests, the one part of the statement that is most important is about Jesus being the Christ/Messiah, and both Michael and Agapius state only that this was the view of some, a statement that Josephus could well have made.

As always, the problem is hypothetical reconstruction based on conjecture rather than actual texts. In the absence of new Greek manuscript discoveries, there will always be uncertainty. Yet based on the general expectation of what Josephus might have written about Jesus and the actual statements found in Michael and Agapius (supported by Jerome and Origen), the following has a reasonable probability of being what Josephus actually wrote (though in English; I have made no attempt to reconstruct the Greek text):

> About this time there was a wise man named Jesus. For he was a worker of glorious deeds and a teacher of truth. Many from among the Jews and the Greeks became his disciples. He was thought to be the Christ. But upon the testimony of the principal men of our nation, Pilate condemned him to the cross. Yet those who had loved him did not cease to love him. They reported that he appeared to them alive after three days. For the prophets of God had spoken with regard to him of such marvellous things. And the people of the Christians, named after him, has not disappeared till this day.

Rabbinic and Medieval References

Since Jesus is said to have interacted with various Jewish groups, including the Pharisees, the basic question is whether in the vast body of rabbinic literature there might be some genuine remembrances of Jesus. A number of studies have been done, mainly by Jewish scholars, but the most recent is P. Schäfer's monograph.[17] He surveys the various references and shows that the aim is counter to the claims of Christianity, as a means of defense against Christian persecutions. Surprisingly, the most detailed attacks come

17. P. Schäfer, *Jesus in the Talmud* (Princeton: Princeton University Press, 2007); see also, G. H. Twelftree, 'Jesus in Jewish Traditions,' in D. Wenham, ed., *Gospel Perspectives. V. The Jesus Tradition outside the Gospels* (Sheffield: JSOT Press, 1985), 289-341.

in Babylonian sources, the rationale coming from the situation of the Jews under Sassanian rule.

For our purposes, though, the references in rabbinic literature all seem to arise from contact with Christians or knowledge of the New Testament or Christian teachings. In other words, there is no evidence that any of the rabbinic passages show knowledge of the historical Jesus or his activities. The rabbis often show a good knowledge of Christianity and the beliefs of Christians, but none can be traced with confidence back to the founder of Christianity. There is not the space to go through the various passages, but the place to begin is Schäfer. But in the light of present knowledge, there does not seem to be useful data on the historical Jesus in the rabbinic passages.

In addition, we have two other Jewish sources relating to early Christianity. One is the *Toledot Yeshu*, which is a life of Jesus in Hebrew.[18] It is generally agreed that this is a medieval work (or at best a production several centuries removed from its subject) and, like the rabbinic references, has no claim to information on the historical Jesus. More recently brought to scholarly attention is the 'Hebrew Gospel of Matthew' published by George Howard.[19] It was found in a fourteenth-century treatise of Shem-Tov-ben-Isaac ben-Shafrut but seems to be older. Although Howard argues that it shows a certain independence from the canonical Gospel of Matthew (not identifying Jesus with the Messiah, for instance), there is so far no indication that it has original independent information about Jesus.

Conclusions

The early extra-Christian accounts that might tell us about the historical Jesus are few. This is why the data in such accounts are exceedingly precious: they are a vital check on the Christian sources. An examination of the accounts—most known for centuries—indicates, however, that even the few extant are not all usable. The interesting and useful letter of Pliny the Younger to the emperor Trajan gives important information on the Christianity of his time, but there is no evidence of any data going back to the supposed historical Jesus. Likewise, Suetonius gives us some brief information on the history of Christianity, but it is not clear that he has any actual information on Jesus. Finally, the many references to Jesus in rabbinic literature are of no help because of a lack of any evidence from the early first century. This leaves us with two sources, making them more valuable

18. Schäfer, *Jesus*, 2-4 and notes. Schäfer is preparing a new edition of the *Toledot Yeshu*, but to the best of my knowledge it is not yet available.
19. G. Howard, *Hebrew Gospel of Matthew* (Macon: Mercer University, 1995).

because of their uniqueness: the Roman historian Tacitus and the Jewish historian Josephus. Note the following important data and arguments:

1. Tacitus and Josephus appear to obtain their information independently of each other. Their independent references to Jesus make it very likely that such an individual existed and was known as the founder of the Christian sect.
2. Both mention Jesus' death under the governorship of Pontius Pilate. This suggests some sort of evidence for the event. One might think that Jesus' death, like that of so many executed by the Romans, would have gone unrecorded. But it seems to have been substantial enough to be noted by the Roman administration. Tacitus probably obtained his information from a document or archival source. Josephus' source of information is more uncertain, since he seems to report a number of things from oral tradition, but a Roman source is a distinct possibility.
3. Tacitus' account is hostile to the Christians, as we might expect of an upper-class Roman. Josephus, on the other hand, was often neutral toward such individuals. The present form of the *Testimonium Flavianum* in the Greek tradition is favorable toward Jesus, but this is unlikely to represent what Josephus wrote. Other versions (including Origen, Jerome and one of the Syriac traditions [attested in Michael the Syrian and Agapius]) look more like what Josephus would have written and give a more descriptive and arms-length account, though not unsympathetic.
4. The data emerging from these non-Christian accounts is minimal but nevertheless significant:
   a. Jesus existed and founded the Christian sect.
   b. He gained disciples among both Jews and 'Greeks' (non-Jews in general?).
   c. He was tried and executed by crucifixion during the reign of Tiberius under the governorship of Pontius Pilate, some of the leading Jews apparently helping to gain his condemnation.
   d. His followers reported various supernatural things about him, including that he was seen alive the third day after the crucifixion and that some thought he was the Christ/Messiah.
   e. The Christian sect was still in existence in the early second century CE.

This may not seem much, but its value lies in its independence from the Christian tradition.

- 4 -

The Grand Inquisitor and Christ: Why the Church Does Not Want Jesus

Niels Peter Lemche

In his great novel, *The Brothers Karamazov*, Dostoyevsky includes a short novel within the novel, the story of Christ's return to earth in the time of the Holy inquisition in Spain. The Grand Inquisitor had Christ arrested and visits him in the jail, telling him that they will have to burn him at the stake because he represents a danger to the Church. The story is told by the nihilist Ivan Karamazov, who is normally considered to side with the Inquisitor, which seems strange because Ivan represents a movement that had also questioned the position of the Church. Perhaps there are more layers represented in this novel than appear at first sight. *The Brothers Karamazov* was written around 1879–80, in a period that was theologically divided in its view of the historical person Jesus. The heated discussion reached a climax when David Friedrich Strauss, in 1835–36, published his *Das Leben Jesu, kritisch bearbeitet*, denying Jesus' divine origins.[1] Is Ivan Karamazov and the Grand Inquisitor of his story right in their assertion that Christ would destroy the Church? In what capacity could Christ represent a danger to the Church? As 'Christ', or as 'Jesus' the mere carpenter's son from Nazareth?

David Friedrich Strauss's investigation into the life and career of Jesus belongs to the early phase of historical-critical studies. It would definitely be too early for inclusion in the liberal theology movement that governed the academic theological environment towards the end of the nineteenth century, but it paved the way for this kind of theology and put up fences between advanced academic theology and conservative church-based

1. Tübingen: Verlag von C.F. Osiander.

theology, although it would be wrong to say that the Church was without its liberals, or the academy without its conservatives, having the long career of Ernst Wilhelm Theodor Hengstenberg (1802–69) in mind.[2] Strauss's study of the life of Jesus was symptomatic of exegetes' liberation from the control of the Church that was inaugurated by Philipp Gabler's famous lecture on the division between historical theology and dogmatics—meaning church control—from 1787.

In the more recent theological climate, opposition against historical-critical studies and the turn to reader-response exegesis, post-colonial studies and so forth has—as correctly emphasized by James Barr—forgotten this aspect of historical-critical scholarship. Liberation theology was not something invented in post-colonial studies; it has been around for more than two-hundred years. Historical-critical scholarship is the invention of Western man. However, because modern liberation theology is in opposition to the type of exegesis current in Europe and North America, it has changed the rules. This has consequences for exegesis because historical-critical exegesis was generally in opposition to the dogmatic reading of Scripture in the Church. Liberation theology is part of the general critique of Western tradition in the postmodern third world. However, it can also easily lead to a new kind of control, for example, of an evangelical character, in no need of critical scholarship. In this way a kind of 'holy alliance' has arisen between evangelical Christianity and third-world theology, the evangelicals having found a partner, or so they believe, among other critics of modern theological scholarship. However, basically they are as wrong as the evangelicals themselves, who believe in a historical reading of biblical texts which are believed to represent the *ipsissima verba* of God and therefore are flawless. From a historical point of view, 'that must have happened since God has told us so' is just as estranged to post-colonial exegesis as traditional historical-critical scholarship. Regardless of how we see it, evangelical exegesis represents a *cul-de-sac*, leading nowhere.

On the other hand, we might argue that third-world exegesis in combination with post-modern theology has, in their criticism of historical-critical exegesis as part of Western culture, also identified a split between scholarly exegesis and the Church which was not part of Gabler's original understanding of the relationship between church and exegesis. Gabler aimed at a practical division of work, demanding that the exegetes should be allowed to carry on with their studies without interference from church

2. Henstenberg was in possession of perhaps the most influential position as professor of biblical studies at the University of Berlin. Here he had taken up the chair left vacant by the dismissal of the liberal Wilhelm Martin Leberecht de Wette who had interfered in the affair around the murder of August von Kotzebue in 1819.

authorities. On the other hand, he never said that the story should end there. On the contrary, he formulated what became a kind of dogma among academic theologians that exegetes studied the Bible to explain what is written there, while systematic theologians (dogmaticians according to his terminology) were obliged to explain to the modern world what the exegetes had found in holy Scripture. This was, of course, an idealistic way of looking at the division of the different tasks among theological departments at the universities, and it has never really succeeded, the exegetes often playing systematic theologians—although few of them have really contributed to the development of systematic theology[3]—while systematic theologians have often indulged in exegetical analysis.[4] It would certainly be wrong to maintain that systematic theologians see their task as merely explaining the work of the exegetes.

The accusation sometimes made against critical exegesis is that it has estranged believing Christians from their Bible. This may not only be a problem for evangelical Christians and plain fundamentalists, it is also a general problem for the Church, especially the Protestant part of Christianity with its insistence on, if not plain *sola scriptura* then at least as the Bible's primary importance for understanding the gospel. Since critical studies began some centuries ago, exegetes have been engaged in an uphill battle and have usually been met with resistance, hatred and unbelief from both church authorities and the general public. There is a saying that it takes about thirty years before ideas taught in the classroom at theological faculties become commonplace among the laity (if ever). After 1800, with romanticism and the change from the Enlightenment to the so-called 'modern world', the laity became involved in ideas about nationality bolstered by a new understanding of history as a humanistic discipline. Historians were called on to establish the foundation of the new nation-states. Their criterion was to find out 'what really happened' (Leopold von Ranke). The blending of historical interest with national interest became a governing dogma in the modern age running at least from 1800 to 2000. Because history became a matter of analysing old documents and artefacts to find out the historical 'truth', historical theology, that is, historical-critical theology, was equally obsessed with the idea of reconstructing the past. The acceptance of the laity depended on the academy's ability to present a reconstruction acceptable to the lay-person, but not directly opposing Christian dogma as formulated by the Church. Christian dogma

3. Gerhard von Rad (1900–1971) is one of the few, James Barr (1924–2006) another.
4. Karl Barth being a famous example.

wished more simply that exegetes provide historical proof of its essential elements.

This had important consequences for the historical-critical analysis of biblical texts. It was a given fact that the historical narrative in the Bible, in the Old as well as the New Testament (the division between these two disciplines being itself a consequence of the fundamental historical ideas about their respective backgrounds), relied on historical events, although the reporting of these events was coloured by ancient beliefs and superstition. Once cleared of such antiquated ideas, but also cleared of later embellishments, the Bible would become a reliable source for the construction of Jewish history and the origins of Christianity. Apart from the most conservative part of Christianity, this was accepted by most moderate members of the Church.

However, there has always been a limit to the liberalism of the Christian laity, the clergy, and the majority of university theologians. If historical-critical scholars came too close to deconstructing the biblical narrative as story and not history; that is, if exegetes dared to question the basic historicity of what was related in the Bible, including certain dogmatic issues, they would immediately have difficulties. This happened when Dostoyevsky wrote his novel. To mention one famous example: in 1881, the leading Scottish biblical scholar William Robertson Smith (1846–1894) was removed from his position at a theological college because of his liberal ideas. He never became professor of theology at the University of Cambridge, but, towards the end of his life he did manage to gain employment there as a professor of Arabic. The fate of the Danish Frants Buhl (1850–1932) was similar. Although already employed by the theological faculty in Copenhagen, he left for the more liberal German academic scene to become professor of Semitic philology in Leipzig as the successor of no less than Franz Delitzsch. He later returned to Copenhagen as professor of Semitic philology.

The problem of historical-critical scholarship has always been the selectivity that is involved when it comes to identifying what is really historical and really critical. Historical-critical scholarship usually stops being critical when it does become really historical. Just try to question the historicity of Jesus in front of a group of New Testament scholars! The situation has hardly changed much during the last two-hundred years. Whenever something really new was proposed, trench warfare immediately began, in an attempt to delay the impact of such new ideas concerning, for example, the historicity of Moses or of David, not to mention the patriarchs. His insistence that Abraham is not a historical figure sent the editor of this volume into an academic exile that lasted for many years. His study on the historicity of the patriarchs was primarily intended for the North

American scene. In European scholarship, something similar had already been proposed at the beginning of the nineteenth century. Nevertheless, the North American academic world and its constituency among the religious laity were definitely not prepared for any such lack of 'belief'.[5]

The true face of traditional historical-critical scholarship in general surfaced when, in the last quarter of the twentieth century, a small group of Old Testament scholars began to deconstruct biblical history from one end to the other, thereby exposing the lack of historical foundation for most parts of the historical narrative of the Old Testament. The reconstruction of the history of this development is, however, more complicated than just showing how the deconstruction proceeded. Moving from the patriarchs, every phase of biblical history right down to the story of the Babylonian exile and the return of the Jewish nation to Palestine was shown to be primarily a narrative, though not devoid of historical elements, primarily interested in legitimizing Jewish power in central Palestine.

No one has embodied resistance to this separation of biblical narrative from the real history of ancient Palestine more than the North American biblical archaeologist William G. Dever. His tirades against the members of the 'Copenhagen School' are textbook studies for the conservative reaction against liberal studies.[6] Dever's religious background also became clear from his introduction to one of his recent books.[7] His father was a Protestant lay preacher whom he followed as a child. Dever is symptomatic of a problem that has always infested biblical scholarship; namely, that most of its practitioners come from a religious background.[8] The importance of Sunday school for biblical studies needs to be explored. The kind of religious teaching found in religious institutions has brainwashed children in such a way that only very few will ever be able to break its hold on them.

A liberal-minded theologian like David Friedrich Strauss will face resistance from conservatives. The resistance has many faces and will show up in many forms, some of them violent. When the subject is no less than Jesus, the centre of Christian belief, the resistance against liberalism can

5. T. L. Thompson, *The Historicity of the Patriarchal Narratives: The Quest for the Historical Abraham* (BZAW, 133; Berlin: Walter de Gruyter, 1974).
6. W. G. Dever, '"Will the Real Israel Please Stand Up?" Archaeology and Israelite Historiography: Part I,' *BASOR* 297 (1995), 61-80; idem, '"Will the Real Israel Please Stand Up?" Archaeology and Israelite Historiography: Part II,' *BASOR* 298 (1995), 37-58: idem, *What Did the Biblical Writers Know and When Did They Know It? What Archaeology Can Tell Us about the Reality of Ancient Israel* (Grand Rapids: Eerdmans, 2001); idem, *Who Were the Early Israelites and Where Did They Come From?* (Grand Rapids: Eerdmans, 2003).
7. Dever, *What Did the Biblical Writers Know?*, ix.
8. H. Avalos, *The End of Biblical Studies* (Amherst: Prometheus Books, 2007), sating the religious interests of biblical scholars at the very opening of the book, 15.

sometimes be vitriolic, because the opponents are not remotely ready to listen to the arguments of the liberal. It, however, says something about the world of the German university in the nineteenth century that it had space for both Strauss and Henstenberg, to use these figures as examples of two opposing categories of biblical scholars. In the second half of the nineteenth century it also accepted a Wellhausen and his liberal ideas about ancient Israel, although the resistance against his liberal ideas forced him to lay down his position as professor of the Old Testament in Greifswald in 1882. His academic career continued in Semitic philology. It is, on the other hand, quite interesting that the general theological climate became increasingly more conservative even at German universities in the generation following Wellhausen.[9]

Strauss denied the divine aspect of Jesus' nature and opted for a historical study of his career. This quest has never ended. Today the most marked example of a group of scholars discussing the person of Jesus is probably 'the Jesus Seminar', a group of mainly North American New Testament scholars devoted to the historical study of Jesus and his life. This is certainly not the place to comment on its procedures or theories, but it is symptomatic of a liberal trend within North American New Testament studies which is unparalleled in North American Old Testament studies.

Disregarding the objections from conservative biblical scholarship as well as from the conservative laity with its base in confessional religious teaching, one issue remains which should be taken into account when we later return to our point of departure; and that is the meeting between the Grand Inquisitor and Christ and the reaction from the non-conservative laity to biblical scholarship. When biblical scholarship entered the phase of the 'history of religions school' and liberal theology towards the end of the nineteenth century, the alienation between the Christian community and its Bible became a serious matter. In many ways, the position of the New Testament was not affected—after all, the New Testament would always be at the centre of Christian services—but the position of the Old Testament as part of the Christian Bible was questioned, sometimes in a very serious way, as, for example, by the leading church historian Adolf von Harnack, who in his famous book on Marcion regarded mental laziness as the only reason for the survival of the Old Testament as part of the Christian Bible.[10] Marcion

9. N. P. Lemche, 'Rachel and Lea: Or: On the Survival of Outdated Paradigms in the Study of the Origin of Israel I,' *SJOT* 2 (1987), 127-53; idem, 'Rachel and Lea: Or: On the Survival of Outdated Paradigms in the Study of the Origin of Israel II,' *SJOT* 3 (1988), 39-65.

10. A. von Harnack, *Marcion: Das Evangelium vom fremden Gott* (Leipzig: Hindrichs, 1921), 127.

11. The date 144 CE is the one mentioned by Tertulian. A date in the second century CE, however, seems certain, as Marcion lived from c. 85-160 CE.

had of course denounced the status of the Old Testament and its religion as early as 144 CE, and, for that reason, was excommunicated from the Church.[11] Harnack considered the rejection of Marcion to be well founded in its time but attacked later Christianity for still keeping to the first part of the Bible.

Rejecting the dogma of Christ's two natures, which, as a matter of fact, is a heresy going back to antiquity, would definitely not only question the position of the New Testament within the Church, it would certainly endanger the survival of the Church, making Christianity redundant. When Strauss took up this issue on historical grounds, it would clearly be the reason for resistance, not only from conservative academics and church people, but also from non-conservatives as well, seeing that their beliefs were being squandered by academic analysis. Such a reaction governed the resistance for a long time when it was first proposed that Moses had never lived. The argument was: we cannot explain the history of early Israel without a Moses. If he had not lived, it would be necessary to invent him. The answer is quite simple: and so they did! At the present, the debate about the historicity of David and Solomon is more pressing.

David is doubly important. From a Christian point of view, he is the apical ancestor of the family into which Jesus was born (disregarding the problem that Jesus was not the son of the man, Joseph, descendant of David), but, in modern politics, he has also become the apical ancestor of the modern Israeli nation. Without a David they would have to invent him, and the answer still is: and so they did!

Now, why will a historical Jesus destroy the Church? Is the Grand Inquisitor right? It is often assumed that the Church has, by and large, developed into a mighty institution far removed from its humble origins and its even humbler founder, Jesus of Nazareth (whether he was a carpenter or a rabbi or both). The difference between the Christ of the Church and the Jesus of the Gospels becomes dangerous when explained to the laity. In a recent article, I have argued that the Bible is dangerous to Christianity.[12] It was my proposal that pious people should not be allowed within 90 yards of the Bible. Reading the Bible has not done them much good. The number of believers who would follow in the footsteps of Christ has always been considerable. Some have been made harmless by being incorporated into the Church and tamed there, such as the Franciscans; and some have developed into doomsday movements—the last decade of the twentieth century saw some nasty examples of the effect of such movements.

---

12. Cf. N. P. Lemche, 'Guns Do Not Kill, People Do,' in Roland Boer, ed., *Secularism and Biblical Studies* (London: Equinox, 2010), 51-58, arguing that pious people should not be allowed closer to the Bible than one hundred metres, as it has done them no good.

The position of the Grand Inquisitor is the position of the well-educated clergy of the Church, whether Orthodox, Catholic or Protestant. The Catholic Church managed well, having a Bible which in practice was inaccessible to its laity, kept in Latin until the second half of the twentieth century. The Protestant ministry had a Bible that could be read by the educated laity. This was not too much of a problem as, until the school reforms around 1800, very few could read. The ones who managed the art of reading and writing had mostly visited schools controlled by the Church and therefore followed the Church's interpretation of Scripture. So Protestantism had a Bible for the laity but still controlled the reading of its Bible. This might not have been Luther's or other Reformers' intention, but, Lutheranism in the liberal time of Luther soon developed into Lutheran orthodoxy, which was not very different in its attitude to the Bible and the laity than traditional Catholicism.

In the nineteenth century, when it became normal (at least in the Western world) to read and write, the situation changed drastically and developed into the situation described above, characterized by the strife between liberal interpretation of the Bible and faith-based endeavours to control the interpretation of Scripture. In this respect, not much has changed since the days of Dostoyevsky. He published his novel when the crisis of critical theology had sharpened and some of critical theology's principal figures were forced out of their academic positions because 'they would destroy the Church'. Dostoyevsky's Jesus is not (yet) the Jesus of liberal theology; rather he is representative of the Jesus followed by pious laity having read too much of the Bible. Such movements represent a danger to the survival of the Church. However, the Jesus of liberal academic theology presents another danger, an attack on the central message of the gospel and the confession that God became man. Surely most theologians will side with the Grand Inquisitor.

- 5 -

Jesus and the Mythic Mind: An Epistemological Problem

Emanuel Pfoh

Preliminary Caveat

The following comments are written by a scholar whose main field of interest and research is, in broad terms, the historical anthropology of Syria-Palestine/the Levant during the Bronze and Iron Ages (c. 3300–600 BCE), including the history of that (those) Palestinian entity(-ies) known as 'Israel'.[1] Thus, the reader will find here only general statements and thoughts by an outsider to the field of New Testament studies regarding epistemological and methodological issues for the history-writing of the Near Eastern world, in which the figure of Jesus together with the whole of biblical traditions should be understood. My main aim is to reflect, from strictly historical and anthropological perspectives, on what we can know about the figure of Jesus and what we cannot: about what can be considered historical knowledge and what is to be deemed myth or mythic creation by ancient writers. Both categories, 'history' and 'myth', are to be taken into account seriously and understood as intellectual phenomena, each with its own social and historical contexts and dynamics.

As 'minimalist' as these remarks may be seen, they stand as reflections on the methodological problems of the search for a historical Jesus in New Testament studies that should be acknowledged, addressed and responded to by scholars, but also as a plea for a critical understanding of the nature of ancient literature and the intellectual worlds supporting such.[2]

1. Cf. E. Pfoh, *The Emergence of Israel in Ancient Palestine: Historical and Anthropological Perspectives* (CIS; London: Equinox, 2009).
2. See the perspective in P. R. Davies, 'What *Is* "Minimalism" and Why Do So Many People Dislike It?,' in M. Müller and T. L. Thompson, eds., *Historie og konstruktion. Festskrift til Niels*

The Figure of Jesus

Since the Enlightenment, the figure of Jesus has been the subject of an intellectual quest for historical knowledge, apart from the theological message we find in the Gospels—as related, for example, in the famous distinction between the Jesus of history and the Christ of faith.[3] Nevertheless, very little, if anything, is known about a Yehoshua bar Yosef in the history of Roman Palestine from our primary sources.[4] Accordingly, in the present contribution, an epistemological inquiry is advanced to deal with a situation not always seriously considered by biblical scholars: the presence of the mythic mind in the intellectual world of antiquity. Closely related to this: is historical knowledge of Jesus possible at all? How is Jesus to be understood from the perspective of the mythic mind of the ancient Near East? The main reason for holding to the historicity of the figure of Jesus, as his activities are narrated in the Gospels, resides not primarily in historical evidence but derives instead from a modern theological necessity. Had Jesus not lived among mortals and, more importantly, had he not died and been raised from the dead, the kernel of Christian theology would lose its essence.[5] Yet, theological need hardly counts as either sound historical method or evidence. In order to draw critical conclusions and historical rather than

---

Peter Lemche i anledning af 60 års fødselsdagen den 6. september 2005 (FBE, 14; Copenhagen: Museum Tusculanum, 2005), 75-85. The key issue is related to the departure from concrete and established knowledge. See also, E. Prinzivalli, 'Introduzione,' in idem, ed., *L'enigma Gesù: Fonti e metodi della ricerca storica* (Bibloteca di testi e studi, 457; Rome: Carocci, 2008), 7-18, esp. 11: 'Voglio solo prospettare al lettore, credente o no credente, un'ipotesi: ammetiamo che i fatti su cui gli storici, o meglio la loro maggioranza, si trovi a concordare a proposito di Gesù siano un numero esiguo rispetto ai punti che rimangono in discussione, ma siano pur sempre un certo numero: avremo raggiunto un consenso che prescinde da fede, dottrine, convinzioni particolare, e che si basa solo su metodi e resultati condivisi.'

3. See an evaluation of the 'three quests' for the historical Jesus in V. Fusco, 'La quête du Jésus historique: Bilan et perspectives,' in D. Marguerat, E. Norelli and J.-M. Poffet, eds., *Jésus de Nazareth. Nouvelles approches d'une énigme* (MdB, 38; Geneva: Labor et Fides, 2003, 2nd edn), 25-57.

4. Although very much can be said about that ancient world! Cf., e.g., H. Koester, *Introduction to the New Testament*. I. *History, Culture, and Religion of the Hellenistic Age* (Philadelphia: Fortress Press/Berlin: Walter de Gruyter, 1982 [1980]), esp. 281-412; B. J. Malina, *The New Testament World: Insights from Cultural Anthropology* (Louisville: Westminster John Knox Press, 2001, 3rd edn); A. Destro and M. Pesce, *Antropologia delle origini cristiane* (Bari-Roma: Laterza, 2008, 2nd edn); J. H. Neyrey and E. C. Stewart, eds., *The Social World of the New Testament: Insights and Models* (Peabody: Hendrickson, 2008), among many others.

5. Relevant to such perceptions are the words of R. de Vaux, nearly a half-century ago regarding the historicity of biblical Israel and its relationship to Christian faith: 'si la foi historique d'Israël n'est pas fondée dans l'histoire, cette foi est erronée, est la notre aussi', in 'Les patriarches hébreux et l'histoire', *RB* 72 (1965), 5-28 (7).

religious answers to our questions, a secular perspective on the subject must prevail—which does not prevent, of course, an engagement with more theologically or religiously-driven perspectives.[6]

For the present, let us concentrate on the mythic character of the figure of Jesus. It should be noted that the concept of *myth* or the adjective *mythic*, as they are used in this essay, have nothing to do with 'falsehood', as opposed to *truth*. *Myth*, as a literary and analytical category, refers to a worldview which is different from a modern Western perception of reality and its understanding of historical causality. It refers not only to the interaction of humans with supernatural forces, but also to the ontology of that interaction. Even so, its main analytical use lies in the possibility of interpreting ancient stories, literary compositions and worldviews that are culturally and temporally distant from a modern Western world.[7] In this sense, the following definition by R. Bultmann can be seen as valid as well:

> The real purpose of myth is not to present an objective picture of the world as it is, but to express man's understanding of himself in the world in which he lives. Myth should be interpreted not cosmologically, but anthropologically, or better still, existentially... Myth is an expression of man's conviction that the origin and purpose of the world in which he lives are to be sought not within it but beyond it—that is, beyond the realm of known and tangible reality—and that this realm is perpetually dominated and menaced by those mysterious powers that are its source and limit. Myth is also an expression of man's awareness that he is not the lord of his own being. It expresses his sense of dependence not only within the visible world, but more especially on those forces which hold sway beyond the confines of the known. Finally, myth expresses man's belief that in this state of dependence he can be delivered from the forces within the visible world.[8]

From the perspective of such an anthropological understanding of what a myth is, we encounter a first obstacle to a historicist search for the Jesus of the Gospels; namely, what we can learn from reading ancient literature or, in other words, how we understand ancient stories. Thomas L. Thompson

---

6. Cf. J. G. Crossley, *Why Christianity Happened: A Sociohistorical Account of Christian Origins* (Louisville: Westminster John Knox Press, 2006), esp. 1-34.

7. Cf. M. Eliade, *The Sacred and the Profane: The Nature of Religion* (New York: Harcourt, 1959); idem, *Myth and Reality* (New York: Harper and Row, 1963); also, the analytical use of the term in N. Wyatt, 'The Mythic Mind,' *SJOT* 15 (2001), 3-56; idem, 'The Mythic Mind Revisited: Myth and History—or Myth versus History—a Continuing Problem in Biblical Studies,' *SJOT* 22 (2008), 161-75.

8. R. Bultmann, 'New Testament and Mythology,' in H. W. Bartsch, ed., *Kerygma and Myth: A Theological Debate* (London: Society for Promoting Christian Knowledge, 1953), 1-44 (10-11). I am sure that Bultmann's use of the adverb 'anthropologically' is theological rather than socio-scientific; even though, both understandings are relevant in this context.

has recently taken up the problematic situation that an attempt to search for the historical Jesus in the Gospels presents:

> The problem of the quest for the historical Jesus is not merely the difficulty of identifying him with specific events or sayings, given the length of time between any such figure of first-century Palestine and the gospels. Nor is the problem that the sources have been revised by the theological message of the gospels. The problem is rather that the gospels are not about such a person. They deal with something else.[9]

What do the Gospels deal with? They deal with '[a] great figure—bearing and illustrating a tradition'.[10] But such a great figure as this is ubiquitous in ancient Near Eastern literature:

> The thematic elements of a divinely destined era of salvation, a messianic fullness of time and a day of judgment bringing about a transformation of the world from a time of suffering to the joys of the kingdom are all primary elements of a coherent, identifiable literary tradition, centuries earlier than the gospels, well-known to us from the Bible and texts throughout the entire ancient Near East.[11]

Accordingly, it is legitimate to ask: what kind of concrete historical knowledge can we obtain from a set of stories about a person who imitates the behaviour of previous literary characters? The question of historicity, as Thompson notes, is not relevant in this context. Thompson's analysis, linking the figure of Jesus in the Gospels with a whole set of mythic motifs from the ancient Near East, is indeed a much more promising avenue for future research, providing us with a variety of positive results, as it works with evidence; namely, the extant mythic traditions, rather than with speculations regarding issues about the historicity of these very mythic traditions.

The Mythic Mind and the Problem of Interpretive Demythologization

The first problem with historical knowledge of Jesus—or any attempt to gain such knowledge—is reflected not merely in the nature of our most important

9. T. L. Thompson, *The Messiah Myth: The Near Eastern Roots of Jesus and David* (New York: Basic Books, 2005), 14.
10. Thompson, *The Messiah Myth*, 14.
11. Thompson, *The Messiah Myth*, 28. Further: 'Biblical figures such as Adam, Noah, Abraham, Moses, Joshua, David, Elijah and Elisha, Hezekiah, Josiah, John and Jesus—to name only the most famous—are the bearers of Palestine's ancient Near Eastern intellectual life' (315). The purpose of ancient stories are not historicist but pedagogic: 'Heroic figures and parables, hymns and prayers educate by evoking imitation' (316).

sources, the Gospels, but primarily in the mentality behind these sources. The very notion of a 'historical Jesus' reflects the epistemological matrix behind the search for this figure of the past, an intellectual matrix that is modern and non-existent in earlier references to Jesus. As V. Fusco notes,

> dans l'Église ancienne l'expression «Jésus *historique*» aurait été inconcevable. Le terme meme porte les traces de son origine polémique; il sousentend une opposition à l'image courante, celle de la foi, qui est jugée non historique; il reflète le présupposé d'après lequel tout ce qui est historique est rationnel, et tout ce qui n'est pas rationnel n'est pas historique.[12]

The ideological setting of the impetus in historical research for the Jesus of the Gospels *beyond* the Gospels marks its need for specific results: the truth as real; namely, that the reality of the revelation present in Scripture depends on rational (historical) truth. Hence, the need to rationalize images, stories and teachings, which are otherwise recognizable as mythic and coming from an ancient world of myth. This can be recognized in Bultmann's effort to 'translate' a mythic *kerygma* into something rational: 'If the truth of the New Testament proclamation is to be preserved, the only way is to demythologize it.'[13]

Bultmann's theological understanding of the figure of Jesus Christ can be synthesized in the following excerpts of his words: 'It is beyond question that the New Testament presents the event of Jesus Christ in mythical terms. The problem is whether that is the only possible presentation. Or does the New Testament itself demand a restatement of the event of Jesus Christ in non-mythical terms?'[14] Bultmann's effort, however, was not concerned with Jesus' historicity, but with a proper theological, that is, hermeneutical understanding of the event of Jesus Christ in history:

> How he actually originated matters little; indeed we can appreciate his significance only when we cease to worry about such questions. Our interest in the events of his life, and above all in the cross, is more than an academic concern with the history of the past. We can see meaning in them only when we ask what God is trying to say to each one of us through them. Again, the figure of Jesus cannot be understood simply from his context in human evolution or history. In mythological language, this means that he stems from eternity, his origin transcends both history and nature.[15]

---

12. Fusco, 'La quête du Jésus historique,' 26-27.
13. Bultmann, 'New Testament and Mythology,' 10.
14. Bultmann, 'New Testament and Mythology,' 34.
15. Bultmann, 'New Testament and Mythology,' 35. Of course, this understanding does not mean that Bultmann considered Jesus to be a non-historical figure: 'The agent of God's presence and activity, the mediator of his reconciliation of the world unto himself, is a real figure of history' (44).

This understanding of the *kerygma* should have precluded any further academic theological effort to stress the necessity of a historical Jesus for theological purposes. But it did not. The so-called 'second' and 'third' quests for the historical Jesus during the last half of the twentieth century went beyond the theological necessity of the historical existence of Jesus. Scholars, by such endeavours, considered it ultimately possible to draw historical facts relevant to Jesus' historical existence from the mythic accounts of the Gospels. The sifting of history from myth, so typical of liberal theologians of the nineteenth century, has been transformed into a circular argument, in which *the Gospels' theology is made dependent on a historical Jesus, while the historical details of Jesus' life depend on the Gospels' stories* (see further below)!

It is a truism to note that the particular social, political, ideological and intellectual contexts of scholarship enable us to recognize the historical setting of such scholarship. But a conscious recognition of how much that situation determines the results of scholarship is not always present.[16] The Enlightenment's quest for rational and non-mythic truth (*the* Truth, in fact) produced a rationalization of the very figure of Jesus which was present in the mythic stories of the Gospels. Being aware of the historical milieu of previous scholarship, therefore, must be our starting point for the evaluation of its results. The correct criticism, raised during the last forty years or so by critical perspectives in Old Testament studies concerning the history of ancient Israel, within a broader realm of critical scholarship, should now find its place among New Testament studies—at least as a research perspective that deserves to be pursued.[17]

The problem of the figure of Jesus, as portrayed in the Gospels, is, for the historian of ancient personalities,[18] analogous to those made by ancient

---

16. But cf. W. F. Arnal, *The Symbolic Jesus: Historical Scholarship, Judaism and the Construction of Contemporary Identity* (London: Equinox, 2005); and J. G. Crossley, *Jesus in an Age of Terror: Scholarly Projects for a New American Century* (London: Equinox, 2008).

17. Cf. especially the following studies: T. L. Thompson, *The Historicity of the Patriarchal Narratives: The Quest for the Historical Abraham* (BZAW, 134; Berlin: Walter de Gruyter, 1974); idem, *Early History of the Israelite People: From the Written and Archaeological Sources* (SHANE, 4; Leiden: Brill, 1992); idem, *The Bible in History: How Writers Create a Past* (London: Jonathan Cape, 1999); idem, *The Messiah Myth*; J. Van Seters, *Abraham in History and Tradition* (New Haven: Yale University Press, 1975); P. R. Davies, *In Search of 'Ancient Israel'* (JSOTSup, 148; Sheffield: Sheffield Academic Press, 1992); N. P. Lemche, *The Canaanites and Their Land: The Tradition of the Canaanites* (JSOTSup, 110; Sheffield: Sheffield Academic Press, 1991); idem, *The Israelites in History and Tradition* (LAI; Louisville: Westminster John Knox Press, 1998); idem, *The Old Testament between Theology and History: A Critical Survey* (LAI; Louisville: Westminster John Knox Press, 2008).

18. On ancient personalities, see, for instance, the studies by J. D. Crossan, *The Historical Jesus: The Life of a Mediterranean Jewish Peasant* (New York: Harper San Francisco, 1991); B. J. Malina and J. H. Neyrey, *Portraits of Paul: An Archaeology of Ancient Personality* (Louisville: Westminster John Knox Press, 1996), on Paul, of whom, apparently, we know more than

Egyptian or Assyrian depictions of the kings. If such personalities are constructed within the realm of mythic motifs, distant from an historicist recalling of reality, how can the modern historian deconstruct what is portrayed in ancient stories and attempt a separation of the ideological features of the given figure and its individual features, without 'breaking' it?[19] Regarding Jesus, then, how can we know the *ipsissima verba et facta Jesu* when all we have is a mythic set of stories (the Gospels) whose narrative patterns and thematic motifs depend on ancient literature which addresses comparable themes? This is an important epistemological problem for the historian of ancient ideas, of ancient individual figures, of ancient representations and worldviews—and I am aware of the reminiscence of Heisenberg's incertitude principle implicit in this argument.

I quote a passage from a recent book by William F. Arnal to address the aforementioned questions:

> Investigations into the historical Jesus require, by contrast, that the gospels be used as historical sources, and in fact the main differences between 'conservative' and 'liberal' scholarship revolves around how much legendary accretion is stripped away in order to arrive at the 'historical core,' not whether there is any historical core to be found at all. In seeking to find the real, historical person behind these narratives, we are using these texts as sources for a figure that they themselves show no interest at all. Just as myths and legends about Herakles are simply not about a historical person, so also the gospels are not *about* the historical Jesus.[20]

All this is not a matter of scepticism, but of an awareness of the conditions of our knowledge and of an attempt to treat the extant and available data critically. Dealing with this problem implies an effort to present answers and solutions not always satisfactory for what we want to know from a

of Jesus. Crossan contextualizes Jesus according to economic and social data from first-century Palestine, while Malina and Neyrey place Paul according to the Mediterranean models of behavior and perceptions of the self. Yet, in both cases, we have an example of an 'ethnography of a dead culture (or person)'. We know of Jesus' or Paul's personality due to ethnographic stereotypes, but not—of course—because of individual interview. This procedure creates a spectrum of possibilities, but it does not present historical evidence of Jesus or Paul.

19. The consequences of this for the historical-critical methods of biblical research are evident: cf. T. L. Thompson, 'Das Alte Testament als theologische Disziplin,' in B. Janowski and N. Lohfink, eds., *Religionsgeschichte Israels oder Theologie des Alten Testaments?* (JBTh, 10; Neukirchen: Neukirchener Verlag, 1995), 157-73: 'Die historisch-kritische Schule hat ihr Fundament verloren. Sie ist tot, und wir sollten sie in Anstand und mit Respekt begraben, anstatt uns über etwas zu streiten, was ohnehin ein äußerst klägliches Erbe darstellt' (157); also, G. Lüdemann, *Altes Testament und christiliche Kirche: Versuch der Aufklärung* (Lüneburg: Zu Klampen, 2006), 183-85.
20. Arnal, *The Symbolic Jesus*, 75-76.

modernist and historicist mindset. Accordingly, we need to allow an attempt to translate the cultural meanings of an ancient society that is not ours, following an ethnographic methodological framework.[21]

Inventing Jesus?

From this perspective, the idea of a purely literarily invented Jesus must be explained and re-addressed.[22] Once more, we have to deal with 'etic' and 'emic' anthropological perspectives; namely, with what modern scholars call 'invented' and with what natives of a non-Western culture might regard instead as a fair depiction of reality, in which the categories of 'true' and 'false' are not formed by Aristotelian-Descartian-Kantian logical premises.[23] Thus, not only is the idea of a historical Jesus beyond the central point of our inquiry, but any effort to try to prove his non-historicity, as well. We possess very scarce extra-biblical references concerning a person named Jesus[24] and we can, therefore, say very little, if anything, about him in strictly historical terms. There might have been a person called Yehoshua bar Yosef in the first century and the Gospels might have built their stories on some of his activities, but we cannot base a historical reconstruction of his life on the Gospels' stories. On the other hand, we possess a considerable amount of primary (the Gospels and para-biblical literature) and secondary (ancient Near Eastern and Graeco-Roman literature) data to work with the figure of Jesus *as a mythic persona*. The mythic persona of Jesus, created by

21. See Destro and Pesce, *Antropologia delle origini cristiane*. Cf. also E. Pfoh, 'Anthropology and Biblical Studies: A Critical Manifesto,' in idem, ed., *Anthropology and the Bible: Critical Perspectives* (Biblical Intersections, 3; Piscataway: Gorgias Press, 2010), 15-35; and P. Ariès, 'L'histoire des mentalités,' in J. Le Goff, ed., *Le nouvelle histoire* (Paris: Éditions Complexe, 2006 [orig. edn, 1988]), 167-90. All research on ancient history is about discovery; but, as Ariès indicates, 'découvrir, c'est d'abord comprendre une différence' (184). The function of the Bible in our modern Western culture often makes scholars ignore the cultural differences between the intellectual world of biblical writers and ours.

22. Doubts concerning the historicity of Jesus can be traced back to the French Enlightenment scholars C.-F. Volney (1757–1820) and C. F. Dupuis (1742–1809) and to the German scholars D. F. Strauss (1808–1874) and B. Bauer (1809–1882).

23. Pfoh, 'Anthropology and Biblical Studies'.

24. Notably, Flavius Josephus's *Antiquitates judaicae*, 18.63-64 (the famous passage known as *Testimonium Flavianum*, written c. 93 CE); and Tacitus' *Annales*, 15.44 (written c. 116 CE). From these two sources, and provided that they are truly independent of later Christian bias (something not certain indeed), all that we might know is that by the end of the first century, there was discussion of a Jewish figure of some kind who had attracted followers to his cause and who represented some trouble for the Roman authorities in Palestine. However, if these accounts are in fact dependent on Gospel tradition, we cannot sift history from myth and therefore we cannot know about this referred person in historical terms, but only as a mythic figure.

the Gospels, represents an insurmountable obstacle to any knowledge of a historical Jesus. Whether this creation is based on a real historical person is beside the point for the historian of ancient mentalities. This is not a search for the historical facticity of an ancient human being, but rather a historical search for ancient worldviews. This is what we have evidence of in ancient literature—not more, nor less.

Cultural Memory and the Present Crafting of Past Figures

A final question to bear in mind concerns the sociological and cultural *milieux* of biblical research on the figure of Jesus. Cultural memory has been a topic of study and discussion among historians and sociologists at least since the publication of Maurice Halbwachs's *Les cadres sociaux de la mémoire* in 1925.[25] This analytical perspective has entered biblical studies only very recently, preceded by the Egyptologist Jan Assmann's studies regarding cultural memory and antiquity.[26] In New Testament studies, cultural and/or collective memory approaches are as novel as they are in Old Testament studies.[27] Without going into this issue fully, I believe it possible to differentiate two levels of understanding the figure of Jesus through a critical use of a cultural memory perspective: one for the interpretation of the Gospels and another for the modern socio-cultural setting of that interpretation.

1. *Jesus' Life and Teachings as Memories in the Gospels.* According to this perspective, it is possible to understand what is narrated in the Gospels as reliable information about the historical Jesus because it represents a mnemonic transmission—a remembrance of faith—about the Jesus of history by the ancient creators of the Synoptic tradition.[28] This is more a theological observation than a

25. M. Halbawchs, *Les cadres sociaux de la mémoire* (Paris: Librairie Felix Alcan, 1925); also idem, *La mémoire collective* (Paris: Presses Universitaires de France, 1950); see also, J. Le Goff, *Histoire et mémoire* (Paris: Gallimard, 1988); J. Candau, *Anthropologie de la mémoire* (Paris: Presses Universitaires de France, 1998).

26. P. R. Davies, *Memories of Ancient Israel: An Introduction to Biblical History—Ancient and Modern* (Louisville: Westminster John Knox Press, 2008); J. Assmann, *Religion and Cultural Memory: Ten Studies* (Stanford: Stanford University Press, 2006).

27. See A. Kirk, 'Social and Cultural Memory,' in A. Kirk and T. Thatcher, eds., *Memory, Tradition, and Text: Uses of the Past in Early Christianity* (Semeia, 52; Atlanta: Society of Biblical Literature, 2005), 1-24.

28. Cf., for instance, J. D. G. Dunn, *Christianity in the Making*. I. *Jesus Remembered* (Grand Rapids: Eerdmans, 2003); and R. Bauckham, *Jesus and the Eyewitnesses: The Gospels as Eyewitness Testimony* (Grand Rapids: Eerdmans, 2006); see also, A. Kirk and T. Thatcher, 'Jesus Tradition as Social Memory,' in Kirk and Thatcher, eds., *Memory, Tradition, and Text*, 25-42. Cf. the criticism in E. Norelli, 'Considerazioni di metodo sull'uso delle fonti per la ricostruzione della figura storica di Gesù,' in Prinzivalli, ed., *L'enigma Gesù*, 19-67 (20-33).

historical understanding of a process of religious diffusion. Cultural memory shapes the past according to needs in the present. Cultural memory does not replicate the past as it really happened, but rather as it is needed to be remembered by the active community that evokes it.[29] In sum, ancient cultural memories—if we are willing to understand the Gospels in that way—cannot lead to a modern historical interpretation of the past because they constitute *a part* of the modern construction of that ancient past. From an ethnographic point of view (to clarify this perspective with an example), the native informant's opinion (i.e. the Gospels) offers us a view on a particular reality (i.e. Jesus), but it does not constitute the bulk of a scholarly interpretation; it is rather a piece of data analysed through scholarly methodologies and frameworks. The canonical Gospels constitute *an ancient view of Jesus* but they do not necessarily represent for the historian of antiquity the correct, the best or the only view, because the Gospels are also data submitted to the historical dissection and analyses of ancient sources. They constitute narratives addressing a literary figure through a plethora of mythic motifs and scenarios, whose historicity cannot be confirmed by analysing them—and this caveat also applies, of course, to non-canonical traditional texts, such as the *Gospel of Thomas*.[30] Theological insight concerning this historical analysis is irrelevant.

2. *Jesus as Western Cultural Memory's Figure*. The discussion deals precisely with the place Jesus has in Western culture and, no less, in Western (especially religious) scholarship in search of the historical Jesus. What follows is a first draft of a preliminary sociology of the modern quest for the historical Jesus.[31]

In the *first quest*, during the nineteenth and early twentieth centuries, we find, in the liberal spirit of the Enlightenment with its rational necessity for a historical Jesus, a Jesus who is both 'within the limits of reason' and inscribed in history.[32] If Jesus had been a real person in history, all of the miracles and mythic details of his narrative should be kept apart from any serious historical depiction of his persona.

---

29. Kirk, 'Social and Cultural Memory,' 10-24.
30. See C. Gianotto, 'Il *Vangelo secondo Tommaso* e il problema storico di Gesù,' in Prinzivalli, ed., *L'enigma Gesù*, 68-93.
31. Cf. Arnal, *The Symbolic Jesus*; Crossley, *Jesus in an Age of Terror*.
32. 'On peut y distinguer trois moments: celui des Lumières, celui de l'idéalisme, représenté par l'école de Tübingen, et enfin l'école libérale. Ce qui est constant dans les trois, c'est la recherche d'un Jesús «limites de la raison», dépouillé de ses atributs divins mais en même temps chargé de valeurs susceptibles d'en faire encore un point de repére, en particulier pour la conscience moderne' (Fusco, 'La quête du Jésus historique,' 27).

With the end of the first quest in the early twentieth century, the search for the historical Jesus enters an *intermezzo*. By that time, Bultmann had proposed a critical theology in which he acknowledged that we do not know historically much about Jesus, but rather have his message culturally encoded in mythic shape. The search for historical knowledge about Jesus of Nazareth was beyond the point of exegesis. From a theological perspective, Bultmann's attempt to demythologize the *kerygma* can be praised as an effort to understand an ancient theological truth in modern terms.[33] However, from a historico-anthropological point of view, his analysis is ethnocentric. We should rather try to understand the myth in its original social and intellectual (religious) context rather than attempt (for modern theological purposes) to retrieve a theological perspective from a world (and from its literary products) which is culturally different from our own.

The *second quest*, launched by Ernst Käsemann's lecture, 'Das Problem des historischen Jesus' in 1953,[34] had a post-Bultmannian character, with the *theological* need for a figure of the historical Jesus. As Marcus Borg explains, 'without a connection to Jesus of Nazareth, Christianity risks falling into docetism and/or an ahistorical piety'.[35] In this quest, theology has hijacked the Jesus of history to accomplish theological enlightenment. In doing so, theology has set the agenda for historical questions and their answers. Critical historical research, however, must shake off all theological insight from its methodology.

With the *third quest*, since the 1980s, this situation has not altered much. In fact, one might suggest a *religious* need rather than a *theological* one, for the reality of a historical Jesus, due to socio-cultural conditions that need to be explored systematically.[36] I use the term *religious* after Clifford Geertz's

33. As was done by some of his contemporaries; cf. F. K. Schumann, 'Can the Event of Jesus Christ be Demythologized?,' in Bartsch, ed., *Kerygma and Myth*, 175-90.

34. Published as E. Käsemann, 'Das Problem des historischen Jesus,' *Zeitschrift für Theologie und Kirche* 51 (1954), 125-53 (English trans.: 'The Problem of the Historical Jesus,' in *Essays on New Testament Themes* [Minneapolis: Fortress Press, 1982], 15-47).

35. M. Borg, *Jesus in Contemporary Scholarship* (Harrisburg: Trinity Press, 1994), 189. Let us recall G. E. Wright's words: 'In biblical faith everything depends ultimately upon whether the central events actually occurred...to assume that it makes no difference whether they are facts or not is simply to destroy the whole basis of the faith' (*God Who Acts: Biblical Theology as Recital* [London: SCM Press, 1962], 126 and 127).

36. The development of sociology of modern and contemporary biblical scholarship is a serious need of modern scholarship, as the fabric of an intellectual discourse which cannot be divorced from socio-religious phenomena in the Western world (especially in the United States and Europe). Antecedents of this reflexive analysis in academic *milieux* can be found in the realms of professional anthropology and sociology: see, for instance, J. Clifford and G. E. Marcus, eds., *Writing Culture: The Poetics and Politics of Ethnography* (Berkeley: University of California Press, 1986), and P. Bourdieu, *Homo academicus* (Cambridge: Polity Press, 1988).

definition of religion, which could certainly be of use to a sociological understanding of the preferences of biblical research about Jesus. A 'religion is a system of symbols, which acts to establish powerful, pervasive, and long-lasting moods and motivations in men by formulating conceptions of a general order of existence and clothing these conceptions with such an aura of factuality that the moods and motivations seem uniquely realistic'.[37] I would propose, then, the existence of a religio-cultural reason for accepting the Jesus of the Gospels as necessarily rooted in the actions of a historical character, clothed with scholarly-made identities and agency, such as Jesus as an apocalyptic prophet (J. P. Meier, P. Fredriksen), a peasant and wisdom sage (J. D. Crossan), a political activist and social revolutionary (R. Horsley, M. Borg), a Cynic philosopher (B. L. Mack), a feminist (E. Schüssler Fiorenza) and so forth.[38] His social role varies as socio-religious example, but his real historicity, built on Gospel 'testimonies' of his life, is entirely unquestioned, because it is already a part of the Western cultural worldview. Sheer faith in the Gospels' accounts seems not to be enough. Rather, one has a more modern necessity for understanding Jesus in *social* and *historical* terms.[39]

The reasons for this, I argue, are cultural rather than historical and indeed not based on any historical evidence. They have to do more with Western culture than with the nature and contents of ancient sources. There is a need in the modern Western world for Jesus to be historical. Otherwise, as noted already, religious dogma based in a mythic world is threatened with the loss of its essence and legitimacy. Theological argument has become a cultural feature, assisted by the modernist understanding of a true reality of Jesus in historical terms. In this sense, the first and the third quests for the historical Jesus were and still are driven by a need to represent Jesus according to the characteristics of the interpretive present, which is modernist, theologically and religiously driven, and unwilling to renounce the status of historicity for the Gospels' literary figure of Jesus. As

---

37. C. Geertz, 'Religion as a Cultural System,' in *The Interpretation of Cultures* (New York: Basic Books, 1973), 87-125 (90).

38. See J. P. Meier, *A Marginal Jew: Rethinking the Historical Jesus*, I-III (New York: Doubleday, 1991–2001); P. Fredriksen, *Jesus of Nazareth, King of the Jews: A Jewish Life and the Emergence of Christianity* (New York: Vintage Press, 2000); Crossan, *The Historical Jesus*; R. Horsley, *Jesus in Context: Power, People, and Performance* (Minneapolis: Fortress Press, 2008); M. Borg, *Jesus: Uncovering the Life, Teachings, and Relevance of a Religious Revolutionary* (New York: HarperCollins, 2008); B. L. Mack, *A Myth of Innocence: Mark and Christian Origins* (Philadelphia: Fortress Press, 1988); E. Schüssler Fiorenza, *In Memory of Her: A Feminist Theological Reconstruction of Christian Origins* (New York: Crossroad, 1983). So too, the introduction of this volume.

39. See the popular treatment in J. D. Crossan and R. G. Watts, *Who is Jesus? Answers to Your Questions about the Historical Jesus* (New York: Harper Collins, 1996).

H. Berg and S. Rollens, in a comparative article on the reconstructions of the historical Jesus and the historical Muhammad, indicate, the

> endeavours of the scholars, whether religious or not, are also often overtly and covertly theological in their methodological framework. That is to say, they are theological in their need to see each of these two 'founder' figures as *the* unique and central *raison d'être* of the respective movements that claim them. Similarly, the need to see the extant sources as historical texts, albeit ones in which the historical facts lie hidden, shares the worldview of the believers—and hardly seems befitting those who consider themselves sceptics.[40]

These socio-cultural foundations of the ideological articulation of the figure of Jesus in religious as well as secular societies of the modern Western world have not, to my knowledge, been researched in any systematic way. If they were, however, it would be clear why it is possible to witness in several histories about Jesus a form of religious nostalgia for the founding events of Christianity. But this kind of academic yearning cannot be supported as a research impetus for, as Thompson suggests, 'nostalgia, that historiographic description of the past, as it informs us about ourselves, also creates both amnesia and myopia in the need to reduce the past's otherness. We only rediscover what we are able to recognize.'[41] This search for Jesus is thus more a reflection on the present status of Christianity in the Western world (especially in its northern hemisphere) than a critical attempt to understand the historical process that led to the rise of Christianity. In this way, any faith-driven search for the historical Jesus creates an apologetic, pseudo-historiographical discourse intended to strengthen a modern religious need for a historical Jesus. A search, on the contrary, based on critical historical perspectives, needs to be fully secular, devoid of any religious anxiety, ready to discover the unexpected and freed from traditional and institutionalized conceptions of the origins of a religious movement on the eastern shore of the Mediterranean around the first centuries of our era.[42]

Concluding Remarks

Without concrete evidence, our historical conclusions regarding an individual named Yehoshua bar Yosef, who started a religious revolution

---

40. H. Berg and S. Rollens, 'The Historical Muhammad and the Historical Jesus: A Comparison of Scholarly Reinventions and Reinterpretations,' *Studies in Religion/Sciences Religieuses* 37 (2008), 271-92 (272).
41. Thompson, *The Bible in History*, 377. Cf. also the methodological remarks in Norelli, 'Considerazioni di metodo,' 19-67. As Norelli notes (30-33), this is a blatant confusion of memory and history; cf. further, Le Goff, *Histoire et mémoire*.
42. Cf., e.g., the studies by Crossley, *Why Christianity Happened*, and P. Veyne, *Quand notre monde est devenu chrétien (312-394)* (Paris: Albin Michel, 2007).

in the first century which would develop for some two millennia, cannot be very positive. How can we know if the Jesus from the Gospels is the Yehoshua of ancient history? My opinion is that such an inquiry is doomed to failure due to clear methodological and epistemological reasons: we cannot test a mythic figure historically, an individual who—despite his central religious role in early Christianity's rise in the Eastern Mediterranean and Western Asia—does not reflect the world of historical evidence but dwells rather in the ancient world of tradition and faith, miracles and beliefs, a world in which whatever the figure of Jesus might embody does not need our tests for historicity in order to exist! We may write many histories and socio-anthropological treatises on early Christianity, but we cannot write any about a concrete historical Jesus. On the other hand, we have the Jesus of tradition (the Christ of faith), who is at home within ancient Near Eastern mythic figures who evoke the themes of death and resurrection, divine sonship and the salvation of warrior kings. That is a world from which the modern historian of ancient mentalities can profit by attempting to understand the societies, beliefs and customs behind it. But of a person named Jesus who inhabited that society's historical world, we cannot have concrete historical knowledge of him. All we have are ancient presentations of faith in a mythic figure.[43]

43. The historico-anthropological arguments presented in this article force me to dissent from Bultmann's theological perspective, although it is not my wish to tread theological paths: 'A blind acceptance of the New Testament mythology world is irrational and to press for its acceptance as an article of faith would be to reduce Christian faith to the level of a human achievement' ('New Testament and Mythology,' 3-4). Otherwise, I think Bultmann expresses very well, *though in negative form*, my views on this matter.

Part II

Paul and Early Christianity: Historical and Exegetical Investigations

- 6 -

Does the Christ Myth Theory Require an Early Date for the Pauline Epistles?

Robert M. Price

Epistles versus Gospels

One of the pillar arguments of the Christ Myth Theory as usually put forth today is the absence from the Pauline Epistles of any Gospel-like teaching ascribed to Jesus. If the Gospels' Jesus Christ, Jesus of Nazareth, the itinerant sage and thaumaturge, was well known, at least among Christians, it would stand to reason that such a Jesus would meet us throughout the apostolic letters by way of quotations and anecdotes. But we find no such material. Suddenly, however, such a Jesus portrait appears in the Gospels, written after the epistles, and the explanation for this discrepancy, according to Mythicists, is that, between the composition of epistles on the one hand and Gospels on the other, the popular Christian imagination (as well as the inventiveness of Christian scribes) 'historicized' the originally suprahistorical, spiritual (mythical) saviour of whom Paul and the rest had earlier written so much of a dogmatic nature, but none of a historical-biographical nature. For various reasons it had become desirable in some quarters to posit a recent historical Jesus of Nazareth to whom one could trace oneself and one's institutional claims of authority. And in this window of time between epistles and Gospels, various unnamed prophets (and borrowers and tall-tale-tellers) supplied the many things this Jesus would have, must have, done and said. Such a figure had not existed as far as the epistolarians knew, and so of course there was no such material with which to lard their epistles. But now that the newly minted material was available, it found the epistle genre altogether too confining and called for a more appropriate format, that of the Hellenistic hero or saint biography, and so the Gospels were born.

Parenthetically, it is worth pointing out that we possess two striking analogies for the rapid generation of 'filler' sayings and stories. Think of the imaginative fabrication of episodes of the child Jesus preserved in the well-known apocryphal infancy gospels (attributed to Thomas, Matthew, James and others); as soon as Christians came to believe that Jesus had not merely been adopted (as an adult) as God's Son, but that he had been born divine, they went to work filling in the imagined gap: what super-deeds must the divine child have been doing during those years? Secondly, after the promulgation of the Qur'an, a swelling flood of spurious hadith, stories of the words and deeds of the Prophet Muhammad, burst the levees of historical probability to correct and supplement the teaching of Scripture.[1] It is by no means far-fetched to suggest, then, that all the Gospel stories of a mortal Jesus walking the earth swiftly arose to fill the newly discerned gap once such a Jesus was posited. It is no stretch to imagine Christian scribes and prophets supplying what their new earthly Jesus would have said, either. If it sounded good, Jesus said it.

This understanding of the epistles as preceding the Gospels grounds the arguments of the two greatest Christ Myth theorists of our day, George A. Wells and Earl Doherty. Their views differ significantly at many points, but they agree here. Let me quote the venerable Wells:

> It is generally agreed that the NT epistles addressed to the Romans, Corinthians, Galatians, Ephesians, Philippians, Colossians and Thessalonians were written before the gospels... These early epistles exhibit such complete ignorance of the events which were later recorded in the gospels as to suggest that these events were not known to Paul or whoever it was who wrote the epistles.[2]

Doherty agrees:

> The story told in the Gospel of Mark first begins to surface toward the end of the first century CE. Yet the curious fact is that when we search for that story in all the non-Gospel documents written before that time, it is nowhere to be found... If we had to rely on the letters of the earliest Christians, such as Paul and those who wrote most of the other New Testament epistles, we would be hard pressed to find anything resembling the details of the gospel story. If we did not read Gospel associations into what Paul and the others say about their Christ Jesus, we could not even tell that this figure, the object of their worship,

---

1. J. Burton, *The Collection of the Quran* (New York: Cambridge University Press, 1977), shows how the stories of the early collections of Qur'anic surahs were fictions posited in the course of attempts to legitimate readings ostensibly accidentally omitted from the copies used in these 'official collections', and so to claim the authority of Scripture for this or that traditional belief or practice.
2. G. A. Wells, *The Jesus of the Early Christians: A Study in Christian Origins* (London: Pemberton Books, 1971), 131.

> was a man who had recently lived in Palestine and had been executed by the Roman authorities with the help of a hostile Jewish establishment.[3]

Wells goes on: 'Orthodox writers sometimes claim that [Paul] omitted references to Jesus' views and behaviour because they were irrelevant to the matters discussed in his letters... But this is hardly plausible.'[4] Paul everywhere proclaims the stultification of the Torah. Would none of the Gospel Sabbath controversies have been relevant? Not even the Matthean antitheses? 'In II Cor. viii, 9, in order to induce the Corinthians to contribute liberally to the collection for the poor in Palestine, he mentions Jesus as an example of liberality', but it is an appeal only to the doctrine of the Son's descent from heavenly glory to share the rude lot of mortals: nothing truly biographical. And why no citation of the uncomfortably many admonitions of the Gospel Jesus to sell one's possessions and turn the proceeds over to the poor (e.g. Lk. 18:22)?[5] When Paul recommends celibacy (1 Cor. 7:7), why doesn't he quote the saying now found in Mt. 19:10-12?[6] When he urges Christians, though citizens of heaven, not to evade Roman taxes (Rom. 13:1-6), why does he not reinforce the point with a citation of the now-famous 'Render unto Caesar' logion (Mk 12:15-17)?[7] Had the vexing business of dietary laws arisen (Rom. 14:1-4; 1 Cor. 8; Col. 2:20-21)? Quoting the saying in Mk 7:15 would have made short work of that one. Was there controversy over circumcision? There was in Rom. 3:1 and Gal. 5:1-12, but Paul never thinks to cite the saying preserved in *Thomas* 53, which would have closed the book on that one fast. 'Precisely where the author of Romans might be expected to invoke the authority of Jesus, he does not.'[8]

But suppose there were originally no dominical sayings to settle these questions; it is not hard to imagine that soon people would be coining them—or attaching Jesus' name to a saying they already liked, to make it authoritative.

Wells deftly parries one of the predictable thrusts against his argument: 'It is often alleged that Paul would not specify details with which his readers were already familiar. Yet he repeatedly specifies the incarnation, death and resurrection with which they were, in the terms of the case, familiar.'[9] Not only that; see 1 Cor. 2:1-5 and 15:1, 15 (recollection of his initial preaching);

---

3. E. Doherty, *The Jesus Puzzle: Did Christianity Begin with a Mythical Christ?* (Ottawa: Canadian Humanist Publications, 1990), 2.
4. Wells, *Jesus of the Early Christians*, 131.
5. *Jesus of the Early Christians*, 147.
6. G.A. Wells, *Did Jesus Exist?* (London: Elek/Pemberton, 1975), 19.
7. *Jesus of the Early Christians*, 147
8. *Jesus of the Early Christians*, 133.
9. *Jesus of the Early Christians*, 147.

5:9-11 (shunning backsliders); 6:3 (the chaste will one day judge the fallen Sons of God); 2 Cor. 2:1-4 (his previously announced travel plans); 13:2 (former disciplinary warnings); Gal. 1:13-14 (his pre-Christian life); 3:1 (their first graphic encounter with the Christian Mystery); 4:13-15 (their kind reception of him in his hour of suffering); 5:21 (a familiar list of mortal sins); Eph. 4:20 (their first catechism); Phil. 3:1 (on repeating what he has previously written them); 3:18 (his old rivals); Col. 1:5-6 (the well-known spread of the gospel); 2:7 (their roots in Christ); 1 Thess. 1:5; 2:5-12 (his solid reputation among them); 4:1 (the pattern of Christian living); 5:1-11; 2:5 (eschatology of which they should require no reminder, *but do*). So the Paul of the epistles had no compunction about repeating himself and his teaching. There is no reason to believe that, had he initially laid a foundation of Gospel-style materials about Jesus, he would not have had ample occasion to revisit it, any less than a modern preacher does.

Some say that the epistles display extensive awareness of the Gospel teachings of Jesus but paraphrase them without indicating that Jesus first said them. Romans 12 and the Epistle of James are full of such logia. James D. G. Dunn[10] maintains that Paul and James intended the reader to sniff out the dominical origin (and authority) in these cases, leaving them as allusions for those who had ears to hear ('wink, wink, nudge, nudge'). But this is one of those arguments no one would offer if they were not trying to wriggle out of a tight spot. Think about it: if you want to settle a question by appealing to the words of Jesus, you are going to make sure the reader understands that they are indeed words of Jesus, and you are going to do that by the simple expedient of *saying so*. Given the whole point of appealing to dominical words, who would neglect to attribute them explicitly to the name of Jesus? If one trusted simply to the self-evident force of an argument or a principle, why seek to undergird it by an appeal to authoritative words in the first place? It seems quite reasonable to suggest that in the epistles we find early Christian sayings, just *before* they were ascribed to Jesus.

But does Paul not derive at least the Lord's Supper pericope from Synoptic tradition? No, he says he received it immediately, by direct revelation, from the Lord himself.[11] In the same way, it is utterly gratuitous for apologists[12] to point to Paul's 'commands of the Lord' as representing a Q-like list of dominical maxims.

> To the married, I give charge (not I but the Lord), that the wife should not separate from the husband, but if she does, let her remain single or else be

---

10. J. D. G. Dunn, 'Jesus Tradition in Paul,' in B. Chilton and C. A. Evans, eds., *Studying the Historical Jesus* (Leiden: Brill, 1994), 177-78.
11. *Jesus of the Early Christians*, 273: cf. Hyam Maccoby, *Paul and Hellenism* (Philadelphia: Trinity Press International, 1991), 90-128.

> reconciled to her husband, and that the husband should not divorce his wife. To the rest, I say, not the Lord, that if any brother has a wife who is an unbeliever, and she consents to live with him, he should not divorce her. (1 Cor. 7:10-12)
>
> Now concerning the unmarried, I have no command of the Lord, but I offer my opinion as one who by the Lord's mercy is trustworthy. (1 Cor. 7:25)
>
> But in my judgment she is happier if she remains as she is. And I think I have the Spirit of God. (1 Cor. 7:40)
>
> The Lord commanded that those who proclaim the gospel should get their living by the gospel. (1 Cor. 9:14)
>
> If anyone thinks he is a prophet or a pneumatic, he should acknowledge that what I am writing to you is a command of the Lord. (1 Cor. 14:37)

Especially in view of the last of these snippets, it becomes obvious that the first, fourth and fifth have originated in prophetic bulletins, 'words of knowledge' or 'words of wisdom' vouchsafed to Christian prophets, oracles of the Risen Christ, probably to the writer himself. This becomes especially clear in light of the second and third statements, which define the 'commands of the Lord' by contrast. It is not that the 'commands' have some origin elsewhere than Paul; it is only that his 'opinion' and 'judgment' have not emerged from a prophetic state as the 'commands' did. It seems gross over-interpretation even to hold open the possibility that in his 'commands of the Lord' the writer should be referring to sayings of the historical Jesus. What we are seeing is a Christian rebirth of the Old Testament practice of the priests 'giving Torah' via oracular judgments on matters brought to them. The result is what Noth[13] called 'apodictic' law as opposed to casuistic or circumstantial law. Again, they would be what Käsemann[14] dubbed 'sentences of holy law.'

There are other, perhaps equally important, foundations of today's Christ Myth Theory, such as the absence of extra-canonical witnesses to Jesus' historical existence, as well as the striking parallels between Jesus and the purely mythic dying and rising god cults, whose divine heroes and saviours had never existed as historical characters. But these do not concern us here. It would scatter the focus of this essay's argument to consider the merits of these arguments here.

12. F. F. Bruce, *The New Testament Documents: Are They Reliable?* (Grand Rapids: Eerdmans, 1972), 78; J. N. D. Anderson, *Christianity: The Witness of History* (London: Tyndale House, 1969), 29.
13. M. Noth, *The Laws in the Pentateuch and Other Studies* (trans. D. R. Ap-Thomas; London: SCM Press, 1984), 7, 243.
14. E. Käsemann, 'Sentences of Holy Law,' in idem, *New Testament Questions of Today* (trans. W. J. Montague; Philadelphia: Fortress Press, 1979), 66-81.

Yesteryear and Beyond

The Mythicist scholars of a past generation used many of the same arguments as their successors do today, but there are many differences as well. Our business here is to compare the way in which the date of the Pauline epistles figured into the Christ Myth Theory as it used to be argued. It will have been noted that Wells and Doherty uphold the traditional dates and (for the most part) authorship ascriptions of the epistles. Wells and Doherty are willing, indeed eager, to take for granted traditional claims for assigning age and authorship. This makes them admirably early and leaves plenty of time for Gospel story-tellers to have done their subsequent work, historicizing Jesus and pillaging the epistles for sayings to reattribute to Jesus. One feels that things would begin to blur if the Gospels and epistles had to be placed as more or less contemporary. That condition would open up the possibility or need to find another solution for the lack of Gospel-type tradition in the epistles.

In the estimation of Paul-Louis Couchoud,[15] the Pauline epistles, at least in their shorter, Marcionite editions, are genuine. This means leaving out more than a third of Romans as Catholicizing padding.[16] But Marcion, Couchoud believed, added 2 Thessalonians as a corrective to 1 Thessalonians's apocalyptic urgency and penned Laodiceans (=Ephesians) as a commentary on Colossians.[17] In addition, 'Marcion is probably the author of a life of St. Paul which was to form the framework of the Acts of the Apostles';[18] that is, the itinerary. Shortly before Marcion, and under pagan influence, Jesus was historicized in popular belief. Christians began to believe Christ had lived on earth, among humanity, in the recent past. His death had been a mundane, political execution, though occurring according to divine providence. Marcion's gospel (of which Couchoud speaks as if Marcion himself wrote it) was the first literary embodiment of the new notion. The notion came in handy because it fit Marcion's idea of Jesus having *recently* revealed his *new God.*

Marcion's gospel reflects the Bar Kochba revolt and stems from c. 133.[19] Mark (c. 133–134, or shortly after 135) abridged Marcion's gospel at some

---

15. P. L. Couchoud, *The Creation of Christ: An Outline of the Beginnings of Christianity* (trans. C. Bradlaugh Bonner; London: Watts, 1939).
16. Couchoud, *The Creation of Christ*, 65.
17. Couchoud, *The Creation of Christ*, 125.
18. Couchoud, *The Creation of Christ*, 126. As far as I know, this arbitrary claim was a tree falling in a forest with no ears to hear it. I know of neither subsequent discussion of the claim nor what possible basis Couchould might have had for suggesting it.
19. A view newly upheld in H. Detering, 'The Synoptic Apocalypse (Mark 13 par): A Document from the Time of Bar Kochba,' *JHC* 7.2 (Fall, 2000), 161-210.

points, expanding it at others. Only a few years later (140), Matthew did the same. Marcion lived to read the four Gospels, all dependent upon his. Couchoud's thinking raises a crucial point he seems not to have recognized, but with which we absolutely must come to terms: on Couchoud's reading, Marcion would have been the author of at least two of the 'Pauline' epistles as well as a Gospel, and this means that one might indeed be familiar with the teaching of the Gospel Jesus, ascribed to Jesus, and yet have reasons for omitting any of it in one's epistles. *If Marcion could have known Gospel tradition and yet mentioned none of it in his epistles, so could Paul.*

To be fair, Couchoud has characterized Marcion's hypothetical epistolary efforts in such a way as not to entail Gospel-quoting: Ephesians as a mere commentary upon Colossians, a writing ignorant of Jesus-attributed teachings, need hardly introduce any of them. And if the goal of 2 Thessalonians was only to correct the hot-head eschatology of 1 Thessalonians, all Marcion need have done was to write what looks like a second version of 1 Thessalonians, differing only in this matter of de-apocalypticizing. As he intended to stick as close to the look and feel of the original, almost to the point of replacing it, in penning 2 Thessalonians Marcion might have had added reason to avoid any ostensible Jesus-teachings he might have known, since including them would make 2 Thessalonians seem needlessly different from its model, 1 Thessalonians. But we will see that there are other reasons to posit Marcionite authorship of still more 'Pauline' material, and the same solution will not suffice.

Edouard Dujardin[20] sees the same epistle-to-Gospel discrepancy, though his view of a Pauline historical Jesus is a bit different. He has Paul envisioning a Jesus who descended to earth only very briefly, and not in a fleshly body. 'It can be shown that the Jesus of St. Paul is a god who took the appearance, and only the appearance, of a man during the few days that the sacred drama lasted.'[21]

> We find nothing in these epistles except the abstract affirmation that Jesus was crucified. The only precise indication is contained in the First Epistle to the Corinthians, ii. 8, in which we read that Jesus was crucified by the demons.[22] St. Paul speaks unceasingly in all the pages of his epistles of the crucifixion of Jesus, and never directly or indirectly refers to the actors who play their parts in the gospel drama; never refers to the intervention of the Jews or Romans; never for an instant conjures up any of the episodes of the Passion. St. Paul knew that Jesus was crucified, but was wholly unaware that

20. E. Dujardin, *Ancient History of the God Jesus* (trans. A. B. Sanders; London: Watts, 1938).
21. Dujardin, *Ancient History of the God Jesus*, 23; cf. 62-63.
22. Dujardin, *Ancient History of the God Jesus*, 32.

> he was arrested, that he was arraigned before one or several tribunals, that he was condemned, and that his death took the form of a judicial crucifixion.[23]

Arthur Drews[24] first dismisses the question of authenticity (did Paul actually write the letters bearing his name?) as irrelevant since impossible to solve. He thus anticipates Derrida's metaphor of 'the Postcard', a literary object whose detachment from any knowledge of origin and authorial intention becomes integral to its character and interpretation.[25] Drews says:

> Let us leave completely on one side the question of the authenticity of the Pauline epistles, a question absolute agreement on which will probably never be attained, for the simple reason that we lack any certain basis for its decision. Instead of this let us turn rather to what we learn from these epistles concerning the historical Jesus...[26] [T]he Jesus painted by Paul is not a man, but a purely divine personality, a heavenly spirit without flesh and blood, an unindividual superhuman phantom.[27] Christ, as the principle of redemption, is for Paul only an allegorical or symbolical personality and not a real one.[28] Christ's life and death are for Paul neither the moral achievement of a man nor in any way historical facts, but something super-historical, events in the supra-sensual world.[29]

Date, it seems, is not so irrelevant as authorship. Drews continues:

> It must be considered that, if the Pauline epistles stood in the edition of the New Testament where they really belong—that is, before the gospels—hardly any one would think that Jesus, as he there meets him, was a real man and had wandered on the earth in flesh and blood; but he would in all probability find therein the detailed development of the 'suffering servant of God,' and would conclude that it was an irruption of heathen ideas into Jewish religious thought.[30]

But even the question of authorship/authenticity creeps back in, having been ejected too soon.

> If Paul refers in his Epistles to an historical Jesus, these Epistles, bearing his name, cannot possibly have been written by the apostle who was changed from Saul to Paul by the Damascus vision. For it is inconceivable that an

---

23. Dujardin, *Ancient History of the God Jesus*, 33.
24. A. Drews, *The Christ Myth* (trans. C. DeLisle Burns; Westminster College, Oxford: Classics in Religious Studies, 1910; repr. Amherst: Prometheus Books, 1998).
25. J. Derrida, *The Post Card: From Socrates to Freud and Beyond* (trans. A. Bass; Chicago: University of Chicago Press, 1987).
26. Drews, *Christ Myth*, 168-69.
27. Drews, *Christ Myth*, 180.
28. Drews, *Christ Myth*, 204.
29. Drews, *Christ Myth*, 206.
30. Drews, *Christ Myth*, 208.

> historical individual should, so soon after his death, be elevated by the apostle to the dignity of a second God, a co-worker in the creation and redemption of the world.[31]
>
> If the Epistles were really written by Paul, the Jesus Christ who is a central figure in them cannot be an historical personality. The way in which the supposed Jew Paul speaks of him is contrary to all psychological and historical experience. *Either the Pauline Epistles are genuine, and in that case Jesus is not an historical personality; or he is an historical personality, and in that case the Pauline Epistles are not genuine, but written at a much later period.* This later period would have no difficulty in raising to the sphere of deity a man of former times who was known to it only by a vague tradition.[32]

But if the letters are that late, late enough for the real historical facts to have passed from collective memory, are the epistles still to be dated earlier than the Gospels? Why would the spurious traditions collected in the Gospels have waited *this* long to rear their heads? Would hagiographic embellishments have begun only in order to replace a complete loss of remembered facts? Actually, that is not unnatural. After all, we hypothesize that a number of myths have attached themselves to rituals in order to provide some sort of an explanation long after the original reason for the ritual has been forgotten.[33] A total eclipse of a historical Jesus and a subsequent substitution with mythology would not be that different.

Mythology versus Methodology

Another consideration: remember that Bultmann[34] suggested that originally many sayings ascribed to Jesus circulated with no narrative introduction, with the result that it was anybody's guess what the sayings were about. We still have trouble being sure what was meant by 'Take care not to cast your pearls before swine or holy things to dogs, lest they trample them underfoot and turn on you to maul you.' Bultmann posited that at first many such isolated sayings made the rounds, and that people supplied hypothetical contexts to lend them some meaning. 'The sound have no need of a physician, but only the sick. I came not to call the righteous but sinners.' 'The son of man is lord even of the Sabbath.' 'The son of man came to save human lives, not to destroy them.' Once narrative introductions were

---

31. Drews, *Christ Myth*, 116.
32. A. Drews, *The Witnesses to the Historicity of Jesus* (trans. J. McCabe; Chicago: Open Court, n.d.; repr. Amsterdam: Fredonia Books, 2003), 117.
33. H. Gunkel, *The Legends of Genesis: The Biblical Saga and History* (trans. W. H. Carruth; New York: Schocken Books, 1964), 30-31, gives a host of examples.
34. R. Bultmann, *History of the Synoptic Tradition* (trans. J. Marsh; New York: Harper & Row, 1968), 39-40, 47-50, 57, 61-62.

added, such enigmatic aphorisms became 'pronouncement stories'. This means sayings were prior to stories. And it is not hard to picture the sayings originating (à la Wells and Doherty) as comments by the epistle writers and only subsequently picking up added *meaning* by a supplied narrative context and added *authority* by a connection to Jesus. We require no absolute dates here. It is simply the logic of the process, and it implies that epistle material is earlier than Gospel material, whatever the actual date of any of it.

Yet another criterion from Gospel criticism may come to our aid. In any case, where we entertain two versions of a story (or two rival stories) and one is more spectacular than the other, the historian must reject the more spectacular as the more likely to have been made up to enhance the story's hero.[35] If the more spectacular version were first known, what would motivate anyone to fabricate the less impressive? But if an original, more modest story had failed to impress, it is easy to imagine that someone might want to replace it with something more impressive.[36] For example, Mark tells us both that the prophecy of Elijah's return was fulfilled figuratively in John the Baptist (9:12-13), *and* that Elijah himself returned, along with Moses, on the Mount of Transfiguration (9:4). Clearly, the figurative John the Baptist version was first, but anyone could see how lame it was: no proof of anything, a reinterpretation of evidence in light of faith, not something to create faith. So they invented a way in which they could swear up and down that Elijah himself, his footprints matching those at Mann's Chinese Theatre, did appear before witnesses! Ah, too bad you were not there, but what are you going to do? If the tradition had begun with the Transfiguration version, who would have bothered for a split second with the Baptist figurative version? No one, that's who.[37]

Well, that is the way it is in the case of epistle material versus Gospel material. Claims of spiritual upheavals in unseen worlds are as old as the hills, and admittedly unverifiable. On the other hand, a bag full of stories of

35. D. F. Strauss, *The Life of Jesus Critically Examined* (trans. George Eliot [M. A. Evans]; Lives of Jesus Series; Philadelphia: Fortress Press, 1972), 229. Of course, Strauss does not suppose that at least one version must be true and accurate. The point is rather that at least one must be *fictive*. And both might be.

36. For a counter example one might point to Lk. 17:6 and 13:6-9, figures of speech, thus less spectacular than the original, miracle-story version (as per standard source criticism) in Mk 11:12-14, 20-21. But this case must be understood differently: by adding Mk 11:22-26, Mark is already engaging in damage control, shifting attention from the original, offensive extravagance of the fig tree tale, akin to 2 Kgs 2:23-25, trying to make it into a polite bromide about faith in prayer. Luke is merely moving farther in the same direction. In both the Markan and Lukan redactions we are dealing with a stage of Gospel transmission subsequent to that which Strauss is considering, i.e., the oral circulation of the original stories.

37. Strauss, *Life of Jesus*, 543.

virgin births, angelic interventions, demon exorcisms, nature miracles and a resurrection from the dead? Well, that is more spectacular, hands down. One might protest that an ostensible war in heaven, or a contest in which the Light-Man defeated the Principalities and Powers in the lower heavens, is pretty spectacular! But really it is like the difference between claiming that Uncle Frank has died and gone to heaven and claiming that Uncle Frank has ascended into heaven in plain sight of many witnesses. By this criterion, then, as I think Drews implies, the vaguer epistolary version still trumps the Gospel version as the earlier. And this remains true no matter when each text was first written down.

It is interesting that, no matter the date of the underlying document, Drews reasons that 1 Cor. 11:23-32, the Last Supper episode, must be an interpolation,[38] presumably because it stands out like a sore thumb: epistles just do not include such materials except as barnacles on the hull. Here, a historical accident (epistles lack Jesus narratives because, at the time, none existed) becomes a genre convention (epistles *do* not, i.e., *can*not contain Jesus narratives).

William Benjamin Smith is equally willing to grant an early date to the epistles, as long as one allows for interpolations. Even if the epistles on the whole predate the Gospels, it can be shown (and he argues the point in great detail) that the two historicizing passages in 1 Corinthians (11:23-27 and 15:1-11) do not.[39] As we have seen, Wells is even more conservative than this, as he is willing to allow the Last Supper passage to stand as authentically Pauline as long as we realize that the scene came to him in a vision, presumably like those breaking upon Anna Katherine Emmerich, compiled in her *The Dolorous Passion of our Lord Jesus Christ.*

John M. Robertson sees things in much the same terms as Arthur Drews, like him, entertaining a much more radical estimate of the date and integrity of the epistles than our recent Christ Myth advocates, Wells and Doherty.[40]

> The fact is that the higher criticism of the New Testament has thus far missed the way... by taking for granted the general truth of the tradition. [n. at this point: 'An emphatic exception, certainly, must be made as regards the Pauline epistles, which by the late Professor van Manen and others are rejected as entirely spurious.]... it clings to the conception of a preaching and cult-founding Jesus, when an intelligent perusal of the epistles of Paul can suffice to show that the preaching was created after they were written.[41]

---

38. Drews, *Christ Myth*, 175.
39. William Benjamin Smith, *Ecce Deus: Studies of Primitive Christianity* (London: Watts, 1912), 146-57.
40. Wells, *Jesus of the Early Christians*, 131; Doherty, *Jesus Puzzle*, 13.
41. J. M. Robertson, *Pagan Christs: Studies in Comparative Mythology* (London: Watts, 1911, 2nd edn), 237.

The implication, if not the main point at issue, is that even if the epistles are quite late, as Bruno Bauer and the Dutch Radicals made them, the Gospels may be dated still later, as per some of the same critics. And in this case, we would still have the same relative dating: earlier epistles without Jesus narratives, followed by later Gospels complete with Jesus narratives, a spirit-Jesus having been historicized in the meantime. In all this, Robertson is echoed by Georg Brandes: 'as far as it is possible to tell, the gradually constructed and repeatedly edited compilations known as the Synoptic Gospels must be at least fifty years younger than the genuine parts of the epistles ascribed to Paul.'[42]

> The epistles which bear his name, genuine or not, are far older than the Gospels. The author of these epistles had never seen Jesus, and he neither knows nor communicates anything at all about the real life of Jesus. The man called Paul has a purely theological conception of Jesus.[43] The likelihood seems to be that only the epistles to the Galatians, the Romans, and parts of the first one to the Corinthians can be held genuine. [But] Even if they should be older than the gospels, the Pauline writings may be antedated. [Referring to the work of Van Manen, implying a second-century date.][44]

At the same time, Rylands anticipates the conclusion of Maccoby and others that even a Jesus narrative like that occurring in 1 Cor. 11:23-27 is pure dogma, not history. It is a piece of cult legend, not biographical information.

> The Pauline writers are interested only in the death and resurrection of Jesus. The writer of Galatians, whom theologians, except those of the Dutch radical school, believe to have been Paul, says not only that he had not learnt what he taught upon this subject from men, but that he did not wish to obtain from men any information with regard to it. A sufficient proof that what he taught was pure dogma.[45]
>
> Not only in the Pauline Epistles, but in all the Epistles, there is not the faintest trace of any impression that had been made by any human personality. If the supposed impression had been made, the experiences through which the disciples had lived in the company of Jesus would have been handed down and the thought of early Christians would have been full of them. But these early Christian writers never reinforce their arguments by anything they had heard that Jesus had done. He is never set before those to whom these Epistles are addressed as an example which they should follow in any human relationship, by pointing to his behaviour on some particular occasion. For the writers of these Epistles Jesus is not a man whose example other men

42. G. Brandes, *Jesus a Myth* (trans. E. Björkman; New York: Albert & Charles Boni, 1926), 42.
43. Brandes, *Jesus a Myth*, 44.
44. Brandes, *Jesus a Myth*, 45.
45. L. G. Rylands, *Did Jesus Ever Live?* (London: Watts, 1935), 23.

could follow. He is the 'Son of God's love, in whom we have our redemption, the image of the invisible God, the firstborn of all creation.'[46]

Robertson avers:

The question of the general genuineness of 'the four' epistles [the so-called *Hauptbriefe*, or principle epistles which F. C. Baur considered largely authentic: Romans, Galatians, 1 and 2 Corinthians] I have left open, while leaning more and more, though always with some reserves, to Van Manen's conclusions. But my case was and is that, whether the epistles to the Corinthians be genuine or spurious, they betray a general ignorance of the purport of the gospel narratives. As thus: (a) the passage 1 Cor. xv, 3-9 cannot well have been current as it stands before the gospels, else they would surely have given the 'five hundred' story;[47] [though] (b) verse 5 must have been written before the Judas story was added to the gospels, since it speaks of Jesus as appearing to the whole 'twelve,' where the Synoptics say 'the eleven';[48] (c) the non-mention of the women also [implies] the ignorance of the gospel story; (d) the specification of 'all the apostles' tells of an interpolation either of that phrase or of 'the twelve'; and (e) the specification of James is again independent of the gospel story... If the writer of the epistle knew the facts, and if the gospels give the facts, how came he to ignore the central role of Judas? If he drew on a current report concerning the 'five hundred,' how came the gospels to ignore that?... Be the epistle genuine or spurious, how can it be held to show knowledge of the gospel story?[49]

Robertson is especially close to Drews when he defines the alternatives this way:

It does not indeed follow that Paul's period was what the tradition represents. The reasonable inference from his doctrine is that his Jesus was either a mythic construction or a mere tradition, a remote figure said to have been crucified, but no longer historically traceable. If Paul's Jesus, as is conceivable, be merely a nominal memory of the slain Jesus ben Pandira of the Talmud (about 100 B.C.),[50] Paul himself may belong to an earlier period than that

46. Rylands, *Did Jesus Ever Live?*, 26.
47. It is thus a later interpolation, as I argue in 'Apocryphal Apparitions: 1 Corinthians 15:3-11,' in R. M. Price and J. J. Lowder, eds., *The Empty Tomb: Jesus beyond the Grave* (Amherst: Prometheus Books, 2005), 69-104.
48. See A. Loisy, *The Birth of the Christian Religion* (trans. L.P. Jacks; London: George Allen & Unwin, 1948), 82; idem, *The Origins of the New Testament* (trans. L.P. Jacks; London: George Allen & Unwin, 1950), 100; F. Kermode, *The Genesis of Secrecy* (Cambridge: Harvard University Press, 1979), 84-88; H. Maccoby, *Judas Iscariot and the Myth of Jewish Evil* (New York: Free Press, 1992).
49. Robertson, *Pagan Christs*, 399.
50. A. Ellegard argued something like this in his *Jesus One Hundred Years before Christ: A Study in Creative Mythology* (London: Century, 1999): the Gospel Jesus is a fiction, though there is, dimly discernable behind the epistolary references, the Essene Teacher of Righteousness. Wells moves to a similar position in *The Jesus Myth* (Chicago: Open Court, 1999), 102-103.

> traditionally assigned to him. Certainly the most genuine-looking epistles in themselves give no decisive chronological clue. But such a shifting of his date would not finally help the case for 'Jesus of Nazareth.' Escape the argument from the silence of Paul by putting Paul a generation or more earlier, and you are faced by the fresh incredibility of a second crucified Jesus, a second sacrificed Son of God, vouched for by records for the most part visibly false, and containing but a fraction of plausible narrative. The only conclusion open is that the teaching Jesus of the gospels is wholly a construction of the propagandists of the cult, even as is [Jesus] the wonder-working God.[51]

Myths versus Legends

But Robertson shows signs of a very different argument he might have employed when he notes that 'the bulk of the cumulative argument of the examination of "The Gospel Myths" in *Christianity and Mythology* remains to be dealt with even if the problem of the Pauline Epistles be put aside... The acceptance of the tradition by "Paul" would not establish the historicity of the tradition.'[52] Robertson refers to his comparative-mythology analysis of the Gospel stories in an earlier work. Even if all of these stories were to be found verbatim in the epistles, even if the epistles should all prove to be authentically Pauline, we would still be dealing with the (rapid) accumulation of stock, predictable hagiographic legends. We would still have to offer some pretty compelling reason for an impartial historian to accept the Gospel versions as historically true while rejecting medieval, classical, Buddhist or Hindu parallels as false. That is what the principle of analogy is all about.

One might put this valuable insight of Robertson's a bit differently. Suppose one concluded that the Gospels were not so much later than the epistles after all, making both products of the late-first, early-second century. Suppose the late Gospels were even *earlier* than the epistles. That alone would still mean little. How shall we describe what we find in the Gospels? Would one call it sober biographical and historical data, even by ancient standards? Or would we not recognize it rather easily as a set of barely historicized hero myths? Consider the major features of the *Mythic Hero Archetype* compiled from the hero myths (both Indo-European and Semitic) and delineated by Lord Raglan, Otto Rank, Alan Dundes and others. Here are the twenty-two recurrent features, *highlighting* those appearing in the Gospel story of Jesus. They make it pretty clear that it is not merely the death-and-resurrection complex in which the Jesus story parallels myth more than history:

51 Robertson, *Pagan Christs*, 237.
52 Robertson, *Pagan Christs*, 398.

1. *mother is a royal virgin*
2. *father is a king*
3. father related to mother
4. *unusual conception*
5. *hero reputed to be son of god*
6. *attempt to kill hero*
7. *hero spirited away*
8. reared *by foster parents* in a far country
9. *no details of childhood*
10. *goes to future kingdom*
11. is victor over king
12. marries a princess (often daughter of predecessor)
13. *becomes king*
14. *for a time he reigns uneventfully*
15. *he prescribes laws*
16. *later loses favour with gods or his subjects*
17. *driven from throne and city*
18. *meets with mysterious death*
19. *often at the top of a hill*
20. his children, if any, do not succeed him [i.e. *does not found a dynasty*]
21. *his body is not buried*
22. *nonetheless has one or more holy sepulchers*[53]

Jesus' mother, Mary, is indeed a virgin, though she is not of royal blood (though later apocrypha, as if to fill the lack, do make Mary Davidic). Joseph is 'of the house of David', though he does not sit on the throne; but of course the point is that David's heir, the true king, is *coming*. Mary and Joseph are not blood relatives. Jesus' conception certainly qualifies as unusual, being virginal and miraculous. Jesus is the Son of God, and more and more people begin to recognize it. He is at once persecuted by the reigning monarch, Herod the Great. In most of these hero tales, the persecutor is also the hero's father who fears, like Kronos did, that his son will one day overthrow him. This role is divided between Joseph, a royal heir but not king, and Herod, who occupies Joseph's rightful throne. Escaping persecution, our hero disappears into distant Egypt. Mary is not a foster parent, though Joseph is. The story supplies no details about Jesus' childhood or upbringing. (The one apparent exception, Jesus visiting the temple as a youth, Lk. 2:41-52, is itself a notable hero theme: the child prodigy.) Sure enough, eventually Jesus goes to Jerusalem to be acclaimed as king, though rejecting political power. But he comes into conflict with the rulers anyway. He does not marry (though, again, as if to fill the gap, pious speculation has always believed he married Mary Magdalene). Does Jesus have a peaceful reign, issuing decrees? Not exactly. But he does enjoy brief popular favour as King of the Jews and holds court in the Temple, giving teachings and moral commands. All of a sudden his once-loyal followers turn on him, demanding his death. They

53. A. Dundes, 'The Hero Pattern in the Life of Jesus,' in Robert A. Segal, ed., *In Quest of the Hero* (Princeton: Princeton University Press, 1990), xxiv. The late Professor Dundes also discusses the relevance of the Mythic Hero Archetype to the Gospel Jesus in an interview on the DVD, *The God Who Wasn't There*.

hound Jesus outside the city, where he is crucified on Golgotha's crest. He is temporarily buried, but his tomb winds up empty, and later various sites were nominated as his burial place. He has no children, except in modern legends which make him the progenitor of the Merovingian dynasty of medieval France.

In other words, there is a lot less difference between the Jesus story of the Gospels and the Christ myth of the epistles than we usually assume. Neither is the stuff of history. But what is the difference between myth and legend?

> Myth operates by bringing a sacred (and hence essentially and paradoxically 'timeless') past to bear preemptively on the present and inferentially on the future ('as it was in the beginning, is now, and ever shall be'). Yet in the course of human events societies pass and religious systems change; the historical landscape gets littered with the husks of desiccated myths. These are valuable nonmaterial fossils of mankind's recorded history, especially if still embedded in layers of embalmed religion, as part of a stratum of religion complete with cult, liturgy and ritual. Yet equally important is the next level of transmission, in which the sacred narrative has already been secularized, myth has been turned into saga, sacred time into heroic past, gods into heroes, and mythical action into 'historical' plot.[54]
>
> Myth can be transmitted either in its immediate shape, as sacred narrative anchored in theology and interlaced with liturgy and ritual, or in transmuted form, as past narrative that has severed its ties to sacred time and instead functions as an account of purportedly secular, albeit extraordinary happening... This transposition of myth to heroic saga is a notable mechanism in ancient Indo-European traditions, wherever a certain cultic system has been supplanted in living religion and the superannuated former apparatus falls prey to literary manipulation.[55]

The logic of development from pure myth, accounts of gods pure and simple, taking place in the heavens or primordial times, to quasi-historical legend, featuring super-powered demigods on earth in the past, only reinforces the conclusion that the epistolary version of the myth-god Christ is prior to the Jesus hero version found in the Gospels. While it is conceivable that the latter managed to take literary form before the former, the former must still be judged the earlier version. If the original mythic form did reach written form only later, that would probably indicate that a community maintaining the original mythic version survived alongside that which cherished the newer, more evolved version, uncontaminated by it. We would have a particularly clear case of this in Phil. 2:6-11. Suppose the epistle as a whole is historically posterior to the Gospels. Even so, as virtually all scholars agree,

---

54. J. Puhvel, *Comparative Mythology* (Baltimore: Johns Hopkins University Press, 1987), 2.
55. Puhvel, *Comparative Mythology*, 39.

it preserves an older hymn fragment, crystallizing a form of Christ-faith that had otherwise perhaps been forgotten:

> Who, though he was in the form of God,
> Did not count equality with God a thing to be grasped,
> But emptied himself, taking the form of a slave,
> Being born in the likeness of men.
> And being found in human form, he humbled himself
> And became obedient unto death [even death on a cross].
> Therefore God has highly exalted him,
> And bestowed on him the *name* that is above every name,
> That at the *name* of Jesus, every knee should bow,
> In heaven and on earth, and under the earth,
> And every tongue confess that Jesus Christ is Lord
> To the glory of God the Father.

The hymn text is based ultimately on Isa. 45:22-23:

> Turn to me and be saved,
> All the ends of the earth!
> For I am God, and there is no other.
> By myself I have sworn,
> From my mouth has gone forth in righteousness
> A word that shall not return:
> 'To me every knee shall bow,
> Every tongue shall swear.'

The Philippians hymn thus depicts the divine enthronement of the vindicated Christ. But scholars traditionally read the text as if God had bestowed the divine title *Kurios*, 'Lord' (equivalent to Adonai in the Old Testament, often substituted in Jewish liturgy for the divine name Yahve) on someone already named Jesus. Couchoud noticed that this is not quite what the text says. Instead, what we read is that, because of his humiliating self-sacrifice, an unnamed heavenly being has been granted a mighty name which henceforth should call forth confessions of fealty from all beings in the cosmos. At the name 'Jesus' every knee should bow, every tongue acknowledging his Lordship. And, Couchould[56] reasoned with relentless logic, does not this piece of early Christian tradition presuppose a theology of a saviour who received the name Jesus only *after* his death struggle, even as Jacob received the honourific name Israel only after wrestling with God (Gen. 32:24-28)? In that case, there can have been no Galilean adventures of an itinerant teacher and healer named Jesus. The antique myth/Christology had managed to survive even after most readers no longer knew how to understand it, what to make of it. And in the same way, even if the Christ

56. Couchoud, *Creation of Christ*, 438.

myth version were textually attested only later (e.g. if the epistles should turn out to have been written later than the Gospels), the nature of the thing can still be recognized in contrast with the hero legend of Jesus, even if the former be embedded in the latter.

Had the partisans of the pure Christ myth heard of the demigod Jesus and his adventures they might have rejected it all as degrading heresy, just as some Ebionites rejected the virginal conception Nativity which other Ebionites had embraced. The only way we happen to know that some Ebionites rejected the Virgin Birth is that Origen (in *Contra Celsum* 5.61; *In Matthaeum* 16.12) mentions the to him strange fact in the course of discussing the doctrine, so for us the non-Virgin Birth version is attested only subsequently by the Virgin Birth version. Yet, if we compare the inherent logic of the two positions, anyone can see that the later-attested version (the natural birth version) must be the earlier version. Legends grow; they do not shrink.

Marcion and the Gospel Story

Once again: what if Marcion was one of the authors of the Pauline epistles? If he also knew a version of Luke's Gospel, as we usually assume, does that not prove that someone might well be familiar with Gospel traditions yet avoid mentioning them (for whatever reason) when writing epistles? Let us pause to take stock of what we believe we know about the content of Marcion's own canon, as opposed to that of the Marcionite church, in case there may have been a difference.

We always read that Marcion came to the theological fray armed with a sheaf of Pauline letters plus a single Gospel, a shorter version of canonical Luke. Church apologists[57] said Marcion's version was shorter than Luke because Marcion abbreviated it, removing what he deemed 'false pericopes'. Others believe Marcion possessed an original, shorter Gospel, with which he tampered only minimally, an Ur-Lukas. Couchoud[58] argued forcefully that Marcion's Gospel was very nearly what B. F. Streeter and Vincent Taylor called Proto-Luke,[59] though with just a bit of other Synoptic material. G. R. S. Mead hypothesized that Marcion had no actual Gospel text but rather

57. Tertullian, *Adversus Marcionem*, Books 4 and 5; Epiphanius of Salamis, *Panarion* I, Haer. xlii.; Adamantius' *Dialogus de recta in deum fide*.

58. P. -L. Couchoud, 'Was Marcion's Gospel One of the Synoptics?,' *HibJ* 34.2, 265-77. Matthias Klinghardt argues a similar case in 'The Marcionite Gospel and the Synoptic Problem: A New Suggestion,' *NovT* 50 (2008), 1-27.

59. B. F. Streeter, *The Four Gospels: A Study of Origins* (London: Macmillan, 1924; rev. edn, 1939), Chapter 8, 'Proto-Luke,' 199-222; V. Taylor, *Behind the Third Gospel: A Study of the Proto-Luke Hypothesis* (Oxford: Clarendon Press, 1926).

only a collection of sayings, something like the hypothetical Q.[60] This diversity of opinion translates into the uncertainty as to whether we are dealing with Marcion's own canon or whether we are hearing, in this or that secondary source, of the canon of subsequent Marcionites. Harnack observed: 'his pupils constantly made alterations in the texts—sometimes more radical than his own, sometimes more conservative—perhaps under his very eyes, but certainly after his death.'[61] John Knox adds: 'It has been clearly established that the text of the Marcionite Scriptures underwent continuous and extensive changes after Marcion's own time. How confident can we be that the Marcionite text criticized by Tertullian in A.D. 200 or by Epiphanius a century and a half later is the text of the original Marcionite Scriptures?'[62] We know the Marcionites were not exactly hidebound traditionalists. It is my opinion, for two reasons to be explained directly, that Marcion's Scripture contained only epistles, with no Gospel. His followers added Proto-Luke (or Ur-Lukas, or something) later on.

First, it appears to me both that Marcion is responsible for significant portions of the epistolary text and that the epistles are quite innocent of the Gospel tradition of sayings and deeds by an earthly Jesus. Therefore, Marcion not only possessed no Gospel but knew nothing of our Jesus tradition.

The second reason for doubting that Marcion knew any written Gospel is the astonishing phenomenon of the near-total dependence of the Gospel stories upon corresponding Old Testament passages. A raft of scholars, including Randel Helms, Thomas L. Brodie, John Dominic Crossan and others,[63] have shown again and again how this and that Gospel passage

60. G. R. S. Mead, *Fragments of a Faith Forgotten: The Gnostics: A Contribution to the Study of the Origins of Christianity* (New Hyde Park: University Books, n.d.), 244.

61. A. von Harnack, *Marcion: The Gospel of the Alien God* (trans. John E. Steely and L. Bierma; Durham: Labyrinth Press, 1990 [orig. 1924]), 30.

62. J. Knox, *Marcion and the New Testament: An Essay in the Early History of the Canon* (Chicago: University of Chicago Press, 1942), 47-48.

63. J. Bowman, *The Gospel of Mark: The New Christian Jewish Passover Haggadah* (StPB, 8; Leiden: Brill, 1965); T. L. Brodie, 'Luke the Literary Interpreter: Luke–Acts as a Systematic Rewriting and Updating of the Elijah–Elisha Narrative in 1 and 2 Kings' (PhD dissertation, Pontifical University of St Thomas Aquinas, Rome, 1988); J. D. Crossan, *The Cross That Spoke: The Origins of the Passion Narrative* (San Francisco: Harper & Row Publishers, 1988); J. Duncan M. Derrett, *The Making of Mark: The Scriptural Bases of the Earliest Gospel*, vols. 1 and 2 (Shipston-on-Stour, Warwickshire: P. Drinkwater, 1985); R. Helms, *Gospel Fictions* (Buffalo: Prometheus Books, 1989); D. Miller and P. Miller, *The Gospel of Mark as Midrash on Earlier Jewish and New Testament Literature* (SBEC, 21; Lewiston/Queenston/Lampeter: Edwin Mellen Press, 1990); W. Roth, *Hebrew Gospel: Cracking the Code of Mark* (Oak Park: Meyer-Stone Books, 1988); W. R. Stegner, 'The Baptism of Jesus: A Story Modeled on the Binding of Isaac,' in H. Shanks, ed., *Abraham & Family: New Insights into the Patriarchal Narratives* (Washington: Biblical Archaeology Society, 2001); R. E. Watts, *Isaiah's New Exodus and Mark* (WUNT, 2; Reihe, 88; Tübingen: Mohr Siebeck, 1997).

likely originated as a Christian rewrite of this or that Old Testament passage. What one Testament had Moses do, the other had Jesus do. Fill in the name. What did David do? Joshua? Elijah? Elisha? Turns out Jesus did it, too, and even in the same descriptive words. When one assembles the best and most convincing of these studies[64] the results are startling indeed: one can make a compelling argument for virtually every Gospel story's derivation from Old Testament sources. How do we account for this? Why the sudden interest in rewriting the Jewish Scripture as a book about Jesus?

The Catholic policy was to retain the Old Testament but to reread it as a book about (predicting) Jesus and Christianity. If this procedure were cut off, as Marcion did, what remained? One had to *rewrite* the Old Testament to make it *explicitly* about Jesus! In this way, even the Old Testament of the Jews became, as Martin Luther would say, *was Christum triebt.*

But this had not happened by Marcion's time. Marcion would never have raided the Old Testament in this way, given his antipathy for the book. Such rewriting must have seemed too close to the allegorical Christianizing of Catholics (of which it was, after all, but another version, creating antitypes to justify typology!). As we will see, Marcionites joined the game once they saw others playing it, but this would have been a retrenching move, like Lutherans who could not bring themselves to go the whole way with Martin Luther and relegate James and Jude to a quasi-canonical limbo. By fabricating new Scripture (Gospel traditions) they could co-opt what they still (guiltily) liked of the old. So there were yet no Gospels for Marcion himself to include in his new Scripture, only epistles which show no sign of acquaintance with any Gospels. But soon there was Marcionite involvement in the production of Gospels.

Mark's Gospel, for instance, holds what can hardly be called other than a Marcionite view of the buffoonish twelve disciples and a Gnostic view of secret teaching which, despite their privileged position, the twelve simply do not grasp. Or think of the Transfiguration (Mk 9:1-8): how can one miss the Marcionite implications of Mark's setting up Jesus, Moses (the Torah) and Elijah (the Prophets) as in a police line-up, followed by the Father's urging that, of the three, Jesus alone is to be heard and heeded? And Mark, of course, refers to Jesus giving his life a ransom for many (Mk 10:45). Though Mark fails to tell us to whom Jesus would be paying this ransom, Marcion tells us. He paid it to the Creator, and no non-Marcionite theologian has produced a better candidate.

---

64. R. M. Price, 'New Testament Narrative as Old Testament Midrash,' in Jacob Neusner and Alan J. Avery-Peck, eds., *Encyclopedia of Midrash: Biblical Interpretation in Formative Judaism* (Leiden: Brill, 2005), I, 534-73.

One wonders if even the name of the Gospel of Mark reflects awareness of the fundamentally (though not completely) Marcionite character of the book. Mark the secretary of Peter (as Papias makes him), the John Mark of Acts, would be too early for us to identify with Marcion, but it is quite possible that Mark the secretary of Peter is an unhistorical character, a 'safe' version of Marcion to have authored the Gospel, much as Eusebius posited a 'John the Elder' as the author of Revelation once he no longer wanted to ascribe that book to John son of Zebedee.

The Gospel of John is heavily Marcionite: Moses and his Jews knew nothing of God. Despite all that Deuteronomy says about Moses seeing God face to face, John denies that any mortal has ever seen the true God (Jn 1:18). Jesus' Father is not the same God the Jews worship (8:54-55). All who came to the Jews before Jesus, presumably the Old Testament prophets, were mere despoilers (10:8). The Father is unknown to the world (17:25). The Torah had nothing to do with grace and truth (1:17). Jesus raised himself from the dead (10:17-18).

The Q Document has Jesus exclaim that no one knows his Father but him (Mt. 11:27//Lk. 10:22). What? Not Israel? Not Moses? Not John the Baptist? It would take quite a lot of ingenuity to come up with some other interpretation of this one. 'No one knows the Father except for the Son and any to whom the Son may deign to reveal him.' That's straight Marcionism. Is it not?

Thomas 52 has 'His disciples say to him, "Twenty-four prophets spoke in Israel, and every one of them predicted you!" He said to them, "You have disregarded the Living, who is right in front of you, to prattle on about the dead!"' Augustine, who wrote up the encounter in *Contra adversarium legis et prophetarum* 2.14, found the second half of the saying, Jesus' reply, quoted in an explicitly Marcionite pamphlet handed him on the street in Carthage. The first half of the saying, the set-up remark of the disciples, was unknown till 1945 when the *Gospel of Thomas* was discovered. Looking at the truncated version, Joachim Jeremias[65] surmized that, while Marcionites must have taken 'the dead' to refer to the prophets, Jesus was really refuting rabbinic arguments that the messiah to come would be a returned Old Testament personality, perhaps Joshua or Hezekiah. No, here he is right in front of you! Have you forgotten? Jeremias's theory must be judged an extreme harmonization, an attempt to preserve an attractive saying by scrubbing away the Marcionite tint. And the discovery of *Thomas* proved him wrong. Or rather, he was right the first time, about the Marcionite reading. The Marcionites

65. J. Jeremias, *Unknown Sayings of Jesus* (trans. Reginald H. Fuller; New York: Macmillan, 1957), 74-77. All discussion of the saying has vanished from the 1964 edition of the book.

were right, and they were only reading what was before them, while Jeremias was prating on about the dead.

So the composition of Gospels, being rewrites of the Old Testament, was a counterblast to the Marcionite rejection of the Old Testament. Once the trend began, Marcionites made their own contributions to it, and thus to the process of historicizing an originally mythic Jesus. Marcion himself, then, had no Gospel. It must have been subsequent Marcionites who ascribed the choice of one to him. Thus we retain the pillar of the Christ Myth hypothesis that the writer of the Pauline epistles (even if Marcion, not Paul) did not know the (historical or historicized) Jesus tradition on display in the Gospels, as he must have if Marcion either composed or adopted the narrative Gospel subsequently used by his followers.

Conclusion

Though today's leading proponents of the Christ Myth Theory tend to hold to a conventional, mid-first-century dating of the epistles, a good twenty to forty years before the (conventional) dates assigned the Gospels, one suspects this is almost a circumstantial ad hominem fallacy, accepting conventional dates mainly for the sake of argument in order to embarrass the orthodox who hold to these dates for apologetical reasons. Christ Myth theorists are not above pursuing an apologetical agenda of their own, which may explain their reluctance to apply the same ruthless scepticism to the Pauline epistles as they do to the Gospels. If they did (like their nineteenth-century forbears did), they would find the picture becoming a bit fuzzier, to be sure, but there might also be significant gains. In a brief survey of remarks on the age and integrity of the Pauline epistles by Robertson, Couchoud, Smith and others, we have detected pregnant hints of arguments for the historical priority of the Christ Myth as attested in the epistles over the Jesus epic met with in the Gospels, and this regardless of either the relative or the absolute dates of the Gospels and epistles.

- 7 -

Paul: The Oldest Witness to the Historical Jesus

Mogens Müller

Asking the question about the historicity of Jesus one naturally first turns to the Gospels. Also, their physical placement as the beginning of the New Testament invites this. However, the fact that the Gospels contain the story about the beginning should not be allowed to hide the fact that the oldest Gospel, the Gospel of Mark, was written 35–40 years after the death of its story's main figure, Jesus of Nazareth. This means that the Gospels belong to a later stage in the history of reception, as do the genuine letters of Paul. If we at least consider the later Gospels as examples of the genre 'rewritten Bible', it becomes obvious that they are theological elaborations of the Jesus tradition. This, however, is already so with the Gospel of Mark.[1] As such, the Gospels of Mark, Matthew and John all identify, in one way or another, their earthly Jesus with the risen and exalted Christ. Only the relatively late Gospel of Luke, which was, according to my understanding, written around 120–130, also allows its Jesus to be a historical person of the past, with the apostolic church replacing him as the authority.[2] This change in perspective could be one reason why the interpretative tradition stopped expressing itself in the writing of Gospels.

When, however, my friend and former colleague, Thomas L. Thompson, in *The Messiah Myth: The Near Eastern Roots of Jesus and David* from 2005[3] seeks

1. Thus, more than a hundred years ago William Wrede, in his seminal *Das Messiasgeheimnis in den Evangelien: Zugleich ein Beitrag zum Verständnis des Markusevangeliums* (Göttingen: Vandenhoeck & Ruprecht, 1901; 3rd edn, 1963, 131), said that the Gospel of Mark belongs to the history of dogma.
2. See M. Müller, 'Lukasevangeliets iscenesættelse af en historisk Jesus,' in M. Müller and T. L. Thompson, eds., *Historie og konstruktion* (FS Niels Peter Lemche; Copenhagen: Museum Tusculanum, 2005), 286–305.
3. New York: Basic Books.

to dissolve the Jesus figure of the Gospels as a historical figure, making him, so to speak, the epitome of biblical and other—far older—Near Eastern concepts of a royal Messiah, the question of historicity invites us to look in other directions for an answer, rather than to try to identify *ipsissima verba Iesu* or situations which could have been historical recollections. This is not to deny that the Jesus story in the Gospels is saturated with reminiscences of Old Testament figures and events, the Old Testament being the medium of the Near Eastern Messiah myth. Moreover, in this respect, Thomas L. Thompson's book is an abundant and impressive arsenal of evidence. However, with regard to New Testament reception, these concepts and traditions are almost exclusively channelled through what became the Bible of Judaism and the reception of it in the other literature of early Judaism. However, just as in the days of the History of Religions School a hundred years ago, one still needs to distinguish between parallels and sources. The fact that what we find in the Gospels certainly is more or less a semi-divine 'preacher preached' does not negate the fact that it all began with a historical preacher-prophet.

The declaration that the apostle Paul was the founder of Christianity is not as far-fetched as it might sound. Not only is he the author of the oldest documents in the New Testament, his letters, that is, the genuine ones, are also the only New Testament documents of which we know the author as a person whose life and teaching can be reasonably sketched. Furthermore, Paul is the oldest witness to the transformation of the historical person, that is, Jesus of Nazareth, into a heavenly saviour, although this transformation occurred in such a way that Jesus, as a historical person of the past, has nearly disappeared.[4]

There are also good reasons to think that all four canonical Gospels have been influenced more or less by the Pauline interpretation, which gives meaning to the historical Jesus as providing salvation to humankind.[5] This transforming interpretation was necessitated by the faith in the resurrected as being, with his life and death, an integral part in the saving act of God and

---

4. The meaning of Paul in this respect is clearly set out in an article by my late teacher, B. Noack (1915–2004), 'TESTE Paulo: Paul as the Principal Witness to Jesus and Primitive Christianity,' in Sigfred Pedersen, ed., *Die paulinische Literatur und Theologie. The Pauline Literature and Theology* (Teologiske Studier, 7; Århus: Aros/Göttingen: Vandenhoeck & Ruprecht 1980), 9–28.

5. There is a growing literature analysing the possible impact of Paul and his 'theology' not only on the Synoptic Gospels but also on the Gospel of John. As correct as it may be of Maurice Casey to emphasize that the oldest Jesus tradition was in Aramaic, so unwarranted is it to date the Gospel of Mark as early as around 40. See M. Casey, *Aramaic Sources of Mark's Gospel* (SNTSMS, 102; Cambridge: Cambridge University Press, 1998), 259–60.

not merely having a role as messenger, whose message could be separated from its bringer. The old masters of critical scholarship, Julius Wellhausen (1844–1918) and Rudolf Bultmann (1884–1976), were right in their judgment that the Jesus of history was not a Christian, because being a Christian implies confessing faith in Jesus as resurrected Lord.[6] Just as the author behind the Gospel of Mark was the first known to us to draw this faith's picture of the earthly Jesus, we have to respect the later evangelists as people who wanted to improve and thereby eliminate the predecessor(s),[7] in which venture, however, they did not succeed.[8]

It seems, therefore, futile to construct a religious gap between Paul and the Jesus of history, which claims that Paul created a new religion that effectively drowned the simple preaching of Jesus in complicated speculations. Since the Enlightenment, this position has, however, been put forward with a broad spectrum of variations, from declaring Paul as the great corrupter of an originally simple faith and practically making the apostle an object of contempt to a respectful acknowledgement of his accomplishment in creating the necessary transition of the message after the death of Jesus.[9] Thus Bultmann, in his *Theology of the New Testament* (1948–1953), only allowed the Synoptic traditions to form the presuppositions of its theology, while, according to him, in the New Testament genuine theology is practically only represented in the Pauline letters and Johannine writings.

But not least, redaction criticism has shown that the Synoptic Gospels also represent a far-reaching theological interpretation of the preaching,

6. See J. Wellhausen, *Einleitung in die drei ersten Evangelien* (Berlin: Reimer, 1905; 2nd edn, 1911), 102; R. Bultmann, *Das Verhältnis der urchristlichen Christusbotschaft zum historischen Jesus* (SHA, 1960); repr. in idem, *Exegetica Aufsätze zur Erforschung des Neuen Testaments* (ed. E. Dinkler; Tübingen: Mohr Siebeck, 1967), 445–69: 449.
7. Cf. T. Heckel, *Vom Evangelium des Markus zum viergestaltigen Evangelium* (WUNT, 120; Tübingen: Mohr Siebeck, 1999).
8. In Thomas Thompson's book, I miss an account of his views on the genesis of the four Gospels; that is, on the dependence of the later on the earlier, because—as I see it—they are chapters in an ongoing tradition process. Sometimes, in the *The Messiah Myth*, it seems as if they are independent witnesses. This is so in spite of Thompson's highly relevant criticism of the procedures of the Jesus Seminar. I find it symptomatic that Paul is hardly mentioned in the book.
9. Cf. J. W. Fraser, *Jesus and Paul: Paul as an Interpreter of Jesus from Harnack to Kümmel* (Nashville, TN: Abingdon, 1974). Also Frank Holzbrecher, *Paulus und der historische Jesus: Darstellung und Analyse der bisherigen Forschungsgeschichte* (TANZ, 48; Tübingen: Francke Verlag, 2007). Of older literature could be mentioned Joseph Blank, *Paulus und Jesus. Eine theologische Grundlegung* (StANT, 18; München: Kösel, 1968); Hans Hübner, 'Paulusforschung seit 1945. Ein kritischer Literaturbericht,' *ANRW* II.25.4 (Berlin: de Gruyter, 1987), 2649–2840, esp. 2745–49: 'Exkurs: Paulinische Christologie und der vorösterliche Jesus'; A. J. M. Wedderburn, ed., *Paul and Jesus: Collected Essays* (JSNTSup, 37; Sheffield: Sheffield Academic Press, 1989).

teaching and actions of Jesus and should be regarded foremost as sources for the theologies of anonymous authors. The historical person is absorbed in this enterprise to such a degree as to overrule Bultmann's verdict on this figure as merely a presupposition for theology. However, attempts have been made at finding a common denominator between Paul and the historical Jesus, as for instance in Eberhard Jüngel's classic *Paulus und Jesus* from 1962.[10]

To treat Paul as a witness to the historical Jesus should not primarily be an attempt to find in his letters traditions which later became a part of the Gospels.[11] It has long been noticed that such 'remnants' are remarkably seldom not only in Paul's letters but also in the New Testament writings outside the Gospels. The first to reflect on this fact was Ferdinand Christian Baur (1792–1860), who offered a theological solution to the problem,[12] but in the same period a few took it as an indication that Paul had not known of any historical Jesus because Jesus had never existed as a historical person. The best known is Bruno Bauer (1809–1882),[13] but a Dane, the otherwise famous literary scholar Georg Brandes (1842–1927), also was himself a spokesman for this view.[14]

We need, however, a broader understanding of the predicate 'historical' as used in connection with the person of Jesus. Thus, 'historical' should not be employed simply in connection with attempts to reconstruct details in the life and teaching of Jesus, treating him solely as a figure of the past. The

10. Published as HUTh 2 (Tübingen: Mohr Siebeck, 1962, with several reprints); peculiarly enough, it has never been translated to English.

11. Cf. D. L. Dungan, *The Sayings of Jesus in the Churches of Paul: The Use of the Synoptic Traditions in the Regulation of Early Church Life* (Philadelphia: Fortress Press, 1971).

12. See F. Holzbrecher, *Paulus*, 15–18, with references to F. F. Baur, *Das Christentum und die christliche Kirche in der ersten drei Jahrhunderte* (Tübingen, 1853), 49; cf. *Vorlesungen über neutestamentliche Theologie* (ed. F. F. Baur; Leipzig, 1864; repr. with intro. by W. G. Kümmel, Darmstadt: Wissenschaftliche Buchgesellschaft, 1973), 173.

13. To be sure, Bauer even doubted the historicity of Paul. See his three small contributions to the *Kritik der paulinischen Briefe* (1st part, 'Der Ursprung des Galaterbriefes' [1850; 74]; 2nd part, 'Der Ursprung des ersten Korintherbriefes' [1851; 76], 3rd part dealing with the other 'Pauline' letters [1852; 129]). Cf. F. Holzbrecher, *Paulus*, 22, but also A. Schweitzer, *Geschichte der Paulinischen Forschung von der Reformation bis auf die Gegenwart* (Tübingen: Mohr Siebeck, 1911; 2nd edn, 1933), 94–96. Most of the letters, according to Bauer, are written after the Acts of the Apostles, but 1 Corinthians is written before and probably on the basis of the same sources. Schweitzer resumes the 'results' of Bauer (95): 'Ob es einen Jesus und einen Paulus gegeben hat, mag dahingestellt bleiben. Sicher ist jedenfalls, dass der eine nicht gesagt hat, was ihm die Evangelien in den Mund legen, und der andere nicht als Verfasser der Briefe anzusehen ist.'

14. In his *Sagnet om Jesus* (Copenhagen: Gyldendal, 1925; German: *Die Jesus-Sage* [1925]; English: *Jesus: A Myth* [1926]). Cf. M. Müller, *Jesu-liv-litteratur i Danmark* (Copenhagen: Anis, 2008), 85–88.

predicate 'historical' should be allowed also to include his impact as it has been conveyed to us through the meanings attached to his life and conduct in the different interpretations of the Christ-faith represented in the New Testament Scriptures.

Presupposed as historical cause, it should be possible to deduce various characteristics of the 'historical' Jesus through the interpretations he received from his first followers. Although it seems safe to assume that Paul never met Jesus personally (*pace* 1 Cor. 9:1; on 2 Cor. 5:16, see below), according to his own utterances he did meet with and therefore personally knew two of his first followers, namely, Peter (Gal. 1:18; 2:9; cf. 1 Cor. 3:22; 9:5; 15:5) and James, the Lord's brother (Gal. 1:19; cf. 2:12; 1 Cor. 15:7; further below). The whole of his understanding must have been channelled through followers and adversaries when he acted as persecutor of the new faith (1 Cor. 15:9; Gal. 1:13, 23; Phil. 3:6). In his self-understanding as an apostle of Christ, however, he claimed not to have his calling through any human person, but directly from the resurrected and exalted Lord (Gal. 1:1). In this way, Paul is himself witness to the circumstance, that, for faith, Jesus is only relevant in his impact—according to which he, through his life, teaching and fate, brought about faith in the lives of those believing in him. Accordingly, the term the 'historical Jesus', in this context, should be extended to include also such effects as a valuable source.

To put it another way, what sort of a historical person is implied by Paul's preaching of the crucified and resurrected Lord? In the midst of all the obvious discontinuities, not to assume a profound continuity between the message of the Jesus of history and its effect on Paul, the apostle as well, raises more questions than it answers. Therefore, a working hypothesis could be that precisely what seems to establish discontinuity was the means for disclosing the meaning of what the Jesus of history had brought about. In this context, explicit Christology thus is to be viewed as secondary in relation to ethics, being the attempt to encircle and define the legitimizing of the authority crucial to ethics. Christology, in this respect, has no 'Selbstzweck'. The essential problem of ethics is that it depends on its obviousness. This authority, however, is an experienced authority, which totally changes its character if one attempts to establish it as an outward authority, functioning with external power.

The genuine letters of Paul seem to be written within a few years in the beginning of the fifties.[15] In these writings, among many other things, we meet his staging of himself as an apostle of the risen Jesus Christ. That we, in later writings in the New Testament, especially the Pastorals and the Act

15. Fundamental with regard to this problem is the profound study of N. Hyldahl, *Die paulinische Chronologie* (AThD, 19; Leiden: Brill, 1986).

of the Apostles, meet him as created by other people should open our eyes to the fact that Jesus was not alone in being transformed in the process of reception. And while the Acts of the Apostles do not tell us anything about Paul as a letter writer—although the author seemingly knew and used at least some of them—in another likewise late New Testament writing, 2 Peter, we meet him in exactly that function; together with a warning that the apostle is difficult to understand, some have misinterpreted him to their own destruction (2 Pet. 3:15–16). As intensely as we might know Paul and his activities in the beginning of the fifties and have some knowledge as well of the period yet earlier from his own hints, we have to admit that we lose track in Romans, where we can only suppose that the apostle actually did reach Rome. Information about his later fate, not least his death as a martyr in the sixties during the reign of Nero, is entirely spurious.

On the basis of the letters of Paul, not much of a life of Jesus can be written. However, so sparse as are the hints, just so clearly is it presupposed that Paul's Jesus Christ has lived the life of a human being on this earth. Thus, in Galatians 4:4–5 it is said, 'But when the time had fully come, God sent forth his Son, born of woman, born under the law, so that we might receive adoptions as sons.'[16] The presupposition is that God's son became a human and even so a Jew. In the prescript to Romans, in sayings which seems to stem from a confessional formula, it is said that Paul was set apart by God to preach 'the gospel concerning his Son, who was descended from David according to the flesh and designated Son of God in power according to the Spirit of holiness by his resurrection from the dead' (Rom. 1:3–4). This is the only place where Paul writes that Jesus is a descendent of King David and in the context it stands in contrast to his status as Son of God, which he achieved at his resurrection from the dead. Later on in the same epistle, his human descent is also referred to in Paul's comment on his fellow countrymen, 'the Israelites', as those to whom belong all the salvation-historical privileges including 'the patriarchs', stating: 'and of their race, according to the flesh, is the Christ' (Rom. 9:5).

Only once does Paul mention an event from the life of Jesus—apart from his death and burial (1 Cor. 15:3–4)—namely, the institution of the Eucharist on the night he was delivered (1 Cor. 1:23–25). Of course the death of Jesus is implied each time Paul mentions him as the one crucified (for instance 1 Cor. 2:2; further in 'the word of the cross', 1 Cor. 1:18). In some way, Paul is also talking about the Jesus of history when he enumerates witnesses to the resurrection, namely Cephas (Peter) and then, further, the twelve, five-hundred brethren at a single time and James and the other apostles (1 Cor. 15:5–7), because the function of a witness also includes the identification of

16. The Bible is quoted according to the RSV.

the one seen as the resurrected—when Paul adds that the resurrected last of all was also seen by himself. Of course, this function is of another nature.

The James mentioned here is neither one of the twelve nor one of the apostles, but, rather, the one whom, as we have seen, Paul tells us of in Galatians he met three years after his call as an apostle, when he visited Jerusalem to see Cephas, with whom he stayed for fifteen days (Gal. 1:18–19). As expressed by Charles Harold Dodd (1884–1973), presumably 'they did not spend all the time talking about the weather' at this meeting[17] and the same should be assumed with regard to the meeting with James who, according to the Acts of the Apostles, took over the leadership of the congregation in Jerusalem after Cephas/Peter (Acts 15:13; 21:18; according to Gal. 2:9, Paul also meets James again when he visits Jerusalem eleven years later at the so-called apostolic council in 53 CE). Just as the 'brother of the Lord' was a historical figure, his brother was as well. And even if being the brother of Jesus had also meant a great deal for James' status in the congregation, it goes without saying that his knowledge of Jesus contributed to this status. This in spite of the tradition in the Gospels that Jesus was not respected by his family in his lifetime.[18]

The authority and power, which the resurrected and glorified exercises in the theological universe of Paul, corresponds to his obedience to the will of God, which is created by preaching and which is understood as participation in salvation. Obedience is also the turning point in the sequence which the hymn in Phil. 2:6–11 draws of the life of Jesus. In the beginning he renounces his divinity; that is, he abandons his so-called pre-existence that he might be a human. Moreover, the only thing we come to know of his human life is that he was obedient, even as it meant death on a cross. This obedience, then, is rewarded with an exaltation which results in the bowing of every knee in heaven and on earth and under the earth and the confession of every tongue 'that Jesus Christ is Lord, to the glory of God the Father'. In this context, the mythical portrayal follows as the justification of an ethical admonition to the Philippians: 'Let each of you look not only to his own interests, but also to the interests of others. Have this mind among yourselves, which you have in Christ Jesus' (Phil. 2:4–5). And the conclusion is that the Philippians shall show the same obedience 'and work out your own salvation with fear and trembling; for God is at work in you, both to

---

17. *The Apostolic Preaching and Its Developments* (London: Hodder & Stoughton Ltd, 1936), 26.
18. See Mk 3:21, 31–35; Jn 7:5; cf. Mt. 12:46–50; Lk. 8:19–21; the names of the brothers are mentioned in Mk 6:3; Mt. 13:55–56; we see a certain retouching of the disbelieving brothers in Mt. 12:45–50, and, in Luke, there is no parallel to this pericope (cf. Lk. 4:22), and later on, in Acts 1:14, the brothers, without further ado, figure as part of the congregation.

will and to work for his good pleasure' (Phil. 2:12–13). Also, in 2 Cor. 8:9 Jesus Christ is included as an example, this time for the Corinthians. They are admonished to offer an abundant gift of money to the collection for Jerusalem, and that because 'you know the grace of our Lord Jesus Christ, that though he was rich, yet for your sake he became poor, so that by his poverty you might become rich.'

The few times Paul adduces words of Jesus—in his terminology they are 'words of the Lord'—it is always in the context of admonition. Just so, in 1 Cor. 7:10, Paul quotes the Lord prohibiting divorce for married women, and later, in the same epistle, he mentions another commandment of the Lord (1 Cor. 14:37), although it is not quite clear to what is referred. As we have seen, only once in his letters does Paul relate an event from the life of Jesus; namely, the institution of the Eucharist on the night he was delivered (1 Cor. 1:23–25), and characteristically this reference is made in connection with an admonition to the Corinthians to regard each other when coming together for the Eucharist.

Accordingly, when Paul relates what is basic for Christian life, it is new conduct in life which is emphasized as important, as in Gal. 5:6: 'For in Christ Jesus neither circumcision nor uncircumcision is of any avail, but faith working through love.' And later in the same letter (Gal. 6:15) we find a similar formula: 'For neither circumcision counts for anything, nor uncircumcision, but a new creation.' Lastly a third saying in the same vein occurs in 1 Cor. 7:19: 'For neither circumcision counts for anything nor uncircumcision, but keeping the commandments of the Lord.' The interpretation of the law, which according to Paul is included in faith in Christ, thus concentrates on the commandments with regard to one's relation to one's fellow man, while the whole legislation concerning ritual things and what makes a Jew a Jew is abandoned as not constituent for one's relation to God. Thus, in Rom. 13:8–10, Paul is able to conclude his admonition in the following way:

> Owe no one anything, except to love one another; for he who loves his neighbour has fulfilled the law. The commandments: 'You shall not commit adultery, You shall not kill, You shall not steal, You shall not covet', and any other commandment, are summed up in this sentence, 'You shall love your neighbour as yourself.' Love does no wrong to a neighbour; therefore love is the fulfilling of the law [πλήρωμα οὖν νόμου ἡ ἀγάπη].

However, it is not merely a new ethic Paul is preaching. His preaching always consists of quotations from the laws of Moses, namely the ten commandments and the commandment to love one's neighbour as oneself. When, for instance, in Gal. 6:15, a new creation is mentioned, it is with regard to the recreation of the mind and will which happens in meeting the gospel. It concerns the indicative behind the imperative. The proclamation of God's love to humanity aims at creating a new obedience, the reason for which is no longer fear of punishment or the attempt to make oneself in God's eyes deserving of salvation. But belief in God's love, so to speak, brings about the obedience which becomes apparent in love for one's fellow man.

If one looks for a complex of concepts which connects gift and duty, it is to be found in connection with the concept which (not without reason) supports the name of the special Christian part of the Bible, the 'New Covenant' or 'New Testament'. The letters of Paul also contain the oldest indications of the fact that the earliest Christian communities regarded themselves as fulfilling the prophecy in the Book of Jeremiah (31:31–34), bearing the concept, namely, that, in the future, God will make a *new* covenant with his people:

> 'Behold, the days are coming', says the Lord, 'when I will make a new covenant with the house of Israel and the house of Judah, not like the covenant which I made with their fathers when I took them by the hand to bring them out of the land of Egypt, my covenant which they broke, though I was their husband', says the Lord. 'But this is the covenant which I will make with the house of Israel after those days', says the Lord: 'I will put my law within them, and I will write it upon their hearts; and I will be their God, and they shall be my people. And no longer shall each man teach his neighbour and each his brother, saying, "Know the Lord", for they shall all know me, from the least of them to the greatest', says the Lord; 'for I will forgive their iniquity, and I will remember their sins no more.'

In the Book of Ezekiel, 36:26–27 (cf. 11:19–20), the concept of a new covenant—although not explicitly called a 'new covenant'—is expanded with such features as a new heart and a new spirit, which God will offer his people: 'A new heart I will give to you, and a new spirit I will put within you; and I will take out of your flesh the heart of stone and give you a heart of flesh. And I will put my spirit within you, and cause you to walk in my statutes and be careful to observe my ordinances.' This covenant theology is obviously the presupposition of Paul's entire understanding of the new life.[19] In 2 Corinthians 3 it becomes explicit. In this chapter, Paul speaks of his letter to the Corinthians as a letter from Christ, delivered by the apostle,

---

19. While the concept of the new covenant earlier did not play any substantial role in the understanding of New Testament theology, the picture has changed in the last decades. Pioneering was L. Hartman in the article 'Bundesideologie in und hinter einigen paulinischen Texten,' in S. Pedersen, ed., *Die paulinische Literatur und Theologie. The Pauline Literature and Theology* (Teologiske Studier, 7; Århus: Aros/Göttingen: Vandenhoeck & Ruprecht, 1980), 103–18. Cf. also M. Müller, 'The Hidden Context: Some Observations to the Concept of the New Covenant in the New Testament,' in Tord Fornberg and David Hellholm, eds., *Texts and Contexts: Biblical Texts in Their Textual and Situational Contexts: Essays in Honor of Lars Hartman* (Oslo: Scandinavian University Press, 1995), 649–58.

'written not with ink but with the Spirit of the living God, not on tablets of stone but on tablets of human hearts' (2 Cor. 3:3). Clear enough it is the imagery around the institution of a new covenant, not least from the Book of Ezekiel, which here shows its influence. When Paul is not quoting Jer. 31:31 explicitly, he is only speaking of the new covenant here and in 1 Cor. 11:25, in connection with the institution of the Eucharist, because the aspect with the Spirit is fundamental in his employment of the concept. Thus, Paul, in what follows, speaks of himself—in *pluralis maiestatis*—as the one whose 'sufficiency is from God, who has qualified us to be ministers of a new covenant, not in a written code but in the Spirit; for the written code kills, but the Spirit gives life' (2 Cor. 3:5–6). I think that his self-designation as a 'minister of a new covenant [ὁ διάκονος καινῆς διαθήκης]' stands at the very heart of Paul's self-understanding.

Later in the same letter, in connection with his speaking about the contrast of having one's pride in one's position and not in the heart, and of no longer living for oneself but for him who died and was raised for us, Paul can say, 'From now on, therefore, we regard no one from a human point of view; even if we once regarded Christ from a human point of view, we regard him thus no longer. Therefore, if anyone is in Christ, he is a new creation; the old has passed away, behold, the new has come' (2 Cor. 5:16–17). Just as, for example, in Rom. 1:3 and 9:5, we translate 'from a human point of view', whereas the Greek is literally 'according to the flesh [κατὰ σάρκα]', which, at times, has been understood as if Paul did not know of the 'historical Jesus', but only a risen Christ.[20] If 'according to the flesh' is associated with 'Christ', this would be the correct understanding, but today, most interpreters agree that it is to be connected with the verb. Thus the meaning is that it is not enough to know Christ only on human premises because it is crucial that this knowledge becomes an occasion for faith; thus: 'If one is in Christ, he is a new creation' (cf. Gal. 6:15).[21]

Admission into the new covenant took place in baptism, the origin of which is difficult to map, but which nonetheless happens as a matter of course in the letters of Paul (cf. 1 Cor. 1:13–17, the 'baptism theology' in Rom. 6, and Col. 2:11–15, where baptism is said to replace circumcision, being itself a circumcision made without hands). In baptism the baptized partake in the Spirit which makes the new life possible and unfolds it. Proclamation and Spirit are bound together by unbreakable ties (cf. 1 Cor. 2:4–5) and 1 Corinthians bears witness to the fact that the manifestation

20. Thus, for instance, Johannes Weiss, *Paulus und Jesus* (Berlin: Reuther & Reinhard, 1909), 23–32. I owe the reference to Holzbrecher, *Paulus*, 27.

21. A thorough discussion in J. Blank, *Paulus und Jesus*, ch. 6, 304–26: '"Was heisst: Christus nach dem Fleische nicht mehr kennen?" Kor 5,16 (5,10–21)'.

of the Spirit in congregational life could be hard to administer. Therefore, Paul more than once has to 'suppress' what sounds like a Corinthian slogan; namely, 'all things are lawful', adding: 'but not all things are helpful', on one occasion, claiming that nothing should enslave anyone (1 Cor. 6:12) and on another occasion that 'not everything builds up' (1 Cor. 10:23). For Paul, to be a Christian is obviously to live in the manifestations of the Spirit, living a life in accordance with the will of God, concerning how everyone is to behave towards their fellow man.

If we only had the genuine letters of Paul, we would not know much about the earthly, not to say the 'historical', Jesus. We would know that, the night he was delivered, he held a Passover meal with his disciples, during which he instituted the Eucharist, that he died on a cross and was buried, but was believed to have risen from the dead. We would also know that he gave commandments (in spite of the evidence being very slender).

Thus, it is possible to deduce that Paul did know of the existence of the man Jesus and it is reasonable to deduce that, in his preaching and teaching, he told his congregations more than a little about what this Jesus, the Lord, had said and done. However, the letter genre was not appropriate for such descriptions, which are, rather, presupposed. What these letters contain is above all else the theological consequences which Paul drew from this human life and its fate as an expression of the salvific will of God. With regard to the expectation of finding traces of references to the historical person of Jesus in the letters of Paul, one could perhaps take a hint from the First Epistle of Peter. Here the pseudonymous author, in spite of hiding behind a figure, suggesting not only an eyewitness, but also one who had been very close to the Jesus of history, does not in any single case take advantage of such pretended first-hand knowledge to quote directly any particular saying of Jesus or refer to any personal experience from their time together. Such an allusion occurs only in the even later Second Epistle of Peter, with its reference to the transfiguration scene (2 Pet. 1:17–18). Thus, one might conclude that the letter genre hardly invites such allusions.

On the other hand, the author of the Acts of the Apostles finds it natural to reiterate important stations in the life of Jesus in Paul's missionary preaching in the synagogue of Pisidian Antioch (Acts 13:23–31). This is done in a manner that is similar to the speech of Peter in the house of Cornelius (Acts 10:36–43). In both cases, the setting is bound up with the proof from Scripture, which is characteristic of Lukan writings. Earlier, for example, C. H. Dodd thought that the speeches in Acts were representative of the original 'kerygma'.[22] But today we might consider that these speeches are rather more 'Luke' than Peter and Paul.

22. See *Apostolic Preaching*, ch. 1, 'The Primitive Preaching'.

The inclusion of the prophetic concept of the institution of a new covenant seems fundamental, as this concept frames the understanding as a whole. At the same time, it is possible to conclude, indirectly, that the special preaching of the law that originated with Jesus, especially if not solely implying the ethical part of the Law of Moses, was still in force, while the ceremonial part (regulations about purity, offerings, Sabbath and, not least, circumcision) was no longer seen as binding. This is a natural consequence of writing the commandments on the tablets of human hearts with the result that they are fulfilled. It is in this way that the commandment of love is made the greater. In the letters of Paul, Jesus Christ appears not only as the bringer of the commandment of love, together with all that it implies. He also—and foremost—makes the fulfilment of that commandment possible. That is what Paul means by 'a new creation' (besides 2 Cor. 5:17, also Gal. 6:15) and that is what he expresses in his saying about faith working through love (Gal. 5:6).

Already in Paul's letters, this historical figure is put within a mythic frame in his description as the Son of God, who became man, died and was raised from the dead to be exalted to the right hand of God, wherefrom he will return to erect God's kingdom once all his enemies have been annihilated (1 Cor. 15:20–28 and Phil. 2:9–11). It is also incorporated in a theological interpretation which explains the impact of this course of events for the realization of salvation in the life of men. Accordingly, Christ—the Greek form of the Hebrew *hammashiah*, the Anointed; that is, the one with God's spirit and power—has become a proper name. There absolutely is a point in insisting on Paul's confession being rendered 'Lord is Jesus', not 'Jesus is Lord' (Rom. 10:9; 1 Cor. 12:3; Phil. 2:11; in 2 Cor. 4:5, just as in Col. 2:6, 'Lord' stands in apposition), even if the last mentioned order is the traditional.[23] It is what Christ is for faith which defines him as Lord, not any already existing concept of what 'Lord' implies that has been transferred to Jesus. He is not revealing that he is other than he appears. It is specifically as he is seen and experienced that he is Lord. Paul brings this out by claiming that it is the crucified he has preached (1 Cor. 1:23; 2:2, but the thought is found throughout Paul's letters).

What we meet in the letters of Paul is Jesus Christ as faith sees and experiences him. And if we look for a *tertium comparationis* between a

23. M. Karrer, in *Der Gesalbte. Die Grundlagen des Christustitels* (FRLANT, 151; Göttingen: Vandenhoeck & Ruprecht, 1991), 369–70, makes the observation that the saying Χριστὸς ἀπέθανεν should be understood as 'he was anointed, who died', the subject in an emphatic way being placed before the verb (cf. F. Blass, A. Debrunner and F. Rehkopf, *Grammatik des neutestamentlichen Griechisch* [Göttingen: Vandenhoeck & Ruprecht; 17th edn, 1990], § 472.2).

historical figure and the preaching of the apostle, it could be the new life of the believers. It thus makes absolute sense to understand the Jesus of history as a prophetic figure, preaching a new understanding of what it means to fulfil the will of God. Of course it should not be excluded that this person was also a charismatic figure and that he perhaps thought of himself in a special way as anointed with the spirit of God. However, we only have access to him through the reception; that is, through the experience of him as that has been expressed in confessional utterances. In any case, the perception of the Jesus-figure in New Testament writings is not an expression of a direct taking over of the historical person's eventual self-understanding. It renders an experience in the form of a confession. This confession will always be shaped according to what was believed to have been the actions of Jesus as Christ.

It is, therefore, worth-while to think about Paul, not as one who, in an unnecessary way, complicated what in Jesus had been straightforward, but rather as the first theologian, known to us, who put the Jesus of history within an interpretative frame, which made it possible, also after his death, to maintain his importance for the salvation of humanity. Perhaps, then, there is good reason to memorize the famous saying of the Catholic modernist Alfred Loisy (1857–1940), 'Jesus preached the Kingdom of God, and it is the Church which has come.' This was not—as it is often taken[24]—ironically meant in the mind of Loisy. To him the coming of the church was the necessary means to maintain what Jesus had brought about.

Christological thinking also serves this goal. Interestingly, it has been possible to observe in the last decades a shift in the understanding of Paul's letters. Earlier interpreters saw their importance primarily in their 'dogmatic' parts, while they saw the paraenetic chapters mainly as routine. Today the tendency is to admit that this interpretation confused what especially interested a modern theologian with what was most important in the mind of the author. For example, the main thrust of the Letter to the Romans had earlier been seen in the dogmatic exposition in chs 1–8, while the discussion of the fate of Israel in chs 9–11 was perceived as a more or less irrelevant excursus, while the admonitions in chs 12–15 was judged as traditional material of no special importance to Paul. Today, however, the prevailing point of view is that the paraenesis in really the main goal, the

---

24. A. Loisy, *L'Évanglige et l'Église* (Paris: Chez l'auteur, 1902; 4th edn, 1908), 153: 'Jésus annonçait le royaume, et c'est l'Église quie est venue. Elle est venue en élargissant la forme de l'Évanglie, qui était impossible à garder telle quell, dés que ministère de Jésus eut été clos par la passion.' Surprisingly, this misunderstanding is also found in Joseph Ratzinger/ Benedikt XVI, *Jesus of Nazareth: From the Baptism in the Jordan to the Transfiguration* (trans. by A. J. Walker; London: Bloomsbury, 2007).

dogmatic exposition in the previous chapters being but the unfolding of theological presuppositions. The ethical teaching has not a philosophical justification but a theological one.

If we take the intended new life as *tertium comparationis*, we accordingly find behind the letters of Paul—though in an indirect way—the Jesus of history, not as a mythic figure but as a charismatic interpreter of the will of God. And this is just as the authors behind the Synoptic Gospels are casting their Christ as an earthly figure. There is, therefore, no necessary reason to see an unreasonable discrepancy between Paul and the later Gospel authors with regard to their view about Jesus as the Christ. They represent two different parts of the foundation message of the new belief: theological reflection and a narration of the earthly fate of Jesus as seen through the eyes of faith. And just as Paul must be presumed to be a historical person, who lived and worked in the forties and fifties of the first century, so the Jesus of the apostle's preaching and teaching is likewise to be taken as a historical figure, having been crucified under the reign of Tiberius in the beginning of the thirties. Thus, my conclusion is that if Paul is assumed to have been a historical person, the same must be assumed with regard to Jesus of Nazareth.[25]

25. For valuable and indispensable help in improving my English I want to thank Revd Jim West, ThD, and Thomas L. Thompson most heartily.

- 8 -

Born under the Law: Intertextuality and the Question of the Historicity of the Figure of Jesus in Paul's Epistles

Thomas S. Verenna

Preliminary Remarks

> Who then is Paul's Jesus? Paul identifies him only briefly in ways that, decades later, dominated the gospel narratives: as a human being...though from 'heaven'...a man born of woman, under the Law, that is, a Jew...a descendant of King David...and thus the Messiah.
>
> —Paula Fredriksen[1]

Paula Fredriksen sees Paul's Jesus as a heavenly being sent down to earth to take human form. This makes Paul a witness to an earthly Jesus through those who knew him even if, Fredriksen admits, he does not much dwell on Jesus' earthly life. However, it is clear that by her list above, Fredriksen mentions 'only briefly' of a historical figure. Because Paul says his Jesus was 'born under the law', he must have been a Jew, as the law is understood as the Jewish Scriptures. Paul states that Jesus was 'born of a woman' and thus he had to have been human with a human mother that gave birth to him.[2] He was a descendant, according to Fredriksen's reading of Paul, of David, and therefore claimed (or perhaps others portrayed Jesus as one claiming)

1. P. Fredriksen, *From Jesus to Christ* (New Haven/London: Yale University Press, 2000, 2nd edn), 55.
2. B. Witherington III, *Grace in Galatia: A Commentary on Paul's Letter to the Galatians* (Grand Rapids: Eerdmans, 1998), 288–89; J. L. Martyn, *Galatians* (AYBC, 33A; New York: Bantam Doubleday, 1997), 309–10, 327; B. R. Gaventa, 'Galatians,' in *Eerdman's Commentary on the Bible* (Grand Rapids: Eerdmans, 2003), 1380–81; R. N. Longenecker, *Galatians* (World Biblical Commentary, 41; Dallas: Word Books, 1990), 170–71.

to be the Messiah.[3] Fredriksen reads that Jesus came in 'the likeness of sinful flesh', that he was a man, a descriptive which expressed a historical, human Jesus. Many scholars accept that Paul's image of Jesus was a historical human being that Paul elaborates upon, and with only a few exceptions many also agree that Paul does not seem to busy himself with historical information. Paul's ignorance of Jesus' human qualities and his human crucifiers is because, per Fredriksen, Paul's focus was on the resurrected Jesus, the 'divine preexistent son of God'.[4] To put it simply, the assumption Fredriksen, specifically, and many historical Jesus scholars, generally, makes is that Paul just did not care about the *historical* Jesus, and this is why Jesus' historical past does not come up in Paul's letters.

This essay will argue something different; that Paul[5] did not believe his Jesus was ever historical in the first place.[6] It will also attempt to show that a critical examination of Paul's epistles lead to the conclusion that Paul's Jesus was taken from the Jewish Scriptures. By using a method formed from analysing intertextuality, I will show that the models used by Paul to form his figure of Jesus are none other than the books which now make up the Hebrew Bible. As a consequence, this article means to suggest that the current, historically dogmatic, exegetical interpretations of Paul's figure of Jesus are not only inadequate but that they take for granted what Paul is attempting to say and what his readers might have understood. The reason

---

3. B. Byrne and D. J. Harrington, *Romans* (SP, 6; Collegeville: Liturgical Press, 2007), 38–40; J. A. Fitzmyer, *Romans* (AYBC, 33; New York: Bantam Doubleday, 1999), 111–13, 229–30, 234; B. Witherington III and D. Hyatt, *Paul's Letter to the Romans: A Socio-Rhetorical Commentary* (Grand Rapids: Eerdmans, 2004), 34; J. Reumann, 'Romans,' in *Eerdman's Commentary on the Bible*, 1283.
4. *From Jesus to Christ*, 56.
5. For the purpose of this discussion, Paul's historicity will be accepted on a tentative basis; at present, Paul's historicity, like Jesus' historicity, should be examined critically before anyone either accepts or denies it—it should not be taken as a fact until investigated properly, which this study cannot do in the space allowed. While remaining conscious of this, perhaps revisionist interpretation of Paul's place in history and tradition—for the sake of consistency alone—when this treatment refers to 'Paul', it will not refer to a historical individual for which there is substantial evidence, but will instead refer to the traditional individual presumed to have written the letters.
6. By 'historical', I here refer to an actual, physical entity that existed within a chronological framework; i.e., Paul does not see his Jesus as a Jesus which walked through Galilee or overturned tables in Jerusalem, nor does he see his Jesus as one crucified by historical, earthly figures. In fact, as will be shown below, I argue that Paul believes in something quite to the contrary. For the sake of clarity, I must stress that I am not arguing against the historicity of the figure of Jesus in this paper since that could only be done after analysing other subjects, such as the emulative quality of the Gospel narratives, the Pseudepigrapha, and literacy in antiquity for example. I am only arguing that any attempt to build a case for the historicity of the figure of Jesus using Paul will ultimately be unsuccessful.

that it is so difficult for scholars to locate the historical Jesus is not, as Bultmann suggests, because Paul is using a 'traditional formulation' from the early church wrapped in a kerygmatic message that 'Jesus' Messiahship was dated from the resurrection'.[7] Instead, it is evinced herein that Paul is drawing from an already established Jewish tradition; a tradition of rewriting.[8] What Paul is interpreting, what he is expressing, is not an earthly figure, but an allegorical one. Paul's place in the question of the historicity of the figure of Jesus is a large one; for he is considered by many to be the earliest witness to the historical Jesus.[9] His letters, the authentic ones, have long been assumed to be the earliest written accounts of Christian origins in the New Testament,[10] but Paul did not convert to Christianity, as Bultmann supposed. 'Christian' is rather a second century CE designation.[11] According

7. R. Bultmann, *Theology of the New Testament* (trans. K. Grobel; New York: Prentice Hall College Div., 1970), 27.
8. For a detailed investigation of this tradition, see: T. L. Thompson, *The Bible in History: How Writers Create a Past* (London: Jonathan Cape, 1999); idem, *The Messiah Myth: The Ancient Near Eastern Roots of Jesus and David* (New York: Basic Books, 2005); T. L. Brodie, *The Birthing of the New Testament: The Intertextual Development of the New Testament Writings* (NTM, 1; Sheffield: Sheffield Phoenix Press, 2006); J. Van Seters, *In Search of History: Historiography in the Ancient World and the Origins of Biblical History* (New Haven: Yale University Press, 1983); E. S. Gruen, *Heritage and Hellenism: The Reinvention of Jewish Tradition* (Berkley/Los Angeles: University of California Press, 1998).
9. So M. Müller in this collection.
10. Not the least of which is the assumption that all the authentic letters are, themselves, whole and unified. There is the question, raised by the Dutch Radicals, of whether or not the letters should be looked at as singular entities—that is, whether Paul wrote the whole letter to the Romans at one time—or as several letters, written over a period of time, perhaps by different individuals, which were later combined into one; this also raises implicative questions towards authenticity.
11. To echo the words of J. D. G. Dunn, in his *The New Perspective on Paul* (Grand Rapids: Eerdmans, 2007), 347, '*from* what did Paul convert and *to* what did Paul convert?' The descriptor 'Christian' is known only from second-century sources, including Luke–Acts, which exists, in its current form, from the second century (cf. n. 20 below) and from the accounts of Tacitus and Suetonius, both writing in the second century as well. In both instances, of Tacitus' account and of Suetonius' account, they appear to be drawing from the tradition of their period—on the kerygmatic traditions which have stemmed from Christian interpretations of the Gospels' rendering of events and Christian proselytizing—not from any documented history, which seems to be common among both Tacitus and Suetonius. R. Carrier, in his, *Not the Impossible Faith: Why Christianity Didn't Need a Miracle to Succeed* (Raleigh: Lulu Press, 2009), 329–68, argues persuasively that it was normal for ancient historians to ignore their fact-checking responsibilities, often trusting hearsay or less authoritative sources over other means. A quick example would be Tacitus' discussion of the Jewish exodus from Egypt in his *Historiae* 5.2–5; ignoring the rumour he cites regarding Crete as the possible origin of the Jews, there is zero evidence for the exodus, so where did he draw his history of it from? This is a common retelling of a rumour, which is shared by Pompeius Trogus (recounted by M. Junianus Justinus, *Epitoma Historiarum Philippicarum* 36.2.11–13), Lysimachus (preserved by Josephus,

to tradition, Paul converted to a sect of Judaism where he drew on his knowledge of the Scriptures as a former Pharisee to educate and explain the coming of what he understood to be the suffering servant and redeemer.[12]

This, then, raises the question as to whether or not such a discussion about Paul's Jesus is useful. Paul could, after all, be interpreting Scripture to explain a historical event, as John Dominic Crossan believes.[13] But this seems to be a suggestion based on a continuing trend of assumptions rather than one founded on an unbiased investigation of the state of the evidence. Recent and more engaging studies have led to conclusions which suggest that ancient literary traditions have a large part to play in Paul's interpretation of Scripture; perhaps more of a part than those previously associated with Pauline theology.[14] It has already been established among many that the Homeric epics had a significant influence on the literary developments

---

C. Ap. 1.304–11), Diodorus Siculus (preserved by Photius, *Bibliotheca*, Diod. Sic. 34.1), and Apion (recounted by Josephus, *C. Ap.* 2.2–3, cf. 2.2.10–12; 2.2.15–16), that the Jews were kicked out of Egypt due to some disease, generally considered to be leprosy; rumour and gossip, slanderous at that, but not factual by any stretch of the imagination. He even recounts their hatred towards other people, much in the same manner that Diodorus does (ibid.). That Paul never refers to himself or his brethren as 'Christian' adds weight to the probability that the term was just not in use, or at least common use, in the first century.

12. Even if Paul was never a Pharisee, he was well educated at the very least. See the very interesting survey of S. E. Porter, 'Paul and His Bible: His Education and Access to the Scriptures of Israel,' in S. E. Porter and C. D. Stanley, eds., *As it is Written: Studying Paul's Use of Scripture* (SBLSymS, 50; Atlanta: Scholars Press, 2008), 97-124. Though Porter draws heavily on Acts which is peculiar; whatever academic viewpoint still holds that Luke knew Paul and was his follower is quite problematic (cf. n. 20 for sources, specifically Tyson and Pervo). Regardless, Porter's conclusions are rather sound even with his dependence upon Acts, as Paul's use of rhetoric and allegory prove beyond a doubt his educational background in both Greco-Roman materials and his familiarity with the Torah and other Jewish literature.
13. J. D. Crossan, *Jesus: A Revolutionary Biography* (San Francisco: HarperCollins, 1995), 145. So too D. Juel, *Messianic Exegesis: Christological Interpretation of the Old Testament in Early Christianity* (Philadelphia: Fortress Press, 1988).
14. Specifically R. B. Hays, *Echoes of Scripture in the Letters of Paul* (New Haven and London: Yale University Press, 1989), though it is a little dated, and his recent collection *The Conversion of the Imagination: Paul as Interpreter of Israel's Scripture* (Grand Rapids: Eerdmans, 2005). More recently the general overview of modern approaches to intertextuality in the Epistles has been covered by S. Moyise, *Paul and Scripture: Studying the New Testament Use of the Old Testament* (Grand Rapids: Baker Academic, 2010), 111-122. For an evaluation of the terminology and methods used in studies of intertextuality in the Pauline Epistles, consult S. E. Porter, 'Allusions and Echoes,' in S. E. Porter and C. E. Stanley, eds., *As it is Written: Studying Paul's Use of Scripture* (SBLSymS, 50; Atlanta: Scholars Press, 2008) and J. R. Wagner, *Heralds of the Good News: Isaiah and Paul 'In Concert' in the Letter to the Romans* (NovTSup, 101; Leiden: Brill, 2002), 5-13.

of the Gospels,[15] particularly Mark; Luke, it has been argued, uses rhetorical language to persuade his reader[16]—this would mean that both Luke and Mark, at least, had other intentions behind writing the Gospels that had little, if anything, to do with 'telling what happened'. What those intentions were might best reflect the ancient tradition associated with *imitatio* and *aemulatio* (or more appropriately, their Greek counterparts: μίμησις and ζήλωσις and their cognates).[17] More on this further on.

Brief Overview of Methods

That Paul knew of a historical Jesus is taken as a consensus, even though many debate what he might have known, what references he makes in his letters to a historical Jesus, and what can be said about them. Consensus, however, is not an argument in itself. To make this matter more complicated, the discussion which will follow is not something that is inscribed on stelae. Philip Davies reminds his own readers that 'neither "Bible" nor "history" are fixed, objective phenomena, but are constructed by humans within the course of human events, and vary from time to time, place to place, and community to community'.[18] In moving forward, the reader is cautioned to keep in mind the ever-changing trends in scholarship; a consensus means nothing when it comes to method, and what may prove to be historically probable in one decade may shift and become improbable in the next (and, sometimes, the opposite is true).

Indeed, this treatment's goal is to offer an alternative to that consensus. In a sense I am treating this as a retrieval, that is, an attempt to look past modern interpretations of Paul, which are far too focused on discovering what he has to say about an assumed historical entity—Jesus—and less about discovering how Paul's initial audience would have understood his meaning. I take this approach because I believe that our foci as interpreters

15. D. R. MacDonald, *The Homeric Epics and the Gospel of Mark* (New Haven: Yale University Press, 2005); idem, *Does the New Testament Imitate Homer? Four Cases from the Acts of the Apostles* (New Haven: Yale University Press, 2003).
16. G. A. Phillips, '"What is Written? How are You Reading?" Gospel, Intertextuality and Doing Lukewise: Reading Lk 10:25–42 Otherwise,' in G. Aichele and G. A. Phillips, eds., *Intertextuality and the Bible* (Semeia, 69/70; Atlanta: Scholars Press, 1995), 113.
17. Quintilian, *Institutio oratoria* 10.2–3; Aristotle, *Poetica*; Longinus, *De sublimitate*; Demetrius, *De elocutione*; Dionysius of Halicarnassus, *De compositione verborum*; cf. Quintilian, *Inst.* 10.2.1–2: 'It is from these and other authors worthy of our study that we must draw our stock of words, the variety of our figures and our methods of composition, while we must form our minds on the model of every excellence. For there can be no doubt that in art no small portion of our task lies in imitation, since, although invention came first and is all-important, it is expedient to imitate whatever has been invented with success.'
18. *Memories of Ancient Israel: An Introduction to Biblical History—Ancient and Modern* (Louisville: Westminster John Knox Press, 2008), 15.

of Paul have been towards meeting different ends; where many modern studies start with a demand to interpret Paul through a Gospel lens, I believe that Paul stands apart from this and must be interpreted within his cultural *milieux*. Hence one does not start a study expecting Paul to be a Christian; rather one must start with the only actual thing we know about Paul with any certainty—Paul was literate and well educated and had a good grasp of the Jewish scriptures.

This means, ultimately, that Paul was trained in both the practice of μίμησις and ζήλωσις. This has certain implications that are scarcely examined in my predecessors' works.[19] This investigation will examine Paul's epistles within the socio-cultural framework so often ignored in many modern historical Jesus studies which, rather than focusing on what Paul has to say, are more concerned about locating what he does not, that is, the subject of the historical figure of Jesus. Paul is certainly no creature of terseness. His letters are full of esotericism which, when analysed in the context of ancient emulation, offer a glimpse at his meaning, a meaning that runs counter to trends which apply hermeneutics to Paul within a faux historical setting based upon the construct that Paul's ministry followed the accounts depicted in the Gospel narratives; a perspective that has not yet been countenanced among the verisimilitudes of the historical annals.[20]

---

19. With some exceptions, c.f. n. 14. In the context of the paragraphs above, this study wishes to remove the rather constraining and, perhaps, unhelpful perspective that Paul specifically (but also early Christians in general) utilized emulation and exegesis of the Old Testament in order to explain the embarrassing situation surrounding the crucifixion of the messiah (n. 13). Paul's exegesis might have been predicated upon an actual historical event (like the crucifixion), but not necessarily. That stories sometimes imitated realistic scenarios but, none the less, were invented wholly, seems to have been known and appreciated in the days of Aristotle (i.e. Aristotle, *Poetica* 1451b.19–20) and even during the times of the early church fathers (i.e. Origen, *Contra Celsum* 1.42). Some might argue that emulations were ignored, or that cuing the reader was not an actual practice in antiquity, but these sorts of criticisms are left wanting.
20. It appears, in fact, that it is the other way around; the Gospel authors used Paul's letters to create their narratives! See Tyson, *Marcion and Luke-Acts*, 18–19; H. Leppä, 'Luke's Critical Use of Galatians' (PhD thesis, University of Helsinki, 2002); W. O. Walker, Jr, 'Acts and the Pauline Corpus Reconsidered,' *JSNT* 7.24 (1985), 3–23; idem, 'Acts and the Pauline Corpus Revisited: Peter's Speech at the Jerusalem Conference,' in R. P. Thomas and T. E. Phillips, eds., *Literary Studies in Luke-Acts: Essays in Honor of Joseph B. Tyson* (Macon: Mercer University Press, 1998), 77–86; R. I. Pervo, *Dating Acts between the Evangelists and the Apologists* (Santa Rosa: Polebridge Press, 2006), 73–102; T. Penner, 'Civilizing Discourse: Acts, Declamation, and the Rhetoric of the *Polis*,' in Todd Penner and Caroline Vander Stichele, eds., *Contextualizing Acts: Lukan Narrative and Greco-Roman Discourse* (SBLSymS, 20; Atlanta: Scholars Press, 2003), 65–104; T. L. Brodie, 'Towards Tracing the Gospels' Literary Indebtedness to the Epistles,' in D. R. MacDonald, ed., *Mimesis and Intertextuality in Antiquity and Christianity* (Harrisburg: Trinity Press International, 2001), 104–16.

Emulation, in this study, means establishing intertextuality; this investigation will be combining several disciplines in order to make a strong case for intertextual references in Paul's epistles. For the sake of brevity, those interested readers who might not have the background in linguistics or literary theory are encouraged to explore the arguments and discussions from related studies for clarification.[21]

That *imitatio* was part of a students' education is well-established. And it is a well-accepted perspective that earlier literature was emulated wholly by authors in the Greco-Roman period. To quote Thomas Brodie, 'Virgil did not just *allude* to Homer; he swallowed him whole.'[22] Studies by Knight, Hinds, Thomas, Russell, Clausen, Farrell, Brodie, Thompson, Conte and Finkelpearl can attest to this, especially in Greek and Latin texts.[23] In Paul,

---

21. There will be no attempt to define separately the different terms associated with these sorts of studies, that is to say, 'allusion', 'echo', and so forth shall fall under the same category for this paper: intertextuality. For those unfamiliar, please consult the excellent overview by G. Allen, *Intertextuality* (London/New York: Routledge, 2000), and the recent critique of these methods along with a balanced overview by J. J. Collins, *The Bible after Babel: Historical Criticism in a Postmodern Age* (Grand Rapids: Eerdmans, 2005). See also (this list is not comprehensive): F. de Saussure, *Course in General Linguistics* (Chicago/La Salle: Open Court, 1986); V. N. Volosinov and M. Bakhtin, *Marxism and the Philosophy of Language* (Cambridge/London: Harvard University Press, 1986); J. Kristeva, 'The Bounded Text,' in idem, *Desire in Language: A Semiotic Approach to Literature and Art* (New York: Columbia University Press, 1980); idem, *Σημειωτιχῄ: Recherches pour une sémanalyse* (Paris: Éditions du Seuil, 1969); R. Barthes, *The Rustle of Language* (Berkley/Los Angeles: University of California Press, 1989), idem, 'The Death of the Author,' in idem, *Image, Music, Text* (New York: Hill and Wang, 1977); M. Foucault, 'What is an Author?,' in Josué V. Harari, ed., *Textual Strategies: Perspectives in Post-Structuralist Criticism* (Ithaca: Cornell University Press, 1979); M. Heidegger, *Poetry, Language, Thought* (New York, Perennial Classics, 2001); S. Burke, *The Death and Return of the Author: Criticism and subjectivity in Barthes, Foucault and Derrida* (Edinburgh: Edinburgh University Press, 1998); J. Pucci, *The Full-Knowing Reader: Allusion and the Power of the Reader in the Western Literary Tradition* (New Haven/London: Yale University Press, 1998); J. Clayton and E. Rothstein, eds., *Influence and Intertextuality in Literary History* (Madison/London: University of Wisconsin Press, 1991); D. Attridge, G. Bennington and R. Young, eds., *Poststructuralism and the Question of History* (Cambridge: Cambridge University Press, 1987).
22. *The Birthing of the New Testament*, 74.
23. In no particular order: S. Hinds, *Allusion and Intertext: Dynamics of Appropriation in Roman Poetry* (New York: Cambridge University Press 1998); E. Finkelpearl, *Metamorphosis of Language in Apuleius: A Study of Allusion in the Novel* (Ann Arbor: University of Michigan Press, 1998); V. Knight, *The Renewal of Epic: Responses to Homer in the Argonautica of Apollonius* (Leiden: Brill, 1995); R. F. Thomas, 'Catullus and the Polemics of Poetic Reference,' *The American Journal of Philology* 103.2 (Summer, 1982), 144–64; W. Clausen, 'Callimachus and Latin Poetry,' *Greek, Roman, and Byzantine Studies* 5 (1964), 181–96; J. Farrell, *Vergil's Georgics and the Traditions of Ancient Epic: The Art of Allusion in Literary History* (New York and Oxford: Oxford University Press, 1991); T. L. Brodie, *The Crucial Bridge: The Elijah-Elisha Narrative as an Interpretive Synthesis of Genesis-Kings and a Literary Model for the Gospels* (Collegeville: The Liturgical Press, 2000); idem, *The Birthing of the New Testament*; Gian

there should be no exception and, as Richard B. Hays notes, there is none to be found:[24] 'Despite the substantial theological differences between Paul and the Rabbis, then, their actual interpretive practices are less divergent than their hermeneutical theories might suggest. Both...presuppose the legitimacy of innovative readings which disclose truth previously latent in scripture.' With that said, Ellen Finkelpearl reminds us to utilize caution, as 'at times the author wishes allusions to be recognized, yet at other times he unconsciously evokes the language and motifs from the sources he has read'.[25]

Intertextuality, Μίμησις and Ζήλωσις in Paul's Epistles

In order to avoid the problems associated with this sort of investigation, like those discussed above, the reader should be reminded that the question, 'why has this story been written?' can never be answered with 'because it happened'. Some questions need to be asked as a result: (1) 'What is this literature if it is not history?' (2) 'Why is this story being told?' (3) 'What is the reader required to believe?' and (4) 'Why should it be believed?'[26] The first two questions deal with authorial intent. What did the author intend to write and how did he or she expect their readers to interpret it?[27] The second two deal with the reader's application of the data; or rather, how they perceived the literature. To answer these questions in Paul, this essay will take into account the rhetorical models and imitative practices associated with μίμησις and ζήλωσις; how did Paul utilize these in order to express ideas, cue his readers and educate his audience? What, if anything, can then be said about what he believed about his Jesus?

To that effect, one should keep in mind these questions when Paul's epistles are approached in this essay. Perhaps it would be good to start with Paul's thoughts on his own experiences. In Galatians 1, Paul's conversion, brought upon by the revelation of salvation from God, is a problem for many

---

Biagio Conte, *The Rhetoric of Imitation: Genre and Poetic Memory in Vergil and Other Poets* (Ithaca: Cornell University Press, 1986); D. A. Russell, 'De Imitatione,' in D. West and T. Woodman, eds., *Creative Imitation and Latin Literature* (Cambridge: Cambridge University Press, 1979), 1–16; and T. L. Thompson, *The Messiah Myth.*

24. *Echoes of Scripture in the Letters of Paul*, 4.
25. E. Finkelpearl, 'Pagan Traditions of Intertextuality in the Roman World,' in MacDonald, ed., *Mimesis and Intertextuality in Antiquity and Christianity*, 81.
26. P. R. Davies, *In Search of 'Ancient Israel'*, 13. Davies writes, 'stories do not neatly reproduce 'what happened', but the fact of something happening does not of itself provide an adequate reason for telling it.'
27. R. B. Hays, in *Echoes of Scripture in the Letters of Paul*, writes that 'the implied readers of these letters appear to be primarily Gentile Christians with an extensive knowledge of the LXX and an urgent interest in its interpretation' (29).

historical reconstructions.[28] Paul explains that, 'For neither did I receive it from man, nor was I taught it, but it came to me through revelation of Jesus Christ' (οὐδὲ γὰρ ἐγὼ παρὰ ἀνθρώπου παρέλαβον αὐτὸ οὔτε ἐδιδάχθην ἀλλὰ δι' ἀποκαλύψεως Ἰησοῦ Χριστου; Gal. 1:12).[29] Some historians have attempted to link this revelatory experience with accounts in Acts of Paul's conversion,[30] but the discrepancies between them, though probably a deliberate attempt by Luke to differentiate his Paul from the rather Gnostic Paul of Galatians, only really prove that the account in Acts is far from historical.[31]

There is an underlying thematic element at play with Paul's version of his conversion found in Galatians which echoes Abraham's covenant with God in Genesis 17:1–4, and with Moses, first with the burning bush in Exodus 3 and then again on Mount Sinai in Exodus 19. The relationship between these experiences, those of Abraham, Moses and Paul, reinforce Paul's message of faith throughout this epistle. While the motifs of these narratives pepper Paul's conversion story, they also do something else: they give us an understanding of Paul's theology, his source material and his Jesus. The problem, however, is that only recently have scholars started to give Paul a fresh, new look. While the fad of assuming that 'all we can know of Paul has already been said' is passing away with the emergence of new studies, moving forward has still been a difficult process. However, with this fresh exegetical examination, Paul's constant appeal to direct revelation, his desire to infuse Scripture into nearly every theological point he makes, should direct the reader to pause and reflect upon the relevance that this might have on any investigation where someone attempts to show that

---

28. P. Fredriksen is right to remark on this complication, that 'Paul...was very independent [from the followers of Jesus—Ed.]. The source of his Gospel...as distinct from theirs, was neither the earthly Jesus nor a human tradition passed from man to man, but the Risen Christ, who had been revealed to him through a special act of God' (*From Jesus to Christ*, 52).

29. All Biblical translations come from the NRSV unless otherwise specified.

30. It should be noted, even in a passing manner, that Acts contains three different versions of the conversion story (Acts 9, 22, and 26) and all three are varied to the point of contradiction.

31. I would argue that Paul's conversion in Acts 9 is an emulation of Heliodorus' conversion in 2 Maccabees 3. The *topoi* of the narratives are in the same order and reflect the same sort of conversion (i.e. divine intervention): (1) in both stories, a nonbeliever (non-Jew, non-Christian) are on their way to persecute the righteous (loot the Temple, persecute Christians); (2) the two non-believers are knocked down and their companions struck with dread; (3) both suffer at the hand of the lord; (4) and their recovery is only given to them by trusting faithful servants of the lord. This emulation is upheld by a number of scholars, though I find N. T. Wright's claim (*The Resurrection of the Son of God* [Minneapolis: Fortress Press, 2003], 188–93) that Luke believed this act to be a historical event—while Wright himself argues for the allusion—to be a little disingenuous.

Paul has something important to say about a historical Jesus. Is Fredriksen, quoted at the beginning of this essay, correct that Paul can grant us some historical information about this figure of Jesus? The next few sections will ask that question, examining each bit of Scripture where scholars like Fredriksen believe allusions to a historical figure of Jesus lie.

Pierced Hands and Feet: The Crucifixion

There is little doubt that the crucifixion is the starting point for any consensus-defying essay which deals with the historical value of Paul's epistles on the figure of Jesus. Even if one could show that Paul knew nothing else about the historical Jesus, the crucifixion must at least be the last shimmer of hope that Paul knew *something*. And there is little doubt; Paul knew of a crucifixion, though he never suggests it happened on earth. He speaks of Jesus as one crucified quite often, albeit only in passing. But these brief passages are formalistic in language, often in an awkward context that cannot make sense historically.

This raises the question: what is the value of crucifixion? What purpose could a death by impalement, followed by the humiliation that came with it, possibly serve Paul if this were not a historical event? This question has had an unfortunate impact on the interpretations of the subject by many historical Jesus scholars. For one thing, many believe, falsely, that Jews of the day were not expecting a crucified Messiah and, as a result, this story must have happened historically—who would invent a story if no one would understand the meaning?[32] But this perspective presumes a lot, and much of what it presumes goes against more recent endeavours to discover the socio-cultural background of the period. Consider that in order for this perspective to be correct, a reader of the Hebrew Bible should find no mention of a humiliated saviour figure, no prophecy at all concerning a righteous Messiah who is to suffer and die. In addition, we would expect to see some dogmatic or unified expectations of the Messiah in ancient Judaism. In order for these scholars to suggest that no Jews would have expected a crucified or humiliated Messiah, they would need to show that Judaism was dogmatic enough that this belief—the belief in a crucified and humiliated Messiah—would not have penetrated a single sect, regardless of how assimilated that sect might have been within its cultural *milieux*. One would expect that no other literature would allow for a resurrection or ascension either; at least there should not be any that would predate

32. This perspective is generally accepted. See the discussion in B. Ehrman, *Jesus: Apocalyptic Prophet of the New Millennium* (New York: Oxford University Press, 1999), 93; see also, R. Stark, *The Rise of Christianity: A Sociologist Reconsiders History* (Princeton: Princeton University Press, 1996), 44–45.

Christianity. The concept of the brutal and humiliating death of a god figure would have to be near entirely absent from any literature with which Paul or a Gospel author might have had contact.

When one looks at the evidence, however, this is not what one sees at all. Contrary to this virtual history, what one sees in antiquity is a segmented, fractured Judaism where local assimilation and acculturation influenced, by varying degrees, Jewish 'religious' belief.[33] Jewish perspectives on the Messiah were just as diverse, meaning that there had not been one or two dogmatic expectations about who would be the Messiah.[34] It is probable that some sects were not even expecting a Messiah at all.[35] Most important is the amount of Jewish scriptural references there are to a saviour figure or righteous individual who must undergo a humiliating and brutal

---

33. J. M. G. Barclay, *Jews in the Mediterranean Diaspora: From Alexander to Trajan (323 BCE–117 CE)* (Berkeley/Los Angeles/London: University of California Press, 1999], 8–9: 'Old notions of "orthodoxy" have been challenged, as well as the assumption that faithful Jews lived largely in social isolation. In fact new evidence, along with new assessment of the old, suggests that Jews were by no means universally despised or isolated, and the mixture of philo-Jewish and anti-Jewish attitudes in the Graeco-Roman world has had to be reassessed.' See also, E. Gruen, *Diaspora: Jews amidst Greeks and Romans* (Cambridge: Harvard University Press, 2002), 5–7.
34. J. H. Charlesworth, ed., *The Messiah: Developments in Earliest Judaism and Christianity* (Minneapolis: Fortress, 1992); see also the discussion in G. W. Bromiley, 'Messiah,' *International Standard Bible Encyclopedia: K–P* (Grand Rapids: Eerdmans, 1986), 333: 'This survey of the intertestamental period has shown that Judaism had never reached agreement on what to expect of the future, except that all believed that God would eventually vindicate His people. In turn, none of the eschatological or messianic views claimed exclusive authority; thus divergent views could easily coexist. Modern attempts to reduce this multiplicity to one system do violence to the evidence.' In addition, J. Neusner, *Messiah in Context: Israel's History and Destiny in Formative Judaism* (Philadelphia: Fortress Press, 1984), ix, and J. Neusner, W. S. Green and E. Frierichs, eds., *Judaisms and Their Messiahs at the Turn of the Christian Era* (Cambridge: Cambridge University Press, 1987), provide excellent discussions of this subject.
35. There is no discussion in any of the source material extant, the Qumran literature aside (I do not believe them to be the literary works of the Essenes), from Josephus to Pliny, that the Essenes were expecting a messianic figure. Even if the sect of the Essenes were just fictional Jewish ideologues, a fantasy Jewish sect which Josephus utilizes, a possibility which is not improbable, Josephus felt no need to include an ideology focused on the coming of a Messiah. Either it was not important enough to him to warrant a discussion or he recognized that some sects found that the subject was not important. Regardless of the particulars, the lack of a discussion leads to some interesting implications. Indeed, the lack of a Messiah in a great deal of Jewish literature was intriguing enough for W. S. Green, in 'Messiah in Judaism: Rethinking the Question,' in *Judaisms and Their Messiahs at the Turn of the Christian Era*, to make the following point: 'The term "messiah" has scant and inconsistent use in early Jewish texts. Most of the Dead Sea Scrolls and the Pseudepigrapha, and the entire Apocrypha, contain no reference to "the messiah."... a messiah is neither essential...nor a prominent feature of ancient apocalyptic writings.'

death.[36] What makes this situation more provocative is the realization that one finds when examining the conversations surrounding these scriptural passages from the Gospel authors and Paul. Not only do we find striking parallels between Psalm 22 and Isaiah 50–53 in Mark's passion account, he tells us explicitly that he is drawing from these passages at the very beginning of the Gospel (cf. Mk 1:2, 11).[37]

It is important for any reader of the Pauline epistles to recognize that it is never *just* the crucifixion alone that Paul discusses. Not even in the Gospels is the crucifixion a singular event, isolated from any other theological or epistemological function. Instead, both Paul and the Gospel authors, who had copies of the Pauline epistles, create a narrative linked forever with the death and resurrection, followed by the appearance of Jesus to certain individuals. There exists no narrative where Jesus simply dies; while some may suggest this is due to the belief held by early Christian followers that Jesus really did resurrect and did appear to his disciples, one should not be so quick to discount the value of intertextuality. This is not the first time a deity has been crucified, followed by their resurrection and ascension, with appearances to individuals shortly after.[38] In Sumerian mythology, there is a tale of Inanna's descent into the underworld, her crucifixion and death,

---

36. In the Hebrew Bible, the strongest verses are found in Ps. 22, Dan. 9:26 and Isa. 49:7, 50–53; see also, Wis. 2:12–22. Anyone familiar with the Passion narrative from Mk 15 and these selections from Jewish Scripture will surely recognize that one set influences the other to an incredible degree.
37. See T. L. Thompson's contribution in this volume. Mark is not the only Gospel author to do this explicitly; all the Gospel authors are explicit about their source material (e.g., Mt. 3:3; 4:14; 8:17; 13:14; 15:7; Jn 12:38–41; Lk. 4:17; Acts 8:27–29; 28:25).
38. I would like to briefly comment on this section to avoid confusion. What will undoubtedly come up in critiques of this section will be the differences between the accounts of the sources discussed above. To such a critic, I would state that, of these differences, I am much aware and would like to stress that in noting the similarities of these so-called parallels, I am merely expressing, in one vein or another, the cultural ties, long-standing as they were, which fed the journey of these motifs and other thematic elements. I am no fan of parallelism without sufficient data and I certainly would not like it if I were accused of trying to harangue correlation into the category of causation. However, the differences, while important, do not necessarily suggest ignorance on the part of the author. As has been demonstrated by scholars like D. R. MacDonald (*Homeric Epics*, 2) and literary critics like G. Genette (*Palimpsestes. La littérature au second degré* [Paris: Seuil, 1982]), a *hypotext* is specifically designed by its authors to subtly utilize another text or group of texts, altering specific things about the plot in a way that still emulates but does not copy verbatim. This process is better explained below, but despite what some scholars (specifically M. S. Smith's discussion in his *The Origins of Biblical Monotheism: Israel's Polytheistic Background and the Ugaritic Texts* [Oxford: Oxford University Press, 2001], 105–20) might suggest, differences between two texts do not automatically disqualify intertextuality, nor does it remove all chance of emulative characteristics to be found. To the contrary, in some instances it can enhance the argument for emulation and intertextuality.

her resurrection and ascension; after this ascension she appears to local deities.

> The pure Ereckigala seated herself upon her throne, The Anunnaki, the seven judges, pronounced judgment before her. They fastened her eyes upon her, the eyes of death. At their word, the word that tortures the spirit. The sick 'woman' was turned into a corpse. The corpse was hung from a stake. After three days and three nights had passed, her minister Nincubur...fills the heavens with complaints for her.... Before Enki he weeps: 'O Father Enki, let not thy daughter be put to death in the nether world'... Father Enki answers Ninshubur: 'What has happened to my daughter! I am troubled, what has happened to Inanna...! What has happened to the hierodule of heaven!... Surely Inanna will arise'.... Inanna arose. Inanna ascends from the nether world.[39]

It is well known that this story had already permeated Jewish society long before Christianity; Ezek. 8:14 states that women were mourning for Tammuz at the north gate. Tammuz was the one God who refused to bow down at first in front of Inanna after she had arisen and ascended. As a result, she banished him to the nether world.[40]

The purpose of this exercise is to bring to light the fact that a story about a crucified God who rose from the dead and ascended does predate the Passion narrative and Paul's crucified saviour. When scholars rely upon the probability of the historicity of the crucifixion because they cannot understand how a Jew in antiquity would worship a crucified Messiah,

---

39. 'Inanna's Descent to the Nether World,' trans. by S. N. Kramer (*ANET*, 52–57).
40. I should again reiterate that intertextuality and emulation studies are not the same as parallelism (cf. n. 38). I am in no way suggesting that it could be authoritatively proven that Paul or the Gospel authors had access to this narrative—even though they might have—and I am certainly not suggesting that the Passion narrative derives from Inanna. There are many differences between the two stories, as many as there are similarities. The hero who is wrongly accused, only to die and rise again has been a motif that penetrates many different myths from many cultures; whether or not any of these influenced the Passion account is hard to say and even more difficult to prove. None the less, that this event is recorded to have happened in the past, prior to Paul, means that scholars must start to acknowledge that the motif present in Paul, as well as the Gospels, comes before the first century CE and that, to some degree, the belief and worship of a crucified and humiliated deity would have been accepted by some percentage of the population during this time. As R. Carrier (*Not the Impossible Faith*, 37) points out, 'The Septuagint actually has the word *Christos* in [Daniel—Ed.] 9:25, with *Chrisma* in 9:26 (which refers to Christos by metonymy), and the original text has *Mashiyach* ("Messiah") in both passages. Thus, rather than expecting a Messiah to "rout the Romans", some Jews plainly expected a Messiah to be killed, even though innocent, and thus fail to rout Judea's conquerors.' Some might argue that Dan. 9 is a reference to the High Priest, but all one needs to do is read 11Q13 (Melch) 2:18-20; the author is interpreting Isaiah via Daniel 9, discussing its messianic component which suggests that at least some early Jewish groups saw it as a messianic reference.

they are really only showing how little they understand the socio-cultural landscape of the ancient world. This brings the discussion back to the earlier question: what good would the crucifixion serve Paul and his theology? Knowing now that the Messiah must undergo a humiliating, brutal and painful death was expected in some Jewish circles, and recognizing that such a motif had existed and been a part of Jewish culture prior to Christianity, it can be stated with some relative certainty that such a view would not have shocked or disgusted his audience the way some scholars believe it would. There is even a strong chance that his audience was aware of the theological and scriptural invocations of the crucifixion from the Psalms and the suffering and humiliated saviour figure from Isaiah. The answer seems to lie within the Scriptures Paul had interpreted, especially Psalm 22, in which the relevant bits should be quoted here at length:

> But I am a worm and not a man, scorned by humankind and despised by the people. All who see me mock me; they make mouths at me; they wag their heads; 'He trusts in the Lord; let him deliver him; let him rescue him, for he delights in him!'... For dogs encompass me; a company of evildoers encircles me; they have pierced my hands and feet—I can count all my bones—they stare and gloat over me; they divide my garments among them, and for my clothing they cast lots. (Ps. 22:6–8, 16–18)

Mark, whose Gospel is much indebted to Paul's epistles, had certainly understood Paul's dramatic use of Scripture to express the crucifixion.[41] Jesus is Paul's atonement sacrifice, without which Paul's message of salvation would be useless; 'For Christ, our Passover, has been sacrificed' (1 Cor. 5:7).[42]

Some scholars seem to be reading Paul through Gospel-coloured glasses, so it may be difficult for some to separate the creative nuances of Paul's account of his Jesus' death; Paul's crucifixion account did not come from a historical event, but from the Hebrew Bible, like the passage in Psalms above. So much had Mark understood this, he fabricated an *entire narrative*

41. T. L. Brodie's massive tome, *The Birthing of the New Testament*, contains a long but thorough discussion, especially for an appendix, on the subject of Paul's indebtedness to Jewish Scripture, 585–606. He writes, 'the New Testament epistles show significant dependence on the Old Testament. It is not simply a question...of using the Old Testament as some form of adjunct—for instance, to buttress, to explain, to demonstrate, or to indicate continuity. Rather, the Old Testament text is at the heart of the Pauline epistle; it is constitutive' (587).

42. Jesus was for Paul both the Passover and the atonement sacrifice. The latter atonement motif from Lev. 16, Yom Kippur, and the former, securing salvation via escape from the angel of death are combined by Paul, possibly a tradition which stems back to the original Christian movement—whoever they were. The atonement sacrifice motif is also found in Ps. 22.

based on this very Psalm, combined with Paul's understanding of the Messiah (which, incidentally, had also been based partly upon this Psalm). Mark had taken Paul's spiritually impaled saviour figure and placed him in a historical context. The following subsections, then, will examine Paul's discussions of the crucifixion based upon this argument; that Paul's Jesus suffered a spiritual death and resurrection and that Paul is clear about this in his letters.

Crucified by the Archons. It seems as though Paul discusses the crucifixion in two ways. The first manner that Paul discusses the crucifixion is the type most commonly used to justify Paul's knowledge of a historical event. The second way Paul discusses the crucifixion might best be explained as a representation of spiritual renewal or rebirth, not as an account of the past. Galatians actually contains both forms of expression about the crucifixion, sometimes only a few verses apart. Galatians 3:1 is, for example, Paul discussing the crucifixion in the first manner, when he writes, 'Oh foolish Galatians, who did bewitch you, before whose eyes Jesus Christ was forewritten [προεγρά φη] to be crucified?'[43] Choosing instead to perceive προεγράφη to mean that Paul is speaking of witnesses of Jesus' physical death, many scholars have interpreted this verse in a context which is not only unlikely, but not relevant to Paul's direct message.[44] In the very next verse, Paul writes that the issue is one of faith: 'Did you receive the Spirit by works of the law or by hearing with faith? Are you so foolish?' (Gal. 3:2–3). If he is speaking to eyewitnesses, then one must ask why he is focusing on faith over their testimony. To grasp Paul's message, one must examine the whole context of this crucifixion in Paul's intertextual language. This first type of crucifixion will be discussed in greater detail a bit further on.

Just a chapter earlier, one can see the second type of crucifixion. He writes that 'I have been crucified with [συνεσταύρωμαι] Christ; and it is no longer I who live [ζῶ δὲ οὐκέτι ἐγώ], but Christ lives in me; and the life

43. The English translations available dubiously portray the Greek προεγράφη (cf. Rom. 15:4) as meaning 'publically portrayed' or 'openly set forth'. According to commentators Harrington and Metera, the reason for this is due to the Greek οἷς κατ' ὀφθαλμοὺς ('before whose eyes'); they argue that the word προεγράφη, which means 'forewritten', should be translated in another way. But their reasoning is not sound and it seems more like an excuse to historically root this verse rather than understand it within the context of Pauline theology.

44. Gaventa writes on this verse, 'publically exhibited does not mean that any of the Galatians were present for that historical event but that Paul's preaching vividly and powerfully placed it before them' ('Galatians,' 1378). While still a conservative rendering of the verse, Gaventa does indeed correctly suggest that Paul does not mean to suggest what some scholars have said about it, her assumption that this was a historical event notwithstanding.

which I now live in the flesh I live by faith in the Son of God, who loved me and gave Himself up for me' (Gal. 2:20). Paul not only suggests here that he was crucified with Jesus, but that as a result he came to recognize the flesh, with Christ who 'lives in' him (ζῇ δὲ ἐν ἐμοὶ Χριστός). This sort of language is also found in Rom. 6:6, where Paul says that 'our old self was crucified with [παλαιὸς ἡμῶν ἄνθρωπος συνεσταυρώθη] Him, in order that our body of sin might be done away with, so that we would no longer be slaves to sin.' Paul does not just liken everyone's spiritual death to Jesus' own crucifixion; he goes so far as to place himself *with* Jesus at the crucifixion, as an active participant.

The implications should be obvious; Paul surely is not dead if he is writing (even Lucian never created a fiction that brash, not even in his *Philopseudes*), so he must mean he was crucified along with Jesus in a spiritual sense only. But what remains to be determined is if Paul always means a spiritual sense when he discusses the crucifixion. Perhaps there is some intertextual, emulative sense at play here. Indeed, it can be shown that the crucifixion of a righteous being has roots deep in the books of the Hebrew Bible. Often, scholars draw on a select group of verses to attempt to show that Paul was aware of a historical crucifixion; most notably they use 1 Cor. 2:6–8:

> Yet among the mature [τοῖς τελείοις] we do impart wisdom, although it is not a wisdom of this age [αἰῶνος] or of the rulers [ἀρχόντων] of this age [αἰῶνος], who are doomed to pass away. But we impart a mysterious and hidden wisdom of God, which God decreed before the ages [αἰώνων] for our glory. None of the rulers [ἀρχόντων] of this age [αἰῶνος] understood this, for if they had, they would not have crucified the Lord of glory.

The most pressing part of this selection is the esoteric language. Paul is speaking to other initiates (τελειοι) about the 'mysterious and hidden wisdom' (σοφίαν ἐν μυστηρίῳ τὴν ἀποκεκρυμμένην). The context implies a mystery rite, in the same way that the Essenes are said to have practiced their own initiations and mysteries.[45] The knowledge Paul had imparted was

45. Josephus, *B.J.* 2.8.7, 137–42, discusses the initiations, while 2.8.10, 150–53 mentions the 'four grades' or divisions in the initiations. The use of the term τελετή and cognates can be seen in a variety of classical literature. In Aristophanes, Plato, Epictetus, Euripides and others, the use of τελετή has been used to signify the rite of initiation and τέλειος, τελεστής, and occasionally τελετής is used to describe a follower of the mysteries who has completed the rites. For example, according to Iamblichus' *De vita Pythagorica* 3.14, Pythagoras was initiated into the sacred rites in Byblos, Tyre and Syria (*Iamblichus: On the Pythagorean Way of Life* [trans. J. Dillon and J. Hershbell; SBLTT, 29, Graeco-Roman Religion Series, 11; Atlanta: Scholars Press, 1991]); cf. 28.151, which has a reference to Pythagoras being 'from the rite in Eleusis' (Παρὰ τῆς τελετῆς τῆς ἐν Ἐλευσῖνι). These words do have meanings outside the applicable definition given to them by the authors concerning the mysteries, but when used in the manner they are portrayed here, the

not exoteric but implicit, interpreted from his parables to those who would understand—his full-knowing readers. Paul's discussion on the 'rulers [ἀρχόντων] of this age [αἰῶνος τούτου]' in this passage represents one of these parables. These archons, within this context, are not to be confused with earthly rulers.[46] While the origin of the word *archon* is not authoritatively known, it may have some relation to the verb ἀρχω (*to begin* or *to be first*). If this is the case, the context may have a double meaning. They are both the rulers and the initiators of the ages.[47]

This sort of mysticism was not uncommon in Jewish circles. The same sort of language was used by the author of 1 Enoch:[48]

> All the thirsty ones drink...and become filled with wisdom. (Then) their dwelling places become with the holy, righteous, and elect ones. At that hour, that Son of Man was given a name, in the presence of the Lord of the Spirits, the Before Time; even before the creation of the sun and the moon, before the creation of the stars, he was given a name in the presence of the Lord of the Spirits. He will become a staff for the righteous ones.... He is the light of the gentiles and he will become the hope of those who are sick in their hearts.... For this purpose he became the Chosen One; he was concealed in the presence of the Lord of the Spirits prior to the creation of the world, and for eternity. And he has revealed the wisdom of the Lord of the Spirits to the righteous and the holy ones... (1 Enoch 48:1–7)

> For the Son of Man was concealed from the beginning, and the Most High One preserved him in the presence of his power; then he revealed him to the holy and the elect ones. (1 Enoch 62:7–8)

For Paul, there was truth in this thinking. In Rom. 16:25–26, he writes 'Now to him who is able to establish you by my gospel and the proclamation of Jesus Christ, according to the revelation of the mystery hidden for long ages past

---

meaning is symbolic. Philo and Josephus also use the terms, which can be verified using the appropriate concordances and Loeb texts. Further information on this matter can be found in the book by M. B. Cosmopoulos, *Greek Mysteries: The Archaeology and Ritual of Ancient Greek Secret Cults* (London/New York: Routledge, 2003), and E. Pagels, *The Gnostic Paul: Gnostic Exegesis of the Pauline Letters* (Philadelphia: Fortress Press, 1975). This subject deserves to be explored further in greater detail.

46. It is interesting that Paul uses this term as well as others (see above), which signifies the ethereal, as opposed to other Greek words to signify more earthly 'rulers', such as δεσπότης, πρύτανις, τύραννος and γεμών. While Paul does once use *archons* in Rom. 13 to signify earthly rulers (the context implies this. Cf. Rom. 13:5–7 (it is because of this submission to these rulers that people pay taxes), where Paul qualifies 1 Cor. 2:6–8 by specifying that these *archons* are of the ages, not of appointed authority (ἐξουσία) over taxable principalities as he does in Rom. 13.

47. A few examples: Philo, *De cherubim* 2.90; Josephus, *B.J.* 1; Preface, 12; 1.22.10, 419; 3.8.5, 374; 6.2.1, 105; *A.J.* 1; Preface, 16; 1.18.6, 272, 'I say, Lord of all ages' (δέσποτα λέγων, παντὸς αἰῶνος); 3.8.10, 223.

48. J. H. Charlesworth, ed., *OTP* (New York: Bantam Doubleday), I, 35, 43.

but now revealed and made known through the prophetic writings by the command of the eternal God.' Part of this mystery was the hidden truth of Paul's figure of Jesus, his death and his rebirth. Paul's Jesus was not slain by a rabble of angry Jews, by a legion of Roman soldiers, a tetrarch, or a prefect of Rome; these Gospel personalities never arise in Paul's epistles. Rather, those who killed Jesus were the ἀρχόντων. Not earthly beings, *not* those of flesh and blood but the rulers and powers (see early Christian evidence for this tradition in Eph. 6:12: ὅτι οὐκ ἔστιν ἡμῖν ἡ πάλη πρὸς αἷμα καὶ σάρκα ἀλλὰ πρὸς τὰς ἀρχάς, πρὸς τὰς ἐξουσίας), the rulers of the darkness (κοσμοκράτορας τοῦ σκότους); these beings crucified Jesus.

Paul discusses the *Archons* elsewhere, although he also uses another term (στοιχεῖα) in some places. See, for example, Gal. 4:3: 'elemental spirits of the cosmos' (στοιχεῖα τοῦ κόσμου); 4:8–9: 'However at that time, not knowing God, you were slaves to Gods who by nature are not Gods. But now that you have come to know God, or rather to be known by God, why do you turn back again to the weak and miserable elemental spirits, to which you desire to be slaves all over again?' ('Αλλὰ τότε μὲν οὐκ εἰδότες θεὸν ἐδουλεύσατε τοῖς φύσει μὴ οὖσιν θεοῖς· νῦν δὲ γνόντες θεόν, μᾶλλον δὲ γνωσθέντες ὑπὸ θεοῦ, πῶς ἐπιστρέφετε πάλιν ἐπὶ τὰ ἀσθενῆ καὶ πτωχὰ στοιχεῖα οἷς πάλιν ἄνωθεν δουλεύειν θέλετε); and Col. 2:8: 'Be careful that you don't let anyone rob you through his philosophy and vain deceit, after the tradition of men, after the elemental spirits of the cosmos, and not after Christ' (Βλέπετε μή τις ὑμᾶς ἔσται ὁ συλαγωγῶν διὰ τῆς φιλοσοφίας καὶ κενῆς ἀπάτης κατὰ τὴν παράδοσιν τῶν ἀνθρώπων, κατὰ τὰ στοιχεῖα τοῦ κόσμου καὶ οὐ κατὰ Χριστόν); also Rom. 8:38: 'For I am persuaded, that neither...angels, nor Archons...nor powers...' (πέπεισμαι γὰρ ὅτι...οὔτε ἄγγελοι οὔτε ἀρχαι...οὔτε δυνάμεις); and 1 Cor. 15:24: 'Then the end comes, when he will deliver up the Kingdom to God, even the Father; when he will have abolished all rule and all authority and power' (εἶτα τὸ τέλος, ὅταν παραδιδῷ τὴν βασιλείαν τῷ θεῷ καὶ πατρί, ὅταν καταργήσῃ πᾶσαν ἀρχὴν καὶ πᾶσαν ἐξουσίαν καὶ δύναμιν).[49]

Paul believes that through the wisdom attained by direct revelation of Christ Jesus, perhaps a cue name for his 'Anointed Saviour', that these other heavenly principalities will be supplanted.[50] Some scholars might hold some

49. Additional first century Christian evidence: Eph. 2:2: 'in which you once walked according to the ages of the cosmos, according to the Archon of the power of the air, the spirit who now works in the sons of disobedience' (ἐν αἷς ποτε περιεπατήσατε κατὰ τὸν αἰῶνα τοῦ κόσμου τούτου, κατὰ τὸν ἄρχοντα τῆς ἐξουσίας τοῦ ἀέρος, τοῦ πνεύματος τοῦ νῦν ἐνεργοῦντος).

50. Other early Christian evidence: Col. 2:9–10, 'For in him all the fullness of the Godhead dwells bodily, and in him you are made full, who is the head of every Archon and Power [ἀρχῆς καὶ ἐξουσίας].' The author is expressing his God's unlimited authority over the

level of distrust of this interpretation, but it can be shown that at least some early Christians knew of this interpretation, as one of the manuscripts discovered at Nag Hammadi is entitled *Hypostasis of the Archons*[51] (*HypArch*) or the 'Reality of the Rulers'. Some of the content of the narrative also implies a different type of death in a different realm.[52] Origen, in his *De Principiis* 3.2.1, also interprets Paul's words in this way, lending more credibility to the argument that this was a common understanding of Paul's message in 1 Corinthians.[53]

However, assuming this is an accurate interpretation, there is still the question of death. After all, Paul says clearly that his Jesus *died*. Yet death, for Paul, does not represent psychical death in his epistles. Indeed, Paul once again uses this esoteric, formalistic language. After all, Paul believed that his Jesus died the same way he felt he had died.

> For apart from the law, sin lies dead. I was once alive apart from the law, but when the commandment came, sin came alive and I died. The very commandment that promised life proved to be death to me. For sin, seizing an opportunity through the commandment, deceived me and through it killed me. (Rom. 7:8–11)

---

other pagan gods held by his audience. In the same way, Paul feels these other principalities or rulers are the enemies (ἐχθρὸς) of his God which will be abolished by God (καταργεῖται; 1 Cor. 15:25–26), and it is they who crucified his Jesus, which he reveals in 1 Cor. 2:8.

51. This work has been tentatively dated to the third century (see introduction by R. A. Bullard, in J. M. Robinson, ed., *The Nag Hammadi Library* [San Francisco: HarperCollins, 1990, 3rd edn], 161–62). Some of the arguments for this *terminus ante quem* are weak (i.e. the 'midrashic handling of scriptural material' is something that Jewish authors have done since the authorship of the first books of the Pentateuch). However, even if the treatise were completed by this date, and not earlier, this would still show that Christians were reading this tradition in the manner discussed above some two-hundred years later.

52. In this narrative, the author(s) linked both the ἀρχῆς ανδ ἐξουσίας, are equatable according to this narrative. In the same way that the Greeks felt that the Gods warred and fought on ethereal planes or on one of the heavens, the same way Paul believes in elemental spirits or ethereal beings that hold sway over various heavens. See the discussion of the title and the first sentence (via Greek retroversion) also found in the introduction by Bullard to the translation of *HypArch* in *The Coptic Gnostic Library* (Leiden: Brill, 1995), II, 220–21. Cf. the contribution by R. van den Broek, 'Archontics,' in W. J. Hanegraaff, ed., *Dictionary of Gnosis and Western Esotericism* (Leiden: Brill, 2006), 89–91, and Bentley Layton, ed., *Coptic Gnostic Chrestomathy: A Selection of Coptic Texts with Grammatical Analysis and Glossary* (Leuven: Peeters, 2004), 48–49.

53. 'Sed et Salvatorem crucifixum esse dicit a principibus huius mundi'; it is worth noting that some commentators have translated 'huius mundi' as 'this world', though often in the New Testament and the epistles, 'huius mundi' and variations of the phrase often signify the underworld/hell, or any 'world' opposite God's holiness. Indeed a similar wording found in the Latin Vulgate, Jn 12:31 (cf. Eph. 2:2), goes 'precips huius mundi' where the ruler of the cosmos (world) is traditionally Satan (ἄρχων τοῦ κόσμου).

Paul, as was mentioned above, is still alive; this must mean that he beckons his readers to interpret his words figuratively or allegorically. The spiritual death Paul talks of here seems to be much worse than an actual death. This death is not separate from birth, but specifically connected to it. Paul explains these parables through the explanation of his revelation (ἀποκάλυψις) from God, through Jesus Christ. He never once separates his own spiritual death and the death of Jesus; everyone who participates in Jesus' death dies a spiritual death, and for Paul this *includes* his figure of Jesus.

The Allegory of the Two Women

Following the crucifixion, there are a number of other relevant verses from the epistles that scholars will use to suggest that Paul knew of an earthly, historical Jesus. Galatians 4:4 offers a glance at how intertextuality and emulative interpretations often will take a back seat when there are historical Jesus inquiries taking place. For instance, Bart Ehrman writes,[54]

> Paul tells us that Jesus was born of a woman (Gal. 4:4; this, of course, is not particularly useful datum—one wonders what the alternative might have been!), and that he was born a Jew (Gal. 4:4), reputedly from the line of King David (Rom. 1:3). He had brothers (1 Cor. 9:5), one of whom was named James (Gal. 1:19). He had twelve disciples (1 Cor. 15:5...) and conducted his ministry among Jews (Rom. 15:8). He had a last meal with his disciples on the night in which he was betrayed (1 Cor. 11:23). Paul knows what Jesus said at his last meal (1 Cor. 11:23–25). Finally, he knows that Jesus died by being crucified (1 Cor. 2:2).

This treatment has already covered the crucifixion, and it will cover the rest of the claims made here by Ehrman and others (see above), but for now the course of this subsection will focus on Gal. 4:4, as there are two claims which are made concerning its historical content.

> What I am saying is that as long as the heir is a child, he is no different from a slave, although he owns the whole estate. He is subject to guardians and trustees until the time set by his father. So also, when we were children, we were in slavery under the basic principles of the world. But when the time had fully come, God sent his Son, born of a woman, born under law, to redeem those under law, that we might receive the full rights of sons. Because you are sons, God sent the Spirit of his Son into our hearts, the Spirit who calls out,

---

54. *Jesus: Apocalyptic Prophet of the New Millennium*, 79; I will not be touching upon the subject of Jesus' betrayal in Paul's epistles as I believe it has been handled quite well in T. L. Thompson, 'If David Had Not Climbed the Mount of Olives,' in J. C. Exum, ed., *Virtual History and the Bible*, *BibInt* 8.1–2 (1999), 42–58; see also the discussion on the intertextuality between 1 Corinthians, Tobit and Daniel in *The Birthing of the New Testament*, 595–604.

> 'Abba, Father.' So you are no longer a slave, but a son; and since you are a son, God has made you also an heir. (Gal. 4:1–7)

To start, the fact of the matter is that Galatians 4 is not really about Jesus; there is no discussion of the man at all and, rather, Jesus is merely the exegetical example that Paul is using. It seems that when historical Jesus scholarship hijacks a verse, all original context for the whole of the chapter is lost. Instead of Jesus, this chapter is entirely about the law and how to be saved under the law. His treatise on salvation starts from this concept of a slave, of a child—an heir—who will still own the estate even if he is but a child. This is allegorical from the start. Consider the following verses from the chapter:

> Tell me, you that desire to be under the law, don't you listen to the law? For it is written that Abraham had two sons, one by the handmaid, and one by the free woman. However, the son by the handmaid was made according to the flesh, but the son by the free woman was made through promise. These things contain an allegory, for these are two covenants. One is from Mount Sinai, bearing children to bondage, which is Hagar. For this Hagar is Mount Sinai in Arabia, and answers to the Jerusalem that exists now, for she is in bondage with her children. But the Jerusalem that is above is free, which is the mother of us all. For it is written, 'Rejoice, you barren who don't bear. Break forth and shout, you that don't travail. For more are the children of the desolate than of her who has a husband.' Now we, brothers, as Isaac was, are children of promise. But as then, he who was born according to the flesh persecuted him who was born according to the Spirit, so also it is now. However what does the Scripture say? 'Throw out the handmaid and her son, for the son of the handmaid will not inherit with the son of the free woman.' So then, brothers, we are not children of a handmaid, but of the free woman. (Gal. 4:21–31)

The context is very important, and Ehrman seems to miss completely the theological meaning behind Paul's statement about Jesus being 'born of a woman'; his jocularity about other alternatives to being born of a woman shows the level of reluctance in New Testament to examine these sorts of questions more thoroughly, especially when the answers given are presumed to be unassailable. In truth, the *alternatives* are precisely what Paul speaks of in 4:4! Jesus is made under the law—the spiritual custodian (Gal. 3:23)—by a 'woman' or specifically, 'the Jerusalem above' (δὲ ἄνω 'Ιερουσαλὴμ), which also happens allegorically to be the mother to everyone. It is not that Jesus was born of a woman; such formalistic language is rhetorical and allegorical, it is not meant to be taken literally. As Ehrman points out, it makes little sense to state that Jesus was born of a woman, if in fact Paul meant that literally! No, the verse is emulative of Scripture. All of humanity is born of one of these two women. However, not everyone will be an heir to God's throne; only those born of one of the women will become an heir with his

Jesus Christ. Paul makes this distinction quite clear in the majority of his epistles; 'for it is the power of God for salvation to everyone who believes, to the Jew first and also to the Greek' (Rom. 1:16). Paul was speaking specifically to everyone who had been adopted into the death of Jesus Christ: 'but you have received the Spirit of adoption as sons, by whom we cry, "Abba! Father!"' (Rom. 8:15). And here the understanding of the parable comes back around.

We are brought into this world through one woman, the woman under bondage—the slave—by which Paul means sin. However, for those who participate in Jesus' death, we can be saved. We call out to our father, allegorically, as we become kin with Jesus through the spirit. But through this death we are saved, from the flesh which is corrupt, through a *rebirth*. This rebirth is through this allegorical woman in the same way that Paul's Jesus is born through the same allegorical woman. Indirectly we, like Jesus, are born again spiritually by way of the heavens, or directly, by God, but this time free from sin, as heirs to God's kingdom.

Then there is Gal. 4:4: concerning the law, 'God sent out his Son...made under the law.' There are those who exegete this verse without considering what Paul is actually saying here; historical Jesus scholars are particularly guilty of this. The verse is taken for granted, presupposed to be about a person which Paul never claims to have known but through direct revelation. For Jesus was made (γενόμενον), specifically, under the law. What is the law? Paul actually tells us what the 'law' means. 'It was added because of transgressions, until the seed should come to whom the promise has been made. It was ordained through angels by the hand of a mediator [μεσίτου]' (Gal. 3:19). Paul clarifies for us, 'For we know that the law [ὁ νόμος] is spiritual [πνυεματικός], but I am of the flesh [σάρκινός], sold under sin' (Rom. 7:14). Paul believes that what comes from the flesh is corruptible: 'For I know that nothing good dwells in me, that is, in my flesh' (Rom. 7:18). The law is the spiritual custodian of the flesh, a teacher which Paul feels leads one to life. It is through this custodian, the spirit, per Paul, that we are also saved.

This is made more explicit in his epistle to the Romans than in Galatians, where he writes that God sent Jesus to fulfill the prophecies 'concerning his Son, who was born of the seed of David according to the flesh' (Rom. 1:3). Immediately following this verse, Paul states that we can also be called 'to belong to Jesus Christ'. It is just more allegory. Consider again the formalistic style, the sort of language that Paul utilizes to craft his rhetorical point. After all, the reader is faced with two options here: (1) we are left to believe that either David was literally Jesus' father (the Greek is ἐκ σπέρματος Δαυὶδ; literally 'of the seed/sperm of David'), which would mean that Jesus' mother was impregnated by one of David's celestial 'seeds' or that (2) Paul means this allegorically. The answer is probably that the reader is meant to interpret this allegorically since Paul is not Luke—by this I mean that Paul does not try to establish a lineage nor does he attempt to create a genealogy.[55] He is making a metaphorical point about something far more important to him than whether or not he was a physical, human descendant of David.[56]

For instance, he does not say, 'from the womb of Mary' or 'from the seed of Joseph, descendant of David'. Paul does not once mention the names of Jesus' parents in relation to David's lineage (nor does he mention them at all, in any context). Instead, he utilizes this allegorical language. *David* was not the father of Jesus. But that is a testament to the parable of Paul's saviour. David is the representative of Israel for Paul's theological point. Once more, Jesus is not the subject of the chapter; it is about salvation for the chosen. Paul is writing to Rome: 'So, as much as is in me, I am eager to preach the gospel to you also who are in Rome. For I am not ashamed of the gospel of Christ, for it is the power of God for salvation for everyone who believes; for the Jew first, and also for the Greek' (Rom. 1:16). For Paul, the goal is the salvation of all; but specifically his intent here is to show the promise of God fulfilled: that the chosen ones—the Jews—are saved according to Scripture. Paul, shortly after making his intentions clear, goes on about this very issue for the *rest of the chapter*, talking about the wickedness of Israel in the past and about how God gave the wicked up to their 'dishonorable passions' (πάθη ἀτιμίας).[57] The works of humanity are irrelevant to the grace of God. He cements this into his discussion of circumcision, which is also allegory.

Circumcision represents the law and those who follow the law, where as those who are uncircumcised—the Greek who does not follow the law—can still be a part of the chosen if they have faith. The tie in with the seed of David is that Jesus, to Paul, reveals himself to all, just as David counts righteous those who do not follow the law.

---

55. In fact, to interpret this passage in that manner is to read Paul through the lenses of the Gospel genealogies. This is precisely the sort of backwards exegetical practices that must be examined critically; Matthew and Luke were not written before Paul had written this verse. It is much more likely that the Gospel authors, in trying to establish a theological point, probably used this verse to euhemerize Jesus into a historical context, just like the authors of 1 Chronicles, like the discussion of Moses' genealogy in the book of Exodus, or of the genealogies in Genesis.
56. Paul cares little (I would argue that Paul simply does not know) for any physical or historical acts of the figure of Jesus that occurred on this earth, on this plane of existence. That is, after all, the primary frustration of historical Jesus scholars—Paul has absolutely nothing (they would argue that he has 'not much') to say about an earthly, physical Jesus. He is wrapped up completely in the spiritual. This was Bultmann's frustration with Paul as well.
57. Rom. 1:26.

> Even as David also pronounces blessing on the man to whom God counts righteousness apart from works, 'Blessed are they whose iniquities are forgiven, whose sins are covered. Blessed is the man whom the Lord will by no means charge with sin.' Is this blessing then pronounced on the circumcised, or on the uncircumcised also? For we say that faith was accounted to Abraham for righteousness. How then was it counted? When he was in circumcision, or in uncircumcision? Not in circumcision, but in uncircumcision. (Rom. 4:9)

For Paul, the seed of David is likened to the seed of Abraham, the children of Israel, who are deemed righteous by their faith, not through works of the law. 'For the promise to Abraham and to his seed that he should be heir of the world wasn't through the law, but through the righteousness of faith' (Rom. 4:13). Once more we see Paul express his point through an allegory using Abraham (and, consequently, the covenant), of the heirs of the kingdom which we find in Galatians 4. Salvation through rebirth: this is his message.

Paul explains further the concept of his idea of salvation while making it clear that there is a 'partial hardening' (πώρωσις ἀπὸ μέρους) upon the sons of Israel, 'And in this way all Israel will be saved.' According to Paul, this salvation will occur when there are a specific number of Greeks who are also saved (Rom. 11:25–26). Paul speaks this mystery (μυστήριον)[58] to his brethren because he seeks to 'somehow...make my fellow Jews jealous, and thus save some of them' (Rom. 11:14).[59] He relates this back to the patriarchs and the prophets. God is attempting to save a remnant of Israelites, those who have faith and are deemed worthy through grace. He brings up the passage in which Isaiah begs God to destroy Israel for their wickedness. God, recognizing the wickedness of the Jews well in advance, allows for seven thousand Israelites who did not 'kneel to Baal' (Rom. 11:6) to be saved. Paul sums up this allegory: 'Israel failed to obtain what it was seeking. The elect [ἐκλογή] obtained it, but the rest were hardened' (Rom. 11:7). Bringing this allegorical interpretation of Scripture back around, to 'belong to Christ' you must become one of the seed of David, an heir to the covenant which is not bound by circumcision (by law), but by specifically identifying your faith in God through Christ, that is, by dying with him and being reborn. This is

---

58. There is a strong allusion to Greek mystery cults, at least in language, throughout Paul's epistles. Paul likens those to whom he speaks as infants, 'Brothers, I couldn't speak to you as to spiritual, but as to fleshly, as to babies [νήμοι] in Christ. I fed you with milk, not with meat; for you weren't yet ready. Indeed, not even now are you ready, for you are still fleshly' (1 Cor. 3:1–3). This signifies that those to whom he is speaking are not yet of the initiates, or the mature, depending on how you translate τέλειοι. See n. 45.

59. Once more the author of Luke–Acts picks up on the allegory of this, and goes as far as to include this perception of the Jews in Acts. When the Jews see the crowds of Greeks they become 'filled with jealousy' and began to contradict Paul. See: Acts 13:45, 17:5.

accomplished through understanding the mysteries, Paul teaches, and by becoming one of the mature (τέλειοι).

The Vision of the Breaking of the Bread. One final example that needs to be addressed before moving on is that of the meal described in 1 Corinthians 11. This is, like earlier representations, not about Jesus. Instead, it is once more about the salvation of mankind. Jesus, for Paul, is both real and also allegorical; he is the real entity which Paul experiences *through revelation and rebirth*, but also an allegorical being significant for the understanding of Scripture, which Paul is interpreting (emphasis mine):

> For *I received from the Lord* what I also delivered to you, that the Lord Jesus on the night when he was betrayed took bread, and when he had given thanks, he broke it, and said, 'This is my body which is for you. Do this in remembrance of me.' In the same way also he took the cup, after supper, saying, 'This cup is the new covenant in my blood. Do this, as often as you drink it, in remembrance of me.' For as often as you eat this bread and drink the cup, you proclaim the Lord's death until he comes. (1 Cor. 11:23–26)

The allegorical interpretation Paul gives his readers is further understood within the context of the chapter. Paul is speaking of divisions in the church at Corinth.[60] He is angered by the fact that so many people differ in personal belief instead of a unified belief through Jesus Christ (1 Cor. 11:17–19). He is likening a communal meal to the church of God (1 Cor. 11:22). He says, 'When you come together, it is not the Lord's supper that you eat. For in eating, each one goes ahead with his own meal. One goes hungry, another gets drunk' (1 Cor. 11:20–21). Indeed, Paul asks, 'Is Christ divided?' (1 Cor. 1:13). Paul follows this up with more evidence of the allegory of the upcoming passage on the last supper when he asks, 'Do you not have houses to eat and drink in? Or do you despise the church of God...?' Paul's meal with Christ is indicative to his message of faith and renewal for the church at Corinth. He states that he received (παρέλαβον) this message 'from the Lord what I also delivered to you' (1 Cor. 11:23), which is the new covenant. But Paul never

60. Paul opens his letter with this rumour that he has received from Chloe as the purpose behind the letter's composition, 'I appeal to you, brothers, by the name of our Lord Jesus Christ, that all of you agree, and that there be no divisions among you, but that you be united in the same mind and the same judgment. For it has been reported to me by Chloe's people that there is quarreling among you, my brothers' (1 Cor. 1:10–11). I have to take pause and wonder why there were such divisions among the Christians in Paul's day. Paul even makes the curious claim that people were suggesting that he was equatable to Christ (1 Cor. 1:12–14; cf. Gal. 4:14: ἐδέξασθέ με, ὡς Χριστὸν Ἰησοῦν). How odd it is that there was so much confusion, just a few years after the supposed death of the historical Jesus.

met Jesus, so certainly he did not learn of this episode from Jesus the man. And in Galatians he makes it clear 'the gospel that was preached by me is not man's gospel. For I did not receive it from any man, nor was I taught it, but I received it through a revelation [ἀποκάλυψις] of Jesus Christ' (Gal. 1:11–12). He did not get this information from any other individual, such that it might be considered evidence of Paul knowing of a historical supper. Rather, Paul is citing this scene allegorically. Paul has elsewhere said that Jesus is the cup of God.[61] But the scene of the meal is also reflective of the scene in Exod. 24:10–11: 'And they saw the God of Israel. There was under his feet as it were a pavement of sapphire stone, like the very heaven for clearness. And he did not lay his hand on the chief men of the people of Israel; they beheld God, and ate and drank.' It is my understanding of this verse that, for Paul, this supper is the very message of salvation he is offering. Immediately following this story in Exodus, God gives Moses the new covenant, which was made in blood. 'Behold, the blood of the covenant, which Yahweh has made with you in accordance with all these words' (Exod. 24:8). Paul is probably also aware of Zechariah's words on the covenant, 'Because of the blood of my covenant with you, I have freed prisoners from the dry pit' (Zech. 9:11). Through these revelations of God through Jesus, Paul is bringing Isaiah's 'good news' to the world.[62] A new blood covenant, in which Jesus had to shed blood in order to free everyone from the old covenant, is the concept behind Paul's question, 'The cup of blessing that we bless, is it not a participation in the blood of Christ? The bread that we break, is it not a participation in the body of Christ?'[63] Paul shows us he is interpreting Exodus from the very opening of his narrative: 'For I do not want you to be ignorant of the fact, brothers, that our forefathers were all under the cloud and that they all passed through the sea. They were all baptized into Moses in the cloud and in the sea.... Nevertheless, God was not pleased with most of them; their bodies were scattered over the desert' (1 Cor. 10:1–5). Christ is the rock which everyone drinks from in 1 Cor. 10:3–4, because Paul is interpreting Exodus 17. The Hebrew people demand a drink because they are thirsty from walking in the desert for so long. Moses is annoyed that they have challenged God, and asks, 'Why do you quarrel with me? Why do you test the Lord?' The Hebrews were angered and lacked faith, and demanded, 'Why did you bring us up out

61. 'They all ate the same spiritual food and drank the same spiritual drink; for they drank from the spiritual rock that accompanied them, and that rock was Christ' (1 Cor. 10:3–4; cf. 10:16–21). This is language reminiscent of the language found in 1 Enoch above.

62. Isaiah 40:9. Especially Isa. 61:1, 'The Spirit of the Lord God is upon me, because the Lord has anointed me to bring good news to the poor; he has sent me to bind up the broken-hearted, to proclaim liberty to the captives, and the opening of the prison to those who are bound.' This is the Christ of Paul.

63. 1 Cor. 5:7; 10:16; cf. n. 42.

of Egypt, to kill us and our children and our livestock with thirst?' (Exod. 17:1–3). Paul is basing his interpretation of the supper on this Scripture.[64]

James, Brother of the Lord

It seems the strongest case for the idea that a historical Jesus was known to Paul is a reference to his brothers, notably James. In most literature on the historical Jesus, there can be found some reference to James in Gal. 1:19: 'But I saw none of the other apostles except James the brother of the Lord [τὸν ἀδελφὸν τοῦ κυρίου].' The issue here, however, seems to be one of interpretation. Greek ἀδελφός is both a figurative word for 'brother' or 'kin', as well as a having a biological sense. However, in early (and modern, for that matter) Christianity it was common for Christians to call each other 'brother' and 'sister'. Herein abides the problem. A reader can see that Paul talks about James the same way he talks about other 'brothers'. He uses the same word, ἀδελφός, when describing James as he does when talking about 'all the brothers of the Lord' (cf. Rom. 16:23, where Quartus is referred to specifically as 'our brother').[65] Paul viewed his fellow congregation as communal brethren, through the Lord, whom Paul felt akin towards (1 Cor. 8:10–12). Paul states in Gal. 3:26–27, for example, 'For you are all sons of God through faith in Christ Jesus.' The reader is drawn back towards the allegory of the covenant, shared by the heirs of the kingdom. Certainly, if Paul felt everyone had to be sons of God, and Jesus is the Son of God, everyone also happened to be brothers of Christ—in fact, he does actually say this, which has already been discussed above. Christ is their brother as Sosthenes and Chloe and Quartus are family as well. There is nothing at all, anywhere in Paul's letters, suggesting that James had been a blood relative to a historical Jesus, and the context does not suggest this.

This is further explained, for example, in 1 Cor. 1:10, which states, 'I urge you, brothers, in the name of our Lord Jesus Christ...'; Gal. 1:2, 'and all of the brothers who are with me...' One would not suggest that Paul is referring to literal kin here. The use of the language (i.e. ἀδελφός) may be similar to a type of rank in the mystery religions of the day. Early Christianity (in

64. Stockhausen has pointed out that 'Paul's take as the basis for his interpretative task is the Torah; that is to say, narrative texts from the Pentateuch are usually (perhaps always) at the core of his arguments... [Paul] is usually (perhaps always) concerned with the stories themselves, that is, with plot line, character, narrative event and especially the inexplicable, unusual or unmotivated character or action.' C. K. Stockhausen, '2 Corinthians 3 and the Principles of Pauline Exegesis,' in C. A. Evans and J. A. Sanders, eds., *Paul and the Scriptures of Israel* (JSNTSup, 83; Sheffield: Sheffield Academic Press, 1994), 144–46.

65. See also, 1 Cor. 1:1, where Sosthenes is 'our Brother'—just in Romans alone, ἀδελφός is used in 1:13; 7:1, 4; 8:12, 29; 9:3; 10:1; 11:25; 12:1; 14:10–21; 15:14, 30; 16:14, 17—all are in relation to Paul's fellow converts.

accordance with 1 Cor. 15), through the letters of Paul, has the marks of a mystery religion (this is seen also in Paul's use of τέλειοι in 1 Cor. 2:6, a term that has long been associated with Greek mystery traditions as well as the use of μυστήριον).[66]

This might also be yet another instance of certain scholars reading the epistles using their Gospel-coloured glasses. After all, the Gospel authors talk about Jesus having brothers (Mt. 12:46; Mk 3:31; Lk. 8:19; Jn 2:12). But the one Gospel author the reader would expect to have interpreted Paul's words literally, Luke, the author of Acts, does not seem to interpret Paul's James as the biological brother of Jesus. Even when he has the chance to do so, he does not (Acts 12:17). While this may seem to be a fairly inconsequential point, in Luke, Jesus' brothers are mentioned, yet Luke makes no suggestion that *James* is the brother of Jesus. There are several Jameses in his Gospel and in Acts as well, but none are related to Jesus.[67] This is odd precisely because Luke seems to have the most reason to interpret the Pauline epistles, along with having the best access to them, with a motivation to utilize them to the advantage of the Church. He has already mentioned that Jesus had brothers, but why does he not see fit to salvage James as he had Paul and Peter?

On this point one final observation: in the epistles one sees consistent evidence that Paul refers to every other Christian as a brother; there is no other evidence in any other epistle that Paul believed Jesus had an earthly, biological family of any kind. Why would Paul cite the name of Jesus' brother, but not his mother or father? Why a brother? Was Jesus' father, Joseph, dead? Where was Mary (any of them)? This silence speaks volumes, and no sufficient solution exists to deal with these questions in a manner that might lend some credibility to the notion that Paul knew a biological brother of Jesus.

Conclusion

So who is Paul's Christ? Paul's Jesus Christ is exactly what Paul interprets from Scripture. Paul finds his anointed saviour in Isaiah, in Moses, in Daniel,

66. See n. 45.

67. There is a James, son of Zebedee (Lk. 5:10), James the son of Alphaeus (Lk. 6:15), James the father of Judas (not the betrayer; Lk. 6:16), and James the son of Mary (not the mother of Jesus; Lk. 24:10); cf. Acts 1:13. See also, R. M. Price, 'Apocryphal Apparitions: 1 Corinthians 15:3–11 as a Post-Pauline Interpolation,' in R. M. Price and J. J. Lowder, eds., *The Empty Tomb: Jesus Beyond the Grave* (Amherst: Prometheus Books, 2005), 82–88. It may still be that Luke intentionally excluded James to downplay the role of the family of Jesus in the Church—J. Tabor makes this case in *The Jesus Dynasty: The Hidden History of Jesus, His Royal Family, and the Birth of Christianity* (New York: Simon and Schuster, 2007), passim—but this author remains unconvinced by the arguments.

in David; he is in the wilderness, stranded in the Diaspora, a wandering pious Jew, an exile from his own home himself. Paul's Jesus was the provider of spiritual salvation then, but also continuously. He had not been a religious leader in Judea killed three decades prior to the authorship of the epistles, but he was a being who existed on another plane, who died continuously with those who sought him, and was resurrected continuously with them as well. This does not mean that there was not a historical figure of Jesus, though that remains to be seen. What it does indicate is that the identity of the figure of Jesus in Paul's letters is not of a man, crucified under Pilate, born of Mary and Joseph, who walked Galilee and calmed storms. Paul never knew *that* Jesus, and never tells us anything about that Jesus. If Paul believed in such a figure, his message of the flesh would not make sense. How could the flesh be corrupt, and nothing good can come of flesh, if his saviour were of the flesh? Of course, this cannot be. Jesus was in the likeness of flesh, but not human—not of this world. His 'life' is summed up only in his death; with every account of Jesus there follows Scripture. It is not that Paul is recounting fulfilled prophecy, but rather Paul gives us his interpretation of Scripture through the new covenant of God, through his mediator Jesus Christ—his teacher of mysteries.

It is within these emulative structures, these epistles built upon a framework of rhetoric, that the reader locates intertextual echoes of subjects that had been a part of the culture of the ancient Near East, dating back to ancient Mesopotamia, to the Sumerians, the Akkadians, to those who lived and worshipped in Ugarit. There are intertextual threads of Homer, of the rising and dying deity so common in the East. Yet within these echoes, upon a *secunda facie* examination of the epistles, there exists not a trace of an entity which the reader can call the historical figure of Jesus.

Part III

The Rewritten Bible and the Life of Jesus

- 9 -

Can John's Gospel Really Be Used to Reconstruct a Life of Jesus? An Assessment of Recent Trends and a Defence of a Traditional View

James G. Crossley

Before the turn of the millennium, critical historical Jesus scholarship was certainly a chaotic world. There were liberal and conservative disagreements over whether Jesus was something like a Cynic philosopher, an eschatological prophet, a teacher of wisdom, a 'liberal' rabbi and so on. There were also accompanying disputes over sources: can we use something called 'Q'? Can we even define 'Q'? Should we use the *Gospel of Thomas* and certain other non-canonical Gospels? But in the midst of the chaos one thing seemed certain: John's Gospel was not to be used as a source for reconstructing the life and teaching of Jesus and it certainly was not the earliest Gospel. There were differing dissenting voices, such as J. A. T. Robinson and D. A. Carson, but these could be dismissed (rightly or wrongly) as being either too maverick or too evangelical for mainstream tastes.[1] John, with its high Christology, lengthy discourses and disputes with the generalized 'the Jews', was deemed too different from the Synoptic tradition and anachronistic in ways that the Synoptic tradition was not.

Two 1996 publications illustrate this well. Maurice Casey's book, *Is John's Gospel True?*, may have provoked some hostility through its polemical tone but part of its design was simply to make clear what Johannine scholarship had long assumed, namely, that John's Gospel was of little use for reconstructing the life and teaching of Jesus.[2] A very different book is N. T. Wright's

1. E.g. J. A. T. Robinson, *The Priority of John* (London: SCM, 1985); D. A. Carson, *The Gospel according to John* (Leicester: IVP, 1991).
2. M. Casey, *Is John's Gospel True?* (London: Routledge, 1996).

massive *Jesus and the Victory of God*. Wright's book is extremely conservative and in over 700 pages he never, as far as I can see, suggests the possibility that any story about, or words attributed to, Jesus might be the product of the early church. However, despite Wright's well-known conservatism, he also has relatively little to say on John's Gospel and effectively works with the Synoptic Gospels in his reconstruction of the life and teaching of Jesus, or, better, his retelling of the Jesus of the Gospels.[3] Wright may very well believe that the Gospel of John could tell us a great deal more about the life of the historical Jesus but he does not really address the issue in his book.

After the millennium, things changed and the role of John's Gospel in reconstructing the life and teaching of Jesus has now come right into the heart of the mainstream. Richard Bauckham has been one prominent figure and widely known as one of the most learned contemporary British scholars. His work on the role of eyewitnesses and a follow-up book on John's Gospel have not only suggested that we can legitimately use John's Gospel in reconstructing the life and teaching of the historical Jesus but also that John's Gospel actually is the work of an eyewitness.[4] For Bauckham, the author of John's Gospel was also a disciple of Jesus (though not one of the Twelve) called John (but not the son of Zebedee) who used the 'disciple Jesus loved' or 'Beloved Disciple' as a self-reference and who lived a long life before dying in Ephesus. The Beloved Disciple, Bauckham argues, provided a story of Jesus from his own memories, along with the memories of other close followers of Jesus, and blended this with reflection on Jewish tradition, to give a distinctive take on a known story.

But Bauckham was not a lone voice in the wilderness. On the contrary, at the annual Society of Biblical Literature meeting, the recently formed John, Jesus, and History Project hammered out issues of historicity and

---

3. N. T. Wright, *Jesus and the Victory of God* (London: SPCK, 1996). See e.g. xvi.
4. R. Bauckham, *Jesus and the Eyewitnesses: The Gospels as Eyewitness Testimony* (Grand Rapids: Eerdmans, 2006); R. Bauckham, *The Testimony of the Beloved Disciple: Narrative, History and Theology in the Gospel of John* (Grand Rapids: Baker, 2007). Compare also, C. L. Blomberg, *The Historical Reliability of John's Gospel* (Downers Grove: IVP, 2001). Blomberg's position is perhaps less surprising coming from an overtly conservative evangelical perspective and Denver Seminary. I do not mean this to be a slight on Blomberg's work or perspective but I prefer to focus on Bauckham's work because, while certainly having conservative tendencies, Bauckham is more obviously representative of 'mainstream' scholarship as a retired professor of New Testament studies at St Andrews, a Fellow of the British Academy and an influential figure in recent mainstream New Testament scholarship. In other words, Bauckham's move in the direction of the historical reliability is a much clearer sign of the times than something we already knew to be typical of Blomberg's output. Cf. also, C. S. Keener, *The Gospel of John: A Commentary* (2 vols.; Peabody: Hendrickson, 2003); P. N. Anderson, *The Fourth Gospel and the Quest for Jesus: Modern Foundations Reconsidered* (London: T & T Clark, 2006).

John's Gospel. The project began life with 'Consultation' status for three years (2002–2004) where the Project analysed various methodological issues followed by the publication in 2007 of *John, Jesus, and History, Volume 1: Critical Appraisals of Critical Views*, edited by Paul Anderson, Felix Just and Tom Thatcher.[5] 'Group' status followed as did three years of studying aspects of historicity in John's Gospel (2005–2007), culminating in the publication in 2009 of *John, Jesus, and History, Volume 2: Aspects of Historicity in the Fourth Gospel* with the same editors.[6] In 2008–2010 further related work is being undertaken with another publication in the pipeline.[7] This is clearly a popular project. The annual meetings, it is claimed, entertain more than 350 scholars, a broad range of perspectives (theological and methodological), some of the leading scholars from around the world, and include a range of views on the historicity of John (a number of essays actually appear to restate the more traditional view of the historicity of John).[8] Coupling the project's work with the high profile work of Bauckham, there should be no doubt: John's Gospel is now on the agenda for reconstructing the life and teaching of Jesus and no critical work on the historical Jesus can ignore these prominent voices.

Why Is John's Gospel Now Being Used in the Quest for the Historical Jesus?

Before we assess the arguments made by Bauckham and certain participants in the John, Jesus and History Project, it may be helpful to contextualize the emergence of John's Gospel in mainstream historical Jesus studies in order to show that this emergence is no freak occurrence but very much part of the cultural trends affecting contemporary scholarship.

---

5. P. N. Anderson, F. Just and T. Thatcher, eds., *John, Jesus, and History, Volume 1: Critical Appraisals of Critical Views* (Atlanta: Society of Biblical Literature, 2007).
6. P. N. Anderson, F. Just and T. Thatcher, eds., *John, Jesus, and History, Volume 2: Aspects of Historicity in the Fourth Gospel* (Atlanta: Society of Biblical Literature, 2009).
7. This discussion of the history of the Jesus, John and History Project is taken from P.N. Anderson, 'Prologue: Critical Views of John, Jesus and History,' in Anderson, Just and Thatcher, eds., *John, Jesus, and History, Volume 1*, 1-8 (4). For the involvement of scholars related to the John, Jesus and History Project in different contexts, see F. Just, 'Epilogue: Whence, Where and Whither for John, Jesus, and History?,' in Anderson, Just, and Thatcher, eds., *John, Jesus, and History, Volume 2*, 387-92 (390).
8. T. Thatcher, 'Introduction: The John, Jesus and History Project,' in Anderson, Just and Thatcher, eds., *John, Jesus and History, Volume 1*, 9-12 (9, 11). Cf. 11: 'It is...intended to stimulate critical dialogue that will produce a more adequate understanding of the background and development of Johannine literature, to cross the gap between Johannine studies and Jesus studies, to stake out the terrain where a discussion of John's value as a witness to Jesus might become serviceable, as well as clarifying where it might not.'

In broader cultural terms, the past decade has seen the rise of both 'fundamentalism' and its antithesis, a hardened secularism or emboldened atheism. Of course, both trends are hardly new but this past decade they have both risen to cultural prominence in ways in which they were not before. A key moment was the September 11 attacks on the Twin Towers. Often at the expense of, or in direct opposition to, socio-economic understandings of the causes underlying violence in the name of religion, much popular rhetoric focussed on 'religion' being the root of all the problems. This problematic but ideologically convenient argument was effectively Richard Dawkins's position four days after the attacks on the Twin Towers. This move to blame the mysterious 'religion' as the primary factor underlying the world's ills has also been argued by other prominent atheists such as Sam Harris, Christopher Hitchens and Martin Amis.[9] Since September 11, such figures have become part of a movement popularly labelled 'New Atheism' and have published various highly popular and relatively controversial works explaining the apparent wrongness of religion, as well as triggering a mini-industry dedicated to countering New Atheism.[10]

Conservative evangelical Christianity has not stood idly by, however. In the USA, such a form of Christianity has been in the ascendency since the 1970s and such Christians were deemed significant enough for Karl Rove and the Republicans to take them very seriously. This past decade has seen the remarkable rise, especially in the USA, of Intelligent Design and some highly polemical disputes over evolution. Significantly, despite evidence overwhelmingly to the contrary, there have been a number of voices claiming that a cold secularism has taken over North America and the UK with (inaccurate) suggestions, for instance, that Christmas and religiously themed Christmas cards have been abandoned by various public figures and local councils in favour of secular themed festivals and greetings.[11] The fact that such scaremongering about the role of secularism can be made so prominently at least shows the cultural prominence (and, some of might add, the conveniently distracting nature) of such 'religious versus secular' discourse in contemporary culture, and is echoed in various high profile media stories such as wearing religious symbols, the role of faith schools and, of course, the *burqa*.

9. R. Dawkins, 'Religion's Misguided Missiles,' *Guardian* (15 September, 2001); Martin Amis, 'The Voice of the Lonely Crowd,' *Guardian* (1 June, 2002); S. Harris, *The End of Faith: Religion, Terror, and the Future of Reason* (London: Simon & Schuster, 2004); C. Hitchens, *God Is Not Great: How Religion Poisons Everything* (New York: Twelve, 2007).
10. For an excellent treatment of the issues, see T. Beattie, *The New Atheists: The Twilight of Reason and the War on Religion* (London: DLT, 2007).
11. O. Burkeman, 'Mulled Whine,' *Guardian* (12 December, 2006).

Scholarship is hardly immune to broader cultural trends. In addition to a range of analyses of contemporary scholarship in historical and cultural contexts,[12] I would add that the secular versus religious discourse of this past decade has had a major impact on scholarly outputs.

For instance, a number of scholars have now been defined by themselves or others as 'secular', 'atheist' or 'agnostic' in work which has received a notable degree of scholarly and public attention. We might think of Jacques Berlinerblau's *The Secular Bible*, Hector Avalos's *The End of Biblical Studies*, Bart Ehrman's hugely popular *Misquoting Jesus* and *Jesus, Interrupted*, William Arnal's article on dividing confessional-driven biblical studies and the academic study of religion, my own suggestion that New Testament studies has historically missed out on different scholarly approaches due to the numerical dominance of Christians, SBL/AAR sessions dedicated to 'secular' approaches, the debates sparked off by a Michael Fox article on scholarship and faith for the *SBL Forum*, and Roland Boer's edited volume on secularism and biblical studies which picks up key debates from the past decade.[13] The very idea of Jesus not existing was not even entertained seriously on the fringes of academic New Testament study, but now there have been some voices suggesting such a thing, including some of the voices present in the Jesus Project (e.g. Thomas Thompson, Robert Price, Richard Carrier), a scholarly gathering backed by the explicitly secular/atheistic Scientific Examination of Religion and the Center for Inquiry.[14] In fact, all the above views are not necessarily new but collectively this is distinctive and there ought to be little doubt that the 'secular' trend is as prominent as it has been for over a century.

An opposite movement of equal prominence has also gathered pace. A number of works from evangelical and conservative scholarship have now entered into the heart of the mainstream in ways which would have been

12. J. G. Crossley, *Jesus in an Age of Terror: Scholarly Projects for a New American Century* (London and Oakville: Equinox, 2008).

13. H. Avalos, *The End of Biblical Studies* (Amherst: Prometheus Books, 2007); J. Berlinerblau, *The Secular Bible: Why Nonbelievers Must Take Religion Seriously* (Cambridge: Cambridge University Press, 2005); B. D. Ehrman, *Misquoting Jesus: The Story behind Who Changed the Bible and Why* (New York: Harper One, 2005); idem, *Jesus, Interrupted: Revealing the Hidden Contradictions in the Bible (and Why We Don't Know about Them)* (New York: Harper One, 2009); Z. A. Crook and P. A. Harland, eds., *Identity and Interaction in the Ancient Mediterranean: Jews, Christians and Others: Essays in Honour of Stephen G. Wilson* (Sheffield: Sheffield Phoenix Press, 2007); J. G. Crossley, *Why Christianity Happened: A Sociohistorical Account of Christian Origins* (Louisville: Westminster John Knox, 2006); M. V. Fox, 'Bible Scholarship and Faith-Based Study: My View,' *SBL Forum*, http://sbl-site.org/Article.aspx?ArticleID=490; R. Boer, *Secularism and Biblical Studies* (London and Oakville: Equinox, 2010).

14. Cf. R. Price, *The Incredible Shrinking Son of Man: How Reliable is the Gospel Tradition?* (Amherst: Prometheus Books, 2003); T. L. Thompson, *The Messiah Myth: The Near Eastern Roots of Jesus and David* (New York: Basic Books, 2005).

unimaginable in the heyday of Bultmann-influenced scholarship. Indeed, certain extremely conservative books have now found themselves among the most influential and widely discussed books in New Testament studies. In addition to Richard Bauckham's *Jesus and the Eyewitnesses* (2006), this past decade has seen books such as Larry Hurtado's *Lord Jesus Christ* (2003), arguing for an extremely early date for Christ devotion, and N. T. Wright's other massive book, *The Resurrection of the Son of God* (2003), arguing that a supernatural explanation for the resurrection of Jesus is the only way to explain the evidence for the emergence of the Christian movement. All these books were reviewed at article length in major New Testament journals.[15] Bauckham's book effectively implies that there were not only eyewitnesses to the Gospel tradition but that there were eyewitnesses to miraculous events.[16] Wright's book is perhaps most surprising of all and, with its emphasis on apparently proving the role of the divine in history, might be described as being what Intelligent Design is to the academic study of evolution, if it were not for the obvious point that Intelligent Design is not part of the scientific mainstream. Some of Wright's points on the supernatural push conventional historical reasoning to its extremities. On the story of the dead saints rising from their tombs in Mt. 27:51-53, Wright claimed, 'Some stories are so odd that they may just have happened. This may be one of them, but in historical terms there is no way of finding out.'[17] I do not think it is going too far to suggest that a very conservative evangelical agenda might be interfering too much with historical research.[18]

Much more could, and will, be said on such matters, but for present purposes there should be little doubt that the recent emergence of John's Gospel as a significant source for the study of the historical Jesus owes something to these polarizing scholarly and cultural trends. This is clearest in the case of Bauckham.[19] While he accepts that 'the finished Gospel has

15. E.g., M. Bockmuehl, 'Complete History of the Resurrection: A Dialogue with N. T. Wright,' *JSNT* 26 (2004), 489-504; M. Casey, 'Lord Jesus Christ: A Response to Professor Hurtado,' *JSNT* 27 (2004), 83-96. Major space and several articles are devoted to the works of Wright and Bauckham in *JSHJ* 3 (2005), *JSHJ* 6 (2008) and *JSNT* 31 (2008).

16. Bauckham, *Eyewitnesses*, 343-45, 399, 405, 504.

17. Wright, *Resurrection*, 636.

18. Cf. D. C. Allison, 'Explaining the Resurrection: Conflicting Convictions,' *JSHJ* 3 (2005), 117-133 (121).

19. See also Bauckham, *Beloved Disciple*, 9: 'The essays collected in this volume...cohere with an approach to the Gospel that differs very significantly from the approach that has been dominant in Johannine scholarship since the late 1970s, though there are signs that this dominant approach is now being undermined or at least considerably modified by very recent trends in Johannine scholarship.' Bauckham locates his own work under the heading 'Something Completely Different' (12). The idea of a distinctive movement in scholarship comes through throughout the volumes of the *John, Jesus and History Project*, particularly in the summary essays by Paul Anderson.

a high degree of highly reflective interpretation',[20] Bauckham argues that the Beloved Disciple—an eyewitness according to Bauckham—is claiming that the thrust of the sword into Jesus' side produced a flow of blood and water, that the resurrected Jesus prepares breakfast, and that there was a huge catch of fish. Bauckham claims that 'these details do help to give readers the impression that the Gospel portrays the Beloved Disciple as an observant witness of what happened'.[21] There is also a similar suggestion about eyewitnesses to the wedding at Cana where, according to John, Jesus famously turned water into wine.[22] These arguments made by Bauckham seem to come close to implying that these miraculous events really did happen and this clearly goes well beyond traditional mainstream views on John's Gospel.

Bauckham and the Eyewitnesses

But cultural context only gets us so far. Cultural context only explains, to an extent, why scholarly movements emerge when and where they did. Certainly cultural context can help explain why mistakes were made (the Nazi Jesus being the most obvious example), but it is possible that the influence of cultural contexts could potentially provide ignored insights (it may well be possible that scholarship on the Synoptic tradition has overlooked the possibility of eyewitnesses). To make a more complete evaluation we now need to turn to some of the details of the arguments made in the turn to John.

If Bauckham is right, what do we do with a passage such as Jn 5:1-18? John 5:1-18 presents Jesus as divine in an exceptionally strong sense and as a figure who endorsed the breaking of *biblical* Sabbath commandments in accepting that a burden may be carried (cf. 'For this reason the Jews were seeking all the more to kill him, because he was not only breaking the Sabbath, but was also calling God his own Father, thereby making himself equal to God'). In John's Gospel we have further high christological sentiment, as we see in Jn 5:1-18, such as Thomas' exclamation, 'My Lord and my God' (Jn 20:28), and 'the Jews' claiming that 'It is not for a good work that we are going to stone you, but for blasphemy, because you, though only a human being, are making yourself God' (Jn 10:33).

If we were to follow Bauckham, this retelling of a Sabbath dispute by one eyewitness stands in sharp contrast to another person deemed to be an eyewitness, namely, Peter, assumed to be a key eyewitness for Mark's Gospel.

---

20. Bauckham, *Eyewitnesses*, 411.
21. Bauckham, *Eyewitnesses*, 399.
22. Bauckham, *Eyewitnesses*, 405.

Mark's Gospel did not see fit to mention the monumental claims of explicitly high Christology in (say) his retelling of Sabbath disputes in Mk 2:23–3:6, which do not endorse the breaking of a single *biblical* commandment. Here Jesus defends his disciples plucking grain on the Sabbath against criticism from Pharisees. There is nothing in biblical law prohibiting such actions but there were those who interpreted biblical law to include various actions similar to plucking grain (e.g. Philo, *De vita Mosis* 2.22; CD 10.22-23). There were, however, those who did not, such as the 'men from Jericho' who, like Jesus' disciples, saw fit to pick fruit from the ground on the Sabbath in dispute with the Sages (m. *Pesah* 4:8). Mark then has Jesus defend his actions with a 'son of man' saying in Mk 2:28. Here there is good evidence of the use of the generic Aramaic idiom (including reference to the speaker), hence the echo in Mark's parallelism with the generalizing Mk 2:27 (the Sabbath being made for humankind), a sentiment closely paralleled in early Judaism (e.g. Exod. 16:29; *Jub.* 2:17; *Mek. Exod.* 31:12-17; b. *Yoma* 85b).[23] This interpretation is strongly supported by Matthew and Luke dropping the generalizing context of Mk 2:27 and thus turning the Markan 'son of man' saying into a christological title. Mark 2:23-28 is then followed by a healing on the Sabbath where Jesus extends the well-known principle of saving life overruling the Sabbath (cf. 1 Macc. 2:32-41; 2 Macc. 6:11; m. *Yoma* 8:6) to include his healings (Mk 3:4), with similar sentiments echoed elsewhere in the Synoptic tradition (Lk. 13:10-17; 14:1-6). These disputes over the details of the interpretation of the Law lead to a plot to kill Jesus by Pharisees and Herodians (Mk 3:6).

Theoretically, it is possible that both the Sabbath traditions in the Synoptic Gospels and John's Gospel were fictional creations of the early church. However, if one tradition were more obviously representative of the historical Jesus, it is the Synoptic tradition. The Synoptic disputes are fairly typical halakhic disputes which do not seem to have been of interest to the early church outside the Gospel tradition and Jesus provides justification for his and his disciples' behaviour, at least in the earliest tradition, in terms of a known Aramaic idiom, and with conflict being with defined groups (Pharisees and Herodians). The Johannine dispute justifies non-observance of the Sabbath commandment, something we know was happening already in mid-first-century Christianity (e.g. Rom. 14:5-6), and justification comes through overtly Christianized claims in distinction from 'the Jews'. Whatever we make of the Synoptic tradition and its historicity, or the Johannine material, with its justification of Christian practice and extremely high Christology, it is particular to John and not in the Synoptic tradition, which

23. On the Aramaic background for 'son of man' sayings, see now M. Casey, *The Solution to the 'Son of Man' Problem* (London: Continuum/T & T Clark, 2007).

at the very least suggests that such ideas were not available in the Synoptic tradition. Otherwise, why leave such hugely relevant material out? Is not the explanation that the Johannine material is largely the product of either a Christian dispute or a creative mind (or both) by far the most plausible one?[24]

In fact, this brings us back to questions which have haunted Christianity from its first centuries. Some of the major Johannine problems will not go away. The Synoptic Gospels have Jesus' action in the Temple as the immediate cause of Jesus' death (Mk 11:15-18) while John puts the Temple action at the beginning of his narrative and has the raising of Lazarus as the immediate cause of Jesus' death (Jn 11). A standard explanation in terms of the issue of historicity is that the Synoptic tradition is more historically plausible than the highly distinctive Johannine tradition. Based on his work on eyewitnesses, Bauckham provides counter-arguments to the most prominent scholarly views of the (non-) historicity of the story of the raising of Lazarus:

> the occurrence and nonoccurrence of names in stories in the Gospels may be partially explained by supposing that the named characters were members of the early Christian communities and themselves told the stories of the events in which they had been participants. So long as they were known figures, their names remained attached to their stories as indications of eyewitness sources of these stories. The same explanation easily fits the case of Lazarus, Martha, and Mary.[25]

Bauckham admits that the 'weightiest argument against the historicity of the raising of Lazarus (apart from the naturalistic objections to the miraculous) has always been its absence from the Synoptics.' Bauckham rightly points out that the presence of a given tradition in one Gospel only is not necessarily an argument against historicity and that there may have been reasons why the Synoptic writers did not feel the need to include another 'resuscitation miracle', like that of Jairus' daughter, and he adds that the raising of Lazarus is 'an especially impressive miracle and also gives it a key role in the sequence of events that led to Jesus' death'. To deal with such issues, Bauckham suggests that we could be dealing with something like a theological evaluation of historical events and that the raising of Lazarus is

---

24. But cf. Bauckham, *Beloved Disciple*, 240: 'These debates in the Gospel [of John] are often thought to reflect debates going on in the Gospel's context between Christians and non-Christian Jews who found the Christian claims for Jesus incompatible with Jewish monotheism. There may be something in this, but the passages in question are too integral to the Gospel's developing narrative and its sophisticated narrative revelation of Jesus' identity to be mere reflections of external debates.'
25. Bauckham, *Beloved Disciple*, 176.

the culmination of conflict against a backdrop of Jesus' popularity. Bauckham argues that this is a '*historical* form of explanation, which is arguably more convincing than Mark's, in which it seems to be Jesus' demonstration in the temple alone that provokes the authorities to plot his death (Mark 11.18).'[26] An explanation for Mark leaving out the Lazarus story could have been, Bauckham suggests, due to 'protective anonymity' where figures such as Lazarus were not named (or discussed at all) in a passion story originating in Jerusalem in the 40s.[27]

I am not convinced that this provides a satisfactory counter-argument to the view that the raising of Lazarus is fictional. The supernatural is glossed over too quickly by Bauckham. The raising of Jairus' daughter is subtly different. The girl is, after all, not dead but 'sleeping' (Mk 5:39) and it has long been noted that such resuscitations are paralleled cross-culturally so in themselves do not have the conventional barriers to historicity of something that would have to be miraculous. The story of the raising of Lazarus, however, makes it perfectly clear that Lazarus is not sleeping but very, very dead and in the tomb for four days (Jn 11:13-14, 17), with the fourth day being the time required for the certainty that a person be deemed well and truly dead, so the soul cannot return to the body, according to a later rabbinic tradition (*Lev. Rabbah* 18:1). So, this now means we have, on the one hand, a Markan-based tradition where authorities want to put Jesus to death because he did something particularly provocative in the Temple during a major festival; on the other hand, we have a Johannine tradition where the demonstration in the Temple is pushed to the beginning of the Gospel and the direct cause of Jesus' death is replaced with a supernatural miracle.

It seems to me that, irrespective of what we make of the historicity of the Markan story, the idea that someone overturning tables of moneychangers and dovesellers at Passover could lead to a less direct means of securing his arrest (a more direct attempt there and then might lead to disorder) is far more believable than a supernatural miracle, with the more mundane action in the Temple pushed to the beginning of the Gospel. At this point, the argument that the raising of Lazarus occurs only in John becomes more significant. Not only is John late first century at the earliest, but the fact that the story of a stunning miracle is missing in Luke and Matthew, not to mention non-Christian sources, is very suspicious and 'protective anonymity' only gets us so far. Why would no other source include this spectacular miracle used to explain Jesus' death, especially as we move further and further away from the 40s CE? And is there not a profound problem in suggesting that a man who had previously been dead was walking around Jerusalem but was

26. Bauckham, *Beloved Disciple*, 181-83.
27. Bauckham, *Beloved Disciple*, 189.

being protected through anonymity?[28] In terms of conventional historical judgment at least, should we not stick with the obvious and suggest that the idea of a formerly dead man walking around Jerusalem is too problematic for historical research?

Bauckham suggests that 'As with any other historical source, what needs to be assessed is its general reliability... If the Gospel is judged trustworthy so far as we can test it, then we should trust it for what we cannot verify. That is ordinary historical method.'[29] This seems reasonable enough and this is precisely what has led so many scholars into believing that John's Gospel is of minimal value for reconstructing the life and teaching of the historical Jesus. I have already given old and supplementary reasons, but more general points ought to give collective weight. Let us take the story of Nicodemus (Jn 3). Even if we were to assume that there was a historical Nicodemus active around the time of Jesus,[30] this story contains the only two Johannine references to the 'kingdom of God' (Jn 3:3, 5). This is, of course, in sharp contrast to the Synoptics where the phrase is famously common. Not only that, but these two references stand in stark contrast to the predictions of the imminent kingdom in Mark and Matthew because the Johannine verses speak of entry into the kingdom in terms of being 'born again'/'from above'. In addition to removing all the kingdom of God sayings, John 21 shows that

---

28. Ben Witherington III goes one better in suggesting that Lazarus, after being raised from the dead, wrote the bulk of John's Gospel:

> Lazarus is the Beloved Disciple...no better solution better explains all the interesting factors in play here than the proposal that the Beloved Disciple was someone whom Jesus had raised from the dead... If our author, the Beloved Disciple, had been raised by Jesus not merely from death's door but from being well and truly dead, this was bound to change his worldview! It became quite impossible for our author to draw up a veiled-Messiah portrait of Jesus, as we find in Mark. No, our author wanted and needed to shout from the mountain tops that Jesus was 'the resurrection,' not merely that he performed resurrections... He had had a personal and profound encounter of the first order with both the historical Jesus and the risen Jesus, and he knew they were one and the same. This was bound to change his worldview... Lazarus had become what he admired, and he had been made, to a lesser degree, to be like Jesus... John of Patmos was the final editor of this Gospel after the death of Lazarus. ('What's in a Name? Rethinking the Historical Figure of the Beloved Disciple in the Fourth Gospel,' in Anderson, Just and Thatcher, eds., *John, Jesus and History, Volume 2*, 209-212)

While, presumably, it is a reasonable thing to suggest that being raised from the (well and truly) dead would dramatically change almost anyone's worldview, I suspect some historians might have a few problems with a zombie-like figure writing the bulk of John's Gospel, though the suggestion that John of Patmos edited the final version might be even more difficult to believe.

29. Bauckham, *Beloved Disciple*, 27.
30. Bauckham, *Beloved Disciple*, 137-72.

there were obvious problems with predictions of the second coming of Jesus not happening, whereas the Synoptics still expect the second coming within the lifetime of Jesus' audience (Mk 13; Mt. 24; Lk. 21). Notice that John's Jesus can also speak of 'my kingdom' not being of this world (Jn 18:36). This is not 'the kingdom of God' of the earliest traditions and we can notice the development from 'the kingdom of God' to Jesus' kingdom in the development of Mark's tradition (compare Mk 9:1 with Mt. 16:28). Again, John's wording presumably points away from the earliest tradition.

We might further add that the Nicodemus dialogue looks like a classic case of Johannine replacement theology where Jewish ethnicity is replaced with some kind of Christianizing practice (baptism?), hence Nicodemus asks quizzically about being literally born again (Jn 3:4). Again, such dramatic claims are not found in the Synoptic tradition. So, again, we are left with, on the one hand, the Synoptic tradition expecting the imminent coming of the kingdom, alongside the return of Jesus within a generation; on the other hand, we have a removal of the imminent kingdom replaced with what is effectively a theological replacement for Jewish ethnicity at a time when other Christians were clearly experiencing problems with eschatological predictions not materializing. Ironically, there may actually be some use for John here in terms of the development of the earliest Jesus tradition because the Nicodemus story and the problems with imminent eschatology in John obviously suggest that there were earlier predictions concerning end times. It is extremely difficult to avoid the conclusion that the Nicodemus story has at the very least been written to reflect first-century (or later) issues.

Eyewitnesses and 'Gist'

It might be countered that a Bauckham-style reading works with the idea of eyewitnesses providing a generally accurate recollection of Jesus. While Bauckham accepts the storyteller's licence, he argues that eyewitness testimony retains the 'gist' of the story through memory and with fidelity to past events: 'the "gist" of an event that is remembered even when details are inaccurate... Those who recall the past really do intend to recall the past, not to create it to suit present needs and purposes.'[31] Though certainly not without qualification, much of Bauckham's methodology seems to be geared toward general historical accuracy and, more specifically, the Gospels as recalling unique, unusual, memorable and salient *historical* events. Generally speaking, Bauckham may well have a point, but when we apply this sort of approach to John's Gospel we start to get some problems.

31. Bauckham, *Beloved Disciple*, 339-40.

We have already seen issues concerning 'high' Christology, Nicodemus and the kingdom of God, and Sabbath disputes which are significantly different from the Synoptic Gospels. To this we might add: why are there no 'I am' sayings, with all their replacement theology and with obvious implications of high Christology (Jn 8:12 [cf. 7:2]; 10:7, 9; 11:25; 14:6) in the Synoptic tradition, and does not this John-only appearance suggest later fiction? To this we might add the farewell discourses, the teaching on the 'world', and the promise of the 'paraclete' (Jn 14:16-26; 15:26-27; 16:7-15) and so on: it is very difficult to see how these were missed out of earlier Jesus tradition and they are best explained as Johannine creations.[32] If significant differences are accepted as being significantly different, then it seems to me that 'gist' has the potential to be expanded indefinitely to include almost anything as a kind of 'natural' development. So where does 'gist' end? Can people not simply invent inaccurate things?

It ought to be added that even if we assume that underlying John's Gospel and Mark's Gospel are eyewitnesses, the old problems of different sources telling us different things remain and thus the same questions of historical accuracy remain. Can we say that the Beloved Disciple invented material or got a little too creative in his recollections? Or do we have to suggest that this material was always implicit in Jesus' teaching, that it was not really made so explicit in the other canonical Gospels and that it took the Beloved Disciple to make it explicit? These are serious problems which remain for anyone wanting to use John's Gospel as a source, irrespective of whether such sources are eyewitness testimony. Even if we were to accept that an eyewitness wrote John's Gospel, it seems to me that we would have a highly creative eyewitness who wrote creative fiction concerning Jesus.[33]

We have now covered major issues in John's Gospel and increasingly collective weight is being amassed. If we follow Bauckham on the importance of general reliability, then we would have to suggest that things do not look hopeful at all for those wishing to use John's Gospel to reconstruct the life and teaching of Jesus.

---

32. Cf. D. Catchpole, 'On Proving Too Much: Critical Hesitations about Richard Bauckham's Jesus and the Eyewitnesses,' *JSHJ* 6 (2008), 169-81.
33. For a helpful critique of memory and John's Gospel, see J. Painter, 'Memory Holds the Key: The Transformation of Memory in the Interface of History and Theology in John,' in Anderson, Just, and Thatcher, eds., *John, Jesus, and History, Volume 1*, 229-45. Painter also suggests a parallel in Plato providing a firsthand account of Socrates for a similar reflexive and interpretative account of a historical figure. Painter does not discuss Bauckham's work but the critique applies nonetheless.

John, Jesus and History Project

The John, Jesus and History Project participants are more systematic in their treatment of issues surrounding John's Gospel and historicity, unsurprisingly given the scope and nature of the different projects. In a lengthy essay in the first edited volume, Paul Anderson assesses the big issues, including those discussed above, and accepts that some of the criticisms against historicity have a degree of strength. However, Anderson argues, they also have significant weaknesses. On the virtual absence of 'the kingdom of God' in John's Gospel, Anderson makes the following counter:

> do we have a Johannine representation of the essential kingdom teaching of Jesus, even as represented in the fuller Synoptic accounts? After all, the spiritual workings of God's active and dynamic reign are indeed contrasted with the human scaffoldings of the religious quest in the Synoptics and the truthful and penetrating activity of God's present-and-ultimate reign is contrasted to all worldly powers—political and otherwise. In that sense, rather than leaving out Jesus' teachings on the kingdom, it could be said that John *summarizes* them.[34]

This may be fair as a (very general) generalization but if we were to push this further in terms of use for the study of the historical Jesus, then the generalization would not work well because the future aspect of the kingdom in John does not have the crucial issue of the imminence of the kingdom we find in Mark and Matthew at least. It is well known that John keeps the future kingdom but it is presumably not thought to be coming in power within the lifetime of Jesus' audience (cf. Mk 9:1) and this is why John removes the precise phrase 'the kingdom of God' and, for not unrelated reasons, why we get John 21. To refer back to the arguments made against Bauckham, there may be general similarities between John and the Synoptics, but once the specifics are brought in, the most obvious explanation is that the predictions of the imminent kingdom are early and the avoidance of these predictions are late and more obviously secondary. If we refer back to the argument that the discussion of the kingdom in John 3 has implications which replace Jewish ethnicity as a means of belonging to the 'in-group', then, on this topic at least, John's Gospel tells us much more about Christianity at the turn of the first century than it does about the historical Jesus. There is certainly nothing John adds to help in the quest for the historical Jesus on this issue, if this is the direction we wish to take Anderson's argument.

---

34. P. N. Anderson, 'Why This Study Is Needed, and Why It Is Needed Now,' in Anderson, Just and Thatcher, eds., *John, Jesus and History*, *Volume 1*, 13-73 (23).

Anderson also tackles other issues, but there is again the problematic tendency to make the arguments too generalized so that crucial details are omitted. To use an example already discussed, Anderson suggests that 'Jesus' healing on the Sabbath and challenge of religious authority is presented as clearly in John as it is in the Synoptics, despite its many distinctive features.'[35] But the distinctive features are crucial. John may agree with the Synoptics over healings on the Sabbath, but the example of John 5, at least, takes it in directions that are much more obviously reflective of the early church and the Johannine situation (the acceptance of the breaking of biblical law by carrying a burden and claiming equality with God) and has less chance of telling us anything significant about earlier tradition. As with Mk 3:1-6, the Lukan Sabbath healings are not against any biblical law, and are disputes over whether the healing activity itself is permitted on the Sabbath and if life is at risk (Lk. 13:10-17; 14:1-6). Once specifics are observed, we can see why John is deemed suspect for some in historical Jesus studies, at least in the instance of healing on the Sabbath.

This generalizing becomes a further problem when Anderson turns to historical Jesus scholarship. Based on Marcus Borg's summary of the different possible portraits of Jesus, Anderson suggests that John's Gospel is coherent with the different models. Anderson suggests that John's Jesus is a 'non-eschatological prophet...the prophet-like-Moses'. The Johnannine Jesus fits 'within the portraiture of a wisdom-imparting sage' and an 'institution-challenging Cynic, in that Jesus cleanses the Temple at the beginning of his ministry, heals on the Sabbath, confronts religious authorities in Jerusalem prolifically, and is willing to challenge the Roman governor in the name of God's transcendent truth and reign.' Anderson adds that Jesus 'comes across with spiritual power, as a holy man in John. While he does not perform exorcisms, the Johannine Jesus is encountered by people epiphanically... Jesus as a holy man cannot be said to be incompatible with the Johannine presentation of Jesus.' Adding to Borg's list, Anderson suggests John's Jesus also comes across as 'an apocalyptic messenger...and the entire ministry of Jesus is presented eschatologically.'[36]

Assuming for the moment the validity of using such disputed categories from historical Jesus scholarship, it is questionable whether Anderson's points help us in any significant way in terms of the quest for the historical Jesus. The idea of an apocalyptic and eschatological Jesus in John may well give a general insight into Jesus (and earliest Christianity, of course) but, as I have pointed out, it potentially gives us a distorted one in that the imminent predictions of 'the kingdom of God' have gone. Furthermore, is it

35. Anderson, 'Why This Study Is Needed,' 36.
36. Anderson, 'Why This Study Is Needed,' 63-65.

really any surprise images of Jesus as a prophet, an eschatological prophet and of a wisdom-related figure turn up in earliest Christianity, irrespective of whether Jesus generated such images of himself? In its struggle with identity in relationship to Jewish groups, it is no surprise that the Christian movement (or whatever we want to call it) tried to monopolize Jewish ideas for the figure of Jesus. After all, as Anderson points out, 'Jesus not only brings light to penetrate the darkness of the worldly thought; he *is* the Light of the world (John 1:4, 5, 8, 9; 3:19; 8:12; 9:5; 12:46).'[37] This could, of course, be plausibly explained as later Christian theology with only a very general connection to the historical Jesus.

The description of a Cynic Jesus highlights well the problems in working with such generalities. None of the features described by Anderson are particularly Cynic, or at least in the sense that numerous non-Cynic people could have been likewise. The Bible, the Dead Sea Scrolls, Josephus and rabbinic literature, for instance, give plenty of examples of institution-challenging figures. Many of the portraits of the Gospel contexts, including the Johannine contexts, and the contexts of the earliest Christians, suggest institution-challenging figures and groups, perhaps inevitably given that a new religious movement was to emerge. It is difficult to see how this very general parallel means we should be including John in historical Jesus discussion. Much more precise and detailed evidence is needed. One point is worth re-emphasizing in response to Anderson: putting the cleansing of the Temple at the beginning of the ministry in John is done by putting the raising of Lazarus as the immediate cause of Jesus' death, and again, if anything, this detracts from using John as a source for understanding the cleansing of the Temple in relation to the historical Jesus. In all these portraits of Jesus, and against Anderson, we probably *cannot* say that 'One might even make the case that any of these portraits might be sketched *more clearly* from Johannine material than from any of the other Gospels.'[38]

Similarly, when Anderson points out that 'In all four Gospels, Jesus comes across as a Jewish prophet healing the sick, challenging the religious institutions, speaking with prophetic urgency, and suffering death at the hands of the Romans in Jerusalem', we miss out on the key distinctive features of John versus the Synoptics and how the Johannine version is clearly building on and altering earlier versions. Anderson, however, adds further Johannine contributions to the quest for the historical Jesus:

1. Jesus' simultaneous ministry alongside John the Baptizer and the prolific availability of purifying power

37. Anderson, 'Why This Study Is Needed,' 63.
38. Anderson, 'Why This Study Is Needed,' 65.

2. Jesus' cleansing of the temple as an inaugural prophetic sign
3. Jesus' travel to and from Jerusalem and his multiyear ministry
4. Early events in the public ministry of Jesus
5. Favourable receptions in Galilee among Samaritans, women, and Gentiles
6. Jesus' Judean ministry and archaeological realism
7. The Last Supper as a common meal and its proper dating
8. Jesus' teaching about the way of the Spirit and the reign of truth[39]

Certainly we may grant potential specifics. It may be the case that there was a simultaneous ministry with John the Baptist, as has also been noted in analysis of material particular to Luke and Matthew.[40] While some of us are not convinced, arguments in favour of Johannine chronology will no doubt continue on the dating of the 'Last Supper'. While there are other aspects, such as Jesus' prediction of a rebuilt Temple (Jn 2:13-22),[41] which may be early tradition, it is notable that we are dealing with arguments which effectively assume historical Jesus 'results' based on the analysis from the *Synoptic* tradition and then corrected or modified using John's Gospel.[42] This may be an important point to emphasize, but the implication has to be that if we used John's Gospel as *the* source then we would have a view of the historical Jesus which was far more reflective of later Christian theology.

Some points raised by Anderson (and others) are too general to give a precise response, though partly because Anderson understandably wants to ground the issues in historical Jesus and Johannine scholarship. The 'multi-year' ministry and numerous visits to Jerusalem may have been the case, but we work that out by looking at first-century cultural contexts. If it were the case that it is more likely Jesus would have visited Jerusalem more than once, then it may simply be assumed in Mark (cf. Mk 11:2-6; 14:12-14) and not worthy of mention because it was assumed, perhaps, that nothing

---

39. Anderson, 'Why This Study Is Needed,' 69-70.
40. M. Casey, *An Aramaic Approach to Q* (Cambridge: Cambridge University Press, 2002), 105-45. See also, Andrew Lincoln's careful qualifications concerning Jesus and baptizing, in A. T. Lincoln, '"We Know That His Testimony is True": Johannine Truth Claims and Historicity,' in Anderson, Just and Thatcher, eds., *John, Jesus and History, Volume 1*, 179- 97 (187-91).
41. See e.g., J. F. McGrath, '"Destroy This Temple": Issues of Historicity in John 2.13-22,' in Anderson, Just and Thatcher, eds., *John, Jesus and History, Volume 2*, 35-43.
42. Cf. D. Moody Smith, 'John: A Source for Jesus Research?,' in Anderson, Just and Thatcher, eds., *John, Jesus and History, Volume 1*, 165-78. See also 178: 'the Jesus who talks the Christology is not the Jesus of Nazareth. Despite all the historical difficulties they may present, as well as their narrative and christological bias, the Synoptics nevertheless more faithfully represent the historical figure of Jesus as he was.'

particularly interesting happened in other visits, and if so then we are back with John being the less useful.[43]

We might develop such ideas to include the Passion chronology and the trial in John's Gospel as compared to Mark; a common issue raised in the publications of the John, Jesus and History Project. Mark's trial scene may well contain historical inaccuracies (Mk 14:53–15:1; cf. m. *Sanh.* 4:1) that cast strong doubts about the validity of its historical accuracy and it may well be a fictional polemic designed to persuade people that Jesus was unjustly killed—but this does not mean John is necessarily more helpful. If John provides a more plausible outline of chronology and procedure then this only need mean, like John's geographical knowledge, that he knows the right details, in this case procedural. John's trial and crucifixion still contain all sorts of issues which may be motivated more by Johannine interests than fidelity to, or reflections on, earlier theological tendencies and historical realities, such as a revelation of Jesus' 'true identity' (compare Jn 18:19 with 13:36-38) and a theological construction of superiority over against the high priest.[44] We might also observe that another disciple, in addition to Peter, managed to get in on the act of Jesus' trial, indeed into the court of the high priest as Peter stood by denying Jesus (Jn 18:15-17). Is there no reason to be a little suspicious of this Johannine addition, written, perhaps, to explain

---

43. Cf. M. M. Thompson's summary of the historical Jesus by E. P. Sanders. Sanders claims:

> Jesus' case—briefly put, that he was God's spokesman, knew what his next major action in Israel's history would be, and could specify who would be in the kingdom—put him equally obviously against any reasonable interpretation of the scripture. If we give full weight to Jesus' extraordinary statements about the kingdom and about the role of his disciples—and thus, by implication, about himself—we have no trouble seeing that his claims were truly offensive... [E]xegesis indicates that there were specific issues at stake between Jesus and the Jewish hierarchy, and that the specific issues revolved around a *basic question*: who spoke for God? (E.P. Sanders, *Jesus and Judaism* [London: SCM, 1985], 280-81).

Thompson adds, 'I have often thought that no better summary could be given of the Gospel of John than this one' (M. M. Thompson, 'The "Spiritual Gospel": How John the Theologian Writes History,' in Anderson, Just and Thatcher, eds., *John, Jesus and History, Volume 1*, 103-107 [107]). This only works at the very general level with some very general statements (e.g. God's spokesman, truly offensive, exegetical differences), but if for the moment we assumed Sanders's portrait of Jesus in only a little more detail, it starts to break down. Sanders's Jesus preaches the imminent kingdom of God; John's does not. John's Jesus makes comments deemed offensive on the issue of being equal with God; Sanders's Jesus does not; both may have claimed to have spoken for God, but are their messages really the same? Note also the reference to 'kingdom' in Sanders's summary, the very term so downplayed and reapplied in John's Gospel.

44. See H. Bond, 'At the Court of the High Priest: History and Theology in John 18:13-24,' in Anderson, Just and Thatcher, eds., *John, Jesus and History, Volume 2*, 313-24 (318-21).

how a reliable Johannine source got into the heart of the trial, and that it is not a genuine historical remembrance?

Some of this is, of course, speculative, but we have little to go on and so little can actually be said. Elsewhere, Anderson points out that 'Mark mentions only one Passover, the one at which Jesus was killed, implying that Jesus' ministry and opposition were all mounted within a relatively short period of time rather than over a period of several years' and argues that 'This could have been the case, but John's rendering here seems more plausible.'[45] But there is no reason why John should be more plausible. Why would it be less plausible for Jesus to have done something provocative in the Temple once and then be killed for it? Why is it less plausible that there was a relatively short ministry (assuming Mark is implying this)? Is it not plausible that John's Gospel introduced extra visits to Jerusalem for theological reasons (e.g. replacement theology) which had no grounding in actual visits to Jerusalem and only happen to reflect the very general point that some Jews went to Jerusalem more than once?[46] Further problems arise when we note that the Johannine conflicts involve the raising of Lazarus, disputes over Jesus being equal with God and the displacement of the Temple scene to the beginning of his ministry. In this light, it is not difficult to see why scholars have been so sceptical in using John as a source for historical Jesus studies.

Similarly, John may record earlier events but these include things like the wedding at Cana which are not helpful, and earlier events may simply be legendary additions, as we usually imply from Luke's story of Jesus as a youth and from apocryphal stories. Archaeological realism tells us little other than details of the place. This may be helpful in understanding the physical world, but fictional stories can, of course, be crafted in very real settings and all such Johannine material shows us is familiarity with Jerusalem.[47] Some suggestions raised by Anderson are at least confronted with old problems. The idea of an 'inaugural prophetic sign' in the cleansing of the Temple again faces the massive historical issue of the location of the raising of Lazarus. The idea that Jesus found favourable receptions in Galilee, 'among Samaritans, women, and Gentiles', poses big problems. It may have been that Jesus attracted women, but this is mentioned in the Synoptics (e.g. Mk 15:40-41; Lk. 8:1-3) and the argument is again too general, as we know that in a later context, Celsus looked down on Christianity partly through seeing it as a lure for women (e.g. Origen, *Contra Celsum* 3.10, 44).

---

45. Anderson, 'Why This Study Is Needed,' 40.
46. Similar points apply to John's portrayal or Jesus associating with Samaritans (cf. Jn 4) because Jesus would have had to travel through Samaria to get to and from Jerusalem (cf. *A.J.* 20.118; *B.J.* 269). All this shows, of course, is that John knew his geography.
47. See the points made by Painter, 'Memory Holds the Key,' 233-34.

Johannine illumination of early Galilean tradition in general is certainly possible, perhaps with reference to Bethsaida, even if the tradition has been heavily reworked and we only have the core of the idea that, say, Bethsaida was initially a significant centre (cf. Jn 1:43-51; 12:20-22).[48] However, the idea of favourable reception among Gentiles and Samaritans is most likely Christian fiction, or at least faces the problem that earlier material did not think this was the case, at least in any enthusiastic way. Mark 7 provides the explicitly exceptional example of the Syro-Phoenician woman, while Mt. 10:5-6 has Jesus saying, 'Go nowhere among the Gentiles, and enter no town of the Samaritans, but go rather to the lost sheep of the house of Israel.' Given that the debates in earliest Christianity were about *how* Gentiles were to be incorporated, not *if* they were to be incorporated, then it is much more difficult to see how the favourable reaction among Gentiles and Samaritans is to be deemed more likely to go back to the historical Jesus than Mt. 10:5-6. Moreover, if material concerning a favourable reaction among Gentiles and Samaritans were available, is this not exactly the sort of thing Mark would have craved (cf. Mk 6–8; 13:10)?[49]

History versus Theology?

A final point involving history and theology needs to be addressed. Where Bauckham was concerned with eyewitness testimony and history, underlying much of the John, Jesus and History Project is the idea that theology does not necessarily equal historical inaccuracies.[50] The 'gist' of an earlier story can still be found in theologically framed texts. Anderson argues that the 'assumption that theologization and spiritualization necessarily imply ahistoricity' is a 'fallacy' and to say that 'symbolization, spiritualization, or theologization displaces originative history is terribly flawed as a historiographic procedure'. Anderson qualifies this and claims, 'equating John's spiritualization of events in the ministry of Jesus cannot be considered a

48. See e.g., M. Appold, 'Jesus' Bethsaida Disciples: A Study in Johannine Origins,' in Anderson, Just and Thatcher, eds., *John, Jesus and History, Volume 2*, 27-34, but with the response by Koester, 'Aspects of Historicity in John 1–4,' 95-97.

49. S. Miller makes some general points of comparison between Jesus' message and Samaritan theology and suggests reasons why Samaritans might have been attracted to Jesus' message. See S. Miller, 'The Woman at the Well: John's Portrayal of the Samaritan Woman,' in Anderson, Just and Thatcher, eds., *John, Jesus and History, Volume 2*, 73-81. General similarity, however, cannot function as a strong argument in favour of the historical Jesus attracting and interacting with Samaritans because more precise arguments in favour of historicity, and how to deal with the problem of Mt. 10:5-6, are required. See also the points raised by Koester, 'Aspects of Historicity in John 1–4,' 100-101.

50. Bauckham also pushes this idea. See e.g., *Beloved Disciple*, 14, 19, ch. 4.

solid proof of its ahistoricity'.[51] Anderson is, of course, correct, but I am not sure that the approach critiqued by Anderson is advanced by too many contemporary scholars. However, a more precise target is mentioned in the same volume, in D. A. Carson's critique of the work of Casey on Johannine theological and christological development over against the historical Jesus: 'one thing that stands out in Casey's work is the way he pits history against theology. In contrast, Marianne Meye Thompson constantly endeavours to show the ways in which history and theology should not be pitted against each other.'[52]

I am not sure this is a particularly valuable critique. Casey can defend himself, of course, but it seems to me that the general issue is not simply one of pitting theology against history but rather the historical location of a given type of theology. So, in the case of a theology which has Jesus cast as being equal with God, it is highly likely to be theological reflection sometime after the death of Jesus, whereas a theology which defends what is deemed a correct legal interpretation with reference to an idiomatic Aramaic saying has more chance of being from the historical Jesus (again, I leave the issue of precise historicity to one side for now). Of course, things, including theology, do not necessarily develop and grow in precise and neat chronological order (and 'low' Christology alone did not die out so quickly and can be invented, too), but the question here, it should be stressed, is dating and locating theology and not pitting theology over against history. If we are not careful then we are getting close to the idea that all interpretation is correct interpretation. As with Bauckham and 'gist', is it not possible that things are murkier than that and that certain interpretations could have been at odds with the ideas of the historical Jesus?

Concluding Remarks

It does not give me great pleasure to disagree with a challenge to a consensus and non-creatively reaffirm a traditional position. And I hope I am not damning Bauckham, Anderson and others in praising them for bringing scholarly assumptions to the fore. It is certainly important to keep questioning established ideas and force defences of them. However, this

51. Anderson, 'Why This Study Is Needed,' 42-43.
52. D. A. Carson, 'The Challenge of the Balkanization of Johannine Studies,' in Anderson, Just and Thatcher, eds., *John, Jesus and History, Volume 1*, 133-159 (147); cf. M. M. Thompson, 'The Historical Jesus and the Johannine Christ,' R. A. Culpepper and C. Black, eds., *Exploring the Gospel of John: In Honor of D. Moody Smith* (Louisville: Westminster John Knox, 1996), 21-42; idem, 'The "Spiritual Gospel";' C. S. Keener, '"We Beheld His Glory!" (John 1:14),' in Anderson, Just and Thatcher, eds., *John, Jesus, and History, Volume 2*, 15-25; Koester, 'Aspects of Historicity in John 1–4'.

forcing has not, I think, shown that the Johannine tradition offers anything significant for the study of the historical Jesus; certainly not in any way that would provide a significant rewriting of lives of Jesus. Even if we are dealing with eyewitness testimonies in reconstructing the life of the historical Jesus, the old problems of fictional rewriting (or remembering) will not go away (e.g. the raising of Lazarus as the catalyst for Jesus' death), no matter how subtle the framing of the questions in terms of memory, eyewitnesses and theology may be. It may well be the case, as several participants in the John, Jesus and History Project make clear, that there is a strong argument to be made for John historicizing his story and not simply being interested in all things symbolic, but this does not, of course, mean we are dealing with evidence of the historical Jesus' life and teaching. While specifics of interpretation and the historical location of John will no doubt continue to breed perhaps necessary disagreements, it would seem that the major scholarly trend since the nineteenth century of largely avoiding John for reconstructing the life and teaching of Jesus appears to be correct. This may be a modernist assumption, as we are sometimes told, but it is not necessarily a wrong one.

- 10 -

Psalm 72 and Mark 1:12-13: Mythic Evocation in Narratives of the Good King

Thomas L. Thompson

In this essay, I present a brief analysis of the construction of a single episode in Mark's Gospel and of the methods which were effectively used in the development and use of a significant building block[1] of his Jesus narrative, reflecting an allegorical technique which reiterates earlier biblical narratives similarly composed within a biographical mode. I have earlier illustrated how specifically allegorical function of such biography has roots in the ancient Near Eastern and early Mediterranean world of narratives, particularly in narratives reflecting royal ideology.[2] I have found the genre's allegorical function most accessible in the development of the figure of Job,[3] but it can also be recognized, for example, in the narratives about Abraham and Esau,[4] as well as in those of David, Solomon and Jesus.[5] While considerable progress has been made in regard to such Samaritan and Jewish

1. On the use of building blocks as an explanatory analogy for the segmented structure of biblical composition, see T. L. Thompson, '4QTestimonia and Bible Composition: A Copenhagen Lego Hypothesis,' in F. H. Cryer and T. L. Thompson, eds., *Qumran between the Old and New Testaments* (CIS, 6; Sheffield: Sheffield Academic Press, 1998), 261-76.
2, T. L. Thompson, *The Messiah Myth: The Ancient Near Eastern Roots of Jesus and David* (New York/London: Basic Books/Jonathan Cape, 2005/2006).
3. T. L. Thompson, 'Job 29: Biography or Parable?,' in T. L. Thompson and H. Tronier, eds., *Frelsens Biografisering* (FBE, 13; Copenhagen: Museum Tusculanums Forlag, 2004), 115-34.
4. T. L. Thompson, 'Reiterative Narratives of Exile and Return: Virtual Memories of Abraham in the Persian and Hellenistic Periods' (forthcoming); idem, 'What We Do and Do Not Know about Pre-Exilic al-Quds,' in E. Pfoh and K. W. Whitelam, eds., *The Politics of Israel's Past: Biblical Archaeology and Nation-Building* (Sheffield Phoenix Press, forthcoming); idem, 'Memories of Esau and Narrative Reiteration: Themes of Conflict and Reconciliation,' *JSOT* 25.2 (2011), 175-200.
5. Thompson, *The Messiah Myth.*

functions of commentary and prophecy in the development of the Gospel narratives through a reiteration or rewriting of the Old Testament,[6] I here wish to pay as much attention to mythic functions which were developed in the broader literary world of antiquity.

A Summary of an Untold Story

The brief account of Jesus' temptation in the desert, which we find in Mk 1:12-13, appears at first to do little more than evoke a story which remains, however, untold. Although lacking a proper narrative, it, nevertheless, offers four clearly presented and distinct thematic elements of a plot-line: (1) the spirit who drives Jesus into the desert; (2) the forty days he is tempted by Satan; (3) he lived with the wild animals and (4) angels cared for him. Although each of these elements have been clearly related in what remains a mere paraphrase of a story, the significance and function of this clustering of motifs is uncertain, implicit or blind. This mere projection of a story untold stands in striking contrast to the three-fold debate narratives in which these same elements function in the Gospels of Matthew and Luke. The purpose behind the spirit that drives Jesus into the desert, the functional specificity of Satan's temptation and the implicit intertextuality of Jesus' living in the desert with wild animals in both Matthew and Luke's version of this story appear as blind motifs in Mark's Gospel. This striking difference encourages me to look more closely at the interactive symbol-system which can be identified with these elements in the hope of evoking something of the relevant meaning of what are obviously significant elements introducing Mark's Jesus. For example, the echo of the Elijah narrative from 1 Kgs 19:7-8 evoked in Mark's reference to angels caring for Jesus in the desert is surely to be associated with the citation of Isaiah's proclamation in the opening words of the gospel of the 'good news' of God's kingdom (Mk 1:1). This ancient, well-known inaugural proclamation[7] is reused by Mark to illustrate Isaiah's announcement of the opening of holy Zion's utopian new world

6. See, for example, especially, J. Bowman, *The Gospel of Mark: The New Christian Jewish Passover Haggadah* (Leiden: Brill, 1965); J. D. Crossan, *The Cross That Spoke: The Origins of the Passion Narrative* (San Francisco: Harper & Row, 1988); J. D. Levenson, *The Death and Resurrection of the Beloved Son: The Transformation of Child Sacrifice in Judaism and Christianity* (New Haven: Yale University Press, 1993) and further, R. M. Price, 'New Testament Narrative as Old Testament Midrash,' in J. Neusner and A. Avery-Peck, eds., *Encyclopedia of Midrash. I. Biblical Interpretation in Formative Judaism* (Leiden: Brill, 2005), 534-73 and his article in this volume: 'Does the Christ Myth Theory Require an Early Date for the Pauline Epistles?,' nn. 62-63.

7. This trope dates at least to the New Kingdom inaugural songs of Merneptah and Ramses IV's reigns: J. B. Pritchard, *ANET*, 378-79. The text from Ramses IV will be discussed further below.

(Isa. 6:1-7; 61:1-6). With it, Mark presents a significant reiteration of the central theme of the Elijah-Elisha tradition: life's victory over death, which is reiterated throughout the miracle stories of his gospel. This evocation of the divine kingdom is also clearly concentrated in Mark's assigning John Elijah's role of the converting angel of Malachi, who is to bring reconciliation to Israel and avoid the coming day of Yahweh's terror and judgment (Mk 1:2-3; cf. Mal. 3:1, 23-24!; also Isa. 40:3).[8] One might understand, thereby, Mark's periphrastic episode of Jesus being driven into the desert as serving an explanatory, introductory function within Mark's Gospel, paired as it is with the coming of the spirit in the episode of Jesus' baptism we find in Mk 1:9-11. It presents Jesus' first *inspired* engagement: a clear reiteration of the role as driving force which 'Yahweh's spirit' has in the Book of Judges, not least as it is presented in the form of a leitmotif for the saving events of Samson's tale (Judg. 13:25; 14:6, 19; 15:14), a function which is well recognized in motifs implied in Pss. 3:10; 6:34 and 18:2, 21. Mark 1:14-15, accordingly, closing John's Elijah-inspired role in Mark's introduction, appropriately follows upon Jesus' departure from the desert. Jesus, driven by the spirit, preaching the good news of the kingdom, is now fit to be the successor of John in taking up the Elijah role from Malachi: the preaching of repentance. The theme of proclaiming the 'good news' dominates. 'The time is ripe' as a chain-narrative is directed through its opening episodes towards the declaration of Jesus' fame, so appropriately illustrated by the growing awareness of his authority over 'unclean spirits' (Mk 1:23-28).

Read in this way, within the context of rewritten narrative, Mark's episode of Jesus in the desert functions as an integral part of the introduction and, in particular, as an illustration of the spirit's power in determining Jesus' role in the story of the kingdom that Mark had announced in his Gospel's opening proclamation. Nevertheless, the key to the integration of the narrative within the introduction to Mark's Gospel implicates only its opening and closing elements: the driving spirit and the care given to him by the angels as it had once been given to Elijah in I Kings 19. The opaque periphrastic rendition of the story as such still threatens to empty the episode of any meaning it might have had apart from this introductory function. Why did the spirit drive Jesus into the desert, rather than elsewhere? Why forty days? Certainly this number, pregnant with meaning and allusion, is meaning-bearing. Are specific biblical narratives reiterated or is it a more generically divine plan or destiny which are signified by this motif? Why and in what way does Satan test Jesus? What role do the wild animals play and why does Jesus need the care of angels while he is in the desert? Just such questions

8. Thompson, *Messiah Myth*, 37. For a discussion of the Gospels' rewriting of the Elijah and Elisha stories, see, *Messiah Myth*, 27-65.

are addressed in Matthew and Luke's constructions. Was Jesus driven into the desert to be tempted in imitation of Israel's lost generation in Numbers, when Israel was driven back into the desert by Yahweh for forty years? Within Mark's Gospel, such questions do not immediately help; for this text hides every narration-explicit function of relating an episode as meaningful within a plot. Merely a reiterative and evocative role seems active, a role which bridges and relates the transition between the coming of the spirit to Jesus at the Jordan and the driving out of the unclean spirit from the man in the synagogue of Capernaum. As an effective narrative segment within Mark's chain narrative, however, the cluster of elements lacks content and, with that content, meaning; it alludes rather to an untold story.

Rewritten Torah or an Allegory on the Wilderness Generation?

In Mt. 4:1-11, the motif of Jesus driven into the desert is also presented. As in Mark, it immediately follows the scene of the spirit's descent over Jesus after he was baptized by John. However, that scene closes with the words of a 'voice from heaven', which quote an amalgam of Ps. 2:7 and Isa. 42:1: 'This is my beloved son, with whom I am well pleased' (Mt. 3:17), helping to create a scene which finds its closest reiteration in Matthew's transfiguration story (Mt. 17:5). This is the context given to our episode. Jesus is driven by the spirit into the desert 'to be tempted by the devil' (Mt. 4:1). The temptation takes the substantial form of a threefold debate story. The integration of the debate's first round with the narrative's context and specifically Matthean development is thorough. The number forty is used as the number of days of Jesus' fast and this provides an integrated and fitting occasion for the first of three temptations. Having fasted forty days and forty nights, Jesus is hungry! From this, the 'tempter' (Mt. 4:3) takes his cue for his opening challenge: 'If you are God's son [as the foregoing scene's quotation from Isaiah had implied], let the stones become bread'—a strikingly relevant reiteration of his rebuke to the Pharisees and Sadducees when he was at the Jordan: 'God can indeed raise up children to Abraham from these stones' (Mt. 3:9)! If he is divine, surely Jesus can make bread from such stones as well as children to Abraham—a theologically intelligent and perceptive introduction to a discourse on Yahweh's promise in Jeremiah always to answer Israel's prayer and provide for them in their need (Jer. 29:12-13), which Matthew will come to emphasize in Jesus' sermon on the mount, where God is likened—in surprisingly detailed contrast to the temptation story's devil—to a father who *gives bread rather than stones* and fish rather than snakes to his children (Mt. 7:12-13), a likeness of the divine which is also narratively reiterated and expanded in two stories about Jesus' feeding the crowds with both bread and fish: to 5000 (in a story Matthew has in common with Mark: Mt. 14:16-21; cf.

Mk 6:30-44) and to 4000 who are hungry (a story in which Matthew, with Mark, retells an Elisha miracle story from 2 Kings: Mt. 15:32-39; Mk 8:1-10; cf. 2 Kgs 4:42-44).[9] Jesus' successful response to the tempter's challenge in Matthew 4 appropriately cites Deuteronomy's discourse on the already engaged lost generation of Numbers: 'Man does not live by bread alone, but by every word that comes from the mouth of God' (Mt. 4:4). Indeed, the passage brings together Deut. 8:3's reiteration of the narrative of Exod. 34:28 in order to structure the entirety of this first part of Jesus' debate with the devil as a reiterative allegory: 'Yahweh had humbled Israel [Jesus as fasting] and let you hunger [the occasion which gave rise to this particular temptation], and he fed you with manna, which you did not know [reiterating Exodus' playful pun on manna; i.e. in Hebrew, *man hu*, 'What is that?']... that you might learn that man does not live by bread alone, but by all that comes from Yahweh's mouth.' After this devastating first round, the debate continues as the devil takes Jesus out of the wilderness, to the pinnacle of the Temple, where he asks Jesus to demonstrate that Yahweh cares for him as he would for his own son: 'If you are God's son, throw yourself down.' He provocatively quotes from the Psalter: 'He will give his angels charge over you and they will bear you up on their hands, lest you strike your foot on a stone' (Mt. 4:5-6; Ps. 91:11-12). Jesus tops the devil's quotation: 'You shall not tempt the Lord your God', deftly citing Ps. 95:8-9, which, by reiterating Deut. 6:16, appropriately fits Matthew's context with the help of Mic. 3:11. He closes the second round of the debate by again returning to the lost generation's fateful tempting of Yahweh in the wilderness (Exod. 17:2-7)! In the third and final temptation, Jesus is taken to a high mountain, where the devil shows him all the riches of the world and their glory. The expected conditional clause, 'If you are God's son', is left off and the story turns instead directly to its dramatic closure. Heaven is once again stormed by Matthew's Lucifer-like Satan as Jesus is unconditionally challenged: 'All these will I give you, if you fall down and worship me' (Mt. 4:8-9). Jesus summarily dismisses his opponent by again turning to the wilderness discourse of Deuteronomy: 'You shall worship the Lord your God and serve him alone!' (Mt. 4:10; Deut. 6:13; 10:12, 20; 1 Sam. 7:3). Matthew's Torah-reiterating story closes with the angels coming to care for him as the angel had cared for Elijah before him, when he was given food and drink at Horeb to strengthen him for his forty days' journey into the wilderness (1 Kgs 19:5-9).

9. For an earlier discussion of the feeding stories, see Thompson, *Messiah Myth*, 51-55.

Filled with the Holy Spirit: God's Son

In Luke's Gospel, the temptation story of Lk. 4:1-13 is linked to an expansive baptism narrative (Lk. 3:1-22), which closes in a reiteration of Isa. 42:1-2, the opening of the first of the 'servant songs',[10] which identify Isaiah's suffering servant as God's chosen one, his first-born and beloved son, Israel (cf. the related, allegorical representation of Isaac in the opening of the etiological allegory for the sacrifice of the first-born in Gen. 22:2; cf. Exod. 13:2, 11-16; 22:29; 34:19-20). Having established this allegorical understanding of his Jesus, Luke links this figure with his birth story by means of a reversed genealogy, centred on Genesis 5, for one 'who had been understood as son of Joseph' (Lk. 3:23-38). Taking up the implied discourse of Genesis 5's complex association of this genealogy with the ironic portrayal of humanity as created in the image of God, the Lucifer tradition implicated by reference to 'the fallen ones' of Gen. 6:1-4, in order that his Jesus might be understood in light of the mythic and messianic roles of son of God, just ruler and new morning star (Ps. 82:6-7; Isa. 14:12-15; 2 Sam. 23:3-4),[11] Luke traces his genealogy for Jesus from Joseph back to God.[12]

With this introduction in place, Luke expands his narrative by drawing on Mark's thematic element of the driving spirit as Luke presents his temptation story as the first of four tales dealing with the divine qualities of one filled with the Spirit (Lk. 4:1-13, 16-30, 31-37 and 38-41), creating, with the help of this narrative chain, a scene of growing uncertainty and ambivalence over Jesus' reputation and identity (4:14-15, 28-30, 40-41, 42-44). In Luke's version of the temptation story, Jesus is led by the spirit in the desert for forty days, where he is tempted by the devil (Lk. 4:1-2). Luke's Jesus does not undertake a fast for forty days, but rather, more simply, 'did not eat during this time', making his story parallel more immediately the narrative in Exod. 34:28, which Deut. 8:3 refers to and interprets. In the Pentateuchal version of the story, Moses had been with Yahweh for forty days, *without eating or drinking*, and he wrote the words of the covenant on the tablets (Exod. 34:28).[13] In this way, Luke, much as Matthew had done in his way, prepares his audience for Jesus' answer to the devil's first challenge that the stones be made into

10. Isa. 42:1-4; cf. 49:1-6; 50:4-11 and 52:13–53:12.
11. On this discursive understanding of the genealogy of Gen. 5 and the opening of the flood story, see now T. L. Thompson, 'Imago Dei: A Problem of Pentateuchal Discourse,' *SJOT* 23.1 (2009), 135-48.
12. On this context, see, further, J. VanderKam, *Enoch and the Growth of the Apocalyptic Tradition* (CBQMS, 2; Washington: CBA, 1984); H. S. Kvanvig, 'Genesis 6,3 and the Watcher Story,' *Henoch* 25 (2003), 1-20; Thompson, *Messiah Myth*, 231-32.
13. For an alternative use of the 40 days and eating and drinking or the lack thereof, see 1 Kgs 19:8.

bread. 'Not by bread alone', but—echoing implicitly the story of Moses in the wilderness, while citing explicitly the commentary in Deut. 8:3—'by all that comes out of Yahweh's mouth'. Luke similarly follows Matthew in the other two temptations, presenting, however, first his variation of Matthew's third temptation on the high mountain, where Jesus views the authority and glory of all the world's kingdoms at one time (Lk. 4:5). Although Luke's version of the debate emphasizes the devil's claim to have both the authority and glory he offers Jesus, if only Jesus would worship him, Jesus' response, citing Deuteronomy, follows Matthew's version closely (Lk. 4:7-8; cf. Deut. 6:13; 10:12, 20). The distinctiveness of Luke's version of the temptation story lies primarily in his story's closing rhetoric. The placement of the scene on the pinnacle of the Temple as the temptation story's final exchange and especially, when it is compared with the stories of both Mark and Matthew, the absence of the theme of angels caring for Jesus, increases emphatically the weight which is placed on the quotation from Deut. 6:16 and draws the temptation story into Luke's larger narrative's context of four tales supporting the theme of widespread questioning, uncertainty and ambivalence about Jesus' identity and authority. The citation of Ps. 91:12, with the Greek's euphemistic translation of the name, Yahweh, as 'Lord', as his narrative's closing message, allows Luke to lay emphasis on the conditional clause of the devil's question: 'If you are the son of God'. In Luke's narrative, it evokes a more complex association with sons of god, as teasing as it is ambiguous, especially tied as it is with Deut 6:16's commandment that one 'must not tempt the Lord, your God' (Lk. 6:13)!

Two Biographical Tropes

Each of the versions of our narrative is well integrated within the central themes and structures of their respective Gospels. At the same time, all three could be understood as drawing on a recognizable template or tale type,[14] if we abstract from the fact that the version as presented in Mark lacks the debate which so dominates the presentations we find in Matthew and Luke's Gospels. The tale which is shared in common is clearly defined not by the debate, but by the four very specific thematic elements we discussed at the beginning of this essay—absent any obvious integral narrative function. The primary difficulty arising from this first reading is the lack of a meaning-bearing plot progression in Mark's version, in spite of the quite competent

14. I am using 'tale type' in the sense developed by the Folklore Fellows. See, for example, S. Thompson, *The Types of the Folktale: A Classification and Bibliography* (FFC, 74 Helsinki: Folklore Fellows, 1927); idem, *The Folktale* (Berkeley: University of California Press, 1946); V. Propp, *The Morphology of the Folktale* (Austin: University of Texas Press, 1968).

role it plays within the larger introduction to Mark's Gospel. Is it helpful to read Mark's episode as an identifiable segmented narrative which reflects an identifiable stereotypical tale type and which is shared by the versions offered in Matthew and Luke or has the inclusion of the threefold debates in Matthew and Luke effectively altered Mark's tale? Do these four elements, which present Jesus as being driven into the desert by the spirit, tested by Satan for forty days, living with wild animals and having angels to care for him, belong together? Do they create a signifying cluster of motifs within the symbol system[15] that underlies the narrative world Mark's Gospel serves?[16] As we have already seen, these specific motifs can readily be understood as both comparable to and echoing such narratives of the Pentateuch as the testing of the lost generation or as the scene of Moses on Mount Sinai, the role the spirit plays in the Samson narrative of Judges or the motif of the angel caring for Elijah in a cave on the edge of the wilderness of Horeb. All, in one way or another, reiterate a variety of Old Testament thematic elements. One might also point out the messianic roles which are played out in connection with such motifs as the spirit and the wilderness in the Elijah-Elisha succession narrative (1 Kgs 19; 2 Kgs 2). However, can Mark's episode bear its own weight as a story in its own right? Is Mark's version of the story of the testing of Jesus in the desert—in contrast to the debate narratives of Matthew and Luke—to be understood collectively as a cluster of motifs, which bear their own, distinct meaning within Mark, given that any other comparable meaning-bearing narrative is absent? I must ask the reader, at this point, to allow a brief excursus on some characteristics of biographical tropes in biblical literature.

There are two central ancient Near Eastern tropes, related to the development of biographical portraits of royal saviour figures, which I believe are identifiable in the introductory narrative of Mk 1:1-13 and which, in their reiteration through biblical literature, appear in ways that evoke an implicit mythic narrative. The first trope is not immediately apparent in Mk 1:12-13, the temptation segment of his introduction. It is, however, implied

15. On the symbol system of biblical mythology, see M. Liverani, *Myth and Politics in Ancient Near Eastern Historiography* (Ithaca: Cornell University Press, 2004); N. Wyatt, 'The Mythic Mind,' *SJOT* 15 (2001), 3-56; idem, *The Mythic Mind: Essays on Cosmology and Religion in Ugaritic and Old Testament Literature* (London: Equinox, 2005); idem, 'The Mythic Mind Revisited: Myth and History—or Myth versus History—a Continuing Problem in Biblical Studies,' *SJOT* 22 (2008), 161-75.

16. On the issue of motif clusters and narrative patterns, see D. Irvin, *Mytharion: The Comparison of Tales from the Old Testament and ancient Near East* (Neukirchen: Neukirchen Verlag, 1978); T. L. Thompson and D. Irvin, 'The Joseph and Moses Narratives,' in J. H. Hayes and J. M. Miller, *Israelite and Judean History* (Philadelphia: Westminster, 1977), 147-212; T. L. Thompson, 'Kingship and the Wrath of God: Or Teaching Humility,' *RB* 109 (2002), 161-96.

already in the opening words of the Gospel, which gives the opening of the introduction in the proclamation, 'The beginning of the good news of Jesus Christ, the son of God.' This proclamation not only identifies its narrative figure as saviour, messiah and son of God, but also links this saviour figure with Isaiah's 'one who prepares the way of Yahweh in the desert' (Isa. 40:3) with the promised messenger of Exodus (Exod. 23:20-33; cf. Mal. 3:1) and thereby identifying him as one sent to lead Israel in its eschatological war against the nations (Exod. 23:20-24; cf. Ps. 2). Supporting this opening with the story of John in the wilderness, allegorically illustrating Isaiah's voice, which identifies Jesus as the promised messenger sent to guide Israel, is the trope, with historical roots in ancient Egypt's royal ideology and specifically witnessed in celebratory proclamations of the accession to the throne by Pharaohs Merneptah and Ramses IV. The proclamation, announcing Ramses IV's accession to the throne, reads as follows:

> O Happy Day! Heaven and earth are in joy. They who have fled have returned to their homes; they who were hidden live openly; they who were hungry are filled and happy; they who were thirsty are drunken; they who were naked are clothed in fine linen; they who were dirty are dressed in white; they who were in prison are set free; they who were chained rejoice; the troubled of the land have found peace.... The homes of the widows are open (again), so that they may let wanderers come in. Womenfolk rejoice and repeat their songs of jubilation...saying, 'Male children are born again for good times, for he brings into being generation upon generation. You ruler, life, prosperity, health! You are for eternity!'[17]

The 'good news' announced and inaugurated in the proclamation of Ramses IV are illustrated by an eightfold list of the reversals of fate and fortune. They are signs of the royal saviour's divine rule over his empire. These reversals stereotypically mark the king's coming reign as salvation for the poor and oppressed, for widows and orphans, the lame and the blind. In an earlier study, I collected examples of this trope under the banner 'the poor man's song', which reflect a trope that not only plays a significant role in hundreds of biblical and extra-biblical texts, but which typically has played a defining role in many modern scholarly representations of the historical Jesus.[18] A typical list of such reversals is not used in Mark's introduction, but is rather only implied by the proclamation of the 'good news'. In Mark's Gospel, generally, this trope is not represented by lists but is rather found in narratives, illustrating such reversals, especially in the healing and

17. See Pritchard, *ANET*, 378-79, for a discussion of this and the many parallels from both ancient Near Eastern and biblical texts. For a survey of similar texts, see also Thompson, *Messiah Myth*, 107-35 and 323-35.
18. Thompson, *Messiah Myth*, 107-13.

feeding stories, which take their point of departure from the introduction (e.g. Mk 1:29-31, 32-34, 40-45; 2:3-12; 7:32-37 and 8:22-26; 10:46-52), but it is also implied in the instruction stories regarding the rich and poor (as in Mk 10:17-22 and 10:23-31). In Matthew, the 'poor man's song' occurs far more frequently. One also finds similar illustrating stories and exhortations as in Mark (e.g. Mt. 18:1-5; 20:25-34; 23:1-12), but the best examples in Matthew involve lists, closely comparable to the eightfold list in Ramses IV's song, most famously, the 'sermon on the mount' and the signs of the kingdom (e.g. Mt. 5:3-12; 11:4-6; 13:14-17 and 25:31-46). In Luke's Gospel, such a list is used to define the figure of Jesus himself as saviour of the poor and oppressed, most notably as expressed in the birth story, to define what the messiah's 'good news' is by the 'blessings and woes' in his sermon on the plain (Lk. 1:46-55, 76-79; see also, Lk. 4:18-19; 6:20-27).

The second literary trope, which I see as supporting significance in Mark's episode of Jesus in the desert, is also a well-known mythic element of ancient Near Eastern royal ideology, which has had profound influence on the development of the biographical figure of the 'good king'. In a thematic analysis of some twenty ancient Near Eastern royal biographies,[19] it is particularly in the plot-opening theme of 'past suffering' in such biographies, establishing a national crisis prior to the king's succession to the throne, which the ensuing narrative first needs to overcome. In surviving and overcoming this crisis, the long-suffering king is presented as fit to take the throne, when he is called and chosen by the divine at a divinely appointed time. This theme of 'past suffering' typically opens when the future king was a young man. His life is threatened and he is forced to flee or is driven into the desert, where he lives with the wild animals in exile for a determined period of time where he is tested: most typically in a duel between the heroic future king and a giant or great warrior, representing evil. It closes, most frequently, with signs of divine protection and care for the chosen saviour, who is then called from the wilderness to enter his kingdom and inaugurate his reign, bringing a reversal of fortune to his people. Of the twenty royal biographies I analysed, four of the biographies contained clear narrative episodes of this type: Idrimi of Alalakh, Panamuwa of the land of *Y'dy*, Esarhaddon of Assyria and Nabonidus of Babylon.[20] As plot elements of story, however, this tale-type is ubiquitous, expressed both by a testing of the future king in the desert and a duel with a hero or giant. The tale

19. T. L. Thompson, 'A Testimony of the Good King: Reading the Mesha Stele,' in L. L. Grabbe, ed., *Ahab Agonistes: The Rise and Fall of the Omri Dynasty* (London: T & T Clark, 2007), 236-92; see further, concerning the issue of the historicity of such life stories of historical persons, T. L. Thompson, 'Mesha and Questions of Historicity,' *SJOT* 21.2 (2007), 241-60.

20. Thompson, 'Mesha and Questions of Historicity,' 250-52; see also, idem, 'Archaeology and the Bible Revisited: A Review Article,' *SJOT* 20.2 (2006), 286-313, esp. 290-97.

type goes at least as far back as the Egyptian story of Sinuhe in the Middle Bronze Age and the segmented tales of Gilgamesh and Enkidu's meeting with Humbaba. In biblical tradition, it is most clearly and fully developed in the stories of David, involving both his duel with Goliath in 1 Samuel 17 and his exile and flight into the desert in 1 Samuel 20–27. Although the figure of David, who fled to the desert to become a bandit leader, has been thought to reflect memories of a historical David from the tenth century in a recent work of Israel Finkelstein and Niels Asher Silberman, as the tenth century offers what they see as a unique archaeological-historical context for what they refer to as a 'memory' of the liberation of Keilah (= *Kh. Qeilah*) and a historical David,[21] this literary narrative about David's flight into the desert and his duel with the evil giant, Goliath, which also includes the well-known fairy-tale pattern of David's three-fold trial to win a princess for his bride, directly reflects the theme from ancient Near East royal ideology of the divinely chosen king, known from royal biographies.[22]

Job 29 as Biography and Parable

My observation that these two tropes—the kingdom's good news of a reversal of fortune for the poor and the oppressed and the testing of the future king through a heroic duel in the desert—belong together and underlie the brief fourfold cluster of thematic elements in Mk 1:12-13 is supported most significantly in the figure of Job, the wise man from the land of Uz, who also was put to the test by Yahweh's Satan.[23] Not one driven out into the desert by the Spirit, Job is native to the desert; he has his home there. At the very beginning of the Book of Job, the reader is introduced to the 'historical' Job, one who, in wealth, was 'the greatest of all the sons of Qedem', with sons and daughters and large numbers of sheep, camels and oxen (Job 1:3-4). He is described in Yahweh's own words as a peer of Noah, Abraham and Josiah: 'my servant', of whom, there is 'none like on earth, a blameless and upright man, who fears God and turns away from evil' (Job 1:8). However, in the society of Yahweh and his sons, Job is but a puff of wind, threatened Abel-like to vanish before the chapter is out (cf. Eccl. 1:18). Job is a man, naked; just so had he once come from his mother's womb and so will he just as certainly return (Job 1:21). The die was cast by Yahweh, and his son

---

21. I. Finkelstein and N. A. Silberman, *David and Solomon: In Search of the Bible's Sacred Kings and the Roots of the Western Tradition* (New York: Free Press, 2006), 26-29, 31-59; for critique, see Thompson, 'Archaeology and the Bible Revisited,' 290-93.
22. Thompson, 'Archaeology and the Bible Revisited,' 293-97. Among other biblical narratives, see especially 1 Macc. 1–3: I. Hjelm, *Jerusalem's Rise to Sovereignty: Zion and Gerizim in Competition* (CIS, 14; New York: T & T Clark, 2004), 273.
23. Thompson, 'Job 29.'

Job is driven from his home to his life's debate in the desert: to be tested by both Satan and his wife, whether to curse or to bless Yahweh (Job 2:1-6). For this, the author of Job draws his story, like both Matthew and Luke, from the tradition. While they drew on the Torah, Job takes his reader on a journey which reaches out into the greater world. The wisdom of Ahiqar is given a new context together with gleanings from Sumerian and Babylonian Proverbs, and the Akkadian masterpiece of wisdom, *Ludlul bel Nemeqi*, the 'Babylonian Theodicy'. The author's intellectual reach stretches even as far back as the wisdom of the 'eloquent peasant' from Egypt's Old Kingdom.[24] At the very climax of Job's long debate over his life's meaning, just before Elihu lends his author's interpretive voice as an introduction to Yahweh's bombastic voice out of the whirlwind, and nearing the final summation of Job's arguments against his three friends, Job looks back in memory, nostalgically, to long ago, to the time when God still had watched over him and lighted his way when he walked in darkness (Job 29:2-3). The presentation of this memory from Job's past creates a cameo of his life as parable as Job is presented as the epitome of the ancient Near East's figure of the good king (Job 29:1-25).[25] In this brief, biographical sketch, Job combines the tropes of both 'poor man's song' and the killing of the evil giant as a coherent and bonded whole, linked together as cause and effect.

Job recalls to himself and his audience how he used to be met at the gate of the city with respect by all the town's enlightened princes. They called him 'blessed' (Job 29:11) and he responded much as Luke's Mary responded to Elizabeth's similar greeting, with an eightfold variant of Hannah's messianic song (cf. Lk. 1:46-56; 1 Sam. 2:1-10)! In Job's story, the good news for all those who had lived under his enlightened rule forms one of the finest examples of the ancient world's 'poor man's song': 'I delivered the poor, who cried, and the fatherless, who had none to help. The blessing of him who was about to die came over me and I caused the widows heart to sing for joy.... I was eyes to the blind and feet to the lame. I was father to the poor and I searched the cause of him whom I did not know' (Job 29:12-13, 15-16).[26]

At the center of his eightfold rendition of our ancient trope (v. 14), Job recalls that he had been clothed 'in righteousness, like a judge's cap', reiterating the clothing of the priest in the Psalter (Ps. 132:9) and of the great king of wisdom we find in Solomon's prayer (2 Chron. 6:41). At the close of his song, Job interprets his protection of the poor and the oppressed as effectively creating a mythic and messianic deed, which gave transcendent meaning to his righteous rule and former life. He presents himself as the conquering

24. Thompson, 'Job 29,' 118-20.
25. Thompson, 'Job 29,' 123-27; idem, *Messiah Myth*, 146-50.
26. Thompson, *Messiah Myth*, 146-48.

future king of holy war, his generation's hero, crushing under his foot the head of the serpent of the garden story (Gen. 3:15), keeping constant watch over the earth-lion's sin which once had crouched before Cain's door (Gen. 4:7).[27] Interpreting his whole life's text at the centre of his song, he declaims: 'I broke the jaws of the evil one; I ripped its prey from between its teeth' (Job 29:17)! 'The evil one' is personified, mythically—with teeth, like a crocodile or dragon. With this strikingly powerful evocation, Job opens his song to a wide spectrum of ancient myth which reaches from ancient Babylon's Marduk who defeats the sea monster, Tiamat, with the four winds of ancient cosmology, to the European medieval world's St George who slew his dragon with a sword. Also evoked is the ancient Egyptian myth of the Apophis dragon, who each night seeks to prevent the sacred sun bark's journey towards the rising of the morning star of a new day and who also comes to represent in legend all of Pharaoh's enemies and becoming itself an unlimited personification of evil, whose primeval destruction once provided the world with its creative foundations and still provides the reigning pharaoh with his eternal enemy, who is to be overcome daily, and ultimately to be defeated by the virtues of wisdom; namely, the care for the poor and oppressed, for widows and for orphans. They are the helpless booty that needs to be ripped from the dragon's jaws.[28] The weapons of the good king are mythically defined as care for the poor, the widow and the stranger. This central trope of ancient Near Eastern ethics creates a divine kingdom, in which all the world is at peace: a new world in which all violence is banished. The same mythic and utopian understanding is reflected in the Psalter. For example, Psalm 3 holds Job as an implicit model when it reiterates Job 29:17 to call on Yahweh to rise and strike David's enemies on the cheek, 'breaking the teeth of those who do evil' (Ps. 3:8; cf. also Ps. 58:7!). Job's reflections on his former life become a parable as this figure of the good king presents a Cain transformed by righteousness, a Cain who had listened to Yahweh's advice, one who had guarded his town against the sin crouching at his gate (cf. Gen. 4:7). He was the keeper of his people, the good shepherd of Psalm 23, ever careful to choose for them the good and secure path (Job 29:25; cf. 29:2).[29]

The Central Motifs of Psalm 72 and the 'Biographical' Events in Mk 1:12-13

From the perspective of an analysis of narrative elements in the comparative literature of the ancient world, the first part of Psalm 72, namely, verses 1-11,

---

27. T. L. Thompson, 'Genesis 4 and the Pentateuch's Reiterative Discourse,' forthcoming.
28. See Pritchard, *ANET*, 6a-8a; 11b-12; 253b.
29. Thompson, *Messiah Myth*, 149.

can be seen as embodying the central thematic and interrelated character of various elements which we have seen in both Job 29 and Mk 1:12-13. This, thereby, helps us to identify more clearly both the discourse and the mythic symbol system which Mark's brief sketch of a narrative holds implicit:

1. Psalm 72:1-4: *the good news.* The transforming reversal of destinies, to which the 'poor man's song' gives voice, opens the psalm by identifying the king, in his role as son of God, 'as the judge of righteousness'. As in Isaiah's description of the reign of the Davidic messiah, the eternal and universal reign of the child to come is established 'with justice and righteousness' (Isa. 9:6). Therefore, with the figure of Job established in Job 29 as good king and righteous judge, this association and identification easily becomes an explicit part of the narrative in both Matthew and Luke's wilderness tales, where the devil introduces each of his three challenges with the conditional phrase, 'If you are the son of God'. For, in each of these narratives, the temptation tale bears the identical task of illustrating this role. In the Gospel of Mark, however, that aspect of the messianic figure of Jesus has already been established by the Gospel's opening line. With it, his role as righteousness's judge is established; he comes to reverse the poor man's destiny (cf. Job 29:12, 16). There needs to be offered now only an allusion to the trope as a whole in order for the entire mythological significance to become transparent.
2. Psalm 72:4c: *victory over the dragon.* Psalm 72:1-11 refers twice to the 'slaying of the dragon' motif. The first time occurs in verse 4c, which signifies the summary effect of the reversal of destinies evoked by the judge of righteousness; namely, 'defending the cause of the helpless, giving aid to the poor, he crushes the oppressor'. The orientation is quite comparable to the sketch of the figure Job, where, following an eightfold iteration of the 'poor-man's song' ending with 'I was as a father to the poor and defended the cause of him I did not (even) know', Job 29:17 has Job sum up the recital of the help he has given the oppressed with the myth-evoking declaration of killing the dragon: 'I broke the jaws of the evil one' (Job 29:12-17)! Psalm 72 returns to the theme of the defeat of the evil one after marking the eternal and universal character of the messiah's reign. The psalmist describes the submission of the messiah's enemies to divine judgment in verse 9b: 'His foes will lick the dust', a text which clearly offers its reader an echo of Yahweh's curse of the snake in the garden story in Gen. 3:14. Isaiah uses this same trope in Yahweh's address to his servant, describing his utopian victory over foreign kings and queens: 'They will throw themselves on the ground before you and lick the dust

from your feet' (Isa. 49:23b). In Micah, one comes even closer to Psalm 72's reiteration of the snake-motif, because it is here linked directly to the submission of foreign kings whom the messiah has crushed, much as in the Davidic and messianic Psalm 18: 'As soon as they heard of me, they obeyed; the foreigners came crawling before me; they gave up and came trembling from their caves' (Mic. 7:17; cf. Ps. 18:43, 45-46 = 2 Sam. 22:43, 45-46).

3. Psalm 72:5-7: *the eternal messianic kingdom.* Psalm 72's second stanza takes up the theme of the enduring nature of the new covenant or creation, which the reign of the good king links to the motifs of both the call of the king from his desert exile and that call's divine significance: 'He shall live as long as the sun and the moon exist; he shall be like the rain that falls on new mown hay, like the showers that water the earth. In his days, righteousness will flourish and peace abound until the moon is no more.' This stanza offers a variation of the eightfold illustration of the permanence of Yahweh's promise after the flood, so great was his regret for trying to destroy his creation. He will never again curse the ground 'while the earth exists, seed-time and harvest, cold and heat, summer and winter, day and night will not end' (Gen. 8:22). The mythic potential, evoking the permanence of the covenant, of this thematic element is well expressed in Isaiah 9's summary of the mythic motif of primordial light's conquest over darkness: 'Great is his reign: peace without end over David's throne and his kingdom, that he might found it and maintain it in justice and righteousness from now until eternity' (Isa. 9:1-6 [6]). Although the theme of an eternal promise is not a fixed element of the duel with the evil one in royal ideology's desert story, the Gospel-opening recognition of Jesus in Mark as the son of God, together with the scene of his call by the spirit at the Jordan, does introduce and give cause for his immediately being driven into the desert to be tested by Satan. Building as the stories of Matthew and especially Luke do on the Old Testament tales of Samson and Samuel (Judg. 13:5, 17-20, 24-25; 1 Sam. 1:20; cf. Mt. 1:18-21; Lk. 1:30-35, 41, 67-80; 2:10-11), Jesus is called and marked in these narratives as son of God already 'from his mother's womb'.[30] In the development of the greater tradition of ancient Near Eastern antiquity, from Sinuhe and Thutmosis III to David and Jesus, the testing of the story's hero in the desert typically precedes the motif of divine election, calling the king to his throne at the appointed time. In this way, the desert testing is, therefore,

30. T. L. Thompson, *The Bible in History: How Writers Create A Past* (London: Jonathan Cape, 1999), 337-52.

to be understood as functioning as an introductory trial, testing the hero's fitness to return to his kingdom.[31] The divine decisiveness or any particular quality of the king as eternally chosen has a long history. It is perhaps most strikingly represented by the million years of Thutmosis III's reign, but usually and most typically it resembles the examples related to Esarhaddon and Nebuchadnezzar which are expressed in terms of the eternal aspects of the choice of the king as divine warrior and son of the gods, as well as by the transcendent and utopian peace of their reigns.[32] In the Bible, this theme comes forward most comprehensively when Yahweh recounts his call of David, the shepherd: that he might become king over his people and that his descendent might rule eternally. Yahweh will be his father and David will be Yahweh's son (2 Sam. 7:12-16; Pss. 89:4-5; 131:11-12). The motif of the just and righteous judge is evoked by Jeremiah's metaphor of the 'righteous branch' growing from David's line (Jer. 33:15). As in Psalm 72 and the Noah story, the permanence of this promise is couched in language which echoes nature's rhythms. His reign will be as secure as the succession of day and night (Jer. 33:20-22, 25; similarly, Ps. 89:37-38) and—here echoing the Abraham story (Gen. 15:5; 22:17)—his line will be as fertile as the sands of the seashore and stars of the sky are many.

4. Psalm 72:8-11: *universal empire*. Parallel to the eternal character of the kingdom is its universal quality. This is usually expressed as the victory over all the king's enemies, as in Psalm 18, which in 2 Samuel 22 is sung 'when Yahweh delivered him from the hand of all his enemies and from the hand of Saul' (2 Sam. 22:1). It refers to the myth of the messiah's victory over the nations in uproar and over foreigners until the ends of the earth (Ps. 2), a victory which is symbolically expressed by the slaying of the dragon; the victory over absolute Evil or its representative. In Ps. 72:8, the kingdom stretches from sea to sea, from 'the river' (that is, the Euphrates; 1 Kgs 4:21) to 'the ends of the earth'. Zechariah uses this same description of the universal kingdom of peace in a very similar context: 'Your king comes, righteous and victorious, humble and riding on an ass, on a colt, the foal of an ass' (Zech. 9:9-10) and it provides the basis for Mark's search for just such a foal that offers his readers one of his most original and intimate scenes (Mk 11:1-11; cf. Mt. 21:5; Lk. 19:28-38; Jn 12:14-15). The peaceful character of the kingdom expressed in the messiah's decisive victory over the conquered enemy, who must eat

31. Thompson, 'A Testimony of the Good King,' 258-62.
32. Thompson, *The Messiah Myth*, 165-66, 249.

the dust of the ground as the garden's serpent was condemned to do (Gen. 3:14; Ps. 72:9; cf. Pss. 2:1, 12; 18:40, 45; 110:1) is given parallel utopian overtones by both Isaiah and Micah in their scenes of eternal peace, as swords become ploughshares and spears pruning knives (Isa. 2:4; Mic. 4:3). All the nations of the world will bring gifts and offer the chosen king their allegiance (cf. Pss. 2:11-12; 22:18; 45:13-16; 68:30). This is the defining character of Isaiah's Zion (Isa. 60:1-7, esp. 60:6: Jerusalem's salvation marked by the wealth brought to the Temple). The kings and queens of the world, coming to Jerusalem bearing gifts, find illustration in the stories of Hiram of Tyre and the Queen of Sheba's visits to Solomon in 1 Kgs 5:15-26 and 10:1-13, even as, in the Book of Kings' tragic narrative, both of these scenes are used to presage Solomon's fall from grace (1 Kgs 5:27-32; 10:14-29; fulfilling the implicit prophecy of Deut. 17:14-17).

Reiteration and Mythic Evocation

The thematic development of Psalm 72 closes with verse 11. Psalm 72:12-14 returns the reader to the 'poor man's song's' reversal of fortune as expressing the king's righteous judgment, with which the song had originally opened (Ps. 72:1-4). The following verse (Ps. 72:15) takes up the theme of gifts from Sheba's king (Ps. 72:8-11), epitomizing the wealth of empire. Psalm 72:16-17 then recalls fertility's excess in nature's rhythms and 18-19 closes the psalm with a song of praise for the universal comprehension of Yahweh's glory. Comparable to Psalm 72's own reiteration of the primary thematic elements that have been developed, the closing stanza of Psalm 22 brings together three of Psalm 72's themes (cf. Ps. 22:26-32), linking a variation of the 'poor man's song' directly to the recognition of Yahweh's patronage by all the world's kings and nations—including even the realm of the dead. It clearly holds implicit the victory over evil through the righteousness epitomized in the poor man's song. An interesting variation of the eternal quality of this proclamation of the eternal, divine kingdom can be seen in the closing oath with which the psalmist and his as yet unborn descendents will announce God's justice to the people, creating a mythic evocation which, like its narrative parallel in Mk 1:12-13, calls forth the memory of that myth's many qualities.

- 11 -

'Who Is My Neighbour?': Implicit Use of Old Testament Stories and Motifs in Luke's Gospel

Ingrid Hjelm

I

While Matthew explicitly draws on Old Testament sources in support of his arguments, Luke's use of Old Testament sources is more subtle. The prophecy and fulfillment scheme that directs Matthew's Gospel places Jesus within a dynastic succession that counts Abraham as his most distant eponym (Mt. 1:1–17). The 42 generations that make up the list create a succession through Abraham, Isaac and Jacob, whose fourth son Judah is followed by ten generations down to David. Thereafter, 14 generations of Judah's kings make up another section until the exile and yet another 14 generations are counted until the birth of Jesus, son of Joseph. The tripartite scheme of 14 adds up to a total of 42 generations, the exact number of all Israel's and Judah's kings as recounted in the Books of Kings.[1] The apparent symbolism in these numbers invite consideration of the number 14 as the sum of the digits of the Hebrew consonants דוד of David's name (4+6+4), and the number 42, which in Egyptian mythology corresponds to the number of provinces in Egypt.[2] The fragmentation, death, resurrection and wholeness

1. Twenty Judaean kings and 19 Israelite kings plus Saul, David and Solomon; cf. Ingrid Hjelm, 'Samaria, Samaritans and the Composition of the Hebrew Bible,' in M. Mor, F. V. Reiterer and W. Winkler, eds., *Samaritans: Past and Present* (CS; Berlin: de Gruyter, 2010), 91-103.
2. J. Assmann, *Religion and Cultural Memory: Ten Studies* (trans. R. Livingstone; Stanford: Stanford University Press, 2006; orig.: *Religion und kulturelles Gedächtnis* [München: Beck, 2000]), 75: 'The forty-two provinces correspond also to the number of limbs of Osiris, whom Seth murdered and whose limbs he scattered throughout Egypt. Every year, the parts of the body are brought together from all regions of the land in solemn processions

themes implied in both biblical[3] and Egyptian mythology structure the Gospels as well. Matthew's genealogy might imply these numbers by sheer coincidence based on his reuse of 1 Chron. 2:1–15 and Ruth 4:18–22, both of which count 14 generations. The mythological value of the number 42 might, however, find affirmation in Luke's placement of David as number 42 in his similar, yet quite different genealogy (Lk. 3:23–38). I will return to that below.

David's function as Jesus' royal eponym (1:6) is never concealed in Matthew's Gospel. The book opens with the announcement that this is the 'genealogy' or 'the book of generations of Jesus Christ son of David, son of Abraham'.[4] In the first announcement of Mary's pregnancy, Joseph is addressed 'Joseph, son of David' (Mt. 1:20). The blind, the foreigners and the crowd several times call Jesus 'son of David' (Mt. 9:27; 12:23; 15:22; 20:30; 21:9, 15) and arouses anger and fear among the religious leaders and the priests. These are left with an impossible choice. If they recognize Jesus' royal descent, they face trouble with the Roman administration, but if they admit that the Messiah is more than David, namely the Son of God (Mt. 2:41–46; 26:59–68), their belief systems become shaken. Matthew's genealogy does not disclose that relation, but places Jesus within an Abrahamic and Davidic cycle, universal and particular reign, that connects the patriarchal tradition with Jerusalem's tradition through the Book of Ruth (4:18–22) and 1 Chronicles (2:1–15).[5] Discussion of Jesus' true nature, however, is a recurrent theme throughout Matthew's Gospel. As part of royal and religious nomenclature, 'Son of God' evokes several Old Testament texts that declare the Israelites or the king 'Son of God' and imply a relationship that underlines adoptive and analogous rather than genealogical aspects.[6] Family metaphors are invoked as signs of the reciprocity of the relationship. While God from his heaven twice calls Jesus 'my son' (Mt. 3:17; 17:5), his fate, however, is that

---

and joined together in one body. In this way, the number forty-two is associated with the idea of Egypt as a sacred entity that is constantly being salvaged from fragmentation of history and has to be joined together.'

3. Cf. also the very entriguing chain of scenes in which the spirit-driven Elisha brings both life and death, as in the scene of the two she-bears who kill the 42 children who mocked the prophet in the episode of 2 Kings 2:19-25.

4. The Greek term βίβλος γενέσεως is a reuse of the similar term that opens and closes the Adam cycle in the Septuagint (Gen. 2:4 and 5:1) before the flood. Its Hebrew form, ספר תולדת, however, is only used in Gen. 5:1. In all other genealogies in the Septuagint and the Hebrew Bible, the term 'book' is not used. A more suitable translation of βίβλος γενέσεως might therefore be '(hi)story'.

5. M. Müller, *Kommentar til Matthæusevangeliet* (DKNT, 3; Aarhus: Aarhus universitetsforlag, 2000), 75.

6. The people as 'son' in Exod. 4:22; Deut. 14:1; Isa. 30:1; 43:6, 45, 11; Ezek. 16:20–21; Hos. 2:1; 11:1, 10–12. The king as 'son' in Pss. 2:7; 89:27–28; 2 Sam. 7:14// 1 Chron. 17:13; 22:10; 28:6.

of a presumptive royal scion rather than the honored messiah, known from Near Eastern royal ideology.[7]

II

Luke's genealogy opens with the uncertainty that some 'meant' (ἐνομίζετο) Jesus was the son of Joseph (Lk. 3:23). The list counts down 76 generations until it reaches his ultimate origin: 'Son of God'.[8] David appears as number 42, but the list from Jesus to David is not made up of lists of Judah's kings, we know from biblical tradition. Recognizable are Zerubbabel and his father Shealtiel, heirs to the Davidic throne, who had irretrievably lost their royal prerogatives at the Babylonian conquest. The list enumerates 20 generations from Shealtiel down to David. The same number as Judah's kings from Rehabeam to Jehoiachin in Books of Kings, but David's son in Luke's list is not Solomon, but Nathan (cf. 1 Chron. 3:5). None of the names mentioned by Luke are names of Judaean kings known from biblical tradition. The mention of Nathan as David's son raises suspicion that Luke deliberately avoided mentioning the kings responsible for Judah's fall. Although Solomon is highly praised in Kings' narrative, he is also criticized for leading Israel astray by marrying foreign women and worshipping their gods (1 Kgs 11:3–8; 2 Kgs 23:13). In Neh. 13:26, his example is used as a warning against reiterative disaster. So what's worth remembering about Israel's kings? Nothing, if we follow the accusations expressed in 2 Kings 23's narrative about Josiah's reform. This might be the reason for Luke's choice of Nathan, who was not a Judaean king, but namesake of the prophet, who pronounced David's everlasting kingship (2 Sam. 7:11–17). Such is the interpretation by Eusebius in his *Questiones Evangelicae ad Stephanum* 3.2.[9] Eusebius' interpretation rests on Jer. 22:24–30's curse of Jehoiachin, which pronounces that 'no seed from him should arise to sit on the throne of David'. The conflation of David's son Nathan and the prophet had begun already in Targumic interpretations of Zech. 12:12–14 and appears also in Julius Africanus' *Letter to Aristides*, known by Eusebius.[10] Luke's incorporation of Zechariah's four

7. T. L. Thompson, *The Messiah Myth. The Near Eastern Roots of Jesus and David* (New York: Basic Books, 2005).
8. The number of generations differs in ancient manuscripts and literature from 72–77 names, so one should be cautious to make too much of the exact number in each; cf. the discussion in M. D. Johnson, *The Purpose of the Biblical Genealogies. With Special Reference to the Setting of the Genealogies of Jesus* (Cambridge: University Press, 1969), 231–33.
9. Johnson, *The Purpose of the Biblical Genealogies*, 243–45. The text quoted by Johnson is from J. P. Migne, ed., *Patrologiæ cursus completus omnium SS. Patrum, doctorum scriptorumque ecclesiasticorum, sive Latinorum, sive Graecorum* (221 vols.; Paris, 1844–1855 and 1862–1865), XXII, 895.
10. Johnson, *The Purpose of the Biblical Genealogies*, 240–43.

names—David, Nathan, Levi and Shimei—in his list together with names that usually appear in Levitical and Josephite lists suggests that he was aware of Jewish discussions over the ancestry of the Messiah.[11] The inclusiveness of Luke's list, much in line with 1 Chronicle's inclusiveness regarding Judah's genealogy,[12] points forward to Christianity's supersessionist ambition of mediating and abolishing inner-Jewish as well as Jewish–Samaritan controversies. By incorporating Nathan in his list, Luke fulfills two purposes. He implies a possible royal and political role for Jesus to play and he also places him within the guild of prophets.

Jesus' royal legitimacy is eponymic rather than genealogical, when the 34 generations before David create a lineage from Adam through Seth to Noah to Shem to Arpachshad to Abraham to Judah to David by use of selected names from genealogies such as are found in 1 Chron. 1:24–27; 2:4–15 and Ruth 4:17–22. Luke's enumeration of 22 generations from Adam to Jacob includes Cainan as Arpachshad's son similar to *Jub.* 8:1 and LXX Gen. 10:24 and 11:13.[13] The list invites speculation on the significance of the 22 generations from Adam to Jacob and the 22 kinds of works of the creation such as found in *Jub.* 2:23 and 4Q *Jubilees*[a] (4Q216). Later traditions equate the number 22 with the 22 letters of the Hebrew alphabet and the 22 sacred books,[14] mentioned already in Jos. *C. Ap.* 1.37–41. Luke's entire list indicates a new beginning, a fulfillment of patriarchal promises such as expressed both in the Magnificat sung by Mary and the Benedictus recited by Zechariah (Lk. 1:67–79). Both draw heavily on biblical literature to proclaim the birth of a Davidic saviour to restore Israel's glory and take away her disgrace and reproach. Using 1 Samuel 1–4 as his paradigm, Luke implicitly announces that the glory that left Israel with the loss of the Ark (1 Sam. 4:21–22) will be restored by the birth of prophet and saviour; namely, John and Jesus in the images of Samuel and David.

Luke shares with Matthew the genealogical placement of Jesus within David's and Abraham's ancestry (Lk. 3:32–38) and announces that Mary's

11. Johnson, *The Purpose of the Biblical Genealogies*, 247.

12. S. Schweitzer, *Reading Utopia in Chronicles* (New York and London: T & T Clark, 2007), 48; J. T. Sparks, *The Chronicler's Genealogies. Towards an Understanding of 1 Chronicles 1-9* (Atlanta: Society of Biblical Literature, 2008), 224–27.

13. Neither Samaritan nor Masoretic Pentateuchs mention Cainan in their lists and that part of Genesis is missing in manuscripts of DSS.

14. R. H. Charles's first English translation of *Jubilees* from 1902 restored *Jub.* 2:22–23 on the basis of several text witnesses to align with the fourth-century CE author Epifanius of Salamis' work, *De mensuris et ponderibus*, ch. 22: 'As there were two and twenty letters and two and twenty (sacred) books and two and twenty heads of mankind from Adam to Jacob, so there were made two and twenty kinds of work before the seventh day'; R. H. Charles, *The Book of Jubilees or the Little Genesis, Translated from the Editor's Ethiopic Text and Edited, with Introduction, Notes, and Indices* (London: Adam and Charles Black, 1902).

child shall be given his father David's throne (1:32). The reader is already prepared for this by Luke's comment that Mary was betrothed to 'Joseph, who was of David's house' (1:27) and he repeats Jesus' Davidic ancestry several times throughout his Gospel. His most eminent disclosure of Jesus' royal descent, however, is given in the 'poor man's song' sung and read by Mary (Lk. 1:46–56), Zechariah (Lk. 1:68–80) and Jesus (Lk. 4:18–19).[15] All three texts are composed of Old Testament prophetic and psalmodic literature, which praise the messianic king, and especially David, in his role as saviour and ruler of Israel. It is, however, striking, that Jesus' first public act takes place in the synagogue rather than the palace, and that he announces himself prophet (Lk. 4:24), placed within the guild of Old Testament prophets; first and foremost Elijah and Moses, whom he surpasses (Lk. 9:33–36). As Yahweh announced his chosen king, 'my son' (2 Sam. 7:14; 1 Chron. 17:13; 22:10; 28:6; Pss. 2:7; 89:27–28), a voice from heaven announces Jesus' ministry with the words, 'this is my son, my chosen one. Listen to him' (Lk. 9:35). The scene answers questions asked by Herod in 9:9: 'who is he?', and Jesus' question to his disciples, 'who am I?', and it legitimates Jesus' role as Moses' and Elijah's successor as lawgiver and prophet. Rather than being one of the old prophets resurrected (προφήτης τις τῶν ἀρχαίων ἀνέστη), that some suggested (Lk. 9:8, 19), he—similar to David in Books of Chronicles—serves the role both of prophet and king, and he is definitely not one of the old prophets.

The appearance and disappearance of Moses and Elijah can be read allegorically as the common and specific traditions of Samaritans and Jews,[16] which Christianity surpasses. Recent studies in New Testament attitudes towards Samaritans and Jews have concluded that the Gospels of Luke and John advocate an inclusion of Jews, Samaritans and Gentiles in the new covenant. Christian theology is offered as a solution to the 'either Gerizim or Jerusalem' question asked in John 4.[17] The theology finds it antecedents in Old Testament visions of an 'all Israel' reconciliation in Jerusalem with David as king, such as is found in Chronicles, Isaiah, Jeremiah and Ezekiel. Here, the role of the Davidic king is cultic and spiritual rather than political, as played by the all too mundane kings presented in Samuel and Kings.[18]

---

15. Thompson, *Messiah Myth*, 132–34.
16. Thompson, *Messiah Myth*, 57.
17. J. Zangenberg, *Frühes Christentum in Samarien: Topographische und traditionsgeschichtliche Studien zu den Samarientexten im Johannesevangelium* (TANZ, 27; Tübingen: A. Francke Verlag, 1998), 206–209; 224–25; M. Böhm, *Samarien und die Samaritai bei Lukas: Eine Studie zum religionshistorischen und traditionsgeschichtlichen Hintergrund der lukanischen Samarientexte und zu deren topographischer Verhaftung* (WUNT, 111; Tübingen: Mohr Siebeck, 1999), 310.
18. I. Hjelm, *Jerusalem's Rise to Sovereignty: Zion and Gerizim in Competition* (JSOTSup, 404/CIS, 14; London/New York: T & T Clark, 2004), 248–53; Schweitzer, *Reading Utopia in Chronicles*, 79–88.

III

These themes are most explicitly developed in Chronicles' portrait of David as *Moses redivivus*. In the Books of Samuel, David is presented in the image of an ancient Near Eastern warrior king who concerns himself with political matters. Unlike Chronicles, the book never mentions Moses or the Law, but presents David as instituting his own law and order (2 Sam. 8:15).[19] Already in Chronicles' genealogies, David and Moses are inseparably linked together, when David is credited with instituting the musical service (1 Chron. 6:16–17) and Moses the laws dealing with the priesthood and offerings (1 Chron. 6:33–34).[20] Following the narrative pattern of Moses' plan for the Tabernacle in Exodus 25–40, David plans the building of the Solomonic Temple and its institutions in every detail, combining his own inventions with Moses' design (1 Chron. 22–29).[21] No less imaginary than Moses' Tabernacle, is David's Temple in Chronicles *not* a description of a Yahwist cult place or temple in Persian or Hellenistic Jerusalem. The utopian Jerusalem to which all Israel gathers[22] places David in Moses' footsteps as the expected prophet (Deut. 18:18).[23]

The true competitor to the Masoretic 'no prophet arose again like Moses' (ולא־קם נביא עוד בישראל כמשה; Deut. 34:10) might not be any of the biblical prophets.[24] Although Hosea speaks about the coming prophets,[25] while Amos[26] and Zechariah[27] speak about 'the former prophets', Samuel appears as a candidate, and Jeremiah attempts to replace both Moses and Samuel,[28]

19. Hjelm, *Jerusalem's Rise*, 233–35.
20. Sparks, *The Chronicler's Genealogies*, 56–60.
21. J. Van Seters, 'The Chronicler's Account of Solomon's Temple-building: A Continuity Theme,' in M. P. Graham, K. G. Hoglund and S. L. McKenzie, eds., *The Chronicler as Historian* (JSOTSup, 238; Sheffield: Sheffield Academic Press, 1997), 283–300.
22. Schweitzer, *Reading Utopia in Chronicles*, 57.
23. For the following, see, Hjelm, *Jerusalem's Rise*, 245–48.
24. P. R. Davies, *Scribes and Schools: The Canonization of the Hebrew Scriptures* (Louisville: Westminster John Knox, 1998), 115: 'It remains possible that a 'prophecy' canon originated as a counterweight to the Mosaic canon and that Deuteronomy's presentation of Moses as a prophet like no other and its concern to control prophecy is influenced by the existence of a prophetic canon.'
25. Hos. 12:11; K. Zobel, *Prophetie und Deuteronomium: Die Rezeption prophetischer Theologie durch das Deuteronomium* (Berlin: de Gruyter, 1992), 213.
26. Amos 2:11; Zobel, *Prophetie und Deuteronomium*, 207–208.
27. Zech. 1:4; 7:7, 8.
28. Jer. 15:1–2; LXX^{A}: και Ααρων; The reference seems to have both 2 Chron. 35 and 2 Kgs 23 in mind (cf. Jer. 15:4). See further J. Blenkinsopp, *A History of Prophecy in Israel: From Settlement in the Land to the Hellenistic Period* (Philadelphia: Westminster Press, 1983), 158–60; C. R. Seitz, 'Mose als Prophet: Redaktionsthemen und Gesamtstruktur des Jeremiasbuches,' *BZ* 34 (1990), 234–45; J. Van Seters, *The Life of Moses: The Yahwist as Historian in Exodus–Numbers* (Kampen: Kok Pharos, 1994), 171–75.

the role of the expected prophet seems rather to have found its fulfillment in David as ideal king. As such, David's example and the Mosaic Law were the standards with which the author of Kings evaluated the behaviour of the Davidic kings.[29] As no prophet arose like Moses, so there was 'no king like' Hezekiah (לא־היה כמהו בכל מלכי יהודה; 2 Kgs 18:5) and Josiah (וכמהו לא־היה לפניו מלך...לא־קם כמהו; 2 Kgs 23:25), who followed in the paths of both David and Moses. As Abraham was judged righteous because he believed Yahweh (והאמן ביהוה ויחשבה לו צדקה; Gen. 15:6), so David was judged righteous (יגמלני יהוה כצדקתי / וישב יהוה לי כצדקתי) because he, having Yahweh's ordinances before him, remained blameless (ואהיה תמים לו; 2 Sam. 22:21–25).[30] That righteousness is a variant of Deuteronomy 6:25's righteousness, for in front of Yahweh to keep the commandments Yahweh has commanded (וצדקה תהיה לנו כי נשמר לעשת את־כל־המצות לפני יהוה אלהינו כאשר צונו[31]) and Ezekiel 18:5's definition of a righteous person. The psalmist's characterization of David's righteousness is not conversion theology's return to a whole-hearted obedience or an allusion to the rather innocent inadvertent sin described in interpretations.[32] The characterization rather belongs to a Platonic world of ideals or to Aristotelian philosophy's hierarchic first mover, in which manner David can be seen as just a little less than God (2 Sam. 7:25–27; cf. Ps. 8:5–9),[33] and so closely adherent to Yahweh that Yahweh's will becomes David's (2 Sam. 15:25–26). As such, David's example as a paradigm for the behaviour of succeeding kings parallels Abraham's role as a model of tribal leadership and Moses' role as legislator, conferring divine law unto the people. In canonical chronology, David's role serves to illustrate the king's dependence on the Law and its interpreters, whether it be an implied written Mosaic Law or a message conveyed by prophets. In narrative chronology, however, the Books of Samuel have presented the king as separated from past institutions: temple, priesthood and law. Compositionally, David's transgressions (2 Sam. 9–24) appear only after he has instituted 'law and justice' (2 Sam. 8:15).

IV

Such is not the role played by Chronicles' David, although he is not as perfect as his son Solomon, chosen and fathered by Yahweh. By means of speeches, songs and prayers, Chronicles' David incorporates Moses *and* the prophets, who continuously admonish the people to seek (בקש / דרש) Yahweh, to

29. Hjelm, *Jerusalem's Rise*, 83–88.
30. As did the righteous Noah (איש צדיק תמים; Gen. 6:9), and as Abraham (Gen. 17:1) and the Israelites (Deut. 18:13; Josh. 24:14) should do.
31. Cf. also Deut. 24:13.

repent (שוב) and observe (שמר) the Law, and warn against forsaking Yahweh (עזב) and being unfaithful (מעל).[34]

As Moses did not enter the Promised Land, but handed over the design for living there to Joshua (Deut. 31:7–8, 23), so David does not enter the Temple, but hands the plan for its construction and function to Solomon (1 Chron. 28:11–19). As Moses before him was not found worthy of entering the holy land, so David is not found worthy of entering its central place, but in the Book of Joshua and in Chronicles, neither Joshua nor Solomon are stained with any sin. If there ever were a completely flawless figure in the Hebrew Bible, it is Chronicles' Solomon, whose period of decline is left out of the narrative.[35] He is Yahweh's chosen king, sitting on Yahweh's throne (1 Chron. 29:23; cf. 28:5) and builder of the Temple (1 Chron. 28:5–7, 10). In the Books of Samuel, Saul and David are designed as 'chosen' (בחר),[36] but, in Chronicles, it is David and Solomon, who are 'chosen'.[37] He is 'a man of peace' (איש מנוחה; 1 Chron. 22:9), in contrast to David as 'a man of war' (איש מלחמות, 1 Chron. 28:3; 22:7–8). The dimensions of Solomon's realm are a utopian fulfilment of Yahweh's promise to Abraham, 'from the Euphrates to the land of the Philistines and the border of Egypt' (2 Chron. 9:26; cf. Gen. 15:18).[38] Such is also found in 2 Kings' praise of Solomon, but at the climax of his reign (1 Kgs 5:1, 5) and before the building of the Temple. In Chronicles, the fulfilment is placed towards the end of Solomon's reign and after the building of the Temple and the institution of the cult, to which both David and Solomon contribute exceedingly.[39] In line with Chronicles' general argument that faithfulness to the Torah and the cult brings blessing, the blessing given to Solomon when the ideal Mosaic cult is completed with Davidic additions,[40]

---

32. Hjelm, *Jerusalem's Rise*, 237; G. A. Anderson, 'Intentional and Unintentional Sin in the Dead Sea Scrolls', in D. P. Wright, D. N. Freedman and A. Hurvitz, eds., *Pomegranates and Golden Bells: Studies in Biblical, Jewish, and Near Eastern Ritual, Law, and Literature in Honor of Jacob Milgrom* (Winona Lake: Eisenbrauns, 1995), 49–64.
33. D. F. Murray, *Divine Prerogative and Royal Pretension: Pragmatics, Poetics and Polemics in a Narrative Sequence about David (2 Samuel 5:17-7:29)*, JSOTSup 264 (Sheffield: Sheffield Academic Press, 1998), 208–11; 312.
34. This is most conspicous in David's admonitions to Solomon in 1 Chron. 22:11–16; 28:8–10; 29:10–19; cf. Jer. 29:13–14; Deut. 5:29. M. A. Throntveit, 'The Chronicler's Speeches and Historical Reconstruction,' in M. P. Graham, K. G. Hoglund and S .L. McKenzie, eds., *The Chronicler as Historian. Studies in Text and Texture* (JSOTSup, 238; Sheffield: Sheffield Academic Press, 1997), 225–45; Brian E. Kelly, *Retribution and Eschatology in Chronicles* (JSOTSup, 211; Sheffield: Sheffield Academic Press, 1996), 49–58.
35. Schweitzer, *Reading Utopia in Chronicles*, 81–88.
36. Hjelm, *Jerusalem's Rise*, 294–96.
37. Schweitzer, *Reading Utopia in Chronicles*, 81.
38. Schweitzer, *Reading Utopia in Chronicles*, 88.
39. 1 Chron. 22:14; 29:2–5; 2 Chron. 5:1; 8:12–16.
40. Schweitzer, *Reading Utopia in Chronicles*, 87.

reaches its climax. Chronicles' David is no less a prophet, to whom Yahweh has conveyed his thoughts, when he, like Moses before him, declares the plan for the Temple as written by Yahweh's hand (מיד יהוה; 1 Chron. 28:19). Here, definitely, is more than Moses, but Solomon surpasses both.

V

Although Solomon is not mentioned in Luke's genealogy of Jesus, he definitely is not forgotten, but serves as a comparison to the utmost perfect, as in Luke 12, when the flowers in the field are clad better than Solomon in his entire splendour (Σολομῶν ἐν πάσῃ τῇ δόξῃ αὐτοῦ περιεβάλετο; Lk. 12:27). Placed within Jesus' wisdom sayings, Luke's comparison is not aimed at or restricted to Solomon's riches, but to his wisdom and understanding, which he asked for rather than possessions, wealth and honour (2 Chron. 1:11 // 1 Kgs 3:11). As a reward for that piety, he was given everything else, in addition to riches, possessions, honour, as well as wisdom and understanding. From the ends of the world came the Queen of Sheba to listen to Solomon's God-given wisdom, but Jesus surpasses it: 'Here is more than Solomon' (πλεῖον Σολομῶνος ὧδε; Lk. 11:31). Within such a biblical supersessionist ideology, Jesus imitates, incorporates and surpasses divinely blessed figures of past traditions.[41] As Solomon before him sat on Yahweh's royal throne (1 Chron. 29:23; cf. 28:5), Jesus shall sit at God's right side in heaven and David will recognize their suzerainty (Lk. 22:69; cf. 20:41–44: Acts 2:33–35; 1 Kgs 1:35). Jesus is definitely not one of the old prophets, but their fate will become his fate (Lk. 11:50–51), as it also became Stephan's fate in his imitation of Jesus' prophetic role (Acts 7:58–60).

Such supersessionist ideology also pertains to Christianity's role in Luke's writings. Judaism and Samaritanism are not cast out but reformulated and incorporated. Luke's Good Samaritan narrative (Lk. 10:25–37) is a most elegant example of his subtle use of previous traditions.[42] The story opens with 'a lawyer [νομικός], who stood up to put him [Jesus] to the test, saying, "Teacher, what shall I do to inherit eternal life?"' Jesus' answer is a reference to the Law: 'what is written in the Law. How do you read it?' Meaning, how do you interpret the Law? The lawyer demonstrates his knowledge of the Law by citing from the *Shema* in Deut. 6:5's commandment of loving God 'with all your heart, and with all your soul, and with all your strength and with all your mind' (Ἀγαπήσεις κύριον τὸν θεόν σου ἐξ ὅλης τῆς

41. F. Bovon, *Luke the Theologian: Fifty Years of Research (1950–2005)* (Waco: Baylor University Press, 2006, 2nd edn), 104.
42. For an analysis of Luke's use of Scripture in light of recent research, see Bovon, *Luke the Theologian*, 87–121, 525–31.

καρδίας σου καὶ ἐξ ὅλης τῆς ψυχῆς σου καὶ ἐξ ὅλης τῆς δυνάμεώς σου),[43] and Lev. 19:18's love of one's neighbour (καὶ τὸν πλησίον σου ὡς σεαυτόν). The answer is approved by Jesus as the whole of what is required for inheriting eternal life: 'do this and you shall live (τοῦτο ποίει καὶ ζήσῃ; Lk. 10:28). But the lawyer seems disappointed by the obvious simplicity of his question and he wants to justify himself by asking, 'who is my neighbour?' Jesus' answer is the well-known story about a man, who on his way from Jerusalem to Jericho, fell among robbers who stripped him and beat him, and departed, leaving him half dead. Both a priest and a Levite saw him and passed him on the other side, but a Samaritan 'saw him, had compassion, went to him and bandaged his wounds after having poured oil and wine on them; then he set him on his own beast and brought him to an inn, and took care of him' (10:34). As he left, he gave the inn-keeper money and asked him to care for the man at any cost. Following this story, Jesus asks the lawyer, 'Which of these three men do you think has proved neighbour to the man who fell among the robbers?' (τίς τούτων τῶν τριῶν πλησίον δοκεῖ σοι γεγονέναι τοῦ ἐμπεσόντος εἰς τοὺς λῃστάς; 10:36), and the lawyer answered, 'The one who has showed mercy on him.' And Jesus said to him, 'Go and do likewise.'

Innumerable are the interpretations of this story which extracts a moral lesson of Christian charity as its main point. So much so that '(Good) Samaritan' often is used as a name for a hospital or an aid organization. The Samaritans, of course, love the story, which adds to their ancient reputation of being hospitable, as found in, for example, 2 Macc. 6:2 and Jos. *A.J.* 11.346. The story's culprits are not the robbers but the priest and the Levite, who might have loved God but had forgotten to be a neighbour. Although it has often been claimed that Luke expresses a pro-Samaritan attitude, this story is no more reflective of pro-Samaritanism than the Samaritan leper's return 'to praise God' in Lk. 17:15–16. The primary function of Luke's Samaritan stories is to illustrate the stubbornness of the Jews, and, using Samaritans as the most fitting comparable group, they form the strongest accusation.[44] Luke's story does not aim at making a simple principle about who is the lawyer's neighbour, but calls to mind an unresolved problem of Jewish hatred of Samaritans. Several incidents had nurtured this animosity, most notable of which are the destruction of the Samaritan Temple on Mount

43. Luke's text is slightly different from the LXX, the MT, the SP and DSS, neither of which have the fourth phrase, καὶ ἐν ὅλῃ τῇ διανοίᾳ σου. The addition of 'mind' or 'understanding' to the Hebrew heart, soul or life, and strength is found in similar texts in Mt. 2:37 and Mk 12:30. The Hebrew לבב, 'heart', however, is an expression for the mind also.

44. I. Hjelm, *The Samaritans and Early Judaism. A Literary Analysis* (JSOTsup, 303/CIS, 7; Sheffield: Sheffield Academic Press, 2000), 116–18.

Gerizim by the Jewish king John Hyrcanus around 110 BCE[45] and the Samaritan defilement of the Jewish Temple in Jerusalem about a hundred years later during Polonius' governorship (6–c. 9 CE).[46] The lawyer, who seems to know Scripture, might, however, recognize Jesus' story as a parable of another story about Jews and Samaritans from his tradition.

VI

This story, found in 2 Chronicles 28,[47] tells about Judah's King Ahaz's war with the Aramaeans and Israel's King Pekah, which led to a massive defeat with more than 120,000 Judaeans killed in the battles and 200,000 of their women, sons and daughters brought into captivity in Samaria (2 Chron. 28:5–8). When the army arrives in Samaria, a prophet named Oded together with some of the leaders of the Ephraimites meet them and scold them for their excessive killing of the Judaeans and for having taken captives from their kinsfolk, lit. 'brothers' (אחים; v. 11; cf. v. 8). Oded warns them against adding to their own sin with their intended enslavement of the prisoners (v. 14). The army then let go of the prisoners and the Ephraimite leaders 'rose and took the captives, and with the spoil they clothed all that were naked among them; they clothed them, gave them sandals, provided them with food and drink, and anointed them; and carrying all the feeble among them on asses, they brought them to their kinsfolk at Jericho, the city of palm trees. Then they returned to Samaria' (v. 15). The similarities of Luke's and Chronicles' narratives are thematic and implicit rather than linguistic.

In light of Chronicles' story, Jesus' parable about the 'good Samaritan' gives a radical answer to the lawyer's question, 'Who is my neighbour?' He is the one who did good to you, the one who 'clothed the naked, gave them sandals, provided them with food and drink, anointed them and carried all the feeble on asses' to bring them to their brothers at Jericho (2 Chron. 28:15). What Jesus is asking for is recognition and reconciliation and an ending of the hatred, which, according to Old Testament Scripture, seems to have arisen from the Syro-Ephraimite–Judaean war. Although this war is not the only incident of confrontation between Israel and Judah in the Old Testament, it is the most notable because it marks an absolute nadir in the Israelite–Judaean relationship.[48] Placed within the context of the eighth century upheavals

45. Y. Magen, *Mount Gerizim Excavations.* II. *A Temple City* (trans. E. Levin and C. Ebert; JSP, 8; Jerusalem: Staff Officer of Archaeology, Civil Administration of Judea and Samaria, 2008), 178.

46. Jos. *A.J.* 18.29–30.

47. Although Kings and Chronicles share many details in their portraits of King Ahaz, the differences are even more numerous and 28:9–15 has no parallel in the Books of Kings.

48. Hjelm, *Jerusalem's Rise*, 115–30.

caused by recurrent Assyrian invasions of Palestine, the conflict carries with it a sadness of brothers forfeiting possibilities of warding off foreign invasion because of their internal conflicts.[49] Rather than allying himself with Israel, Judah's King Ahaz brings further disaster upon himself by turning to Assyria for help. His subjugation is not only political, but religious to the extent that he even shut the doors to the Temple and worshipped other gods (2 Chron. 28:24–25). While in the Books of Kings, all Israel's disappearance from the scene at the Assyrian conquest is met with a rationalistic 'they got what they deserved' attitude (2 Kgs 17:7–8, 15–18), the Books of Chronicles, similar to Isaiah's concern for Israel's surviving remnant (שאר ישראל ופליטת בית יעקב), expresses utopian hopes of God's repentance and a return of those Israelites left (וישב אל הפליטה הנשארת לכם מכף מלכי אשורי)[50] to a common worship of Yahweh in Jerusalem (2 Chron. 30:6–8).[51] The account of Hezekiah's reversal of Ahaz's acts in 2 Chron. 29:3–10 hits right at the centre of what is implied: Judah's patronage relationship with Yahweh, to whom their fathers had been unfaithful (מעל; 2 Chron. 29:6; cf. 28:19, 22), had forsaken (עזב; 29:6; cf. 28:6), from whose dwelling they had turned away (ויסבו פניהם ממשכן יהוה) and with whom Hezekiah intends to make a covenant (28:10).

The literary and historical setting of Hezekiah's reign is the eighth–seventh century BCE. However, the situation that gave impetus to the Chronicler's wish for reconciliation is not the division of an Iron Age idealized Davidic–Solomonic kingdom of the past, but the continuous existence of Samaria and Judaea as separate political and cultic entities under Persian and Hellenistic supremacy. The wish for a single cultic centre in the Hasmonaean kingdom eventually led to John Hyrcanus' destruction of the Samaritan Israelites' cult place on Mt Gerizim around 110 BCE. Repercussions of this event and the growing hatred between Jews and Samaritans are not unknown to the authors of the New Testament. Samaritan origins was a much debated subject and especially Josephus made great efforts to deprive Samaritans of any relationship with the Israelite tribes, ten of which he argued had completely disappeared (Jos. *A.J.* 10.183–85).[52] His polemic was levelled against Samaritan claims of being descendants of Joseph, Ephraim and Manasseh.[53] When Jesus tells a story that calls into memory the good deeds

---

49. Hjelm, *Jerusalem's Rise*, 118.
50. 2 Chron. 30:6; Isa. 10:20–22; Hjelm, *Jerusalem's Rise*, 123, 150.
51. Hjelm, *Jerusalem's Rise*, 116.
52. Hjelm, *Samaritans*, 194; I. Hjelm, 'The Samaritans in Josephus' Jewish "History",' in H. Shehadeh and H. Tawa, eds., *Proceedings of the Fifth International Congress of the Société d'Études Samaritaines. Helsinki, August 1-4, 2000. Studies in Memory of Ferdinand Dexinger* (Paris: Societe Nouvelle, Libraire Orientaliste, Paul Geuthner S.A., 2005), 27–39.
53. According to Jos. *A.J.* 9.291 and 11.340, the Samaritans occasionally claim family ties with the Jews and 'call them their kinsmen, on the ground that they are descended from

of the Ephraimite Israelites (the lawyer's 'brother'), the implicit question is, will you recognize and appreciate 'the one who has showed mercy on you' as your neighbour?

Luke's aim, however, is not a return to any past Judaisms. Nor is it an eschatological hope for a revival of Chronicles' utopian Davidic–Solomonic kingdom, with its royal and cultic institutions. Luke advocates rather a replacement of such by a 'Christian Judaism', which disestablishes the borders between 'the way of the Gentiles', 'the town of the Samaritans' and 'the lost sheep of the house of Israel' (Mt. 10:5–6), such as we see illustrated in the dispersion of Christianity in Acts 1:8; 8:1; 8:5–29; 9:31; 15:3.[54]

VII

To conclude, with Luke's implicit use of Old Testament themes and narratives, he exposes an insight into Old Testament ideology, narratives and language that is far more profound and sophisticated than the simple search and mark method employed by Matthew. The key to understanding Luke's hermeneutics is given in the book's closure when the risen Jesus identifies himself with the Messiah, who has been prophesied by Moses, all the Prophets and the Psalms (Lk. 24:27, 44).[55] Fulfilling the prophecies of old, Jesus' life and teaching in Luke does not indicate an ending of history, but an introduction to the Christian mission narrated in Acts.[56] Luke's use of pre-Christian Jewish and Samaritan Scripture not only 'binds the Scripture to the Church',[57] as testimony, witness and heritage, but even more importantly, it is Scripture that offers the paradigms for Luke's composition. Luke's background might, therefore, not be that of a Christianized non-Jew, but rather a Hellenized Jew, well versed in his tradition's Greek editions.[58] His method is not that of rabbinic demonstration of utterance and fulfilment, but rather the use of allusion, typology, parallelism and reiteration, so common in ancient writings, that, from a modern perspective, it dissolves the testimonial values and reliability of the Old Testament, the Apocrypha

Joseph' (*A.J.* 9.291), or 'saying that they are related to them and tracing their line back to Ephraim and Manasseh, the descendants of Joseph' (*A.J.* 11.341).

54. Hjelm, *Samaritans*, 118.
55. P. Schubert, 'The Structure and Significance of Luke 24,' in W. Eltester, ed., *Neutestamentliche Studien für Rudolf Bultmann zu seinem 70. Geburtstag am 20. August 1954* (ZNW, 21; Berlin: Töpelmann, 1954), 165–86.
56. J. Dupont, *Études sur les Actes des Apôtres* (Paris: Cerf, 1967), 246.
57. Bovon, *Luke the Theologian*, 120.
58. In recent years, several studies have created a more nuanced image of Luke by analysing his use of Scripture in Luke–Acts in light of theories of rewritten Bible; cf. Bovon, *Luke the Theologian*, 525–31.

(esp. the Books of Maccabees[59]), Josephus and, as it seems, the Gospels. However, form and genre do not define historicity per se and our unease with reiteration clashes with the reliability assigned to the use of double witness and reiteration in antiquity. In the biblical world, the continuity and confirmation of past prophecies and events were signs of the fulfilment of a historical plan that had been created long ago. It was the interpreter's task to see these signs and communicate them.

59. Hjelm, *Jerusalem's Rise*, 266–88; I. Hjelm, '1 Makkabæerbogs helte mellem fortælling og virkelighed,' in H. Tronier and T. L. Thompson, eds., *Frelsens Biografisering* (FBE, 13; København: Museum Tusculanums Forlag, 2004), 63–78.

- 12 -

The *'Īsā* Narrative in the Qur'an: The Making of a Prophet

Joshua Sabih

The Qur'anic (Q) discourse about the *'Īsā* (عيسى) figure—taken to be identical to the New Testament's (NT) Jesus by most scholars—reveals many salient features, some of which refer to, not borrow from, NT narratives as mock narratives, not as source narratives. While the term 'narrative' is used here in the sense it is by Susana Onega and José Angel Garcia Landa:[1] 'A narrative is the semiotic representation of a series of events meaningfully connected', mock narrative/text, refers to the other(s) narrative(s)/text(s) as implied narrative(s)/text(s) by the Qur'anic narrative. Mock narrative/text represents the counterpart of the Qur'anic narrative/text, functioning as its second narrative/text. I coined this term, on the basis of the term 'mock reader' that Walker Gibson coined in 1950.[2] In a communicative situation, this mock narrative/text presupposes an implied reader, who engages in the reading process from the outside into the inside of the (Qur'anic) text. Both the implied reader and the mock narrative/text are abstractions, but unlike the implied reader, mock narrative/text can actually be heard and seen in the text. Mock narrative/text is intended by the concrete narrative/text, and as such it occupies an intermediate position between the concrete text/narrative, Qur'an—and the non-Qur'anic texts/sources/narratives—Qur'an commentaries, midrashic literature, NT tradition, pre-Islamic oral traditions and so forth.[3]

---

1. S. Onega and J. A. G. Landa, *Narratology: An Introduction* (New York: Longman, 1996), 3.
2. W. Gibson, 'Authors, Speakers, Readers, and Mock Readers,' in *College English* (1950), 265–69. This is mentioned in W. Booth, *The Rhetoric of Fiction* (Chicago: University of Chicago Press, 1961), 138.
3. Mock narratives and mock texts are not features of intertextuality. Nor do mock texts or narratives represent a specific or traceable text or narrative; they have a life of their own.

The literary form of *'Īsā* narratives within the Qur'anic corpus in general, and Suras 3 and 19 in particular, show that the aim of the Qur'anic discourse is not to reconstruct a history/biography of a 'historical' *'Īsā/Jesus. 'Īsā narratives* in the Qur'an appear to be fragmentary, though they are not. This perception, nevertheless, is dominant in modern scholarship, which finds it very difficult to talk about *'Īsā* narratives in comparison to the Joseph narrative in the Qur'an.

Bio-hagiographical units, minimal stories,[4] of which *'Īsā narratives* are composed, are used in 23 Suras in the Qur'an to tell a different story; different in the sense of being conscious, intentional and ideologically motivated. The Qur'anic texts do not speak about themselves in a *narrative mode*. These texts express themselves in a *proclamatory mode* as if it were God/Allah who speaks as in a monologue mode. All voices are invisible, but not absent.[5] In the depiction of *'Īsā*, both mimesis and diegesis are used. It is therefore of utmost importance that one should keep in mind that the primary function of the *'Īsā* narratives, as they are used in the Qur'an, are not to retell the story of Jesus, but to contest and deconstruct it. It is easy for the reader to identify *'Īsā* narratives as fragmentary, heterogenic, repetitive and mythical. Later Muslim exegetes and Western Orientalists and Islamologs have failed to understand that the character of *'Īsā* in the Qur'an serves merely a *hermeneutical moment* and is the product of an anti-historical discourse, contesting the hegemony of a theologically constructed narrative, in which the Pauline theology of salvation dictates the rewriting of history. The Qur'anic discourse about *'Īsā* cannot be divorced from the sectarian milieu in Arabia and the Mediterranean basin of the sixth–seventh centuries. The proclaimed name of the founder of Christianity, namely, Jesus (עושהי/עושי: *he saves, Yahweh saves*) is the first thing that the Qur'anic narrative of *'Īsā* contests and restores. Doing away with the doctrine of Jesus Christ as the ransom for mankind's sins begins with contesting the name as it has been theologically charged.

Centuries after the consolidation and canonization of the foundation narrative of the figure of Jesus, the Qur'anic discourse, re-constructing its prophetic history as salvation history, revived peripheral narratives, which had been silenced, de-canonized and excluded in the process of building orthodox(ies). Most modern scholars, writing on the Qur'anic figure *'Īsā*, identify him as the *Jesus* of the NT. It is obvious, however, for these scholars that the Qur'anic and NT discourses about *'Īsā/Jesus* respectively are on a collision course with one another on many fundamental points. Western

4. S. Rimmon-Kenan, *Narrative Fiction* (Oxford: Routledge, 2002).
5. A. L. De Prémare, *Aux origins du Coran, questions d'hier, approches d'aujourd'hui* (Paris: Téraèdre, 2004), 31.

scholarship in the field of comparative religion, including Qur'anic studies, still insists that the Qur'anic narratives of *'Īsā/Jesus* and other biblical figures simply represent Muhammad's tacky emulation of and debt to the biblical tradition. Medieval and modern Christian and Jewish scholarship has always advanced the idea of the Christian and/or Jewish origin of Islam and its foundational text, the Qur'an. Research along those lines is accordingly a simple demonstration of where, how and why Islam should be a Christian or Jewish sect.

This essay postulates, on the other hand, that the Qur'anic *'Īsā* is not identical with the Jesus of the NT. The *'Īsā* of post-Qur'anic Islamic tradition—that is, Qur'anic exegesis, Hadith, Sufisme, folk story—however, is identical. In fact, Western scholars, including biblical scholars, have simply reiterated traditional Muslim scholarship's narratives about an *interpreted 'Īsā figure*, which had been the product of the post-Qur'anic sectarian milieu rather than of the Qur'anic *'Īsā*. This narrative—at first, apologetic—sought to re-habilitate both the canonized NT and the de-canonized hagio-agnostic narratives about Jesus and claim that the latter and the Qur'anic *'Īsā* are *one and the same*, and, by extension, that the *historicity of Jesus/'Īsā* was established or proven. It is this narrative, not the Qur'anic narrative, which later came to be canonized in the three living orthodoxies within Islam; namely, the *Sunni*, *Shi'a* and *Ibadi* islams. In other words, the figure of *'Īsā in* the Qur'anic discourse is not only different from that figure in post-Qura'nic discourse, but both discourses represent *hermeneutical moments* expressing different sectarian environments. There are two literary systems, though interdependent, which represent two separate worldviews and ideologies. The perception of the religion of *'Īsā*, for example, is neither Jewish nor Christian. Most Western scholars view the Qur'anic use of Maryam the mother of *'Īsā* as an excellent example of the Qur'an's misinterpretation of biblical sources, as the Qur'an is understood to obviously confuse *Mary*, the sister of Moses and Aaron, with *Mary, the mother of Jesus.* Gallez, however, challenges this view by asking and answering the following question: 'In what tradition do the Qur'an and its tradition about the issue of the "two Maries" belong?': 'Il doit s'agir d'une part d'une tradition bien vivant, non seulement pour l'auteur du text, mais nécessairement aussi pour ceux qui l'écoutent; et d'autre part, elle s'est manifestement ni juive-rabbnique ni chrétienne.'[6] There are actually several discourses about the *'Īsā* figure in the Islamic tradition, which, for our purposes, can be reduced to two central ones; namely, Qur'anic and post-Qur'anic (i.e. Islamic) discourses, representing *two different hermeneutical trajectories* about the *'Īsā* figure. The

6. E. M. Gallez, *Le messie et son prophète, aux origins de l'Islam* (Paris: Èditions de Paris, 2005), I, 31.

Qur'anic narratives about the *'Īsā figure* are a literary re-construction of the same bio-hagiographical sources, which NT editors had used to construct the Jesus narratives.[7] The Islamic narrative about the *'Īsā* figure, I should say, is, on the other hand, a hybrid narrative, reflecting a three-hundred year process of *rehabilitation* or *islamicization* of the NT image and identity of the Jesus figure, which had been initiated by the Arab–Islamic conquests in the seventh century CE.

With the exception of very few critical scholars, most modern Muslim scholars are no different from their Western counterparts. They all assume that the Qur'anic *'Īsā* is the Jesus of the NT—not because Western scholars say so, but because classical Islamic tradition had canonized such an understanding. Tarif Khalidi,[8] in his book *The Muslim Jesus*, compiled a number of sayings and anecdotes found in Islamic literature in order to ' introduce an image of Jesus little known outside Arabic Islamic culture... [The] Jesus presented here will in some ways be similar to the Jesus in the Gospels, in others not.'[9] As Marie-Thérèse Urvoy has noticed, Khalidi, goes on record to say, 'The Qur'anic Jesus has little in common with the Jesus of the Gospels, canonical or apocryphal.'[10] Still, Khalidi rightly believes that the Jesus of the Muslim gospel has a different identity from the one we find in the Qur'an.[11]

In a remarkable note, Khalidi sums up the main problem characterizing the Qur'an's relation to the Bible, of which the present essay is a follow-up:

> In Sum, it is difficult to arrive, from all these contrastive images, at a single vivid synthesis, a formula which captures the essence of the image of [Jesus] in the Qur'an on the one hand and certain books of the Old and New Testaments, canonical and apocryphal, on the other. A close reading of the Qur'an which paid special attention to its structure and diction would, I think, convey the impression of a text struggling to establish its authority amid the sneers and sarcasm of the unbelievers or the babble of quarrelsome religious communities... The Jesus of the Qur'an is a trustee of an inheritance but not a relative of the testator. [12]

In 1977, Ata ur-Rahim reiterated the position of traditional Islam by saying that his book, '*Jesus, Prophet of Islam* shows us how "true" Christian teaching was diverted, or one might even say derailed, by the Pauline explosion.'[13] Ata ur-Rahim's thesis was to 'prove' the theological claim of traditional Islamic

7. Gallez, *Le messie*; S. A. Al-Assiouty, *Jésus le Non-Juif: Culte d'Isis Précurseur du Christianisme* (Paris: Letouzey & Ané, 1987).
8. T. Khalidi, *The Muslim Jesus* (Cambridge: Harvard University Press, 2001).
9. Khalidi, *The Muslim Jesus*, 1.
10. Khalidi, *The Muslim Jesus*, 15.
11. Khalidi, *The Muslim Jesus.*
12. Khalidi, *The Muslim Jesus*, 16–17.
13. M. Ata ur-Rahim, *Jesus, Prophet of Islam* (Norfolk: Diwan Press, 1977).

orthodoxies that the Qur'an is the only surviving divine revelation and, therefore, superior to both the Old and New Testaments. 'To the Muslims, Christianity is a historical reality based on a metaphysical fiction. Because its foundations are mythical and invented, as opposed to existential and revealed, it appears to us [Muslims] as a locked system of negation.'[14]

Qur'an as a Corpus, Text and Discourse

Although the Qur'an does not say much about its own history, it is replete with *stories* about characters (prophets), which the Qur'anic discourse calls by their proper names, including the name of Islam's founder, Muhammad (Q. 3:144; 47:2). As to the question of whether one should consider the Qur'an a historical document in regard to the formative period of Islam or not, the position of this essay is that the Qur'anic corpus is a discourse inscribed in a historical reality that cannot be denied. I am looking beyond questions of historicity—the only concern of Orientalists—and adopting, instead, *an open reading*; that is, *a* pluralistic mode of approach, which views the use of the historico-critical method by itself as insufficient.[15]

The Qur'an is a corpus, a text and a discourse. The Qur'an is a corpus in terms of its textual composition. In other words, the Qur'an seems to be 'an assemblage' of text-fragments which have undergone an editorial process.[16] This fact is not new, since Islamic tradition was the first to write about the issue extensively. The Qur'an is also a text in terms of unity and cohesion.[17] De Prémare explains this essential feature of the Qura'nic text: 'It existe pourtant un element qui assure la cohesion de cet assemblage, à la fois quant au contenu et quant au style. Si l'on considère le corpus dans son ensemble, cet element de cohesion est d'abord d'orde rhétorique; il est renforcé par le fait que tous les discours sont pourvus de rimes.'[18] In fact, rhetorical devices, such as rhyme, repetition, metaphor and so forth, do not create cohesion merely between the different text-fragments, but also between various discourse-types and narratives. One must also say that cohesion/coherence is not dependent on simple formal rhetoric alone, but also on other discursive and narratological devices; such as mimesis, diegesis, narrator, implied narrator, narratee and so forth. Unlike the literary structure of the biblical text, one cannot talk of 'literary genres'[19]

14. M. Ata ur-Rahim, *Jesus, Prophet of Islam*, 3.
15. M. Arkoun, *Lecture du Coran* (Paris: Maisonneuve & Larose, 1982).
16. De Prémare, *Aux origins du Coran,* 2004.
17. Arkoun, *Lecture du Coran.*
18. De Prémare, *Aux origins du Coran,* 32.
19. The Qur'an text represents an independent literary genre in Arabic literary theory and history.

within the Qur'anic corpus, but rather of types of discourses, which serve as contexts for the Qur'anic narratives, including the *'Īsā* narrative. It is beyond the scope of this essay to enlist and discuss all the discourse-types in the Qur'an. War, legislative, narrative, polemical, eschatological and theological discourse-types are some primary ones.

'Īsā in the Qur'anic Discourse

Etymological/Origin Argument

The proper name *'Īsā* comes in three various forms in the Qur'an: عيسى *'Īsā* (3:55), عيسى ابن مريم *'Īsā ibn Maryam* (2:87) and المسيح عيسى ابن مريم *al-Masiḥ 'Īsā ibn Maryam* (3:45). The reason that these three forms are considered proper names of *'Īsā* is that the Qur'an says so.

> Q. 3:55:
>
> Behold! Allah said: 'O *'Īsā*! I will take you, and raise you to me, and purify you of those who do not believe. I will make those who follow you above those who do not believe [in you] until the day of resurrection. To me you all shall return and I shall judge between you in matters that you are in disagreement.
>
> Q. 2:87:
>
> Indeed, we gave Moses the book and followed him up with messengers. And we gave *'Īsā ibn Maryam* (*'Īsā* son of Mary) *al bayyināt* (clear signs) and *'ayyadnāhu bil-rūhi al-qudus* (supported him with the holy spirit).
>
> Q. 3:45:
>
> Behold! The angels said to Maryam (Mary): O Maryam! Allah gives you good news, a *word* from him: *his name* is/will be *al-Masiḥ 'Isā ibn Maryam* (Christ/ Messiah *'Isā son of Mary*).

The proper name *'Īsā* is mentioned in both the polemical and narrative discourse. These two do sometimes overlap. In fact, some of the bio-hagiographical elements are used polemically as in the cases of the annunciation, birth and death/ascension of *'Īsā*. Most strikingly, the Qur'anic discourse addresses this figure as *'Īsā* or as *'Īsā ibn Maryam*, or as *al-Masiḥ 'Īsā ibn Maryam*. The question that still puzzles modern scholarship and which has caused many speculations, some of which are unfounded and apologetic, is not only the Qur'an's *use* of the proper name *'Īsā*, but its refusal to use or recognize the NT Gr. *Iesous*, Aram. *Yeshū'*, Heb. *Yeshua'* or Ar. *Yasū'*, as many scholars have expected and still demand. The other problematic issue is that despite the fact that the Qur'an calls *'Isā* by *al-Masiḥ*, the title is not given eschatological content. *'Īsā* has no salvific function within Qur'anic eschatology. The term *al-Masiḥ*, in Qur'anic discourse has, rather, a conflict-function against those who—such as the rabbinates—deny that *'Īsā* is *al-Masiḥ* on the one hand, and those who—namely, Christians—consider *Jesus/ʿĪsā* as the saviour, on the other.

G. C. Anawati begins his article in the *Encyclopaedia of Islam*[20] as follows: "*Īsā*, Ḳur'anic name for Jesus; The Ḳur'an refers to him in 15 suras and devotes to him 93 verses which are the foundation for Muslim Christology.' As mentioned earlier, Anawati—as most Muslim and non-Muslim scholars—identifies Qur'anic *ʿIsā* as *Jesus*. The implication of this assumption can be seen in the discussion about the so-called etymology of the Qur'anic *'Isā*. Anawati presents a number of possibilities for the origins of this etymology.

The Rabbinic Origin. Anawati sums up the Jewish-Rabbinic origin of the proper name *ʿĪsā*, which is used in the Qur'an. He mentions three scholars who are known as precursors for this view: Marracci (d. 1700), Landauer (d. 1937) and Nöldeke (d. 1930): 'Jews induced Mohammed to use the form *ʿIsā* and he did so in good faith. In fact the Jews, in hatred, referred to Jesus as Esau (עשו) maintaining that the spirit of Esau had passed.'[21] It is true that Esau, the twin brother of Jacob in Genesis, has become the archenemy of Israel in later rabbinic literature. He is referred to as 'the wicked Esau' in *Genesis Rabbah*. As Ishmael in his narrative, Esau is the rejected firstborn. He is red (Gen. 25:25), which is connected to Edom, *'adhama*, which becomes his home (Gen. 32:4). In search for the etymology of *ʿĪsā*, Arab lexicographers refer to the colour red. In later rabbinic literature, Ishmael became the father of Arabs and synonymous with Islam, as also Esau became synonymous with Christianity. The pairing of Ishmael–Esau as marginal biblical figures in rabbinic literature does not always allude to a specific religious or ethnic group such as Arabs (Muslims) and Christians. Rather they are used in rabbinic Judaism as an 'imagined other'. In rabbinic literature, one finds two narratives which might represent two different traditions: an Esau narrative, depicting sometimes a wicked and unfit Esau and applied to Christian Romans and a Yeshu narrative (*Toledot-Yeshu*), a polemical counter-narrative about the NT's Jesus narrative. Ishmael is depicted very positively in the Qur'an.[22] The annunciation narrative of Esau and Jacob in Gen. 25:23 and the role of the mother in Esau's rejection are very interesting in comparison with the Qur'an's annunciation narrative of Esau/*ʿĪsā*. The mother, Maryam, single-handedly sticks by her child and risks being rejected by her people together with him. This is an example of how peripheral narratives make their way into the centre, or at least make themselves visible as such.

20. G. C. Annawati, "*Isā*,' in *EI*, IV, 81–86.
21. Annawati, "*Isā*,' IV, 81.
22. It is worth comparing the depiction of Ishmael in the Book of *Jubilees*.

Aramaic-Syriac-Mandaic Origin. The Christian Syriac origin of *'Isā* has been proposed by Derenbourg, Frankel, Vollers and Nestle. Anawati presents this theory as follows: '*Yasū*' derives, by a phonetic change, from the Syriac *Yeshū*', itself coming from the Hebrew *Yeshua*'.'[23] Luxenberg maintains that the present Qur'anic reading of *'Isa* should be read *'Ishay/yishay* (Syr.: ܝܫܝܐ; Heb.: ישיא / ישי), which has an East Syriac-Mandaic origin:

> Daß der heutige Koran jedenfalls *'Isā* liest, beruht sicherlich auf der nachkoranischen arabischen Phonetik, zumal dieser Name, wie Horovitz a.a.O. (S. 129) bemerkt, in der altarabischen Poesie nicht überliefert ist. Die koranische schreibweise entspricht hingegen der ostsyrisch-mandäschen Orthographie und Phonetik des biblisch beslegten Namens. Daher ist *'Isā* sicherlich nicht *'Isā*, sondern eher isay zu lessen.[24]

The implication of this proposition goes beyond being an issue of orthography in the Qur'anic text—being of Syro-Aramaic origin—to become an issue of misreading and confusion on the part of the Qur'an with regard to biblical sources.

> This finding is interesting not only because it once again points to the Eastern Syrian region, but also and especially because it raises the question—relevant to the history of religion—as whether with *'Isā* (= *'Ishay/yishay*) the Koran has intended the connection between the *historical Jesus* and *Isai*, a genealogical ancestor of his, named in Isaiah 11.1, 10 and Luke 3.32, or whether it consciously or unconsciously confused *'Isho* (') with *'Ishay*, or perhaps took them to be dialectal variants of one and the same name.[25]

Robinson[26] notices that Qur'anic orthography of the NT's 'Jesus is strikingly different from any currently used by Christians'. Due to the assumed ethnicity of Jesus as a Palestinian Jew—a *conviction* among Western scholars—his authentic name must have been Hebrew, thus *Yeshū*'. *'Īsā*, however, has travelled from Hebrew through Nestorian Syriac *'Ishū*' or through *Yashū*' into Arabic *Yasū*'. After exploring the whole of the classical 'scholarly' charade, Robinson concludes the debate on a very interesting note: 'It is *not certain* that Jesus' original name was *Yeshua*'. The view that it was, and that it connoted that he was the Savior, cannot be traced back to earlier than around 80 C.E., the time when Hebrews and Matthew were written. *In any case, 'Īsā, the qur'anic form of his name, has no such connotations*.'[27] Parrinder, in 1965,

---

23. Annawati, "*Isā*,' IV.
24. C. Luxenberg, *Die Syro-Aramäische Lesart des Koran: Ein Beitrag zur Entschlüsselung der Koransprache* (Berlin: Verlag Hans Schiler, 2004), 50–51.
25. C. Luxenberg, *The Syro-Aramaic Reading of the Koran: A Contribution to the Decoding of the Koran* (Berlin: Verlag Hans Schiler, 2007), 42.
26. N. Robinson, 'Jesus,' in *EQ*, III, 7–21 (8).
27. Robinson, 'Jesus,' III, 10.

uttered what later would become the main doctrine in Western scholarship: 'The proper name of Jesus in the Qur'an: *ʿĪsā,* is used in the personal sense without explanation.' [28]

The Egyptian scholar, al-Assiouty, writing in French, considers four elements in pinning down the identity of Jesus/*ʿĪsā*. For this scholar, what is at stake and questionable in biblical scholarship is the identity and ethnicity of Jesus/*Īsā*, not his historicity. *ʿĪsā*, the real name of the NT Jesus, is in fact indicative of his *non-Jewish origin*: 'Dans un pays pluri-ethnique comme la Palestine au dédut de notre ère, le nom de chaque individu est un indice prima facie de son appartenance à un groupe ethnique dpnné. Il est vrai que des Juifs avaient adopté des noms grecs; mais, en general, l'Arabe aura un nom arabe, le Grec un nom grec, le Juif un nom juif, jusqu'à prevue contraire.' [29] Faithful in his approach to the question of ethnicity, al-Assiouty[30] seems to think that *ʿĪsā* is 'un nom égyptien, araméen et arabe par excellence.' Al-Assiouty's postulate from the outset seems to contradict what modern initiated and non-initiated readers have been brought up to know and believe. Robinson, at least, seems to think so.[31] Although the questions which al-Assiouty asks seem to challenge the proponents of Jesus' historicity by raising the issue of the ethnicity of Jesus as it is conceived in the NT tradition, the matter will not be settled by 'proving' that he is not. As it appears in bio-hagiographical elements encoded in Qur'anic discourse, the proper name, *ʿĪsā*, reflects an awareness of not only the issue of the name in non-Qur'anic sources, but also the theological and eschatological implications of Christian Christology. It is not that the Qur'an does not happen to know the *Yasuʿ* of Christian Arabs nor the *Yeshuaʿ* of Jews, as Marie-Thérèse Urvoy seems to suggest, it chooses not to know these two different forms of the same name. Hence, the Qur'an insists on the fact that 'his name is *ʿĪsā.*' 'Le Coran ne connaît pas le *Yasûʿ* des arabes chrétiens, ni le *Yeshuaʿ* des juifs. En revanche, il parle beaucoup de *ʿIsa* fils de Maryam.'[32] Gallez paints another picture of what might be the literary sources of the Qur'anic non-use of the NT Jesus under its Arabic transcription *Yasūʿ*. These sources are the *Testaments of the Twelve Patriarchs*. Fragments in Aramaic and in Hebrew of the testaments of Judah, Levi, Joseph and Naphtali have been found at Qumran. What might be suggestive in this regard is that the Christology of the *Testaments* is not Christian. One notices the absence of

28. G. Parrinder, *Jesus in the Qur'an* (Oxford: Oneworld Publications), 16.
29. Al-Assiouty, *Jésus le Non-Juif*, 109–10.
30. Al-Assiouty, *Jésus le Non-Juif*, 111.
31. Robinson, 'Jesus,' III, 8.
32. M.T. Urvoy, (2007), 'Jésus, in M. A. Amir-Moezzi, ed., *Dictionnaire du Coran,*' (Paris: editions Robert Laffon, 2007), 431.

the name *iesous/Jesus* from these *Testaments*, despite the fact that they paint a picture of the Messiah-figure.[33]

Gallez, following a similar approach, considers Islam (Qur'anic discourse about the *'Īsā* figure and eschatology) as 'l'héritier de cette mouvance [Judaéonazaréenne]: il est le continuateur, sous une presentation modifiée'.[34]

Bio-hagiographical Elements in the Qur'anic Discourse about *'Īsā*

The Annunciation Narrative: An Abridged Gospel

Sura 19, being the oldest of text-fragments containing an *'Īsā* narrative, includes the longest story of the annunciation and birth events of *'Īsā.* Chronologically, Sura 19, called *surat Maryam*, is number 58 according to Nöldeke, 60 according to Blachère and 44 according to al-Azhar. According to the Islamic tradition, this Sura emanates from the Meccan period, preceding Muhammad's emigration to Yathrib, which was re-named *Medinah*, a city-state.

Sura 19:2–15 deals with the story of Zechariah, consisting of Zechariah's supplication and Allah's mercy: 'this is a [restorative] account [*dhikr*] of your Lord's mercy on his servant/slave Zechariah' (19:2). Allah's mercy is the very miraculous birth of a unique son, who would be given a new name; that is, a name that has not been used before: namely, *yahya.*[35] In Sura 19:16–21, the story of the annunciation contains the following constituent elements:

1. Location and situation (Q. 19:16–17a): Maryam lives on her own in a secluded place.
2. Event I (Q. 19:17b): God's spirit, taking the form of perfect flesh/a human (*basharan sawiyyan*), pays Maryam a visit.
3. Event II (Q. 19:18–21a): dialogue between Maryam and God's messenger:
    a. She (Maryam) said: 'I seek the protection of the All-beneficent from you, you should be God wary!'
    b. He (Allah's messenger) said: 'I am only a messenger (*rasūl*) of your Lord (*rabbi-ki*) to offer you (a gift), a purified boy (*ghulāman zakiyyan*).'
    c. She said: 'How shall I have a boy, and no human/flesh (*bashar*) has ever touched me, nor have I been a harlot?'
    d. He said: 'So shall it be. Your Lord says: "It is easy for me".'

---

33. Gallez, *Le messie I*, 171.
34. Gallez, *Le messie*, II, 9.
35. This name is also used in *Sidra d-Yahya* of the Mandeans.

4. Event III (Q. 19:21b): commentary:
   a. 'So that we make him a sign for mankind and a mercy from us, and it is a matter [already] decided.'

In Sura 3—Nöldeke (97), Blachère (99), al-Azhar (87)—the annunciation story is more complex. The Qur'anic discourse uses a double annunciation scene. Maryam, *'Īsā*'s mother, was supposed to be the son that should have been set aside to serve God. In Q. 3, the wife of Imran, Marayam's mother, makes a vow to Allah. It is the mother who gave her girl-child the name Maryam, not Allah. The latter, however, decided her sex, put her in Zechariah's care and later gave her a son, *'Īsā*.

1. Q. 3:35:

   'When the wife of Imran said: "my Lord, I dedicate to You what is in my belly, in consecration. Accept it, therefore, from me; indeed You are the All-hearing and the All-knowing."'

2. Q. 3:36a:

   'And when she gave birth to her, she said: "My Lord, I have borne a female."'

3. Q. 3:36b: the narrator's comment, breaking the remarks of Imran's wife:

   'Allah knew better what she had given birth to. The female is not like the male.'

4. Q. 3:36c:

   (She said): 'I have named her Maryam, and I command her and her offspring to Your care against the outcast Satan.'

While in Q. 3:37–44, the life of Maryam and Zechariah intertwines:

Q. 3:37:

'Thereupon her Lord accepted her with a gracious acceptance, and made her grow up in a worthy fashion, and He charged Zechariah with her care.'

'Īsā's annunciation is told first in Q. 3:45–51. This composite narrative, *an abridged gospel* in which the story of *'Īsā*'s birth, identity, nature, prophetic mission, miracles, reform of the Torah and religion are first announced to his mother, Maryam. In other words, Allah outlines in a few lines the program according to which *'Īsā* should work as a prophet. This is an anti-Christian narrative, a *restorative* narrative, in which the NT Jesus figure regains his identity and humanity, *'Īsā the son of Mary*.

Here, it is the angels who pay Maryam a visit, not the messenger of 19:17b—Allah's spirit becoming perfect flesh.

Q. 3:45:

When the angels said: 'O Maryam! Allah gives you good news, a *word* from him: *his name* is/will be *al-Masīḥ 'Isā ibn Maryam, a noble* in this world and the hereafter, and one of those brought to near [to Allah].'

Q. 3:46:

He will speak to people in the cradle and in adulthood, and will be one of the righteous,

Q 3:47:

She (Maryam) said: 'My Lord, how shall I have a son and no human/flesh (*bashar*) has ever touched me?

He said: 'So it is that Allah creates whatever He wishes. When he decides on a matter, that it "Be" and it is.'

Q. 3:48:

And He will teach him the Book (*al-kitāb*) and Wisdom (*al-ḥikmah*), the Torah (*al-tawrāt*) and the Injil.

Q. 3:49:

and [he will be] a messenger to the sons of Israel, declaring: 'I have certainly brought you a sign from your Lord, [which is] "I will create for you out of clay in the form of a bird(s). Then I will breathe into it, and it will become a bird by Allah's leave. And I will heal the blind and the leper and revive the dead by Allah's leave. And I will tell you what you have eaten and what you have stored in your houses. There is indeed a sign in that for you, that you should be faithful."'

Q. 3:50:

Confirming that which is before me of the Torah, and to make permissible (*ḥalal*) for you some of the things that were forbidden you. I have brought you a sign from your Lord; so fear Allah and obey me.

Q. 3:51:

Indeed Allah is my Lord and your Lord; so worship him. This is a straight path.

From the outset, the Qur'anic narratives mentioned above agree for the most part with the Gospel of Luke. However, how does the Qur'anic discourse use these bio-hagiographical elements? *'Īsā*'s annunciation, birth and early life as a baby do appear abnormal and miraculous. The repetitive act of telling and re-telling, telling and showing, as well as the visibility of the narrator render these events very normal by the very fact that they are acts of the divine. The creative act is as divine as the narrative act. This is exactly how the Qur'anic discourse perceives itself. Nothing is special about *'Īsā*, the event of the annunciation of *'Īsā* is repeated several times as in the two cases of his mother and *Yaḥyā* of Zechariah. What if the wife of Imran, Maryam's mother, had a son instead of Maryam (cf. the annunciation of Samuel, John the Baptist/*Yahya*)?

Nativity

Sura 19: 22–33, *Maryam*, encapsulates a series of events in which the child to be will come to his mother's rescue twice. The story is about Maryam's pregnancy, childbirth, return to her people and the child *'Isā*'s *speech.* In all this, *'Isā*, a baby boy, *takes an active role.* He speaks and acts on behalf of Allah. He intensifies the narrator's visibility in the narration.

Q. 19:22:

Thus she conceived him, and she withdrew with him to a distant place.

Q. 19:23:

The birth pangs brought her to the trunk of a palm tree.
She said: 'I wish I had died before this and become a forgotten thing, beyond recall.'

Q. 19:24–26:

Thereupon he [*'Isā*] called her from below her [saying]:
'Do not grieve!
Your Lord has made a spring to flow at your feet.
Shake the trunk of the palm tree.
Freshly picked dates will drop upon you.
Eat, drink, and be comforted.
Then if you see any humans (*bashar*),
say: "Indeed I have vowed a fast to the all-beneficent,
so I will not speak to any human (*'ins*) today."'

Q. 19:27–33:

Then carrying him she brought him to her people.
They said: 'O Maryam,
you have certainly come up with a shameful thing!
O sister of Aaron!
Your father was not an evil man,
Nor was your mother a harlot.'
Thereat she pointed to him.
They said: 'How can we speak to one who is yet a baby in the cradle?'
He [baby *'Isā*] said: 'indeed I am a servant of Allah!
He has given me the Book and made me a prophet.
He has made me blessed wherever I may be,

And He has enjoined (*'awṣaānī*) me [to maintain] prayer (*ṣalāt*)
And to pay the *zakāt* as long as I live,
And to be good to my mother,
He [Allah] has not made me self-willed and wretched.
Peace be upon me the day I was born and the day I die, and the day I am raised alive.'

Sura Q. 19:34–40 is the Qur'anic/divine narrator's comment, which represents a very charged hermeneutical moment. It protests against the views and accounts of others; namely, of Christians and Jews.

The primary function of the annunciation and birth narratives in the Qur'an can easily be seen in the polemical discourse. The immediate context of this discourse is the group that the Qur'an calls *Naṣarā.*

Q. 5:14–17:
Also from those who say (profess): 'We are *Naṣārā*'.
We took their pledge, but they forgot a part of what they were reminded.
...
They are certainly faithless who say (profess):
'Allah is the Messiah son of Maryam'.
Say:
'Who can avail anything against Allah should He destroy the Messiah, son of Maryam, and his mother, and everyone upon earth?'
To Allah belongs the kingdom of the heavens and the earth, and whatever is between them. He creates whatever He wishes, and Allah has power over all things.

It is clear that the *'Īsā* narratives, especially the annunciation and birth narratives, do not emanate from the New Testament. They are independent of them, in the sense that the Qur'an belongs to a different tradition.

Naṣārā in the Qur'an

Another striking feature of the Qur'anic discourse is the consistent use of the term نصارى, *Naṣara* in the plural,[36] referring to *'Īsā*'s followers. The Qur'an does not use the term *Christians* at all. This term occurs only in the Medina suras (from the Medina period). In Q. 19:34–40, a Meccan sura, the groups that disagreed about *'Īsā* were called *al-'ahzab* (parties, groups, sects).

That is *'Īsā*, son of Maryam, expression of truth, whom they are in doubt.
It is not for Allah to take a son. Immaculate is He!
When He decides on a matter, He just says to it: 'Be!' and it is.

---

36. The Singular form of the term *Naṣārā* is نصراني (*naṣrānī*).

Indeed Allah is my Lord and your Lord,
So worship Him.
This is a straight path.
But the parties differed among themselves.
So woe to the faithless at the scene of a tremendous day
...
Indeed we shall inherit the earth and whoever there is on it
And to us they shall be brought back.

Naṣārā, as a term mentioned 15 times in the Qur'an, is problematic. Typologically, there are faithful (Q. 2:62) and faithless (Q. 5:14–17) *Naṣārā.* The latter, Jews (دومي, *yahūd*) and Sabians, are described as *ahl al-kitāb* (people of the book). Etymologically, two forms have been proposed as representing the origin of the Qur'anic term, *nzr* and *nṣr.* In the Jewish Bible, the root *nṣr* as a verb: rcn, *nāṣar* (Ar-Syr. נטר, ܢܛܪ, *ntar*; cf. Ps. 119:22, 34, 56, 60, 100, 129). All the shades of meaning of this verb can be brought back to the idea of *protecting, keeping and watching over.* It is used as a noun rcn (*nēṣr*) in Isa. 11:1; 14:19 and Dan. 11:7, meaning *twig, offshoot.* In Arabic lexicography, the verb رصن, *naṣra*, means to help, assist, protect, defend, watch over. Muslim Qur'anic exegetes present a number of interpretations regarding the meaning and etymology of the Qur'anic term *Naṣārā*, two of which are mentioned by ibn Kathir in his *Commentary*:

> When Allah sent *'Īsā* (peace be upon him), it became incumbent upon the children of Israel to follow and obey him. His companions and the followers of his religion were called *al-Naṣārā.* They were called by that name because *they helped—empowered—one another*; they were also called *'anṣār* (helpers, watchmen). *'Īsā said* (asked) his disciples (*al-ḥawāriyyīn*) in Q. 60:14—'Who will be *my helpers* for Allah's sake?' The disciples said: 'We will be Allah's helpers (watchmen)!' Another view states that they called by that name because they settled in a land called *Nāṣirah.*[37]

It is clear that the Qur'anic term *Naṣārā* seems to originate from *nṣr*, and not *nzr.* Whatever the etymology may be, the term has an indexal/deictic function in the Qur'anic discourse in general and in the 'people of the book' narratives. It is polysemic. Thus the meaning of the term *Naṣāra* depends on its immediate context. It can refer to *Christians*, whose theological system is contested in the Qur'an, orpre-Christian movements, such as the Judaeo-Nazareans. Gallez construes the latter as the ones designated as the *mīinīim* (secterians), who, together with the *nōṣrīim* (Christians), *Birkat ha-mīinīim* are cursed.[38] Jerome describes the Judaeo-Nazareans in his letter to Augustine

37. Ibn Kathir, *Tafsir al-Qur´an al-`Aẓīm I* (Beirut: Mu´assat al-Rayyan, 2001), 139.
38. Gallez, *Le messie.*

'desiring to be both Jews and Christians at the same time, whereas in fact they are neither Jews nor Chritians.' This seems to be re-iterated by the Qur'an as an identity marker of the proto-muslim:

> Q. 2:135:
>
> And they say: 'Be either Jew (*Yahūd*) or Christians (*Naṣārā*), that you may be rightly guided.'
>
> Say (reply): 'Rather [we will follow] the creed of Abraham (*Millat Ibrāhīm*), a *ḥanīf*
>
> and he was not one of the associators.'
>
> Q.2: 140:
>
> Do you say that Abraham, Ishmael, Isaac, Jacob and the Tribes were Jews or Christians?
>
> Say: 'Is it you who know better, or Allah?'
>
> And who is a greater wrongdoer than him who conceals a testimony that is with him from Allah? And Allah is not oblivious to what you do.

The indexical function imposes very clear semantic/hermeneutical constraints upon the reader when it comes to the meaning of Jews and *Naṣārā* in Qur'anic discourse. Being Muslim is the only identity immune from human corruptive forces. The Qur'an's prophetic history becomes identical with Qur'anic Islam and not with post-Qur'anic Islam.

Conclusion

The study of biblical material in Qur'anic and post-Qur'anic Islamic literature has become increasingly a subject of a new approach, which seeks to break away from the traditional 'debt' complex and to study the Qur'anic text instead in its own right, from an interdisciplinary perspective.

These biblical sources are mock texts. Not only are they visible in the Qur'anic text, they are the product of the text–reader relationship. No reader would be able to approach the *'Īsā* narratives in the Qur'an with mock texts. The latter generates other mock texts every time the Qur'anic text is read. The typology of *'Īsā* narratives in Islam expresses this mechanism well. No text is read isolated from other texts, which we have the tendency to construe as source-texts. In Islamic as well as in Jewish and Christian tradition, the notion of an 'Ur-text' is fundamental for the mythic construction of the history of each tradition's own foundational text. The Qur'anic text is no exception.

- 13 -

Investigating Earliest Christianity without Jesus

K. L. Noll

Introduction

My thesis is that any quest for a historical Jesus is irrelevant to an understanding of the earliest social movements that evolved into the religion now called Christianity.[1] This is the case even if a historical Jesus existed and made an effort to found a movement of some kind. Several essays in this volume question the existence of Jesus, and others plead agnosticism. For my part, I can assume for the sake of argument that Jesus existed (which is, after all, a very reasonable option). That assumption enables me to demonstrate from evidence that Jesus was functionally irrelevant to the earliest stages of what contemporary researchers call the Jesus movement, or the Christ cult, or the Jesus-confessing communities (and that I will call early Christianity).

My thesis unfolds in four stages. First I describe my research method, then I evaluate two recent publications about early Christian literature in order to expose a key question, one that is frequently overlooked. With this key question in place, a historical analysis of earliest Christian literature demonstrates that Jesus, even if he existed, played no role in the formation of the movement that bears his name. Last, a comparison of this evidence with earliest Muslim traditions provides an alternate explanation for the data, an explanation that, if correct, renders superfluous any questions about a historical Jesus. If my thesis is accepted, it is reasonable for historians to

1. An early version of this essay was presented under the title, 'Why Does the New Testament Exist?,' to a session of the Ideological Criticism section of the Society of Biblical Literature, 'The Bible as a Construct of Scholarship,' in Boston, 24 November, 2008. My thanks to Hector Avalos for inviting me to participate in this colloquium. Thanks as well to Zeba Crook, Philip Davies and Thomas Verenna for valuable responses to the longer, written draft of that presentation.

dismiss all quests for a historical Jesus from discussion about the process by which the religion of Christianity emerged, evolved and survived.

Method of Evaluation

I write from a Darwinian perspective. This method treats religious ideas as memes, as defined by Richard Dawkins.[2] Memes survive and replicate according to a process that is analogous to biological evolution.

In this analysis, any religious idea is a meme that must be constructed in one human mind after another to avoid extinction. Not only is there a chance of severe mutation each time a meme is re-created in a new brain, there is always a chance that a meme can disappear in a single human generation, so the struggle for survival is intense. A religious meme that is fit for survival and replication is one that is sufficiently simple to be understood and inculcated by the average human mind, yet can appeal to human perceptions of religious need, and is distinctively different from other religious memes so that its character does not dissolve into the fabric of a religiously plural local culture.

Any religion that remains distinct from all other religious options is called a 'doctrinal mode'.[3] Doctrinal modes are clusters of memes that serve as a kind of brand identity for the religion, rendering it distinct from all competing religious ideas and behaviours.[4] To function, a doctrinal mode must be defended by trained leaders who can ensure brand consistency over time and geographical distance. Inevitably, the doctrinal mode will involve some combination of regular teaching events, ritual reinforcement of the teachings and an institutionalized means for guarding against defection from the favoured memes.[5]

From this Darwinian perspective, the most interesting aspect of any religion is its continued existence. Possible causes for extinction are legion. The inherent instability of memes requires of the trained leadership an unrelenting diligence in the defence of their doctrinal mode, lest rank-and-file participants fail to inculcate, retain and transmit the memes that

2. For an explanation of my method and citations of relevant scholarship, see K. L. Noll, 'The Evolution of Genre in the Hebrew Anthology,' in Craig Evans and Daniel Zacharias, eds., *Early Christian Literature and Intertextuality*. I. *Thematic Studies* (London: T & T Clark, 2009), 10–23.
3. K. L. Noll, 'Was There Doctrinal Dissemination in Early Yahweh Religion?,' *BibInt* 16 (2008), 395–427. My thinking on this issue (including the term 'doctrinal mode') derives from H. Whitehouse, *Modes of Religiosity: A Cognitive Theory of Religious Transmission* (Walnut Creek, CA: AltaMira, 2004), 66–68 and context.
4. The concept of 'brand identity' derives from P. Boyer, *Religion Explained: The Evolutionary Origins of Religious Thought* (New York: Basic Books, 2001), 277.
5. Whitehouse, *Modes of Religiosity*, 76, 129–31.

effectively distinguish this doctrinal mode from any other religion.[6] The doctrinal mode faces competition not only from other doctrinal modes (e.g. the self-proclaimed orthodoxy of Irenaeus vs the self-assured orthodoxy of the so-called Gnostics), but from an even more insidious enemy, the 'cognitive optimum'.

The cognitive optimum is produced by a neurological architecture shared by all humans, which constructs a default religious belief that can undermine any doctrinal mode.[7] Just as a child easily invents an imaginary friend, so also rational adults construct invisible agents, whether gods, ghosts, angels or humans with supernatural capacities.[8] We attempt to interact with these invisible agents through our intuitive assumptions about human obligation (moral values) and reciprocal exchange (retribution and/or grace).[9]

In other words, the basic components of a generic theism are part of our evolutionary heritage. This kind of theism runs under the radar of all doctrinal modes, because this theism is universal, constructed by any person in any time or place. The cognitive optimum does not require (in fact, actively dismisses) sophisticated theologies, subtle distinctions in doctrine or complex rationalizations behind a particular ritual.[10]

Paul's frustration with the Corinthians illustrates the competition between a doctrinal mode and the cognitive optimum.[11] Corinthian observance of

---

6. The success of a doctrinal mode depends on the laity far more than on even the most diligent and effective leadership, because any religious movement rarely includes more than a small percentage of zealots or intellectuals. In other words, the doctrinal mode is limited by the intellectual capacity of the average lay participants, whose collective inculcation of a similar set of memes generates the 'critical mass' that perpetuates the doctrinal mode. I. Pyysiäinen offers valuable insights on this aspect of the issue in a penetrating critical evaluation of the 'doctrinal mode' hypothesis, in Pyysiäinen, 'Corrupt Doctrine and Doctrinal Revival: On the Nature and Limits of the Modes Theory,' in H. Whitehouse and L. H. Martin, eds., *Theorizing Religions Past: Archaeology, History, and Cognition* (Walnut Creek: AltaMira, 2004), 173–94.

7. The term 'cognitive optimum' is common in the research, and derives from Boyer, *Religion Explained*.

8. J. I. Barrett, 'Theological Correctness: Cognitive Constraint and the Study of Religion,' *MTSR* 11 (1999), 325–39; idem., *Why Would Anyone Believe in God?* (Walnut Creek: AltaMira, 2004).

9. Boyer, *Religion Explained*, 314.

10. Whitehouse, *Modes of Religiosity*, 23; cf. I. Pyysiäinen, *How Religion Works: Towards a New Cognitive Science of Religion* (Leiden: Brill, 2003).

11. In this essay, the seven letters attributed to Paul that New Testament researchers rarely dispute (Romans, 1–2 Corinthians, Galatians, Philippians, 1 Thessalonians, Philemon) will be treated as composed by a Hellenistic Jew named Paul, active c. 40s to 60s (or perhaps as late as the 70s) CE. Some researchers in this volume doubt the historical existence of Paul (see T. S. Verenna, R. M. Price). Given the evidence for many interpolations in the undisputed letters (e.g. 1 Cor. 13 appears to be an extensive insertion, disrupting the flow of the argument from ch. 12 into 14), it is not unreasonable to suspect that 'Paul' is at

the Eucharist and conceptualizations of the afterlife have drifted away from Paul's intention, which threatens to obliterate the distinctive aspects of Paul's gospel (1 Cor. 11:17–34; 15:1–57).[12] Paul's apostolic authority is central to his concern because a doctrinal mode will dissolve if the community does not distinguish between approved and unapproved sources of divine revelation. To defend his status as the authoritative transmitter of a divinely revealed doctrinal mode, Paul has no choice but to domesticate or defeat all competing claims of revelation, and so he writes, 'Anyone who claims to be a prophet, or to have spiritual powers, must acknowledge that what I am writing to you is a command of the Lord' (1 Cor. 14:37). In other words, one who fails to acknowledge the authority of Paul's doctrinal mode is effectively dismissed as a false prophet. This is similar to, though less violent than, the Torah's attempt to defeat all competing sources of prophecy in Deuteronomy 13.[13]

Paul's frustration generated by the Corinthians is paralleled throughout the undisputed letters of Paul, because Paul's need to construct, define, defend and replicate a doctrinal mode was felt at every stage of his career and in every interpersonal encounter. Paul does not attack the purveyors of mysteries; nor does he slander Jews who have no contact with followers of Jesus. Although these doctrinal modes were genuine competitors in Paul's environment, they were not the immediate concern. Most of Paul's venom is reserved for other followers of Jesus. Anyone who proclaims a gospel other than the one Paul proclaims is to be cursed (Gal. 1:8–9). Christians who advocate religious observances differing from those favoured by Paul's doctrinal mode are 'dogs' or 'evil workers' (Phil. 3:2), and Paul wishes such people bodily harm (Gal. 5:12). Likewise, Paul castigates those who chase after any new Jesus they encounter (2 Cor. 11:4). Paul wants his followers to 'keep an eye on those who cause dissensions and offenses, in opposition to the teaching that you have learned' and to 'avoid them' (Rom. 16:17). In a later generation, if women within the community have threatened (or

---

least partially an invention, but even if this were the case, my approach is not affected. The polemical nature of the literature associated with Paul's name exists in any case. If 'Paul' is a wholly invented figure, my analysis transfers to the scribe(s) who invented him for polemical purposes ('Paul' becomes *functionally* equivalent to mainstream scholarship's hypothesis of 'deutero-Paul').

12. J. Z. Smith suggests that the Corinthian community viewed Paul's teaching as one interesting option among many, a point that Smith stressed particularly in the oral presentation of his essay at the annual meeting of the Society of Biblical Literature, November 2001: 'Re: Corinthians,' in *Relating Religion: Essays in the Study of Religion* (Chicago: University of Chicago Press, 2004), 340–61.
13. On Deuteronomy's doctrinal mode, see K. L. Noll, 'Was There Doctrinal Dissemination?,' 409–26.

might threaten) the doctrinal mode, then they, too, must be silenced (1 Cor. 14:34–35).[14]

All the essential features of a doctrinal mode are illustrated nicely by Paul's letter to the 'foolish' Galatians, in which Paul competes with a rival doctrinal mode. The Galatians are foolish in Paul's eyes because they have been tempted by a brand of Christian observance that no doubt enjoyed its own systematic defence from well-trained leaders, possibly the individuals 'from James'. Francois Tolmie notes that, in spite of the emotional language throughout, Paul is clearly in control of his thought process, for the letter unfolds as a single, linear argument in which the strongest rhetorical strategy comes first, the second strongest is next, and a series of weaker arguments follow.[15] This linear argument illustrates that Paul instinctively realizes which elements to stress and in what order. First, his own status as the one who initiated the regular teaching events (his gospel, as opposed to another gospel) must be defended, so he begins by asserting his independence from all human authority and his authorization by his god alone (Gal. 1–2). Next, Paul appeals to the ritual reinforcements of those teaching events, the corporate activities through which the Galatians transformed Paul's words into their own existential 'truths' (Gal. 3:1–5). Only after reaffirming the regular teaching events and their ritual reinforcements does Paul turn his attention to the kind of intellectual rationalizations that can be used by religious leadership to justify their truth claims (Gal. 3:6–6:18), but even this portion of the argument is peppered with appeals to the Galatians' memory of their attachment to the teacher and his ritual reinforcements (e.g. 4:12–20). In sum, the Letter to the Galatians betrays all three of the essential requirements for an effective doctrinal mode: Paul as teacher, ritual reinforcements for the Galatians and the letter itself as a means for defeating heterodoxy. Paul knew what he was doing—he was inventing an organized religion.

The urgency felt by Paul (and his heirs, the hypothetical deutero-Paul) is palpable because the competition is so trivial, at least from an outsider's vantage point. Variant versions of Jesus remain proclamations of a 'Jesus', as even Paul can admit when he is feeling charitable (e.g. Phil. 1:15–18). The historian has little difficulty noting similarities to which early Christian

---

14. D. Trobisch observes that 1 Cor. 14:34–35 is not from the original author, but a marginal gloss, since its placement varies in some manuscripts and it flatly contradicts 1 Cor. 11:5. See D. Trobisch, *Paul's Letter Collection: Tracing the Origins* (Minneapolis: Fortress, 1994), 39–40.

15. D. F. Tolmie, *Persuading the Galatians* (Tübingen: Mohr Siebeck, 2005), 235–43. Tolmie identifies six objectives in the letter, most of which unfold in several phases. Paul's strongest two arguments are found in the first objective and the first two phases of the second objective (Gal. 1:1–3:5).

heresiologists appear to be blind.[16] Paul and various second-century polemicists (e.g. Irenaeus of Lyon) needed to protect their own versions of Jesus from all competing versions of Jesus, lest the name of Jesus become associated with competing doctrinal modes. An equally present danger was that the name of Jesus might devolve into a common Hellenistic cognitive optimum, rendering Jesus indistinguishable from common invisible agents, such as angels or mystery gods.[17] If the earliest extant Christian literature did not contain vitriol, it is safe to say this literature would not have survived at all (except as fragments of papyri occasionally recovered from the sands of Egypt), for this doctrinal mode would have gone extinct.

To establish a foundation for the application of this Darwinian method of analysis to the question of a historical Jesus, it is necessary to expose a key question that has been overlooked by mainstream New Testament research. The best way to bring that question to light is to survey and evaluate two excellent, but entirely contradictory, academic publications, each of which succeeds beautifully on its own terms, but fails at precisely the locus where this key question comes into play. When this question is in place, a new survey of earliest Christian history will demonstrate the irrelevance of the historical Jesus to this religion.

Why Were the Gospels Defended as Referential Literature?

Richard Bauckham's *Jesus and the Eyewitnesses* and Thomas Thompson's *The Messiah Myth* provide a useful contrast not so much because their conclusions differ radically (which, of course, they do), but because their presuppositions determine the selection of the evidence, with the result that they address the same topic—earliest Christianity's literature—while treating

16. For example, it is a small step from Paul's ability to assume the persona of the Christ (Gal. 4:14) to the proto-Gnostic notion of Judas as a 'Didymus Thomas' (that is to say, a 'twin' of Jesus) in the *Gospel of Thomas*, and eventually to the belief that one who sees Christ *becomes* Christ, as in the *Gospel of Philip* (J. M. Robinson et al., eds., *The Nag Hammadi Library in English* [San Francisco: Harper & Row, 1988], 126, 147). That a Gospel such as John was suspected of heresy in the second century (by Caius of Rome) is hardly surprising.

17. There seems to have been an especially strong tendency to equate Jesus with an angel, as attested by the early fourth-century inscription from Laodicea Catacecaumena: 'First I shall sing a hymn of praise for God, the one who sees all; second I shall sing a hymn for the first angel, Jesus Christ' (S. Mitchell, *Anatolia: Land, Men and Gods in Asia Minor* [Oxford: Clarendon, 1993], II, 46). Paul apparently does not make a clear distinction between Christ and an angel (cf. Gal. 4:14), the Letter to the Hebrews polemicizes against such a tendency in its first two chapters, and the Shepherd of Hermas appears to equate Jesus with the angel Michael (*Herm. Sim.* 8.3.3.69). For discussion of the latter, see J. Pelikan, *The Christian Tradition: A History of the Development of Doctrine*. I. *The Emergence of the Catholic Tradition (100–600)* (Chicago: University of Chicago Press, 1971), 183.

almost entirely separate sets of ancient data.[18] Bauckham has focused on written remnants from, and references to, proto-orthodox and proto-heretic Christians of the first and second centuries CE, while Thompson places the New Testament writings in dialogue with the literatures of the entire ancient Near Eastern world. Both sets of data are essential for understanding early Christianity, and I suggest that an approach that can accommodate both is likely to provide a more reasonable hypothesis than either of these volumes on its own.

Bauckham writes as a Christian, and his foundational concern is the realization that, if belief in Jesus is to avoid the heresy of docetism, the events of Christ's life, death and alleged resurrection necessarily expose themselves to critical scrutiny.[19] An appeal to faith alone for assertions about the past (e.g. 'Jesus has risen') is fundamentally unchristian.[20] Yet, Bauckham's viewpoint places the truth claim of Christianity at risk, for Thompson's research can account for the emergence of early Christianity without appeal to a historical Jesus.[21] Bauckham is motivated to demonstrate that the narratives of the New Testament intend to *describe* or, at least, *make authentic reference to* real events. It is this attempt to establish that the New Testament Gospels are what I shall label *referential literature* that interests me.

Bauckham has surveyed every datum that suggests direct continuity between eyewitnesses of a historical Jesus and the New Testament Gospels, demonstrating that a significant number of the proto-orthodox Christians known to us (e.g. Papias, Polycarp, the [final] authors of the Gospel of John and the Gospel of Luke) attempted to inculcate among their followers a strong belief that such continuity existed. He concludes that the Gospel narratives can be identified with a genre he calls 'testimony', and suggests that historians who require triangulation of independent streams of data are overly sceptical.[22] If the data include 'participant eyewitness testimony', the historian should suspend scepticism and trust the testimony. Bauckham introduces testimonies from Holocaust survivors to illustrate his point, which is an unfortunate choice, since the example clarifies the fallacy he

18. R. Bauckham, *Jesus and the Eyewitnesses: The Gospels as Eyewitness Testimony* (Grand Rapids: Eerdmans, 2006); T. L. Thompson, *The Messiah Myth: The Near Eastern Roots of Jesus and David* (New York: Basic Books, 2005).
19. Bauckham, *Jesus and the Eyewitnesses*, 1–8.
20. In other words, Bauckham aligns himself with self-identified 'conservative' or 'traditional' Christians, but eschews their usual apologetics in favour of an academic approach. For my assessment of history in the service of apologetics, see my *Canaan and Israel in Antiquity: An Introduction* (London/Sheffield: Continuum, 2001), 38–41.
21. Thompson, *Messiah Myth*.
22. Bauckham, *Jesus and the Eyewitnesses*, 472–508.

commits.[23] We trust the testimony of an Auschwitz survivor because similar atrocities are documented by other means (e.g. the facilities at Auschwitz, Nazi records) and because the eyewitness testimony never invokes elements of the supernatural. The usual method of seeking triangulation from independent streams of data is upheld, not undermined, in Bauckham's example. By contrast, the New Testament narratives, if viewed as testimony, ask us to trust a narrative for which there is no external evidence and which expects us to believe that a man was conceived by parthenogenesis, walked on water, rose from the grave and ascended into the sky on a cloud.

Although Bauckham's apologetic goal is a failure, his research is of great interest, because the ways in which Bauckham has failed expose and clarify significant evidence that ought not to be overlooked. First, Bauckham *demonstrates* unequivocal early claims that Gospel narratives derive from eyewitness testimony, but *concedes* that we have no means to determine which ancient testimonies about Jesus can be traced to participant eyewitnesses. For example, Bauckham believes the attribution of a canonical Gospel to Matthew 'is a mystery', and he never attempts an argument against the attribution of a sayings collection to Thomas, which suggests this attribution is a mystery as well.[24] Throughout the monograph, Bauckham compensates for these missing links in the data by introducing questionable judgments of probability. For instance, Bauckham declares it 'likely' that the tradition tracing testimony from Peter through Glaukias to Basilides was invented by someone who was imitating the tradition that moves from Peter through Mark to Papias.[25] But, so far as we can tell, the name of Mark was as obscure as that of Glaukias in the early second century, so Bauckham's reasoning is circular. It is just as likely that Mark was invented in imitation of Glaukias. A third possibility is perhaps even more likely, namely that both Mark and Glaukias were real people, both were genuine disciples of the man Paul calls Cephas (Gal. 1:18), and that each interpreted this man's testimony in different ways, resulting in conflicting conceptualizations about Jesus (cf. 1 Cor. 1:11–12; 2 Cor. 11:4).[26]

---

23. Bauckham, *Jesus and the Eyewitnesses*, 479–99.
24. Bauckham, *Jesus and the Eyewitnesses*, 131–32; cf. 108–12, 300–302. The *Gospel of Thomas* never receives sustained discussion; in fact, Bauckham mentions it only a few times (236–37; cf. 238, 302, n. 28).
25. Bauckham, *Jesus and the Eyewitnesses*, 237–38. Along with incidental references on pp. 35 and 296, this is the only discussion of Basilides in Bauckham's monograph. The peripheral role played by the proto-heretics (e.g. *Gospel of Thomas*, Basilides) suggests that the bias in favour of the proto-orthodox tradition has predisposed Bauckham to marginalize data that might have taken his thesis in a very different direction, and not necessarily an unorthodox one.
26. Bauckham's arbitrary dismissal of a tradent known as Glaukias is echoed by many researchers. For example, Birger A. Pearson gives Glaukias 'little credence' in *Ancient*

Bauckham's second and more devastating flaw is an accidental deconstruction of his own thesis that Gospel testimony consistently intends to be *referential*. With respect to the Gospel of John, which he defends as participant eyewitness testimony, Bauckham concludes that 'there is no epistemological chasm between the eyewitness testimony and the theological significance of the events as this author develops them'.[27] That conclusion is remarkable in light of Jn 19:31–37, which gives the appearance of having been invented in order to match the tale to a pre-existing anthology of Jewish literature.[28] Occam's razor suggests this testimony was not intended to be referential, unless it was designed to deceive a reader into believing it references a real event even though the author knew it does not (cf. the rhetoric of 1 Jn 1:1–5).[29] Bauckham is correct that the 'epistemological chasm' of which he speaks does not exist, yet this very fact muddies the epistemological waters rather than, as Bauckham had hoped, purifying them.

This second flaw exposes a significant reality that any researcher is obligated to keep forefront in the discussion: the claims of eyewitness testimony preserved in the early Christian literature are significant for what they *assert*, but even more for what they implicitly *concede*. For example, both Lk. 1:1–4 and Jn 21:24 *assert* continuity with eyewitnesses and *concede* unreliability of content. Luke's prologue concedes that many accounts about Jesus (perhaps all of them) were not 'orderly' and required improvement or displacement, while the group who call themselves 'we' in Jn 21:24 admit that they have misunderstood the testimony they received and transmitted, a misunderstanding that they admit took place already during the lifetime of their own beloved eyewitness (Jn 21:23).[30] Similarly, the testimony from Papias of Hierapolis about Mark and Matthew (Eusebius, *Hist. eccl.* 3.39.14–16)

Gnosticism: Traditions and Literature (Minneapolis: Fortress, 2007), 135–36. This is puzzling since Pearson believes that (a) Gnosticism began as a sectarian Jewish movement independent of earliest Christianity, and (b) Irenaeus misrepresented Basilides when he claimed that Basilides taught the substitution of Mark's 'Simon of Cyrene' for Jesus on the cross (Mk 15:21; Irenaeus, *Haer.* 1.24.4; Pearson, *Ancient Gnosticism*, 15–19 and 140). If Pearson is correct with respect to these two details, then there is every reason to believe that Basilides received a Jewish-Gnostic tradition from an authentic earlier source and is independent of the Markan Gospel narrative. In other words, there is no logical basis for giving Glaukias 'little credence'.

27. Bauckham, *Jesus and the Eyewitnesses*, 472.
28. New Testament authors routinely invented fictions about Jesus inspired by passages from Jewish literature. On this, see an essay that I regard as required reading for all who are interested in the study of early Christianity: Michael J. Cook, 'Jewish Reflections on Jesus: Some Abiding Trends,' in L. J. Greenspoon, D. Hamm and B. F. LeBeau, eds., *The Historical Jesus through Catholic and Jewish Eyes* (Harrisburg: Trinity Press International, 2000), 95–111.
29. Compare the discussion in Noll, 'Evolution of Genre,' 21–23.
30. Bauckham avoids discussion of these self-evident observations in *Jesus and the Eyewitnesses*, 116–24, 127–29, 369–70, 379–81, 384–90 and passim.

intends to establish continuity with eyewitnesses, but Bauckham believes that Papias deliberately called into question the accuracy of their narrative contents so that Papias could subordinate Mark and Matthew to the Gospel of John.[31] Faced with the evidence Bauckham has so skillfully marshaled, no competent reader of the New Testament, even one who trusts the *sincerity* of these claims about eyewitnesses, can trust the *content* of these narratives, and Bauckham's desire to place trust in Gospel testimony as referential narrative is revealed to be a misplaced trust.

To summarize, Bauckham's careful survey of early Christian texts demonstrates that, from the first half of the second century at the latest, the Gospel narratives later canonized were disseminated and promoted as though they presented participant eyewitness testimony about Jesus. Whatever the origins of Matthew, Mark, Luke, John and the Acts of the Apostles, their handlers (e.g. the 'we' of Jn 21:24; the 'I' of Lk. 1:1–4 and Acts 1:1; the claims of Papias about Mark and Matthew) desired that these books be accepted as *fully referential*. Although this is not entirely what Bauckham set out to demonstrate, the conclusion is established beyond reasonable doubt. In my view, that conclusion is fascinating because, on the surface at least, it seems to be contradicted by the research of Thomas Thompson.

Thompson's thesis is that the Gospel literature is part of a long literary stream that included Mesopotamian, Egyptian, Hebrew, Syrian and Greek rivers, all flowing into one gulf, which was the intellectual and cultural heritage of the ancient world.[32] All such literature had as its goal 'the education of its audience to a set of values and principles'.[33] The influence of commonly known plot motifs, stock scenes, stereotyped characters, popular proverbs, frequently recurring poetic flourishes, as well as perennial religious or philosophical themes, transcended language barriers and political boundaries, so that these motifs appeared in vast numbers of unique combinations from the Early Bronze Age to the Common Era.

In Thompson's view, much of modern New Testament scholarship's effort has been a failure. Researchers have not realized that the extant data are but the tip of a now-lost literary iceberg. For example, efforts to isolate a documentary source common to Matthew and Luke, but unknown to Mark (i.e. the hypothetical Q-source), are quixotic, and such illusions would vanish if the researchers involved would take note of our necessarily limited access to the ancient texts.[34] The Synoptic Gospels do not depend on one another,

---

31. Bauckham, *Jesus and the Eyewitnesses*, 226–27; cf. 12–38, 202–39, 412–37.
32. Thompson, *Messiah Myth*, 3–26 and 315–21.
33. Thompson, *Messiah Myth*, 316.
34. Thompson, *Messiah Myth*, 8–20; cf. 74–80, 107–13. On the Q-hypothesis, see J. M. Robinson, P. Hoffmann and J. S. Kloppenborg, eds., *The Critical Edition of Q* (Hermeneia; Minneapolis:

but are streams from a river of similar literature, all of which are samples of 'rewritten tales'.[35] The authors of these narratives are part of a tradition that 'does not deal with original texts or founding events as much as it reflects a widespread literary discussion that has many other refractions than those we meet in the Bible'.[36]

If this thesis is accepted, it is not difficult to see that any quest for a historical Jesus is misguided. Thompson asserts that characters such as Moses, Job and Jesus are 'interchangeable protagonists', whose tales borrow, modify and recombine elements to probe ageless themes of 'justice, humanity and life'.[37] Thus, in response to those who quest for a historical Jesus, Thompson writes that 'the gospels are not about such a person. They deal with something else.'[38] This 'something else' is a perpetual conversation among an elite group of intellectuals for whom and by whom the literature was produced.[39] These ancient users of texts shared a recondite vocabulary of literary motifs that could be combined in a vast number of ways. For example, the Matthean kingdom parables (Mt. 13) are 'not presenting a historical Jesus or anything he said', but use the 'figure of Jesus to discuss the book of Daniel'.[40] In turn, Matthew's source-text, Daniel, was part of a vast ancient conversation about royalty, divine will and the place of human behaviour in the divine scheme. Even the death and resurrection of Jesus is a reiteration of the ancient myths of dying and rising gods, which are themselves part of a larger cluster of parables 'about new beginnings and a future marked by life'.[41]

Thompson's emphasis on a larger cultural conversation in ancient Near Eastern literature is supported by researchers whose comparative studies have illustrated the ancient scribal subculture's perpetual construction of ever-new, yet always-old, literatures.[42] To be sure, a reasonable objection can

---

Fortress, 2000). For dissent from the Q-hypothesis while still positing Matthew's dependency on Mark, see M. S. Goodacre, *The Case Against Q: Studies in Markan Priority and the Synoptic Problem* (Harrisburg: Trinity Press International, 2002). For a defence of Matthean priority, see A. J. McNicol, ed., with D. L. Dungan and D. B. Peabody, *Beyond the Q Impasse: Luke's Use of Matthew* (Valley Forge: Trinity Press International, 1996).

35. Thompson, *Messiah Myth*, 35.
36. Thompson, *Messiah Myth*, 43.
37. Thompson, *Messiah Myth*, 59.
38. Thompson, *Messiah Myth*, 14. Thompson has in mind, primarily, the Jesus Seminar founded by Robert W. Funk.
39. 'No author of merit...has written apart from a literary community and a common tradition', Thompson, *Messiah Myth*, 65.
40. Thompson, *Messiah Myth*, 29.
41. Thompson, *Messiah Myth*, 217.
42. Recent examples include K. van der Toorn, *Scribal Culture and the Making of the Hebrew Bible* (Cambridge: Harvard University Press, 2007) and D. M. Carr, *Writing on the Tablet of the Heart: Origins of Scripture and Literature* (New York: Oxford University Press, 2005).

be raised: because 'themes' are slippery targets of investigation, Thompson is not able to demonstrate beyond doubt that the themes shared between Jewish and Christian Scriptures result from direct literary dependence in every instance. One researcher sees dependence where another sees only an interesting correspondence of motifs. However, Thompson's thesis rests on a strong foundation, for his observations about shared themes fit exactly with more commonly observed processes of composition in both of the Christian Testaments. For example, much of the Hebrew Bible's literature is 'recycled', such as the variant tales placed side by side in Genesis, the often verbatim overlap between Chronicles and Samuel–Kings in the service of two very different stories, the variant torah-codes in Exodus–Deuteronomy stressing alternative theologies, or the variant tales of warrior-heroes in Joshua–Samuel, in which details are repeated (e.g. 'Goliath' in 1 Sam. 17 and 2 Sam. 21:19, or the killing of a lion in Judg. 14:6 and 2 Sam. 23:20). Although many researchers have become so familiar with this phenomenon that they often overlook its significance, Thompson rightly stresses that recycled literature of this kind is the norm and not the exception. Famously, the Hebrew Latter Prophets display an intricate web of recycled oracles, a datum that would seem anomalous without the insight Thompson's thesis provides: for example, Mic. 4:1–3 is repeated verbatim in Isa. 2:1–4, Obad. 1–7 appears as well in Jer. 49:9–16, and the oracle against daughter Zion in Jer. 6:22–24 becomes an oracle against Babylon at Jer. 50:41–43. More frequently, single phrases or poetic lines are recycled in a variety of ways (e.g. Amos 1:2 and 9:13 are echoed in Joel 4:16, 18 [3:16, 18]). It is a small step to extend this analysis, as Thompson does, to the New Testament.

Regardless of the process by which literary recycling took place (and scholarship has, predictably, generated a variety of plausible hypotheses about this process), Thompson's observation that our extant manuscripts represent but the tip of an unseen literary iceberg is correct. For example, biblical references to now-lost literature (e.g. Num. 21:14; Josh. 10:13 MT; 2 Sam. 1:18; OG 3 Kgdms 8:53; Lk. 1:1–4; Col. 4:16) warn us away from the naïve belief that the absence of extant manuscript variation constitutes evidence for an original composition free from entanglement in an unseen web of literary dependencies.[43] In short, it is not possible to view a book such as Deuteronomy or Jeremiah as the product of historical persons named Moses or Jeremiah; rather, these anthologies of literature are the distillate from a long process of literary recycling. Even in cases where it is reasonable to believe that a historical person, such as a Jeremiah or a Paul, ultimately stands behind the literature, the quest for this figure is, at best, problematic. Likewise, regardless of whether a Q-source existed

43. Cf. Noll, 'Was There Doctrinal Dissemination?,' 422–23.

(and Thompson's dismissal of the hypothesis can be debated), the narrative reiterations in the canonical Gospels are the unsurprising by-product of a literary culture that paid little attention to questions of historical accuracy or original sources.

The genuine contribution of Thompson's monograph is its explication of motifs in the New Testament that appear to be part of the universal ancient literary conversation. The Gospel narratives of the New Testament are fictions constructed from prior literature and betraying only minor influence, at best, from memories of (or, perhaps, gossip and folklore inspired by) real-world events. The researcher must accept, as a necessary methodological foundation, that any tale about Jesus is likely to have a long and rich pre-Christian provenance. The miracle stories have derived from the prevailing literary (and probably folk) culture, as demonstrated by Wendy Cotter; moreover, Jens Schröter observes that 'the distinction between "genuine" words of Jesus and other traditions played no part at all' in the construction of the Gospels' teaching segments.[44] For example, Schröter is able to identify many formulations that appear *firstly* in the letters of Paul, and were only *secondarily* attributed to Jesus himself.[45] Observations of this kind must play a central role in any historical hypothesis that hopes to be plausible. In sum, the variant images of a Jesus are identical to the variant images of a Moses or a Jeremiah, suggesting that attempts to dissect Gospel narratives in quest of a historical Jesus are methodologically unsound.

Bauckham and Thompson have arrived at seemingly incompatible conclusions. Either the canonical Gospel narratives refer to real events pertaining to a man named Jesus, or the figure of Jesus is nothing more than a vehicle through which intellectuals recombined traditional religious and philosophical concepts in order to inculcate traditional values. Yet the data upon which these alternative viewpoints rest are unequivocal. There can be no doubt that proto-orthodox Christians defended the eyewitness veracity of these documents, as demonstrated by Bauckham; and there can be no doubt that much of the content in these New Testament stories was

44. W. Cotter, 'Cosmology and the Jesus Miracles,' in W. E. Arnal and M. Desjardins, eds., *Whose Historical Jesus?* (Waterloo: Wilfrid Laurier University Press, 1997), 118–31. J. Schröter, 'Jesus and the Canon: The Early Jesus Traditions in the Context of the Origins of the New Testament Canon,' in R. A. Horsley, J. A. Draper and J. M. Foley, eds., *Performing the Gospel: Orality, Memory and Mark: Essays Dedicated to Werner Kelber* (Minneapolis: Fortress Press, 2006), 104–22, 222–28 (110).

45. Schröter, 'Jesus and the Canon,' 109–10. For example: 1 Thess. 5:2 = Lk. (or Q) 12:39 (Mt. 24:43; cf. Rev. 3:3; 16:15; *Gos. Thom.* 21:5–7); 1 Thess. 5:13 (cf. Rom. 12:18) = Mk 9:50 (Mt. 5:9); 1 Thess. 5:15 (cf. Rom. 12:14, 17) = Lk. (or Q) 6:28 (Mt. 5:44; cf. 1 Pet. 3:9); Rom. 12:20 (cf. Prov. 25:21) = Lk. (or Q) 6:27, 35 (Mt. 5:44); Rom. 14:14 = Mk 7:15 (Mt. 15:11); 1 Cor. 13:2 = Mk 11:22–23 (Mt. 17:20; cf. Lk. 17:6; *Gos. Thom.* 48, 106).

invented freely through imaginative combinations of pre-existing motifs, as suggested by Thompson.

Can both scholars be correct? I believe that they can, though we must be clear about what each researcher has *not* demonstrated. Just as Bauckham failed to achieve his ultimate goal of tracing the common assertions about eyewitnesses back to actual eyewitnesses, Thompson has overreached as well.

Thompson's graceful explications of narrative motifs do not rule out the probability that these literary flourishes were meant to enhance, not negate, claims that events really have been 'fulfilled among us' (Lk. 1:1). It is not sufficient to note, with Thompson, the literary-cultural provenance of the narratives about Jesus. The researcher is obligated to pay attention to explicit rhetorical clues about the intended function of each text.[46] Matthew and Mark lack rhetorical markers of authorial intention (though in Mark's case, the lack might have resulted from mutilation of the text).[47] Nevertheless, the three other New Testament narrative books (Luke, John, Acts) in received form have been marked as 'testimony' in the sense defined and demonstrated by Bauckham.

Certainly Thompson is correct that literature constructs an imaginary realm, but it does not necessarily follow that every ancient scribe viewed the matter that way. Each scribe used his educational heritage as he saw fit. The fictional provenance of many tales about Jesus does not demonstrate that the genre of a Gospel narrative in its final form was intended to be received as fiction. For example, although it is unlikely that the Gospel of Luke and the Acts of the Apostles were composed by one author, their received form is designed to look that way, and Bauckham correctly points to relevant parallels among ancient historians, such as Polybius and Josephus, to understand the intended genre marked by the two prologues (Lk. 1:1–4; Acts 1:1–2).[48] Even if one accepts Loveday Alexander's alternative suggestion

46. The necessity of explicit rhetorical markers for identification of literary genre is stressed in K. L. Noll, 'Is the Book of Kings Deuteronomistic? And Is It a History?,' *SJOT* 21 (2007), 49–72.

47. On the possibility of Mark's mutilation, see N. C. Croy, *The Mutilation of Mark's Gospel* (Nashville: Abingdon, 2003).

48. Bauckham, *Jesus and the Eyewitnesses*, 119. Many recent researchers have questioned the authorial unity (and commonly assumed dates of composition) for Luke–Acts. See P. Walters, *The Assumed Authorial Unity of Luke and Acts: A Reassessment of the Evidence* (Cambridge: Cambridge University Press, 2009); M. Klinghardt, 'The Marcionite Gospel and the Synoptic Problem: A New Suggestion,' *NovT* 50 (2008), 1–27; R. I. Pervo, *Dating Acts between the Evangelists and the Apologists* (Santa Rosa: Polebridge, 2006); J. B. Tyson, *Marcion and Luke-Acts: A Defining Struggle* (Columbia: University of South Carolina Press, 2006).

that these prologues 'collapse the distinction between outsider (observer) and insider (believer)', so that their historiographical intention could have been grasped only by insiders, the conclusion remains inescapable that Luke and Acts as transmitted in the extant manuscripts expect the reader to accept the events narrated as fully referential in the sense defined by Bauckham.[49] In spite of Thompson's useful insights, Bauckham's insights must not be ignored.

Likewise, the letters of Paul explicitly expect the reader to accept Paul's crucified Christ as a real, flesh-and-blood human who was the victim of execution by real-world authorities (1 Cor. 1:23). Thompson is correct that Paul displays erudite use of mythological and 'apocalyptic' Jewish literature, but Thompson's discussion of this fails to demonstrate that the apostle did not expect his readers to associate his Lord, Jesus Christ, with a specific near-future manifestation (e.g. 1 Thess. 4:14–18; 1 Cor. 15:22–23).[50] In my view, the 'rulers of this age' who crucified the 'Lord of glory' (1 Cor. 2:8) refer to real-world authorities (cf. Rom. 13:1–7) and become associated with a mythological realm only in the later, deutero-Pauline interpretation (e.g. Eph. 3:10), just as Paul's eschatology evolved in deutero-Pauline handling (e.g. 2 Thess. 2:1–12 modifies 1 Thess. 4:13–18). The rhetorical structure of Paul's epistles, as also the apocalyptic passages in the narrative Gospels, implies that readers were expected to place their trust in a god who saves the predestined through a risen Christ in real time. Such tales about Jesus, or attributed to him, were not merely the 'discursive retelling' of 'a cyclical, never-ending story of the imminent kingdom of divine rule to every new generation'.[51]

In other words, Thompson, like Bauckham, advances knowledge even as he falls short of his ultimate goal. Bauckham had hoped to establish continuity with eyewitness testimony deriving, ultimately, from a hypothetical historical Jesus. Thompson had hoped to demonstrate that, because the narrative Gospels partake of a universal conversation among literati of the ancient world, early Christians were not speaking about a historical Jesus. Nevertheless, the question of a historical Jesus remains because the early Christian literature makes explicit claims about such a figure even as they transmit narratives that are too generic to be viewed as reliable information about him.

---

49. L. C. A. Alexander, *Acts in Its Ancient Literary Context: A Classicist Looks at the Acts of the Apostles* (London: T & T Clark, 2005), 133–63 (162–63).
50. Thompson, *Messiah Myth*, 17–18. I place 'apocalyptic' in quotation marks because, in Thompson's view, this literature only seems to be apocalyptic to modern researchers who fail to discern its rhetorical function.
51. Thompson, *Messiah Myth*, 55.

In my view, Bauckham and Thompson have each exposed, but failed to examine, a *key question*, which has to do with these non-referential Gospel narratives for which claims of eyewitness testimony have been made: *What was the intended function of the claims about continuity with eyewitness participants?* It is reasonable to conclude from the preceding discussion that those who made these claims knew that the narratives were non-referential. That is to say, they knew that the content of the narrative Gospels was relatively generic, consisting of common miracle tales and a variety of relatively universal teachings. Therefore we must ask, why did they promote them as referential literature, literature that narrates the revelation of a god through a man named Jesus? Was this an attempt to deceive others? (Many biblical scholars rule out such a possibility a priori, but there are no methodological grounds for doing so.) If there was no intention to deceive, then what was the purpose?

Paul versus the Pillars: Doctrinal Modes in Conflict

In sum, our key question is: why were non-referential narratives about Jesus promoted as eyewitness testimony by, at the latest, the early decades of the second century CE? A Darwinian model can address this question. The emphasis by early Christian leaders on eyewitness testimony about Jesus suggests that the historian should be searching for earliest evidence of a doctrinal mode associated with the name of Jesus so that we can trace its evolution. The goal of this quest is to determine how such a doctrinal mode became linked to narrative Gospels that are largely devoid of unequivocal information about Jesus. This section and the final section will outline the process by which this took place.

If one assumes, for the sake of argument, that a historical Jesus existed, it must be admitted that little can be established about the time or place of his activity. If one trusts the datum provided by Tacitus (*Ann.* 15.44), one might at least locate the death of Jesus in Judea (presumably Jerusalem) under Pontius Pilate (thus, between 26 and 36 CE), but the possibility that this text is dependent, ultimately, on the Synoptic Gospels cannot be ruled out. Paul does not provide information about the place or time of Jesus' activity, nor can one rely on 1 Cor. 5:7b–8 to place the crucifixion in a Passover context since this passage is an afterthought inspired by the quoted proverb in 5:6–7a.[52] It is worth stressing that a Galilean setting for Jesus appears to

52. The association of the crucifixion with Passover was invented by the author of the Gospel of Mark. Elaborate hypotheses can be constructed to avoid this conclusion but, as always, I prefer Occam's Razor. See H. J. de Jonge, 'The Early History of the Lord's Supper,' in Jan Willem van Henten and Anton Houtepen, eds., *Religious Identity and the Invention*

be unknown to Paul. While the possibility that Jesus was from Galilee is not implausible, the undisputed letters of Paul would lead a researcher to assume that Jesus was a Judean, perhaps from Jerusalem, and that any social movement bearing his name migrated to Galilee without Paul's knowledge, or after Paul's time.

Regardless of when or where Jesus was active, any hypothetical historical Jesus can be plausible only if the one who posits this hypothesis affirms that Jesus failed on at least one of two fundamental levels. To establish himself as an enduring authoritative persona (a prophet, a sage, a messiah, an angel or whatever), the historical Jesus would have had to accomplish two things:

1. convince a number of followers that the supernatural agent he proclaims is identical with, or effectively replaces, the supernatural agent these followers previously affirmed, and that this supernatural agent has commissioned Jesus to speak on its behalf;[53]
2. reduce his message to a doctrinal mode, using (at a minimum) a set of regularly recurring teaching events with ritual reinforcements, and institutionalizing a specialized leadership to guard against defection from the doctrinal mode associated with the name of Jesus.[54]

If, for sake of argument, our hypothetical Jesus succeeded in the first endeavour, a glance at Galatians 1–2 is sufficient to realize that Jesus failed with respect to the second task. Presuming these chapters offer a glimpse at a real dispute taking place in the earliest decades of the movement, their content demonstrates that a doctrinal mode associated with the name of Jesus was only beginning to emerge after Jesus had departed from the scene. Likewise, early Christian texts that almost all researchers view as much later than the undisputed letters of Paul demonstrate that no ritual reinforcements of a doctrinal mode were yet in place during the career of Jesus. For example, John's Gospel cannot decide whether Jesus baptized (Jn 4:2; cf. Jn 3:22 and 4:1) or whether a literal understanding of the Eucharist was acceptable to the earliest followers of Jesus (Jn 6:66). The latter detail is fascinating in light of the Codex Bezae version of Luke's Eucharist (Lk. 22:14–22), which suggests that the eucharistic liturgical formulae were slow to develop.[55]

---

of Tradition: Papers Read at a Noster Conference in Soesterbert, January 4-6, 1999 (Assen: Van Gorcum, 2001), 209–37 (218, n. 16).

53. Boyer, *Religion Explained*, 225–26, and context.
54. Whitehouse, *Modes of Religiosity*, 66–68. These are the minimal requirements. Whitehouse notes as well some elements that, while not necessary, commonly occur in a successful doctrinal mode (69–70).
55. For research on the Codex Bezae (with bibliography), see D. C. Parker, *Codex Bezae: An Early Christian Manuscript and Its Text* (Cambridge: Cambridge University Press, 2009).

Therefore, the discussion of earliest Christianity's construction of a doctrinal mode necessarily begins with Paul and his opponents at Galatia, for there is no earlier evidence for early Christian groups.[56] To begin with the dispute among the Galatians is not controversial, as even mainstream scholarship places all other early Christian literature—the deutero-Pauline letters, Acts and the Catholic letters, the canonical Gospels, a hypothetical Q-source and non-canonical Christian literatures—no earlier than, and usually after, the time of the undisputed Paulines.[57] Methodologically, it is not only (or even primarily) that these other texts are chronologically posterior to Paul's texts, but that a consensus of research has concluded that their content is either clearly dependent on Paul's content or reasonably suspected of being dependent on that content. Thus, any attempt to answer our key question and, in so doing, demonstrate the relative significance of the historical Jesus for the emergence, evolution and ultimate survival of the Christian religion depends primarily on Paul.[58]

The only viable evidence for the content of any proselytizing by the 'pillars' of Jerusalem is Paul's assertion that his Gospel received 'the right hand of fellowship' from them (Gal. 2:1–10). Some researchers suggest that the fifteen-day visit with Cephas and James (Gal. 1:18–20) introduced Paul to an extensive set of stories and sayings, so that Paul would have been aware of the traditions now contained in the Synoptic Gospels, but this defies the evidence.[59] The fifteen-day visit does indeed suggest that Paul learned

---

For research on the Eucharist (with bibliography), see D. E. Smith, *From Symposium to Eucharist: The Banquet in the Early Christian World* (Minneapolis: Fortress Press, 2003); Paul F. Bradshaw, *Eucharistic Origins* (Oxford: Oxford University Press, 2004).

56. One might appeal to Tacitus and Suetonius for details about earliest Christians, but these are minimal and potentially misleading, and I doubt that the two passages in Josephus that mention Jesus and James were unmolested by later Christian scribes. For entry into non-biblical sources of the early Jesus, see R. E. Van Voorst, *Jesus Outside the New Testament: An Introduction to the Ancient Evidence* (Grand Rapids: Eerdmans, 2000). In addition to the usual (and significant) arguments against the authenticity of the two passages in Josephus (*A. J.* 18.3.3; 20.9.1), it is worth noting that Josephus never uses the word 'Christ' except when mentioning Christianity's Jesus, which suggests that the word was interpolated in both passages (cf. J. Fitzmyer, *The One Who Is to Come* [Grand Rapids: Eerdmans, 2007], 131).

57. Occasionally, an idiosyncratic voice is heard, such as J. G. Crossley's quixotic attempt to place Mark prior to Paul's debates concerning Torah observance (*The Date of Mark's Gospel* [London: T & T Clark, 2004]). A thesis preferable to Crossley's is presented by Cook, 'Jewish Reflections on Jesus'.

58. Methodologically, my approach is similar to that of D. H. Akenson, *Saint Saul: A Skeleton Key to the Historical Jesus* (Oxford: Oxford University Press, 2000), 134. My conclusions differ from Akenson's, but I recommend his useful and sometimes insightful discussion on 158–70.

59. This idea is widespread in New Testament research. For example, Helmut Koester, *Ancient Christian Gospels: Their History and Development* (London: SCM Press, 1990), 49–55; Bauckham, *Jesus and the Eyewitnesses*, 264–71.

everything Cephas and James deemed essential, but the contents of Paul's letters are the only (and sufficient) measure of that essence.[60]

The rhetorical thrust of Paul's self-defence in Galatians suggests that the pillars approved the very kind of teaching contained in Paul's authentic letters. Admittedly, we do not possess a source for the viewpoint of those pillars, but my assertion is not to be dismissed as an argument from silence; rather, it is an argument from the plain sense of the text. Paul fully expects his opponents to concede this one point, if nothing else, for otherwise there is no value in his narrative at all. In my view, what Paul explicitly tells us provides ample data to formulate a probable summation of both Paul's continuity with and departure from the gospel preached by the pillars. For example, Paul betrays no hint of knowing the types of stories familiar to us from the Gospel narratives, and since he is careful to distinguish his own teachings from sayings of his Lord (1 Cor. 7:10, 12, 25), there is strong foundation for denying that any portion of Paul's letters not explicitly noted by Paul depends on prior traditions about Jesus.

In other words, the gospel preached by the historical Cephas and James the Lord's brother was roughly identical to Paul's 'Christ crucified' (1 Cor. 1:23), along with Paul's recitation of some liturgical formulae (e.g. 1 Cor. 11:23–25), Paul's eschatological doctrine (e.g. 1 Thess. 4; 1 Cor. 15), and probably not much more than that. From this evidence one is not able to assign to Cephas or James any stories about a virgin conception, or a baptism by John, or a miracle-working Jesus, or a ministry in Galilee, or sermons on the mount or on the plain, or a betrayal by one disciple and denial by another, or an arrest at Gethsemane, or a casting of lots for garments at Golgotha, or an empty tomb or any other Jesus-meme.

For those who knew and remembered the historical Jesus, his last meal and death, his resurrection appearances and his future return were the only elements worthy of emphasis.[61] From the evidence, there is no justification

60. Although there is much to commend in his essay, on this issue M. P. Miller tries to problematize what should be a straightforward historical judgment, in Miller, 'Antioch, Paul, and Jerusalem: Diaspora Myths of Origins in the Homeland,' in R. Cameron and M. P. Miller, eds., *Redescribing Christian Origins* (Atlanta: Society of Biblical Literature, 2004), 177–235.

61. Probably the Eucharist evolved considerably even before Paul learned of it from Cephas and James; see D. Smith, *From Symposium to Eucharist*, 188–91 and passim. Nevertheless, Paul's version of the meal remains 'Jewish' in the sense that the words over the cup do not suggest that the wine is blood, as does the non-Jewish modification found in Mk 14:24 and Mt. 26:28, and elaborated by Jn 6:53 (for Luke's Last Supper, follow Codex Bezae). The resurrection appearance formula in 1 Cor. 15:3–7 was modified over time, as is clear by the way Paul adds himself to the list (1 Cor. 15:8–11). This was not a fixed set of witnesses and thus there is no reason to think that a structured set of related resurrection stories or 'eyewitness accounts' circulated. In this very early stage of the religion,

for believing that these people viewed Jesus as a specially gifted teacher, miracle worker or prophet. In all probability he was viewed as a persecuted and vindicated son of David, as charismatic and fallible as the David of hoary antiquity; and Jesus was the one who has been designated by resurrection to be Son of God and eschatological conqueror of the entire world (Rom. 1:3–4; 1 Cor. 15:20–28; cf. Pss. 2; 110). Paul knows Jesus as 'Christ' and 'Lord' precisely because the pillars in Jerusalem proclaimed him the Christ who will come again to establish the kingdom *of* the Jewish god and to deliver that kingdom *to* the Jewish god (1 Cor. 15:24; 16:22b; cf. Rom. 11).[62]

It is necessary to stress that these relatively few Jesus-memes are more than sufficient to build and sustain a viable religious subculture within the orbit of first-century Judaisms. All researchers agree that earliest Christianity was not designed to depart from its Jewish culture, but to win the allegiance of the Jewish people. In that context, a Jesus who departs from Moses or who surpasses David (at least as these figures seem to have been known by first-century Jews) would be unnecessary and potentially blasphemous.

The evidence suggests that James, Cephas, John, Paul and Barnabas shook hands on the doctrinal mode that I have just described, with its very narrow set of easily inculcated, and soteriologically significant, Jesus-memes. Because this doctrinal mode is almost entirely about the fate of Jesus from the night before crucifixion until the eschaton, and lacks the teachings

---

anyone who 'experienced' a resurrected Jesus, and who could convince the defenders of the doctrinal mode that this experience was valid, could add himself or herself to the list and thereby establish credentials as an authority in this movement. It would not be long until the defenders of the doctrinal mode lost what little control they ever maintained over such claims. Note that Paul experienced difficulty finding ways to control personal experiences at Corinth (e.g. 1 Cor. 12–14). For recent discussion of this much-debated creed, see David M. Moffitt, 'Affirming the "Creed": The Extent of Paul's Citation of an Early Christian Formula in 1 Cor 15:3b–7*,' *ZNW* 99 (2008), 49–73.

62. J. J. Collins writes, 'How Jesus came to be identified as the Davidic messiah remains one of the great puzzles of early Christianity' ('What Was Distinctive about Messianic Expectation at Qumran?,' in J. H. Charlesworth, ed., *The Bible and the Dead Sea Scrolls*. II. *The Dead Sea Scrolls and the Qumran Community* [Waco: Baylor University Press, 2006], 71–92 [85]). This is a puzzle only if one assumes that the peaceful Jesus favoured by later Christian preaching was the historical Jesus. Using my conservative research method for evaluating ancient sources, I suggest that the Jerusalem pillars preached a Jesus who claimed to be a son of David and expected to wage holy war on behalf of the Jewish god in the near eschatological future (in other words, a Davidic messiah similar to those in Ps. 2, the Qumran texts or *Psalms of Solomon*). The proclamation of the cross fits very nicely with this hypothetical 'Gospel according to the Jerusalem Pillars', for any Roman governor would have viewed this type of Jesus as a foolish but potentially dangerous criminal, and the pillars would have used the story of the resurrection to affirm how wrong that Roman governor had been (1 Cor. 1:20–25).

and tales that later tradition anchors in the so-called historical ministry of Jesus (e.g. Paul never quotes the actual words of his Lord, never describes a significant event in the life of Jesus and does not even appeal to a miracle-working Jesus to explain or justify his own claims to miraculous capability in, say, 2 Cor. 12:12), it is a moot question whether the historical Jesus, presuming he existed, played any role in the construction of this doctrinal mode.

At the time of the Jerusalem deal in Gal. 2:9–10, the Gospel agreed upon was just another variant of the many common Judaisms of the late Second Temple period.[63] The challenge that Paul faced was how to remain faithful to this doctrinal mode and yet translate it into a set of Jesus-memes that would be comprehensible and attractive to a non-Jewish demographic. His letters demonstrate that he was not entirely successful, but that he tried to accomplish his goal by relaxing Jewish observances and by expressing the gospel in the language of Greco-Roman religions (e.g. Rom. 9:5; 1 Cor. 2:8; 8:6; 10:16; Phil. 2:6–11).[64] However, this required that Paul become all things to all people (1 Cor. 9:19–23), something that was unanticipated and unappreciated by the Jerusalem pillars.

Does this mean that no variant Jesus-memes circulated prior to the first Jewish Revolt? Clearly there were other conceptualizations of Jesus and other Gospels at that early date, because Paul complains about them (e.g. 2 Cor. 11:4); but none of these other Jesus-memes derived from the teachings of the Jerusalem pillars. Werner Kelber and Helmut Koester suggest that

---

63. For the varieties of Judaism, see L. L. Grabbe, *Judaism from Cyrus to Hadrian* (2 vols.; Minneapolis: Fortress, 1992); E. P. Sanders, *Judaism: Practices and Belief, 63 BCE–66 CE* (London: SCM Press, 1994); S. J. D. Cohen, *The Beginnings of Jewishness: Boundaries, Varieties, Uncertainties* (Berkeley: University of California Press, 1999); L. L. Grabbe, *Judaic Religion in the Second Temple Period: Belief and Practice from the Exile to Yavneh* (London: Routledge, 2000).

64. In my view, Paul proclaimed Jesus as the incarnation of the Jewish god, a proclamation that is not orthodox if one defines orthodoxy by appeal to the book of Deuteronomy (and not every Jew of that era would have made this particular appeal). However, there is reasonable Jewish precedent. Exodus 7:1 defines Moses as a 'god' to Pharaoh because Moses is the sole instrument through which Pharaoh will experience the Jewish god. Paul believes Jesus is the sole instrument through which he and his followers experience the Jewish god (whether Paul consciously thought of the analogy with Exod. 7:1 or not). In any religion, the highest supernatural agent need not be the one who matters most. It is the supernatural agent who possesses key insight into human affairs or power over daily life who receives most of the veneration, and Jesus fulfills that role in Paul's version of the Gospel (cf. Boyer, *Religion Explained*, 160 and passim). There is no need to soften Paul's unequivocal identification of Jesus with his god, but it would be incorrect to think of Paul as Nicene (e.g. the binary creed in 1 Cor. 8:6 derives from Paul, but the trinitarian formulation of 2 Cor. 13:13 is a post-Paul gloss). For an opposing view, see J. D. G. Dunn, *Christology in the Making: A New Testament Inquiry into the Origins of the Doctrine of the Incarnation* (Grand Rapids: Eerdmans, 1996, 2nd edn), xviii–xix, 114–21 and passim.

Paul opposed a source roughly similar to (or perhaps a very early draft of?) the *Gospel of Thomas*.[65] Burton Mack and Gerald Downing are undoubtedly correct to identify some Jesus-memes as Cynic.[66] And majority scholarship is correct to view many teachings attributed to the Synoptic Jesus as typically Jewish, including a healthy dose of eschatological and messianic speculation involving concepts like the Son of Man.[67] But none of these additional stories or sayings, be they Jewish or Cynic or Jewish-Gnostic, derive from the pillars in Jerusalem, probably none goes back to a historical Jesus and certainly none was acceptable in the eyes of Paul, to the extent he knew them at all.

The only issue that divided Paul from the Jerusalem pillars was a question of Torah observance. Apparently, James held that the death of Jesus restores Jews to correct observance (perhaps along the lines of Jer. 31:31–34); as for non-Jewish converts, James seems to have assumed that they were acceptable to Jesus but not full members of this new movement, perhaps possessing a kind of God-fearer status.[68] If so, this explains why Cephas could switch his allegiance when those from James required a bris before table fellowship was possible.

Apparently, for Cephas and James, this dispute with Paul was nothing more than a matter of observance (rabbinic tradition would later call it *halakah*), but Paul elevated it to a question of doctrine, thus generating a schism that is unlikely to have healed. Paul was a self-certain believer in his own experience and his own logic—not one to back down.[69] New Testament

65. W. H. Kelber, *The Oral and the Written Gospel: The Hermeneutics of Speaking and Writing in the Synoptic Tradition, Mark, Paul, and Q* (Philadelphia: Fortress, 1983), 176; Koester, *Ancient Christian Gospels*, 55–62.
66. B. L. Mack, *A Myth of Innocence: Mark and Christian Origins* (Philadelphia: Fortress Press, 1988), 67–74; idem, *The Christian Myth: Origins, Logic, and Legacy* (New York: Continuum, 2001), 41–58; F. G. Downing, *Christ and the Cynics: Jesus and Other Radical Preachers in First-Century Tradition* (Sheffield: Sheffield Academic Press, 1988); Downing, *Cynics and Christian Origins* (Edinburgh: T & T Clark, 1992); Downing, 'The Jewish Cynic Jesus,' in M. Labahn and A. Schmidt, eds., *Jesus, Mark and Q: The Teaching of Jesus and Its Earliest Records* (Sheffield: Sheffield Academic Press, 2001), 184–214. Cynicism infiltrated the Jesus-meme pool as non-Jewish Christians began to depict elements from Paul's lifestyle in their newly invented stories about Jesus (contra Downing, 'The Jewish Cynic Jesus,' 212–13).
67. For background on the Son of Man, see D. Burkett, *The Son of Man Debate: A History and Evaluation* (Cambridge: Cambridge University Press, 1999). For entry into the discussion of messianic speculation in the late Second Temple period, see J. J. Collins, 'What Was Distinctive'; idem, *The Scepter and the Star: The Messiahs of the Dead Sea Scrolls and Other Ancient Literature* (New York: Doubleday, 1995); Fitzmyer, *One Who Is to Come*.
68. Akenson, *Saint Saul*, 162–63. M. Zetterholm arrives at a similar position in *The Formation of Christianity in Antioch: A Social-Scientific Approach to the Separation between Judaism and Christianity* (London: Routledge, 2003), 156–64.
69. For useful background on the certainty displayed by a person like Paul, see M. Persinger, 'Egocentrism: The Power behind the Proof,' in idem, *Neuropsychological Bases of God Beliefs* (New York: Praeger, 1987), 41–51.

researchers debate endlessly whether Paul *intended* to break with Judaism, but his personal intentions strike me as a moot question;[70] it is the consequences of his legacy that count.

Paul's letters survived him, their significance was not defined by him and a social movement of mostly non-Jewish readers determined what his letters were permitted to mean. The flow of Paul's logic would lead any neutral observer to predict that a permanent schism between Paul's Christianity and any of the common forms of first-century Judaism was inevitable. If the Torah is reduced to an interim caretaker (Gal. 3), characterized as something that increases 'sin' (Rom. 5:20) and denigrated as a source of death (Rom. 6–7; 2 Cor. 3–5), not even the creative exegetical achievements of modern theological scholarship, had they been available in the late first century, would have achieved reconciliation with emerging rabbinic Judaism after 70 CE.

Those (probably very few) Jewish followers of Jesus who agreed with Paul departed from Judaism and denigrated their own past, and the majority who were non-Jewish disciples of Paul did not retain much admiration for Judaism. Although Paul did not write Hebrews, that early Christian 'sermon' (if that is what it was) is a predictable by-product of Paul's movement, in which a Gentile author sifts through the Jewish literature of his day to provide a systematic rationalization for why Christians claim to venerate the Jewish Scriptures while simultaneously ignoring the plain sense of their words, a process that would continue with the anti-Jewish sentiments expressed by Ignatius of Antioch, the *Epistle of Barnabas* and Justin's *Dialogue with Trypho*.[71]

If, as majority scholarship believes, the dispute between Paul and Jerusalem was not yet resolved when Paul was completing his monetary collection for the city (Rom. 15:25–32; 1 Cor. 16:1–4; 2 Cor. 8–9), then it is reasonable to assume that the schism ended only when the first Jewish War annihilated Jerusalem and most of its inhabitants. Whether Paul ever made it to Jerusalem prior to the war with his offering is unknown (the narrative of Acts notwithstanding), but in any case, the influence of the Jerusalem

70. Representative examples include E. P. Sanders, *Paul and Palestinian Judaism: A Comparison of Patterns of Religion* (London: SCM, 1977); H. Maccoby, *The Mythmaker: Paul and the Invention of Christianity* (New York: Harper & Row, 1986); A. F. Segal, *Paul the Convert: The Apostolate and Apostasy of Saul the Pharisee* (New Haven: Yale University Press, 1990); S. G. Wilson, *Related Strangers: Jews and Christians 70–170 CE* (Minneapolis: Fortress, 1995); J. G. Gager, *Reinventing Paul* (Oxford: Oxford University Press, 2000); J. D. G. Dunn, *The New Perspective on Paul: Collected Essays* (Tübingen: Mohr Siebeck, 2005).

71. For some of the Jewish influences on the author of Hebrews, see H. Attridge, 'How the Scrolls Impacted Scholarship on Hebrews,' in J. H. Charlesworth, ed., *The Bible and the Dead Sea Scrolls. III. The Scrolls and Christian Origins* (Waco: Baylor University Press, 2006), 203–30.

pillars did not survive this disaster. Later Christian documents betray hints that some remnant of the Jerusalem pillars survived (e.g. Eusebius, *Hist. eccl.* 3.5.3), but, even if judged accurate, these hints are not sufficient to posit the continued existence of an element within Christianity that exerted significantly widespread influence.[72]

Among the people who transmitted a conceptualization of Jesus in continuity with those who actually knew the historical Jesus, it was Paul's Christianity *alone* that escaped decimation after the first war with Rome. No document survives from Cephas, James or other acquaintances and relatives of Jesus.[73] However, Paul's Christianity left a disturbing written legacy that suggested a break with those who knew Jesus, and that required a heavy coat of whitewash—a forged record of reconciliation. In the absence of such whitewash, the post-Paul leaders of proto-orthodox Christianity had no means to combat the 'other' Jesuses (2 Cor. 11:4) that circulated in Paul's time and later. These purveyors of competing Jesus images could (and did) claim their own continuity with Jerusalem, either by forging texts in the name of alleged eyewitnesses, such as the *Gospel of Thomas*, or by claiming, as did Basilides (whether truthfully or falsely is irrelevant), to be disciples of the disciples. In that environment, the propaganda we know as the Acts of the Apostles, James and 1–2 Peter (not to mention deutero-Paul) are predictable by-products of a need to protect the image of Paul and defend a threatened doctrinal mode.[74]

---

72. In my view, the Ebionite Christians do not descend from the Jerusalem pillars. For an introduction to the Ebionites, see B. D. Ehrman, 'At Polar Ends of the Spectrum,' in *Lost Christianities: The Battles for Scripture and the Faiths We Never Knew* (Oxford: Oxford University Press, 2005), 95–112 (99–103).
73. In my view, 1–2 Peter are forgeries and perhaps best described as deutero-Pauline. For a cautious assessment of the evidence, see P. J. Achtemeier (who concludes that 1 Peter is pseudonymous but is ambivalent about the Pauline connection), *1 Peter: A Commentary* (Hermeneia; Minneapolis: Fortress, 1996), 1–50 and passim; J. H. Neyrey, *2 Peter, Jude: A New Translation with Introduction and Commentary* (AYBC, 37c; New York: Doubleday, 1993), 120–22 and passim. James and Jude might derive from early Jewish followers of Jesus. However, it is not out of the question that James was a Jewish document borrowed and 'Christianized' by a scribe who added a handful of glosses (e.g. at Jas 1:1; 2:1) or was composed by a non-Jewish Christian with access to Jewish literature. For discussion, see M. Dibelius, *James: A Commentary* (rev. Heinrich Greeven; trans. M. A. Williams; Hermeneia; Philadelphia: Fortress Press, 1976), 20–23 and passim; Neyrey, *2 Peter, Jude*, 29–31.
74. D. Trobisch makes an excellent case for viewing the so-called Praxapostolos (i.e. Acts of the Apostles, James, 1–2 Peter, 1–2–3 John, Jude) as a work of propaganda that was disseminated, at least in part, for this purpose, in Trobisch, *The First Edition of the New Testament* (Oxford: Oxford University Press, 2000). However, Trobisch's thesis that the entire New Testament, along with a complete Christian Old Testament in Greek translation, was published as a single codex by the mid-second century goes beyond the evidence. At the very least, the uncertain position of the Praxapostolos in fourth-century

The Spread of Jesus-Memes in Earliest Christianity

The historical reconstruction presented above can be interpreted fruitfully from a Darwinian perspective. The question is why several collections of narratives and sayings that reiterate themes that were relatively common in the ancient world came to be associated with the name of Jesus and promoted as eyewitness testimony to events allegedly accomplished by Jesus. So far, it has been demonstrated that Paul's letters provide sufficient data to determine the primary content of earliest Jesus-memes (those associated with the Jerusalem pillars) as well as Paul's continuity and discontinuity with those memes, and these provide the foundation for further discussion.

The moment Jesus died, the memes that he carried in his head died with him, and he became irrelevant to the movement that he might have begun. At that moment, the image of Jesus—the surviving Jesus-memes—depended entirely on those who imagined him. According to (certainly very dubious) Christian testimony, Jesus participated in the movement for a maximum of three years, but Cephas, James and others were leaders of the movement for decades and undoubtedly exerted more influence than the founder. In turn, they created new leaders (such as Paul) who, in turn, created other leaders (such as Titus). As these disseminators of Jesus-memes travelled, variant Jesus-memes inevitably emerged and competition between them became inevitable.

Memes that derive from an eyewitness have no advantage over memes invented by newcomers to the movement because the success of a meme depends on its adaptability to the needs of the human brains it inhabits.[75] Even though Paul agonized over the seemingly miraculous multiplication of Jesuses, he was helpless to stop the process. In fact, he contributed to it. His epistles demonstrate that Paul earnestly sought to defend a doctrinal mode that he believed was consistent with Jerusalem's pillars, but was, in fact, already evolving away from that mode. And, of course, it was as easy for the name of Jesus to become one more popular supernatural agent in the Greco-Roman world (e.g. an angel or a Gnostic revealer) as it was for the name of Jesus to become equated with Paul's doctrinal mode (e.g. a Jesus who was pre-existent and who rejects *kashrut*) in conflict with its Jerusalem-based source.[76]

---

codices (i.e. א vs B; cf. Trobisch, *First Edition*, 24–25) suggests that the Praxapostolos and the Pauline Corpus circulated as separate codices, and this implies that the four Gospels and the Revelation of John each circulated as separate codices as well. The addition of an 'Old' Testament was an afterthought and was not constructed until at least one human generation later, as Melito of Sardis attests (Eusebius, *Hist. eccl.* 4.26.13–14).

75. For this process, see Whitehouse, *Modes of Religiosity*.

76. On the invention of supernatural agents (such as the various Jesuses of early Christianity), see Barrett, *Why Would Anyone Believe?*

The preceding analysis demonstrates that, very quickly after the crucifixion, the movement that began with our hypothetical historical Jesus faced, and ultimately lost, a Darwinian struggle for survival among competing Jesus-memes invented by variant presuppositions. These were sometimes Jewish presuppositions (e.g. those of the Jerusalem pillars) or Jewish-Gnostic (perhaps those Paul opposed in 1 Corinthians?). In some cases, they were Cynic presuppositions, or Platonic, or Stoic, or a variation of one of the many Greco-Roman mystery religions; and a few were even modified from Paul's letters. A combination of these is the origin of the four narrative Gospels, narratives that provide no information at all about Jesus or the earliest form of Christianity.

Those who knew Jesus well apparently focused on a relatively limited set of memes and—but for a catastrophic event, the Jewish War—might have evolved into a significant Jewish sect. But like the dinosaurs, the Jerusalem-based meme pool was wiped out by a 'meteorite' and it survived only in a geographically isolated strain, Paul's Christianity. Like a king who desperately seeks a son as his heir but is compelled to settle for a nephew twice removed, the dynasty begun with Jesus found itself in the hands of Paul for better or worse; and even Paul's legacy was reduced to a set of letters and fading memories among his followers, most of whom are unlikely even to have been Jewish.

Paul's strain of the meme pool contained significant mutation from the Jerusalem-based original, and the doctrinal mode it constructs must be viewed as an entirely new species of religion, for it housed a set of memes that logically required a sharp break from Judaism and its traditional observances, as well as consequent modifications in doctrine about the significance of Jesus and his cross. Paul elevated a dispute over observance into a question of foundational doctrine when he insisted that 'if justification comes through the law [Torah], then Christ died for nothing' (Gal. 2:21). It matters not what the author's original intent might have been, these words created their own dynamic. No matter how many coats of whitewash one smears across the surface of Paul's logical reasoning, there is no disguising that Paul's doctrinal mode has broken with the dominant Judaisms of his era and all who accepted his viewpoint were no longer Jews.

Paul was the father of Christianity just as mitochondrial Eve was the mother of all humanity. Although the movement began as a sect of late Second Temple Judaism, and in spite of continued Christian fascination with all things Jewish in later generations (as suggested, for example, by fourth-century church fathers who were compelled to forbid philo-Semitic Christians from attending synagogues), genuinely Jewish elements evaporated quickly after 70 CE. The most significant stage of early Christian development began only after the fall of the Jerusalem Temple, when the Jesus-memes were being preserved and modified, while new ones were being evolved, among increasingly non-Jewish followers of Paul. The literate elite among these Christian *goyim* had access to a limited number of Jewish texts in the Greek language (though not a Jewish canon, for that did not yet exist) and may have engaged in polemics with a fading remnant of surviving Jewish Christians, but their approach to the Jewishness of Jesus became very quickly a 'bookish' matter in which a two-dimensional Jewish backdrop was painted so that Jesus could lead his followers along a path to a new and 'better' kind of religion (e.g. the central narrative thrust in Luke–Acts).[77]

Nevertheless, during the final decades of the first century, no one could have guessed that these non-Jewish Jesus-memes inherited from fading memories about a man named Paul would become foundational for the Christianity of later centuries. Although earliest Christianity (that of the Jerusalem pillars) was already extinct by that time, the new Pauline species was not yet the clear winner of the struggle. In the midst of the varieties of Jesus-memes that Paul opposed, and others that he surely would have opposed if he had lived to encounter them, the Pauline Jesus-memes now faced a struggle for survival that would continue for many human generations. To win this struggle, Pauline Jesus-memes required the protective armour of a defensively oriented doctrinal mode, a network of trained leaders (from deutero-Paul to Irenaeus) who could ensure brand consistency through regular teaching events, liturgical reinforcement and systematic guards against defection from the approved teachings and behaviours.

A key problem for Paul's doctrinal mode was the image of Paul himself. From a purely pragmatic perspective, the authority of a doctrinal mode can be undermined by appeals to a greater authority and, so long as Paul's doctrinal mode rested on Paul's authority, anyone (Basilides, for instance) could invent a Jesus whose teaching would undermine Paul. For example, whether intentionally or not, the almost hyper-Jewish Jesus constructed by Matthew's Gospel seems to attack Paul directly in Mt. 5:19 and 7:21. When competitors are able to go over Paul's head by claiming continuity with someone (anyone) who had actually met Jesus, the doctrinal mode Paul had so carefully constructed and so diligently defended could be annihilated

77. Loveday Alexander argues that the Acts of the Apostles was intended to 'plea for a fair hearing at the bar of the wider Jewish community in the Diaspora' (*Acts in Its Ancient Literary Context*, 183–206 [205]). This is reasonable but not compelling. In my view, the Jews of this narrative are two-dimensional figures and would not have been recognizable by the Jewish audience Alexander posits, with the result that the narrative could not have functioned as Alexander suggests that it did. On the contrary, these simplistic portraits of Jews are designed to convince a non-Jewish readership that there is no need for Christians to embrace a Jewish subculture (e.g. Acts 18:6).

within a single human generation. An evolutionary adaptation was required for this doctrinal mode.

It seems never to have occurred to Paul that a 'historical' Jesus would be necessary for the ultimate success of Paul's doctrinal mode, but it was not long after Paul's time that this innovation appeared.[78] Early post-Pauline writings transmit favourite Pauline doctrines (such as a declaration that *kashrut* need not be observed; Mk 7:19b), but shifted these declarations to a new authority figure, Jesus himself. It is Paul's doctrinal DNA that survives in the Jesus who undermines Torah (Mk 2:23–3:5), trumps the authority of both Moses and Elijah (Mk 9:2–8) and eventually distances himself from Judaism altogether (Jn 8:17; 13:33; perhaps 10:34).[79] By the days of a Papias or a Justin, Paul had faded from the centre of discussion, though his Jesus-memes had become the foundation for something called the *regula fidei* ('rule of faith') that was defended by those whom later tradition would call the apostolic fathers.

From Paul's perspective, the Jewish Scriptures were sufficient to defend Paul's authority to define the 'correct' Jesus. Prophets had promised everything necessary beforehand (Rom. 1:2), so that the Christian can be assured that Jesus died and rose 'in accordance with the Scriptures' (1 Cor. 15:3–4). Christopher Stanley has argued persuasively that Paul's audiences did not have access to the Jewish literature Paul quotes, so they could not have challenged the idiosyncratic uses to which Paul put his citations of the Jewish texts.[80] In the context of my preceding analysis, Stanley's observation is significant for this reason: our earliest accessible leader of the Christian movement, himself highly educated and likely to be familiar with the literary heritage described by Thomas Thompson, was not using that literary heritage in the way that Thompson describes.[81] Rather, Paul was freely manipulating those texts to convince a largely illiterate and non-Jewish audience that the Jewish god had promised an atoning martyr and then fulfilled that promise, creating a message of good news that will save every Jew or Gentile who believes.

In short, there is a clear break discernible between the grand literary tradition expertly described by Thompson and the crude use of that tradition with persuasive intent by early Christian leadership, beginning with Paul and leading ultimately to the explicit rhetoric of eyewitness testimony

78. Consider, as well, the views of Kelber, *Oral and Written Gospel*, 205–207.
79. Cook, 'Jewish Reflections on Jesus,' 99–102.
80. C. D. Stanley, 'Paul's "Use" of Scripture: Why the Audience Matters,' in S. E. Porter and C. D. Stanley, eds., *As It Is Written: Studying Paul's Use of Scripture* (Atlanta: Society of Biblical Literature, 2008), 125–55.
81. Thompson, *Messiah Myth*.

outlined by Richard Bauckham.[82] At some stage after Paul departed from the movement (or otherwise independent of Paul's knowledge), the common ancient literary tradition described by Thompson was co-opted and applied to the image of Jesus, so that the proto-canonical Jesus of alleged eyewitness testimony began to emerge. The motivation was purely pragmatic—the defence of a doctrinal mode by appeal to the greatest possible authority figure. Non-referential writings (about Jesus?) were constructed or adapted (perhaps, e.g., the hypothetical Q-source; a proto-*Thomas* collection of sayings; early collections of miracle tales), and later configured as eyewitness testimonies (e.g. the final versions of the Gospels of Luke and John; claims made about Mark and Matthew by Papias of Hierapolis).

Comparison of the data Bauckham has compiled with similar data from early Islam provides insight into the process by which this literary Jesus was invented, as well as the function performed by early Christian assertions about eyewitness veracity. Although political, social and cultural contexts differ between these two processes of religious formation (not least because Islam was a state religion from its inception, but Christianity remained disestablished for several hundred years), the process of meme construction followed a remarkably similar path. In both cases, a 'historical' religious founder was invented more or less from scratch, even though each founder might have been based on a real person, the memory of whom had faded almost completely.

It is my thesis that the reason for the similarity between the inventions of Muhammad and Jesus has to do with the intended function of each doctrinal mode: both were constructed by a leadership intent on establishing and maintaining the authority to dictate the behaviour of *hoi polloi*. In the case of Muhammad, the process was overtly political, as the Umayyad caliphate struggled with dissenting factions, so that the emergence of Muhammad as *the* authoritative prophet effectively limited the Caliph's power even as it created a successful doctrinal mode.[83] Similarly, the rise of Jesus as the authoritative voice overshadowed and limited the authority of Paul—whose letters were increasingly sidelined in favour of narrative Gospels during the second century—while simultaneously transforming Paul's behavioural ethos into the counsel of Jesus himself. Although the Christian process took place among authoritarian leadership unconnected to imperial power, the motivation to control behaviour among *hoi polloi* was identical to that of the Umayyad era: now, instead of Paul's exhortations, it is Jesus who preaches

82. Bauckham, *Jesus and the Eyewitnesses*.
83. Patricia Crone and Martin Hinds, *God's Caliph: Religious Authority in the First Centuries of Islam* (Cambridge: Cambridge University Press, 1986).

proper Christian conduct and who models that conduct through stories about his deeds.[84]

Muslim *sunna* (common Sunni custom) derives from the Qur'an and collections of *hadith* (tales about Muhammad), and these became the resources for various constructions of a *sīra* (biography of Muhammad).[85] The Qur'an is said to be a record of divine revelations to Muhammad that were compiled by his followers during the decades immediately after the prophet's death in 632 CE.[86] The collections of *hadith* are not revelations, but exemplary teachings and behaviour that provide a raison d'être for aspects of the sunna. Each *hadith* must carry an *isnād* (chain of named authorities) to authenticate its claims about the prophet.

Although Muslim tradition asserts that eyewitnesses began to construct the *hadith* collections shortly after the prophet's death and completed the task within two decades, the evidence demonstrates that this process actually began roughly one-hundred years after Muhammad's time and continued for several generations.[87] The sheer obscurity of the Qur'an was catalyst to a complex process of Muslim exegesis that produced fictional accounts on a massive scale (e.g. the region of Iraq saw *hadith* reports attributed to one source multiply from fewer than 50 to more than 900).[88] Even when a *hadith* appears to preserve a fragment of authentic information about Muhammad, it is lacking essential data about the actual historical context, so that it must be judged useless in the same frustrating way that an unprovenanced artefact is useless to an archaeologist.[89]

This freewheeling process resulted in a historical tradition that stands as a 'monument to the destruction rather than the preservation of the

---

84. For authoritarian tendencies in early Christianity that would later serve the imperial needs of Roman emperors, see L. E. Vaage, 'Why Christianity Succeeded in the Roman Empire,' in L. E. Vaage, ed., *Religious Rivalries in the Early Roman Empire and the Rise of Christianity* (Waterloo: Wilfrid Laurier University Press, 2006), 253–78.
85. For a general introduction, see A. Rippin, *Muslims: Their Religious Beliefs and Practices* (London: Routledge, 2005, 3rd edn).
86. The traditional date for the composition of the Qur'an is disputed by J. E. Wansbrough, whose classic volume was recently reissued: *Qur'anic Studies: Sources and Methods of Scriptural Interpretation* (Amherst: Prometheus, 2004). For an argument that it was the historical Muhammad who composed, edited and disseminated the complete Qur'an, in all its glorious opacity, see J. Burton, *The Collection of the Qur'ān* (Cambridge: Cambridge University Press, 1979), 160–66, 183–89, 238–40 and passim.
87. G. H. A. Juynboll, *Muslim Tradition: Studies in Chronology, Provenance and Authorship of Early Ḥadīth* (Cambridge: Cambridge University Press, 1983), 9–76.
88. Juynboll, *Muslim Tradition*, 29.
89. P. Crone presents an example in which the historian is able to recognize fragments of authentic information about Muhammad embedded within hadith reports that are nevertheless utterly useless in Crone, *Slaves on Horses: The Evolution of the Islamic Polity* (New York: Cambridge University Press, 1980), 7.

past'.[90] Obviously, devout Muslims would disagree with this judgment, but even the earliest Muslim scholar to investigate every *isnād*, Shu'ba b. al-Ḥajjāj (c. mid-eighth century CE), declared that roughly two-thirds of them were fabrications, and relatively moderate modern researchers are less credulous than was he.[91] Not infrequently, an *isnād* was constructed by inventing names freely, although the more ingenious method of falsification was to adopt a preexisting *isnād*, one that had gained the trust of Muslim scholars, in order to introduce a spurious *hadith*.[92]

Because the Qur'an's testimony about Muhammad is famously vague, the later biographies function as a means to fill in details and establish an ideal, albeit fictional, history.[93] It was not unusual for the judgments of a Muslim jurist living as many as one-hundred years after Muhammad to become source material projected backward in time and attributed to the prophet with an authoritative, and completely fictional, *isnād* securely attached.[94] Likewise, as discussed earlier, Paul's letters were mined for material with which to construct images of a Jesus who sometimes speaks Paul's words and often champions Paul's behavioural ethos.

The process of *isnād* invention is relevant to this discussion because Bauckham's work reveals a similar pattern in Christian literature. Mark's Gospel refers to possible eyewitnesses by name, but these are relatively rare (e.g. Mk 3:13–21; 6:3; 15:21, 40), and sometimes rhetorically oblique (esp. 6:3; 15:21), so that Bauckham feels compelled to enhance their number and their importance with extensive argumentation.[95] By contrast, later Christian

---

90. Crone, *Slaves on Horses*, 7.
91. Juynboll, *Muslim Tradition*, 20. M. Cook succinctly summarizes the difficulties that a historian faces when attempting to untangle the web of *isnād* relationships in Cook, *Early Muslim Dogma: A Source-critical Study* (Cambridge: Cambridge University Press, 1981), 107–16. A conservative view of the early Muslim sources is provided by F. M. Donner, *Narratives of Islamic Origins: The Beginnings of Islamic Historical Writing* (Princeton: Darwin Press, 1998), who stresses that a historical consciousness did not emerge among Muslims until after the demise of Muhammad, during a period when Muslims were beginning to view themselves as an identifiable identity-group opposed to similar groups. In other words, Donner believes that Muslim historiography was invented to meet the needs of an emerging doctrinal mode, and Donner dates that process to the late seventh and early eighth centuries CE. His thesis on the invention of Muhammad is roughly equivalent to my thesis about the invention of Jesus.
92. Juynboll, *Muslim Tradition*, 4–5.
93. Burton, *The Collection of the Qur'ān*; see also U. Rubin, *The Eye of the Beholder: The Life of MuHammad as Viewed by the Early Muslims* (Princeton, NJ: Darwin Press, 1995); A. Rippin, 'MuHammad in the Qur'ān: Reading Scripture in the 21st Century,' in H. Motzki, ed., *The Biography of MuHammad: The Issue of the Sources* (Leiden: Brill, 2000), 298–309.
94. Juynboll, *Muslim Tradition*, 15–16; M. Cook, 'The Opponents of the Writings of Tradition in Early Islam,' *Arabica* 44 (1997), i–iii, 437–530 (490).
95. Bauckham, *Jesus and the Eyewitnesses*, 39–66, 93–113, 124–27, 155–201 and passim.

authors freely introduced references to 'disciples' or other eyewitnesses, named and unnamed, and did so very explicitly. The Gospel of Luke, for example, abounds in such references not paralleled in other Gospels (e.g. Lk. 2:25, 36; 6:17; 8:1–3; 10:1; 19:37; 23:27, 49; 24:10, 13–35). Bauckham correctly identifies the rhetorical function of these references: they increase the pool of authoritative informants so that Luke's narrative appears to derive from the research implied by the prologue (Lk. 1:1–4).[96] In other words, Luke's invention of 'disciples' is equivalent to the Muslim invention of an *isnād*. But this kind of invention was not exclusive to those authors later deemed to be orthodox. Second-century heresiologists condemned many texts that positioned themselves as eyewitness testimony, such as the Gospels of Mary and Thomas. That these 'heretical' Gospels exist in manuscript fragments as old as the earliest extant manuscripts of the canonical Gospels suggests that the freewheeling invention of eyewitnesses was common to *all* Christian groups by the early- to mid-second century CE, at the latest.[97]

Bauckham devotes considerable attention to Papias of Hierapolis and draws conclusions that again parallel the Muslim data. Papias appears to have been careful to avoid claiming that he ever met the eyewitnesses whose authority he cites.[98] Also, Bauckham builds a compelling thesis that Papias was familiar with, and favoured, the Gospel of John, even subordinating Matthew and Mark to John's testimony.[99] If Bauckham is correct, it is reasonable to conclude that Papias, who was active roughly one-hundred years after the time of Jesus, used a text (the Gospel of John) to construct an *isnād* for allegedly orally transmitted testimony of earlier decades (Bauckham suggests the 80s CE), and carefully distanced himself from these eyewitnesses to avoid implausibility and ensure a general acceptance of the chain's authenticity. Papias was operating much like later Muslims who tailored each *isnād* for its intended purpose, and it is worth noting that, like Papias' use of John, Muslims also relied excessively on the names of allegedly aged members from the first generation in their effort to invent plausible chains of eyewitness testimony (e.g. Zaid b. Thābit plays a prominent role in stories about the compilation of the Qur'an).[100] Papias appears to have been gathering geographically diverse literary resources during the middle decades of the second century, a process and a time period that parallel

96. Bauckham, *Jesus and the Eyewitnesses*, 30. (John's Gospel employs a similar technique.) Bauckham not only identifies this rhetorical function, he believes in it.
97. C. Tuckett, 'Forty Other Gospels,' in M. Bockmuehl and D. A. Hagner, eds., *The Written Gospel* (Cambridge: Cambridge University Press, 2005), 238–53 (250).
98. Bauckham, *Jesus and the Eyewitnesses*, 19, 32 and passim.
99. Bauckham, *Jesus and the Eyewitnesses*, 15–21, 417–20 and passim.
100. Burton, *The Collection of the Qur'ān*, 118–20, 157–59, 228 and passim.

exactly early Islam's construction of the *hadith* collections for similar purposes.[101]

In sum, the evolutionary imperative answers our question: to avoid extinction, a doctrinal mode must motivate members of the movement who are of average intellect and emotional commitment to understand, accept and transmit the distinctive elements (the memes) associated with that doctrinal mode. Paul's version of Christianity clearly attempted to do that, but necessarily underwent further evolutionary development in order to compete with alternatives that claimed greater authority by invoking not Paul's name, but the name of Jesus. By constructing a 'historical' Jesus and defending him with claims of eyewitness veracity, the memes that Paul favoured survived, though the species of Christianity that emerged obviously could not remain identical to that of Paul.

Conclusion

This essay examined the thesis of Richard Bauckham in light of the contradictory hypothesis of Thomas Thompson. Judging that each scholar is correct as far as he goes, my task became a quest for the missing link between their respective data. The key question is this: given that the Gospels produced after Paul's time are constructed from literary motifs common to the ancient Near East, so that the Jesus who speaks and acts in these Gospels is, for the most part, generic, performing common miracles and espousing common teachings, why was this literature promoted as though it were eyewitness testimony? Using a Darwinian model of analysis, I have argued that the creation, survival and replication of any distinctive religion, such as Paul's version of Christianity, requires a set of well-defined constants (i.e. a doctrinal mode), lest the religion face extinction in a social environment that is indifferent to its existence and therefore unlikely to preserve its distinctive features.

Applying this form of analysis to the earliest Christian literatures, I have argued that the data betray a clear evolutionary process from the proclamation of the so-called Jerusalem pillars, through the teachings of Paul, and ultimately into several competing varieties of post-Pauline Christianity. Earlier Christian doctrinal modes went extinct as later ones evolved. The doctrinal mode favoured by the Jerusalem pillars was extinct by the late first century. Although Paul's doctrinal mode was able to survive, it could do so only by evolving significantly new traits, including a conceptualization of a 'historical' Jesus guaranteed by allegedly eyewitness testimonies. This newly invented 'historical' Jesus effectively replaced Paul as the authority

101. Juynboll, *Muslim Tradition*, 39, 62–70 and passim.

behind Paul's doctrinal mode. Briefly, I discuss parallels in early Islam to demonstrate the probability of this analysis.

This essay demonstrates that Jesus was irrelevant to the construction, consolidation and transmission of the various early Christianities known to us from the sources. Even if one assumes that a historical Jesus existed and attempted to play a key role in the movement that survived him, his own contributions (that is to say, his distinctive memes) disappeared when he passed from the scene. From that moment, the Jesus-memes that survived and replicated were those whose advocates could most effectively construct regular teaching events, ritual reinforcements and institutional structures designed to defeat tendencies toward defection. It was Paul, first and foremost, who was able to do this, and the heirs of Paul (almost exclusively non-Jewish) who were able to build on the foundations he created. To the extent that the Jesus of the canonical Gospels preserves any DNA from pre-Gospel stages of the religion's evolution, that DNA derives from Paul, not from the Jerusalem pillars (whose images have been domesticated to Paul's themes in the Gospels, Acts, James and 1–2 Peter), and certainly not from a hypothetical historical Jesus.

Index of References

Hebrew Bible

New Testament

Index of Authors